The Archaeological Survey of Nubia Season 2 (1908-9).
Report on the Human Remains

About Access Archaeology

Access Archaeology offers a different publishing model for specialist academic material that might traditionally prove commercially unviable, perhaps due to its sheer extent or volume of colour content, or simply due to its relatively niche field of interest. This could apply, for example, to a PhD dissertation or a catalogue of archaeological data.

All *Access Archaeology* publications are available as a free-to-download pdf eBook and in print format. The free pdf download model supports dissemination in areas of the world where budgets are more severely limited, and also allows individual academics from all over the world the opportunity to access the material privately, rather than relying solely on their university or public library. Print copies, nevertheless, remain available to individuals and institutions who need or prefer them.

The material is refereed and/or peer reviewed. Copy-editing takes place prior to submission of the work for publication and is the responsibility of the author. Academics who are able to supply print-ready material are not charged any fee to publish (including making the material available as a free-to-download pdf). In some instances the material is type-set in-house and in these cases a small charge is passed on for layout work.

Our principal effort goes into promoting the material, both the free-to-download pdf and print edition, where *Access Archaeology* books get the same level of attention as all of our publications which are marketed through e-alerts, print catalogues, displays at academic conferences, and are supported by professional distribution worldwide.

The free pdf download allows for greater dissemination of academic work than traditional print models could ever hope to support. It is common for a free-to-download pdf to be downloaded hundreds or sometimes thousands of times when it first appears on our website. Print sales of such specialist material would take years to match this figure, if indeed they ever would.

This model may well evolve over time, but its ambition will always remain to publish archaeological material that would prove commercially unviable in traditional publishing models, without passing the expense on to the academic (author or reader).

The Archaeological Survey of Nubia Season 2 (1908-9)

Report on the Human Remains

Jenefer Metcalfe

ARCHAEOPRESS PUBLISHING LTD
Summertown Pavilion
18-24 Middle Way
Summertown
Oxford OX2 7LG
www.archaeopress.com

ISBN 978-1-80327-636-6
ISBN 978-1-80327-637-3 (e-Pdf)

© Jenefer Metcalfe and Archaeopress 2023

Cover: Image adapted from Firth, C.M. (1912). *The Archaeological Survey of Nubia. Report for 1908-1909 Vol. II. Plates and Plans accompanying Vol. 1*. Cairo: Government Press, Plate 21D.

All rights reserved. No part of this book may be reproduced, stored in retrieval system, or transmitted, in any form or by any means, electronic, mechanical, photocopying or otherwise, without the prior written permission of the copyright owners.

This book is available direct from Archaeopress or from our website www.archaeopress.com

For Ryan and Alex

With All of My Love, Always

Contents

List of Figures v
Acknowledgements vi
Introduction 1
Season Two of the ASN (1908-1909) 2
The Excavation and Recording of Human Remains 4
The Original Season Two Reporting 4
Sources of Evidence 6
The Reconstructed 'Season Two: Report on the Human Remains' 8
A Source for Researchers Today? 9
Burial catalogue 11
Cemetery 58, West bank, Ginari 12
Cemetery 58/100, West bank Ginari 18
    C-group burials 18
    New Kingdom (Dynasty 18) burials 23
Cemetery 59, West bank, Kalabsha 28
Cemetery 62, East bank, Khor Basil 30
Cemetery 65, East bank, Wadi Abiad 30
Cemetery 66, West bank, Abu Regab 30
Cemetery 67, West bank, Dugheish 31
Cemetery 68, East bank, Moalla 32
    C-group burials 32
    New Kingdom (Dynasty 18) burials 34
    X-group burials 35
Cemetery 69/1, East bank, Moalla 36
    A-group burials 36
    C-group burials 37
    New Kingdom burials 44
    C-group/New Kingdom burials 53
    Moslem burial 53
    Burials of unknown date 53
Cemetery 69/100, Moalla, East bank 55
Cemetery 69/200, Moalla, East bank 56

Cemetery 70, West bank, situated between Faragalla and Musa Kolei 58
A-group burials 58
New Kingdom burials 58
Christian burials 58
Cemetery 70/100, West bank, situated between Faragalla and Musa Kolei 61
New Kingdom burials 61
Christian burials 61
Cemetery 71, East bank, Sharaf el Din Togog 64
Cemetery 71/100, East bank, Sharaf el Din Togog 64
Cemetery 72, West bank, Gerf Husein 65
C-group burials 65
New Kingdom burials 86
X-group burials 88
Christian burials 99
Burials of unknown date 105
Cemetery 73, West bank, Gerf Husein 108
A-group burials 108
C-group burials 112
New Kingdom burials 116
Ptolemaic burials 116
Cemetery 74, West bank, Gedekol, Gerf Husein 117
C-group burials 117
Roman-Christian burials 119
X-group burials 125
Christian burials 126
Burials of uncertain date (Christian/X-group) 133
Cemetery 75, East bank, Shalub Batha 136
Cemetery 76, West bank, Gedekol, Gerf Husein 137
A-group burials 137
Burials of uncertain date (A to C-group) 144
C-group burials 144
New Kingdom burials 148
X-group burials 159
Roman-Moslem burials 159
Burials of unknown date 160

Cemetery 77/1, West bank, Gedekol South, Gerf Husein 161
    A-group burials 161
    Burials of uncertain date (A to C-group) 161
    C-group burials 161
Cemetery 77/100, West bank, Gedekol South, Gerf Husein 162
    A-group burials 162
    Christian burials 163
    Burials of unknown date 163
Cemetery 78, West bank, Mediq, Gerf Husein 164
Cemetery 79, West bank, Mediq, Gerf Husein 165
    A-group burials 165
    Christian burials 189
Cemetery 80, West bank, Mediq, Gerf Husein 190
Cemetery 81, Mediq South, Gerf Husein 193
Cemetery 82, Gerf Husein 194
Cemetery 83, Gerf Husein 195
    A-group burials 195
    C-group burials 195
Cemetery 85, Koshtamna 196
    A-group burials 196
Cemetery 86, Hamadab, Koshtamna 199
    Ptolemaic-Roman burials 199
    Roman burials 199
    X-group period 200
    Burials of unknown date 200
Cemetery 86/500, Koshtamna 203
    A-group burials 203
    A to C-group burials 203
Cemetery 87, Koshtamna 204
    A-group burials 204
    C-group burials 204
Cemetery 88, Koshtamna 230
Cemetery 89/1, Awam, Koshtamna 231
    A-group burials 231
    New Kingdom burials 232

Cemetery 89/500, Koshtamna 233
    A-group burials 233
    Ptolemaic-Roman burials 245
Cemetery 90/500, Kuri 256
Cemetery 91, Kuri 256
Cemetery 92, Aman Daud 257
    A-group burials 257
    New Kingdom burials 258
    X-group burials 258
    Christian period burials 261
Cemeteries with no surviving human remains 263
    Cemetery 60, East bank, Aqabaten - Roman period 263
    Cemetery 61, East bank, Nagi-koleh - Roman period 263
    Cemetery 63, West bank, Dendur - X-group and Christian period 263
    Cemetery 64, West bank, Metardul - New Kingdom (early Dynasty 18) period 263
    Cemetery 71/200, East bank, Sharaf el Din Togog - A-group to C-group period 263
    Area 84, the fortified town of Sabagura, East bank - Byzantine period 264

References 265
Index: Pathology, trauma, non-metric traits and minor anatomical variations 267
Appendix I 274
Appendix IIa 277
Appendix IIb 300
Appendix IIIa 323
Appendix IIIb 337

List of Figures

Figure 1: Map of the Nile Valley showing the area covered by the 1908-1909 excavations, from Ginari 3

Figure 2: Anatomical recording card produced by Derry and Smith for grave 384, cemetery 72 5

Figure 3: An example of one of the anatomical recording cards used to record numerous burials from cemetery 72 5

Figure 4: An example of one of the pencil notations made on the long bones in the field 8

Figure 5: The female skull found in cemetery 69, grave 20 46

Figure 6: A desiccated mass preserved in the cranial cavity of body 69:20 which is potentially part of the brain 46

Figure 7: An adult, male skull from cemetery 72, grave 41 that demonstrates extensive destruction of the cranial base due to a nasopharyngeal carcinoma 89

Figure 8: The skull of an adult, male found in cemetery 74, grave 12 128

Figure 9: The ossified larynx of an adult, male found in cemetery 74, grave 15 129

Figure 10: Part of the frontal bone of an adult male found in cemetery 76, grave 87 147

Figure 11: The skull of an adult female found in cemetery 87, grave 89 217

Figure 12: The humeral head and scapula of an adult male from cemetery 89, grave 686 with a benign bony tumour 239

Figure 13: A healed depressed fracture identified by Smith and Derry in an adult male from cemetery 92, grave 114 260

Figure 14: One of the original line diagrams produced by Smith and Derry, detailing three cranial injuries experienced by this adult male (cemetery 92, grave 121) 261

Acknowledgements

Grateful thanks are due to the museum and university collections and archives that permitted access to their human remains collections and archives: The Natural History Museum, London; The Duckworth Laboratory, The University of Cambridge; the Museum of Fine Arts (MFA), Boston; the Royal College of Surgeons, London; The University of Manchester Special Collections, Manchester.

Particular thanks are due to Norman MacLeod and Robert Kruszynski at The Natural History Museum and Marta Lahr and Maggie Belatti at The Duckworth Laboratory for their support during my numerous visits and for enduring endless questions.

Eternal thanks are due to my husband Ryan for taking literally thousands of photographs for me whilst I tried to reconstruct the season 2 excavations, patiently reeling off long-bone measurements and for supporting me in the 10 years it has taken to write this book.

Grateful thanks are also due to those who provided financial support for this work. The initial research for this volume was carried out as a part of a Wellcome Trust funded research grant [WT090575MA]. Further financial support for permission to include several images in this work has been provided by the KNH Endowment Fund, The University of Manchester.

Finally and most importantly, I would like to acknowledge the work of Sir Grafton Elliot Smith and Dr Douglas Erith Derry. Many of the bodies excavated during the early 1900s in Egypt have no surviving burial context or provenance, often because of way in which they were excavated. The dedication of Smith and Derry to recording these burials has allowed us to re-establish some of their identities and to understand a little more about life in ancient Nubia.

Introduction

The first Archaeological Survey of Nubia (ASN), which took place from 1907 to 1911, remains one of the largest and most significant investigations to have been conducted into the ancient population of Lower Nubia. The excavations were directed by George Andrew Reisner, whose team recorded, photographed and studied 151 cemeteries over four working seasons. In one of the first excavations of its kind the survey benefitted from the presence of on-site anatomists who assisted with the excavation and recording of any human remains found. Estimates by the author suggest that ~7500 bodies from ~20,000 graves were discovered during this period based on the archaeological reports (vagaries and inconsistencies throughout the reports do not allow for more precise estimates). At a time when human remains were often discarded by excavators unless they had artefacts associated with them or were attractive mummy bundles suitable for museum display, the ASN demonstrated a remarkable departure from the norm.

Led by the well-known anatomist, Sir Grafton Elliot Smith, a small team of anatomists studied the human remains that were excavated and carried out a systematic study of the anatomical and palaeopathological features of the Lower Nubian population. These covered a period of around 5000 years from the early A-group period to the early Christian period (4th millennium BCE through to the mid-late 1st millennium CE. The methods of study and recording used by the ASN anatomists formed an early base which later anatomists and anthropologists built upon (e.g. Batrawi 1945). The exact methods used by the ASN team have long since been developed and refined, but the use of extensive skeletal measurements is now part of an established procedure for studying ancient populations.

One of the main reasons that the ASN continues to be referenced by osteologists and palaeopathologists today was the production of a detailed anatomical report on the first season's work (Smith and Jones 1910) which took place between 1907-08. This was unlike anything published previously; few anatomists had studied such a large number of bodies and any reports that were produced tended to focus on isolated case studies or the study of bodies from a single cemetery. Only mummified remains appear to have been subject to a broader, more inter-disciplinary approach (e.g. Pettigrew 1834). Rather than focussing purely on bodies that provided evidence of a novel anatomical variation within the human population or a particular disease of interest, Elliot Smith and his colleague at the time, Frederick Wood Jones also recorded measurements of skeletal elements, assessments of age and sex, dental disease and tooth loss, evidence of medical intervention, funerary rituals (e.g. anthropogenic mummification) and trauma. The report was accompanied by a photographic appendix produced by George Reisner and a team of Egyptian colleagues expertly trained by Reisner himself (Berman 2018). The published photographic plates provide extremely clear and detailed images of many of the bodies found, as well as macro images of examples of pathology and trauma.

Osteological methodology has obviously progressed considerably since the time of the ASN; despite this the 1910 anatomical report remains important for those studying the ancient populations of Egypt and Nubia, palaeopathology and the history of excavation in the region. No complete anatomical reports were however produced for the other three seasons, 1908-09, 1909-10 and 1910-1911. The only published records detailing the human remains found are the short bulletin reports produced shortly after each excavation season finished. Unfortunately, this has meant that researchers up until the present day have only been able to focus on the excavations carried out during season one.

A research project funded by the Wellcome Trust [WT090575MA] has now made it possible to produce a reconstruction of the work carried out by the ASN anatomists during season 2 (1908-1909). This volume is the result of that research and pieces together the numbers of bodies found per cemetery, the studies originally carried out on them and provides further context and support to the research carried out during season 1. The work also provides valuable information to modern day researchers including indications of where any known human remains from these particular excavations are located, any research carried out on the bodies that post-date the work of the ASN anatomists and the history of this material in so far as it has been possible to reconstruct.

Season Two of the ASN (1908-1909)

The second season's excavation started on 1 October 1908 with the excavation of cemeteries around the village of Gennari on the east bank of the Nile and Kalabsha on the west bank. Thirty-seven cemeteries were studied in the six months until March 1909, finishing at Aman Daud on the east bank (Figure 1). As with the previous season, the excavations were directed by George Reisner and teams worked simultaneously along either side of the Nile. In contrast to the previous season however Reisner was increasingly absent from the excavations, leaving the direction of work to his deputy Cecil Firth. Firth later succeeded Reisner as director of the ASN excavations during the 1909-1910 season. Similarly, Elliot Smith was rarely present on site during this season; the in-field study and collection of human remains was instead carried out by Douglas Derry, following the departure of Wood Jones from the excavations in 1908. Derry would also remain as the on-site anatomist for the ASN throughout the subsequent two seasons.

Season two was focussed on trying to establish whether the cemeteries further down the Nile reflected a continuity of occupation, both geographically and historically, from those excavated during season one. Two major aims of both the archaeological and anatomical teams were the identification of a Predynastic (A-group) population in the area and the identification of biological distinction between the indigenous Nubian population and Egyptian colonists. The overlap between C-group and New Kingdom populations were subject to particularly intensive focus. Similarly, the discovery of the existence of the X-group as a cultural entity and its incorporation into Reisner's Nubian chronology led to both archaeological and anatomical concentration on remains from this period (Reisner 1909a). These interests affected which cemeteries were chosen for extensive, detailed excavation and which were not, and the human remains that were studied and retained from each cemetery. Some cemeteries, particularly those from the Christian period, were left largely untouched due to time constraints. The anatomists were also of the opinion that the Christian period cemeteries excavated during the previous season had already provided an adequate amount of information about the Nubian population during this time (Smith 1909, 21). Not all periods were well represented in the archaeological record however and Reisner identified no sites as belonging to the 3rd Intermediate and Late periods – the Nubian Napatan period (c. 1000-300 BCE).

Preservation was found to be a significant problem for the anatomists during this season. Sebakh digging was highly prevalent and termite and beetle activity is reported frequently. Sebakh digging is the removal of decomposed mud bricks for use as fertiliser and fuel (Quickel and Williams 2016). The activity is known to cause significant damage and occasionally total destruction of cemeteries in the Nile Valley region. It is unclear whether these problems were more prevalent in the area covered during season two or whether the issues were better recognised and recorded by the excavation team after their experiences the previous year. The impact of these problems does appear to have had a profound effect upon the number of bodies considered suitable for anatomical study. Elliot Smith reported that from 2000 graves only 300 skeletons provided full sets of measurements (Smith 1908, 21). The destruction of context by sebakh diggers was also problematic as Elliot Smith and Derry were hoping to draw comparisons between bodies from secure, dated burials. The recovery of a smaller number of

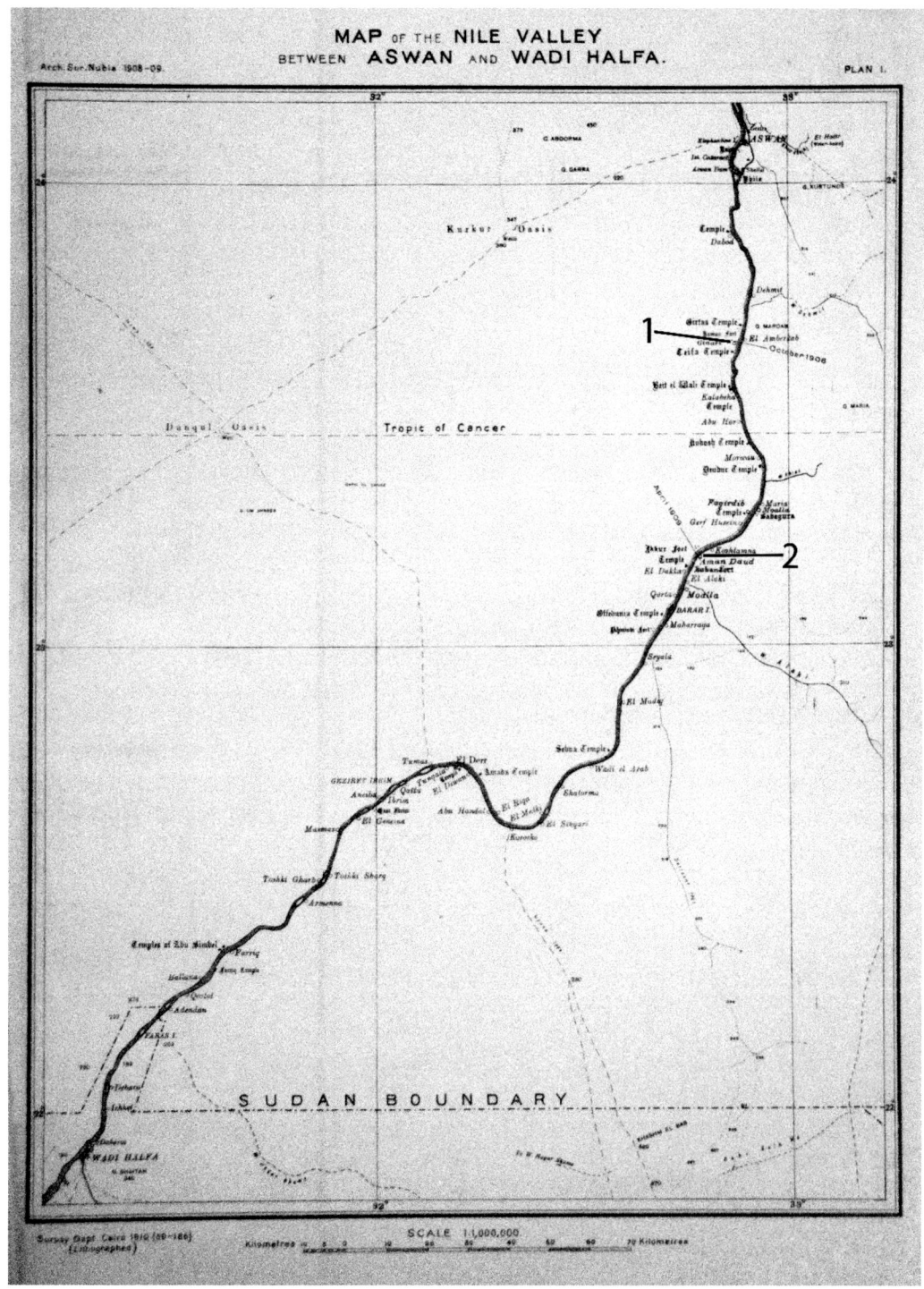

Figure 1: Map of the Nile Valley showing the area covered by the 1908-1909 excavations, from Ginari (1) down to Aman Daud (2) (Amended from Firth 1912b, Plan I).

graves during 1908-09 season than 1907-08 season meant the loss of so many bodies had an impact on the data available to the anatomists and consequently, the conclusions they were able to draw.

The Excavation and Recording of Human Remains

Derry was the only anatomist present on site during these excavations as Elliot Smith remained in Cairo to focus on the development of an Anatomy Department at the University of Cairo. Many of bodies found were packed and sent to Cairo for the two of them to study in a laboratory environment. In 1909 Elliot Smith accepted the Chair of Anatomy at The University of Manchester, UK leaving Derry as the only anatomist not just on site but in Egypt. Only bodies deemed to be in 'good' condition were retained and sent to Cairo, following the protocol developed during season one (Smith 1909). The notion of good preservation seems to be highly variable depending upon the historical age of the skeleton/mummy in question and whether they were considered to be of interest to a member of the anatomical team. For example, relatively rare skeletons from the A-group period were often retained even if the bones were fragmentary and/or fragile.

Although the methods of excavation, recording and subsequent study established for the ASN material were those devised by Elliot Smith, they were maintained throughout despite the change of personnel. Individual recording cards, developed by Elliot Smith for work on an earlier Egyptian cemetery, were used for each body where a significant proportion of the body or skeleton survived. These were inspired by the archaeological recording cards devised by Reisner and used throughout his entire career. The cards recorded the skeletal elements present, skull and long bone measurements and had a free text box for recording evidence of pathology, trauma or anything further of note (see Figure 2 for example). Although well preserved bodies were allocated a detailed record card, those that were very poorly preserved and the majority of child skeletons were recorded only in terms of a grave number, the sex and age of the individual (the latter two are unfortunately recorded inconsistently). A single card may record the existence of several tens of children for example (see Figure 3 for example). Additional notes and corrections were often made to these cards when bodies were more comprehensively studied in a laboratory setting at a later date.

The identification of sex was made using soft tissue preservation in many cases. Where this was not possible the pelvis was used and failing that the skull. Records where both the pelvis and skull were studied to assign gender to a single individual are rare. Age determination was carried out using dental eruption sequences and epiphyseal fusion. These are only ever reported in detail for sub-adults in the ASN reports, but Smith and Jones note that these were assessed for all bodies where possible (Smith and Jones 1910, 7). The appearance of mummified bodies, such as the presence of white hair, was used to assign age. It is unclear how accurate this is likely to have been; most of the mummies where appearance is recorded were natural mummies not subject to the application of resins or natron during the embalming process which may have affected hair colour. However, the natural desiccation process may also have had some inadvertent effect on the body due to extreme heat, sun exposure, fungal growth or other environmental conditions (Aufderheide 2003, 341-42). Particular attention was paid to anomalies of the vertebral column, dentition and cranial sutures. Any perceived asymmetry in the cranium or the long bones was also recorded. Some examples of pathology and trauma were recorded in detail; however, any similar to those identified by Wood Jones during the season one excavations were simply reported on the recording cards (Smith 1910, 13).

The Original Season Two Reporting

Two bulletins were published in 1909 to cover the 1908-09 season, covering archaeological, anthropological and pathological findings. An official full-scale report, with plates followed this

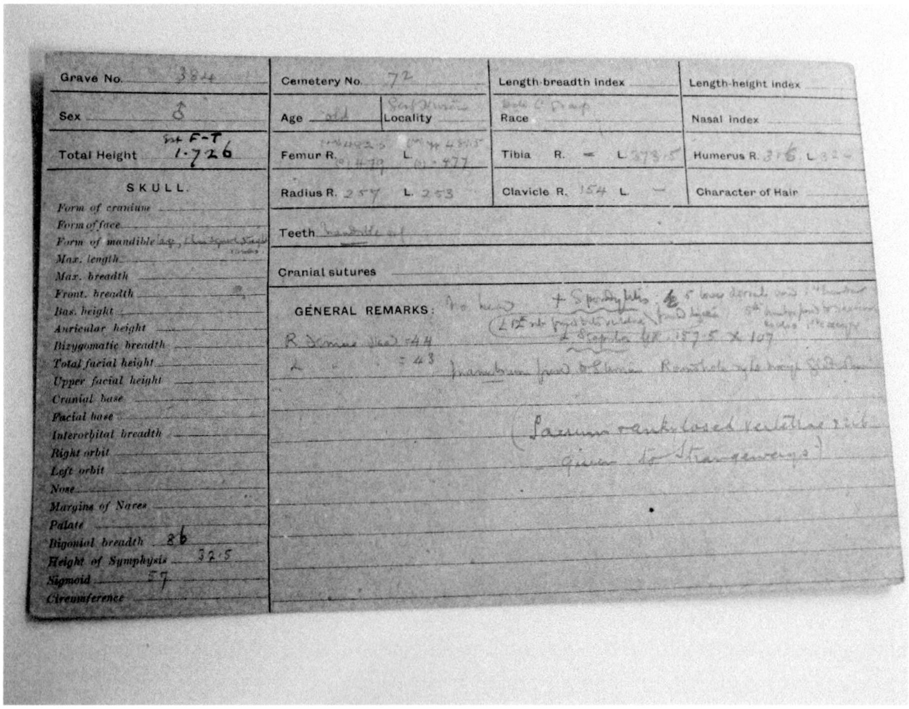

Grave No. 384
Cemetery No. 72
Length-breadth index
Length-height index
Sex ♂
Age old
Locality
Race
Nasal index
Total Height 1·726
Femur R. L.
Tibia R. L.
Humerus R. L.
SKULL.
Radius R. 257 L. 253
Clavicle R. 154 L.
Character of Hair
Form of cranium
Form of face
Form of mandible
Max. length
Max. breadth
Front. breadth
Bas. height
Auricular height
Bizygomatic breadth
Total facial height
Upper facial height
Cranial base
Facial base
Interorbital breadth
Right orbit
Left orbit
Nose
Margins of Nares
Palate
Bigonial breadth 86
Height of Symphysis 32·5
Sigmoid 57
Circumference
Teeth
Cranial sutures
GENERAL REMARKS:

Figure 2: Anatomical recording card produced by Derry and Smith for grave 384, cemetery 72. The card shows the addition of later annotations by both the anatomical team (black ink) and a note by an unknown hand confirming the transfer of part of the skeleton to Thomas Strangeways (in brackets, bottom right). ©The Duckworth Laboratory, The University of Cambridge, 2023.

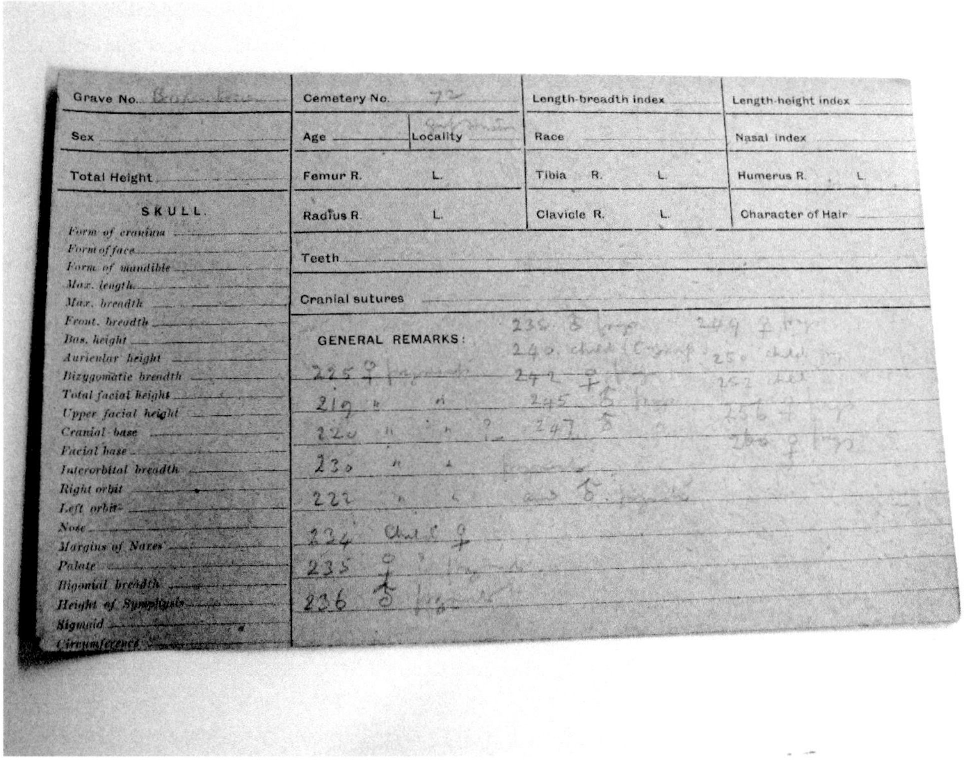

Grave No.
Cemetery No. 72
Length-breadth index
Length-height index
Sex
Age
Locality
Race
Nasal index
Total Height
Femur R. L.
Tibia R. L.
Humerus R. L.
SKULL.
Radius R. L.
Clavicle R. L.
Character of Hair
Form of cranium
Form of face
Form of mandible
Max. length
Max. breadth
Front. breadth
Bas. height
Auricular height
Bizygomatic breadth
Total facial height
Upper facial height
Cranial base
Facial base
Interorbital breadth
Right orbit
Left orbit
Nose
Margins of Nares
Palate
Bigonial breadth
Height of Symphysis
Sigmoid
Circumference
Teeth
Cranial sutures
GENERAL REMARKS:

Figure 3: An example of one of the anatomical recording cards used to record numerous burials from cemetery 72. The numbers in the general remarks section provide the grave number of the body and comments about age, sex and condition. ©The Duckworth Laboratory, The University of Cambridge, 2023.

in 1912. However, contrary to the first season's two detailed reports on both the archaeological and anatomical discoveries made, the season two report was a slightly less extensive archaeological report only. The detailed photographic record of the bodies found, and the existence of anatomical recording cards suggest that an equivalent report for season two was originally planned but this never happened, possibly due to Elliot Smith's relocation to Manchester. There are signs that there was some input from the anatomists into the archaeological report, with a proportion of the bodies identified by sex. These assignments for the most part match those given on the surviving anatomical recording cards, making it highly likely that this is where the data was taken from. Unfortunately, the same style of reporting was not used for the ages of the bodies found and the reader is required to infer their age from the circumstances of the burial and any published photographs or sketches.

The archaeological report for season two continues to be used today as the only comprehensive record of the bodies found during these excavations. It had been assumed until recently that the lack of an anatomical report for seasons two to four was because the anatomists studied very few of the bodies and that those described in the bulletins cover the extent of those investigated. The discovery of 479 anatomical recording cards from season 2 at the Duckworth Laboratory, University of Cambridge testifies that this was not the case.

Sources of Evidence

This report has been produced using a number of sources, most significantly the surviving ASN body cards discovered in the archive at the Duckworth Laboratory, The University of Cambridge. 495 cards from 20 cemeteries were located by the author, mixed in with the body cards produced by Douglas Derry during the 1913-16 excavations at Kerma, Sudan. The reporting cards from these excavations, which were also directed by George Reisner, are curated at the Duckworth Laboratory. Eighteen of the cemeteries covered by the cards were from the season two excavations whilst the other two came from season one. It seems likely that the cards were in the possession of Derry whilst he was at University College London (UCL) between 1910 and the outbreak of World War I. A large number of human remains and their accompanying records were subsequently transferred from UCL to Cambridge during World War II. The ASN cards appear to have been transferred as part of this. Correspondence from Elliot Smith indicates that the cards were retained by Derry, with the exception of the season one cards. The latter were originally located in the Royal College of Surgeons but were largely destroyed, along with the majority of the ASN skeletal collection deposited there when the College was bombed in 1941 (Molleson 1993, 136). These 495 cards are a fortunate survival of what must originally have been a much larger archive, covering the last three seasons of excavation.

The reports on the cards are of variable detail; well-preserved adult bodies are recorded in detail with as many skeletal measurements as possible made and a description of the body. The latter often included further measurements not included in the pre-printed boxes on the card, information on non-metric traits and anatomical variation, evidence of pathology or trauma. The bodies of children and poorly preserved skeletons were recorded in less detail. Some cards are largely empty, others contain records of multiple burials usually noting just the cemetery and grave number and the sex of the skeleton.

The cards must be viewed as working documents. The original notes were made in pencil, frequently in the field. There is often evidence of two different hands being involved in writing the reports and in a small number of cases, the pencil was written over in ink. The measurements recorded were accompanied by ticks or corrections in some instances suggesting the records were checked at a later date. There are notes to indicate that some bodies or skulls specifically were retained as they demonstrated a feature of interest. This in turn also indicates that not all of the bodies from this season were retained following excavation. Three cards contain an additional notation added at a later date by Thomas Strangeways, a pathologist with an interest in rheumatoid arthritis (see Figure 2). He recategorized three examples of pathology found during season two at some point prior to his death in 1926 and added notes to the relevant anatomical card. Strangeways had connections with the Royal College of Surgeons in London, so it is likely that he was able to review the ASN material there. He had in his private collection when he died at least one example of a foot with gout discovered during season one of the ASN excavation (this is now in the Natural History Museum, London) and two skulls.

The photographic record from season two is similarly incomplete; the Boston Museum of Fine Arts, USA which curates the majority of photographs produced by George Reisner during season one also curates a small number from season two. Some of these are copies of the photographs published as part of the official archaeological record and others are contact prints of unpublished images. These unpublished images include additional site photographs of cemeteries prior to excavation and occasional images of individual graves following clearance. The most valuable images however are a range of photographs of skulls – these are usually two or three skulls side-by-side, demonstrating perceived variation between sexes or different historical periods. In all but one instance, the location of the skulls in the photograph is now unknown. There are also a large number of images of artificial mummies, mostly from cemetery 89, many of which are not published. This is the best source of evidence for Lower Nubian anthropogenic mummies found during the ASN as the location of almost all of them is now unknown.

In addition to the published archaeological report and bulletins, there are a small number of published papers which refer to human remains found during these excavations (see for example Derry (1911a); Derry (1911b)). Archival documents relating to both Smith and Derry also survive in the collections of the Royal College of Surgeons, London and University College London (UCL) and the University of Manchester. These contain little discussion of actual human remains, recording instead some information about how skeletal material was brought to the UK and distributed between Smith and Derry for study. The Royal College of Surgeons also preserves a document written by one Watson and dated only to 'pre-1935'. This is a notebook containing osteological measurements carried out by the author on a number of ASN skulls which at the time were curated in The University of Manchester.

The majority of human remains from this season's excavations have sadly been lost. Small collections of material survive in The University of Manchester, The University of Cambridge, The Natural History Museum, London, the Aswan Museum and the South Australia Museum, Adelaide (see Appendix I for a full list). Most of the surviving material comprises individual skeletal elements, except for five intact mummies in Australia and Egypt. It has been possible to assess some of the original descriptions of pathologies and trauma in this small sample set. Archival documents have demonstrated that the collection of season two material originally located in the Anatomy Museum at The University of Manchester was once extensive. This was brought to Manchester by Elliot Smith when he took the Chair of Anatomy position in 1909. Parts of this collection were subsequently transferred to UCL in 1919 when Elliot Smith left Manchester, and then again to Cambridge during World War II. For an in-depth discussion of how the season two material was distributed post-excavation, see Cockitt (2014).

As it is no longer possible to identify significant numbers of bodies from the season two excavations in these collections, it appears likely that over time bodies have become separated from their provenance making it difficult to place them within their correct archaeological context. The major skeletal elements (skull, long bones) of each body were annotated with the cemetery and grave number and often a male or female symbol by the anatomists upon excavation in the field. The smaller bones and any additional tissues that were separated from the body (mummified skin, hair etc.) were not usually individually labelled. The anatomists relied on the use of dedicated packing boxes and the labelling of some bones to correctly identify a body post-excavation. Unfortunately, none of the bodies have survived in their original packing cases. Where bones were annotated, these were usually recorded in

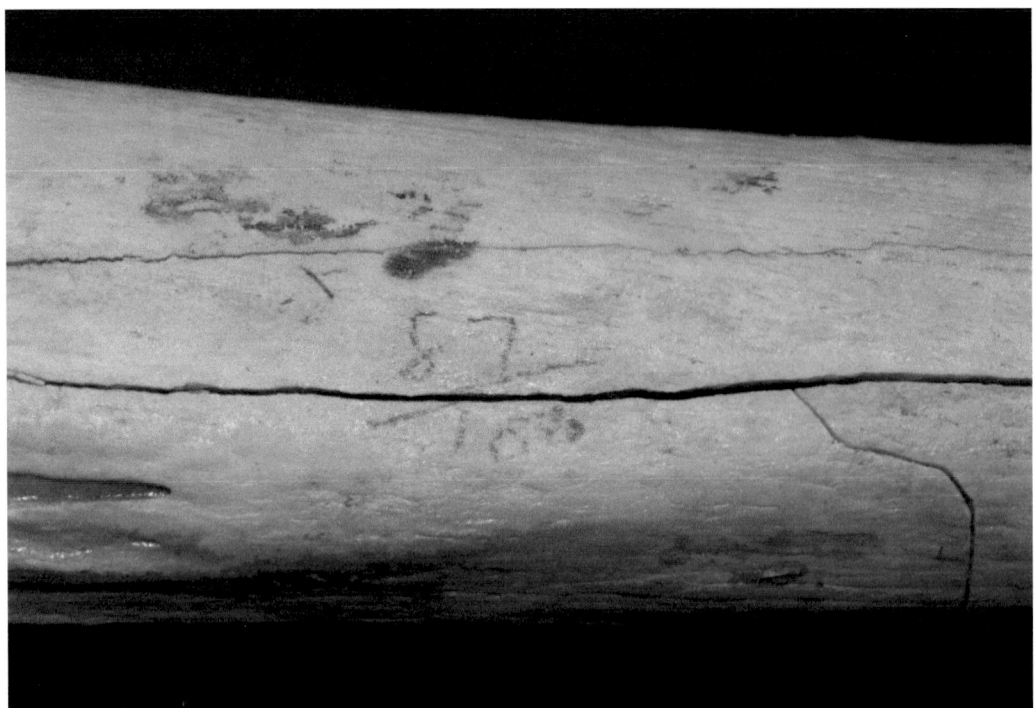

Figure 4: An example of one of the pencil notations made on the long bones in the field. Less than clear original notations, post-mortem fractures, handling and preservation issues have all contributed to making these difficult to read in many cases. ©The KNH Centre for Biomedical Egyptology, The University of Manchester, 2023.

pencil which is prone to smudging or rubbing when bones are handled (see Figure 4). This has led to the loss of provenance for the majority of the bodies found during this season.

The Reconstructed 'Season Two: Report on the Human Remains'

This report is a reasonable reflection of the work of Grafton Elliot Smith and Douglas Derry during season two, along with the inclusion of some more recent updates on individual bodies where this has been possible. A list of the graves that were excavated and the bodies found within them has been produced, using the archaeological report and bulletins as a foundation. This has been amended or adjusted as required when additional information was provided by archival documents or the anatomical recording cards. The archaeological report presents a number of issues; the most significant is that it is not always possible to determine whether a grave was empty or unexcavated. Creating an accurate tally of the number of empty graves can therefore only be considered partially successful.

A record for each body has been produced, giving the available information about the cranial, post-cranial and dental remains as reported by Smith and Derry. A publication/reference list for each body has been included, along with any information about the current location of the body. In some instances, it has been possible to link anatomical or pathological descriptions from the bulletins back to a specific body. The casual reporting style used in the bulletins has made this very difficult in many instances – bodies are often not identified by the grave number, even if they are identified as belonging to a particular cemetery or historical period. Careful evaluation of the bulletin reports, along with additional evidence provided by other documents and photographs has helped with these identifications. It has however not been possible in most cases to reproduce the detailed level of recording seen during season one. The surviving recording cards are clearly not a complete set – some of the bodies recorded in the bulletin/archaeological report are not included. The terminology is now over 100 years old and the authors only intended them as a preliminary record for their own study purposes. The cards were also written in pencil, making them unclear especially where lots of numbers are used (for example, with dental records).

Records of whether a body was naturally mummified, anthropogenically mummified or skeletonised are also poor. It has been possible to improve upon the data provided by the archaeological report, but the records remain incomplete. It is well known that Elliot Smith and Derry autopsied a significant number of mummies in the field, yet only a few detailed reports of these autopsies for season two have survived. The anatomical recording cards testify that infant and child remains were recorded by the anatomists. This focus, although often lacking in detail, is in contrast to the work of many researchers in the field at the time. Sir William Flinders Petrie for example paid little attention to the remains of children found at Kahun, dismissing them almost as a distraction to the main focus of his excavations (Carruthers et al. 2021). Discussion of the mummification techniques used to preserve bodies from Koshtamna was either not produced or did not survive. The lack of detail experienced here may be a reflection of the fact that the level of laboratory study carried out posthumously was much lower after season one. There are likely to be a number of reasons for this – the anatomists were both involved in other projects that required their attention, the skeletal material from the later cemeteries was in poorer condition and much of the excitement with the discoveries made in season one had started to wear off. The number of bodies was in excess of what they had expected when the ASN began and maintaining interest and focus is likely to have been difficult long term. This does not however detract from what they did achieve – some of the surviving anatomical reports are remarkable and the examples of pathology, trauma and anatomical variation they reported is extensive.

A Source for Researchers Today?

The importance of the ASN to both anthropologists and palaeopathologists is well documented (Aufderheide 2003; Baker and Judd 2012). This is due to a number of factors including the sheer size of the project and the high number of bodies discovered, as well as the fact that the survey is one of the earliest investigations into this region. The level of anatomical detail and the reporting of cases of pathology and trauma make the survey truly unique, even by modern standards. Despite this, the focus of scholars has always been on season one due to the existence of a comprehensive anatomical report. The other seasons' work tends to become eclipsed, probably due to the difficulties in reconstructing what excavations were carried out and what was found.

The season two report, as it has been possible to reconstruct, does not compare to season one in terms of the level of reporting or the number of bodies studied. It does however allow a more comprehensive picture of the Nubian cemeteries excavated by Reisner and his team to be built up. For those cemeteries excavated completely, there are a large number of records and the data can be reliably compared against other cemetery populations of similar date. Despite the selection criteria applied to the cemeteries discovered during season two, it does appear that the population in this region was slightly smaller than that found during the previous season. The number of cemeteries containing more than 100 bodies was much lower and there are few examples of cemeteries that remained in use over multiple historical periods.

The archaeological report for the 1908-09 season, although now widely available as a digital copy, does not provide the data required for osteological or palaeopathological studies. The focus of Firth's work was the graves themselves and any surviving grave goods. The report does record the position of the bodies and records important details about any wrappings or coffins present in the grave or tomb.

Although some of these details were recorded on the anatomical recording cards, this information has not been duplicated here. Instead, this report should sit alongside the archaeological report and provide additional, supporting information to those studying the population of Lower Nubia.

This volume contains a detailed record of a range of non-metric traits and examples of anatomical variation identified by Smith and Derry. Although these appear to have been recorded during season one, they were inconsistently recorded and reported in the published report. During season two the absence of an anatomical variation was recorded as well as the presence; features were frequently recorded as either 'normal' or the perceived abnormality was described. This was particularly the case for maxillary prognathism and occipital asymmetry. The number of non-metric traits recorded by the anatomists expanded beyond their initial interests during season one, possibly as a result of their determination to identify physical differences between communities and populations.

There is an obvious racial bias in many of the records and measurements made, in line with the interests of both the archaeological and anatomical teams and as was common at the time (Challis 2013). The supposed racial variations identified by Smith and Derry are no longer considered viable or acceptable. As such, comments such as 'evidence of negroid traits' for some individuals have not been transcribed. The records of actual osteological features and skull and long bone measurements have however been faithfully reproduced from the original records. Many of the anatomical variations recorded are important for continuing anthropological research. Studies of the surviving human remains from the ASN testify that the anatomical descriptions provided by Smith and Derry were usually accurate. The anatomical descriptions of pathologies are extremely good for example, even where a diagnosis couldn't be made. This does not however always extend to osteological measurements and researchers such as Batrawi (1945) have commented upon their inability to replicate Elliot Smith's work.

The data preserved here forms a historical record of the studies carried out – it is important to be mindful of this fact when using this volume. The focus of both the anatomical and archaeological teams on identifying physical and societal differences between the neighbouring Nubian and Egyptian populations affected the progression of the excavations, the selection of different bodies for different purposes (display, dissection, retention, disposal) and as a result, our understanding of the ancient Nubian people and their communities. It is hoped that the recognition and identification of further human remains from these cemeteries in the future will allow researchers to evaluate more comprehensively the work of Smith and Derry. This would, in turn, provide a more appropriate narrative of how the 1908-09 excavations have, and can, contribute to understanding of the ancient Nubian population.

Burial catalogue

The following chapters discuss the burials excavated from cemeteries 58 to 92 during the season 2 excavations. Each cemetery has a location, approximate time range for when it was in use and brief description, where these have been preserved. The cemetery numbering system used by Reisner and Firth was simple and contiguous; each new area under investigation was allocated the next number in the sequence. As a result, some cemeteries that were completely destroyed or areas that proved not be cemeteries upon excavation were still allocated a number. The list of cemeteries covered here is therefore not a complete numerical list. Instead, it reflects those where records of at least graves or tombs were preserved, even if there were no surviving human remains. A list of any empty graves/tombs is provided for each cemetery, as well as descriptions for any of the burials still in-situ. The records of the surviving burials is highly variable, ranging from a simple record that there was a skeleton present in a particular grave to incredibly detailed anatomical records of an individual.

Bodies were assigned a number in the same contiguous way as the cemeteries. Bodies from multiple burials were usually assigned a character to distinguish between them. For example, bodies 1A and 1B would indicate that two bodies were found in grave number 1. The system does occasionally break down – there are some bodies that are recorded but which were not allocated a number. There are a couple of duplications of numbers and in some cases, multiple burials were not properly identified.

To provide clarify the following numbering/naming conventions have been followed:

- A multiple burial identified as such in the archaeological/anatomical record is identified using an upper case character. For example, 1A.

- A multiple burial that was not appropriately labelled at the time the time of excavation but which has been subsequently identified is labelled with a lower case character. For example, as 1(a).

- Duplicated numberings are identified with a 2 in superscript. For example, 1^2.

- Any body not assigned a number is labelled UNKN (unknown).

Where detailed archaeological or anatomical records have survived, these are broken down into brief descriptions of the body, the original anatomical observations records and information on any subsequent studies. A full reference list for each body is given to allow for full reference back to the published archaeological report, any data presented in the bulletins and any later publications. For the small number of bodies or partial bodies still known to exist, a current location for each one is given, detailing which parts of the body have survived and the catalogue number the host institution uses for these.

Cemetery 58, West bank, Ginari

C-group period

The cemetery was located on an alluvial mound between the Nile and the village of Ginari. The superstructures had all been destroyed and the outlines of the graves were no longer preserved (Firth 1912a, 15). This was the first cemetery to be completely excavated during the 1908-09 season. Twenty bodies were recorded from 20 graves.

1 A female 3-year-old skeleton.

   References: Anatomical recording card; Firth (1912a, 55); Firth (1912b, plan VII).

2 A male, adult skeleton with slightly curly hair. The body was contracted on the left, with the head to the east. There were remains of linen and matting under the head. The skull was damaged when discovered. There is a notation on the anatomical card that this body was photographed upon excavation, but this image was not published in the archaeological report or bulletins.

   Original anatomical observations: The teeth of the mandible are perfect, but the 3rd molars are not present on either side. The right 3rd molar is also absent in the maxilla, the left is present but peg shaped.

   The sternal epiphysis of the clavicle is not joined. The manubrium is separate from the gladiolus and is very long. The patellae are notched.

   References: Anatomical recording card; Derry (1909a, 29); Firth (1912a, 55; Fig. 12); Firth (1912b, plan VII).

3 A male, adult skeleton. The body was originally flexed on the right, with the head to the east. It had however fallen onto its front when uncovered. Leather and matting are present. There is considerable insect damage to the body.

   Original anatomical observations: The coronal and sagittal sutures are obliterated but the lambdoid suture is open. A slight prognathism is visible and the chin is prominent. The supraorbital ridges are fairly well marked.

   There is a slight manifestation of an occipital vertebra.

   The teeth in both the maxilla and mandible are all present and perfect, with little wear.

   The scapula is missing. The manubrium is still separate from the rest of the sternum. The right patella is notched. The sacrum is 5-pieced and slightly curved.

   The tibiae are platycnemic.

   Surviving skeletal elements: A badly damaged skull and mandible are currently housed in the Duckworth Laboratory, The University of Cambridge (catalogue ref. NU848). The base of the skull has been destroyed, so it is no longer possible to observe the occipital vertebra. Slight pitting suggestive of cribra orbitalia is visible in the left orbital roof, but the orbital roof is missing on the right. The location of the rest of the skeleton is unknown.

References: Anatomical recording card; Firth (1912a, 55); Firth (1912b, plan VII).

4   A male, young adult post-cranial skeleton. The body was contracted on the left, with the head originally to the north.

Original anatomical observations: The bones are very small. Fusion of the lower epiphysis of the femur is complete, but the lower epiphyses of the radii, ulnae and humerii have recently joined with the line of union distinct. The epiphysis of the iliac crest is partly joined. The sternal epiphysis of clavicle has not joined. The left patella is notched. The sacrum is straight and 5-pieced.

References: Anatomical recording card; Firth (1912a, 44); Firth (1912b, plan VII).

5   A partial probably female skeleton, with no age recorded. The upper part of the skeleton only remains. The maxilla and right scapula were broken when excavated; the implication from the anatomical report is that these breaks were post-mortem although that was not explicitly stated.

Original anatomical observations: The left occipital fossa is much larger than the right.

The sockets of the incisors and 1st molars in the maxilla are apparent but the rest of the alveolus has resorbed. All of the teeth in the mandible are present but much worn.

There is spondylitis deformans of all vertebrae. This is worst in the cervical vertebrae, except for the atlas.

References: Anatomical recording card; Firth (1912a, 55); Firth (1912b, plan VII).

6   A child skeleton, about 2 years old. The body was contracted on the right, with the head to the north east.

References: Anatomical recording card; Firth (1912a, 55); Firth (1912b, plan VII).

7   A fragmentary male, aged post-cranial skeleton.

Original anatomical observations: The manubrium is ossified to the gladiolus.

The coccyx is ankylosed to the sacrum.

References: Anatomical recording card; Firth (1912a, 56); Firth (1912b, plan VII).

8   A female skeleton, with no age recorded. The body was contracted on the left, with the head to the east. The skull was damaged when excavated but it was originally retained by the anatomists due to the dental pathologies observed. The location of the skull is however no longer known.

Original anatomical observations: The teeth are all present in the maxilla except the left third molar which has never appeared, and the right 2nd incisor and the right canine which have gone. A large abscess cavity is present at the roots of the right 2nd incisor and the canine.

References: Anatomical recording card; Firth (1912a, 56); Firth (1912b, plan VII).

9   A male, aged adult skeleton. The body was contracted on the left with the head to the east. There is matting present under the head.

Original anatomical observations: The lambdoid and sagittal sutures and the lower end of the coronal suture are closing. The squamous portion of the temporal articulates with the frontal on both sides.

The super-orbital ridges are very slightly marked, and the lateral walls of the orbits are thin and perforated.

19mm posterior to the bregma, lying right across the sagittal suture is a depression in the bone measuring 35 x 18mm, which at the right extremity perforates the skull. Inflammatory process.

The teeth of the maxilla are curious in appearance as the alveolar margins are absorbed and the fangs exposed. Otherwise, the teeth are in good condition. The teeth of the mandible are all present and much worn, with no caries.

There is marked torsion of the left femur. There is a facet present on the anterior surface of the neck of both femora. The patellae are notched

References: Anatomical recording card; Firth (1912a, 56); Firth (1912b, plan VII).

10 A fragmentary male skeleton, with no age recorded.

Original anatomical observations: There is a facet present on the anterior surface of the neck of the right femur. Torsion very slight.

References: Anatomical recording card; Firth (1912a, 56); Firth (1912b, plan VII).

11 A fragmentary infant skeleton, with no sex recorded.

References: Firth (1912a, 56); Firth (1912b, plan VII).

12	A female skeleton, about 9 years old.

Original anatomical observations: An orthognathous skull with slight subnasal guttering.

References: Anatomical recording card; Firth (1912a, 56); Firth (1912b, plan VII).

13	A possible male, aged skeleton. The skull was found to be broken post-mortem when excavated.

Original anatomical observations: The coronal suture is closed at the lower end and the tables of the skull are extremely thick.

The teeth are completely absent in both jaws. The alveolus in the maxilla is completely absorbed and the mandible is reduced to a horseshoe shaped bar of bones.

The bones are described as 'extremely small and very female but with male characteristics'. Both patellae are notched.

References: Anatomical recording card; Firth (1912a, 56; Fig. 13); Firth (1912b, plan VII).

14	A female, aged skeleton. The bones are stained with a red pigment. The body is sharply contracted on the right, with the head to the east.

Original anatomical observations: The sagittal suture and the lower end of the coronal suture are closing, all other sutures are open. There is a distinct visible prognathism which is not measurable. The mastoids are small and the supraorbital ridges are well-marked.

All teeth are present in both jaws, except the 3rd molars in the maxilla. The teeth are very worn.

Both patellae are deeply notched on the outer side. Torsion of the femur is well marked. The sacrum is 5-pieced.

Surviving skeletal elements: A skull and mandible are currently housed in the Duckworth Laboratory, The University of Cambridge (catalogue ref. EDN80). There has been some damage to the skull and the post-mortem loss of a number of teeth since excavation. The location of the rest of the body is unknown.

References: Anatomical recording card; Firth (1912a, 56); Firth (1912b, Plate 4A; plan VII).

15	A female skeleton, about 4 years old. The skeleton is described as that of an infant in the archaeological report, in contrast to the anatomical record.

References: Anatomical recording card; Firth (1912a, 56); Firth (1912b, plan VII).

16   A male skeleton, with no age recorded.

Original anatomical observations: The sacrum is five pieced and slightly curved. Spondylitis.

References: Anatomical recording card; Firth (1912a, 56); Firth (1912b, plan VII).

17   A female skeleton, under 25 years old. The body was contracted on the right, with the head to the south. The bones of the lower limbs, pelvis and ribs, up to the level of the distal end of the humerus, are in a contracted position. The contracted portion of the body is stained a deep red brick colour, but the bones above this show no staining.

Original anatomical observations: All cranial sutures are open. There is marked visible prognathism which is not measurable. The great cornea of the hyoid is ossified.

The teeth are all present and perfect in both the maxilla and the mandible. The 3rd molars are not quite fully erupted in the maxilla.

A 5-month-old foetus was found above the pelvic rim, head down, lying between the thighs. In this case, as in others recorded by F. Wood Jones (see for example Jones 1910, 260), the sciatic notch is masculine.

References: Anatomical recording card; Derry (1909a, 31); Firth (1912a, 56); Firth (1912b, Plate 4B; plan VII).

18   A male, aged skeleton. The body was flexed and there was a red coloured thick matter present on the bones closest to the floor of the grave, which extended up as far as the scapula. There was also marked staining around the face and forehead, which was attributed to blood by Derry and Smith. The skull was damaged when discovered.

Original anatomical observations: The skull is damaged. The sagittal, lambdoid and left coronal sutures are obliterated, and the right coronal suture is disappearing. The supraorbital ridge is very well marked, and the orbits are horizontal ellipsoids.

There is a hole in the right superior maxilla opening into the Antrum of Highmore, apparently ante-mortem. There is marked staining all around the face and upwards into the orbit and onto forehead - ? blood.

The teeth are very much worn in both jaws, with no evidence of caries. Parts of the alveolus in the maxilla have been absorbed.

There is marked spondylitis in the cervical region. There are apparently only 6 cervical vertebrae, the rest of the vertebrae are normal.

There is a large facet on the anterior surface of the neck of the left femur. The coccyx is ankylosed to the sacrum. All parts of the sternum are ankylosed including the ensiform.

The anterior surface of the left radius shows large callus at the lower end. This inflammation extends into the carpus; all the carpal bones are ankylosed, including the 2nd and 3rd metacarpals and all of the phalanges of the middle finger.

References: Anatomical recording card; Reisner (1909a, 12); Firth (1912a, 57); Firth (1912b, plan VII).

19   A male skeleton, with no age recorded. The body was found contracted on its back, with the legs lying over to back. The head was in a position of acute opisthotones. There is insect damage to the body.

Original anatomical observations: The lower end of the coronal suture is closing, but all others are open. There is a wormian bone present in the left lambdoid suture measuring 39 x 21mm. In each zygomatic fossa there is a bony process coming from the great wing of the sphenoid in the position of attachment of the upper head of the external pterygoid muscle. The supraorbital ridges are very slightly marked and the orbits are oblique ellipsoids. The palate is very highly arched and there is a slight prognathism.

All teeth are present and perfect in both jaws, with little wear. There is an abscess cavity present in the outer alveolar surface of the left 1st molar in the mandible.

The manubrium is separate, but all pieces of the gladiolus have joined. The sacrum is normal and curved.

The posterior arch of the fifth left vertebra is separate from the rest of the vertebra.

References: Anatomical recording card; Firth (1912a, 57; Fig. 14); Firth (1912b, Plate 4C; plan VII).

20   A male child skeleton, around 5 years old found with straight hair preserved. The body was contracted, with the head bent back at an acute angle.

Original anatomical observations: There is a slight prognathism.

References: Anatomical recording card; Firth (1912a, 57); Firth (1912b, plan VII).

Cemetery 58/100, West bank Ginari

C-group and New Kingdom period

This cemetery was the 2nd of two alluvial mounds situated between the village and the river Nile. 58:100 was found west of 58:1 and may have originally been part of the same cemetery. New Kingdom burials are also found in this cemetery and in some instances, these graves cut through earlier C-group burials (Firth 1912a, 15). The condition of this cemetery is similar to 58:1.

Thirty-one bodies from 29 graves were recorded from this cemetery. Thirteen of the bodies were specifically dated to the New Kingdom, whilst the rest were dated to the C-group/New Kingdom.

C-group burials

100 A much disturbed female skeleton, about 25 years old. Short, straight dark hair was preserved. There is an indication on the anatomical recording card that the vertebral pathology was photographed but this image does not appear to have survived to the present day.

Original anatomical observations: All cranial sutures are open.

All teeth are present and perfect in both jaws, with no sign of caries. The 3rd molars in the mandible are cut but below the level of the other molars.

The line of epiphyseal fusion is still visible in both humerii and the sternal epiphysis of the clavicle is not yet fused.

Three of the upper lumbar vertebrae are involved in a pathological change consisting of ulceration of the bodies of the vertebrae, the body of the central vertebra having completely disappeared leaving a large abscess cavity. There is marked curvature owing to falling forward of the upper vertebrae.

References: Anatomical recording card; Firth (1912a, 57; Figs. 15-16); Firth (1912b, plan VII).

101 A partial female skeleton, with no age recorded. The body was sharply contracted on the right, with the head to the south. Only the long bones remain postcranially. The skull was recorded as suffering considerable insect damage.

Original anatomical observations: The coronal and sagittal sutures are completely closed and the lambdoid is closing. There are small wormian bones in each lambdoid suture. There is marked general occipital bulging and marked visible prognathism. The orbits are elliptic and slightly oblique, and the lateral walls of the orbits are complete. There are no supraorbital ridges.

All teeth are present in both jaws and considerable wear is evident. There is no caries.

References: Anatomical recording card; Firth (1912a, 57); Firth (1912b, plan VII).

102   A much disturbed male, aged skeleton. The skull was damaged when found.

Original anatomical observations: The coronal and sagittal sutures are closing, the lambdoid is open. The tori are well-marked and the orbits are elliptic and slightly oblique.

The teeth are very much worn in both jaws, with the alveolus absorbed in some areas. There is no caries.

The sacrum is small, 5-pieced and curved.

Spondylitis is noted.

References: Anatomical recording card; Reisner (1909a, 12); Firth (1912a, 57); Firth (1912b, plan VII).

103   A fragmentary child skeleton, about 12 years old. The archaeological report records the presence of this grave but does not refer to a body being present.

References: Anatomical recording card; Firth (1912a, 57); Firth (1912b, plan VII).

104   A disturbed child skeleton, about 8 years old.

References: Anatomical recording card; Firth (1912a, 58); Firth (1912b, plan VII).

105   A male, adult skeleton. The body is contracted on the right, with the head to the east. The grave is a circular pit. The skull was recorded as being disturbed prior to excavation. The right side of the body was damaged by insect activity.

Original anatomical observations: The coronal and sagittal sutures are closing, the left lambdoid closed and right is open. The tori are prominent and mastoids are large. There is a marked, measurable prognathism. The orbits are horizontal ellipsoids.

All teeth present and perfect in both jaws but fairly well worn.

The manubrium is separate from the gladiolus. There are facets present on the anterior surface of the neck of both femora. The sacrum is fairly straight and flat. Both patella are notched. The right tibia has been broken post-mortem.

References: Anatomical recording card; Firth (1912a, 58); Firth (1912b, Plate 4D; plan VII).

106A   A female skeleton, with no age recorded. The anatomical description of body 106A is not consistent with the archaeological report which records this body as a male skull only. The anatomists noted only that the mandible was missing.

Original anatomical observations: The sagittal and coronal sutures are closing, the lambdoid is closing on the left and open on the right. The supraorbital ridges are slight and there is a very slight prognathism. The orbits are horizontal ellipsoids with no thinning of the lateral orbital walls.

All of the teeth in the maxilla are present and perfect.

References: Anatomical recording card; Firth (1912a, 58); Firth (1912b, plan VII).

106B A male, adult skeleton with black, straight hair preserved. The archaeological report records the presence of two bodies in grave 106 which are numbered 106 and 106A, in contrast to the anatomical records. The mandible is noted as missing.

Original anatomical observations: There is a marked visible prognathism, which was not measurable. The nose is somewhat flat at the root and the orbits are horizontal and elliptic.

All of the teeth in the maxilla are present and slightly worn. The 1st molars on both sides are carious.

The os calcaneus is very long. Both patella are notched.

Surviving skeletal elements: The skull was located in the Anatomical Museum, The University of Manchester when studied by Watson (prior to 1935). The current location is unknown.

References: Anatomical recording card; Firth (1912b, plan VII); Watson (pre-1935).

107 A possible male skeleton, about 1 year old.

References: Anatomical recording card; Firth (1912a, 58); Firth (1912b, plan VII).

108 A male skeleton, with no age recorded. The archaeological report records the post-cranial remains as consisting of a tibia and foot only in contrast to the anatomical records.

Insect damage to the skeleton was reported and the skull was found to be fragmentary.

Original anatomical observations: All of the teeth are present and slightly worn in both jaws, with no caries.

The sacrum is 5-pieced and slightly curved.

References: Anatomical recording card; Firth (1912a, 58); Firth (1912b, plan VII).

109   A male skeleton, with no age recorded. Black, wavy hair is preserved. The body is flexed on its right side, with the head to the east. The skull was damaged when found and the mandible was missing.

   Original anatomical observations: All cranial sutures are open and there is a wormian bone in the left lambdoid. The tori are fairly well-marked. There is marked left occipital asymmetry.

   The remaining teeth in the maxilla are in good condition.

   The manubrium is separate from the gladiolus. The sacrum is 6-pieced (5 sacral bones+1 coccyx)

   References: Anatomical recording card; Firth (1912a, 58); Firth (1912b, Plate 4E; plan VII).

110   A male skeleton, about 19 years old. The anatomical record is not consistent with the archaeological report; the latter reports that the only post-cranial remains are a tibia and the bones of both feet.

   Original anatomical observations: All teeth are present and perfect in both jaws, with all 3rd molars fully erupted. There are the rudiments of a 3rd pre-molar present.

   The epiphyses of the distal femur are not yet joined but all others in the femur are. A similar pattern is seen with the head of the humerus. The epiphysis of the distal radius is fusing but the lower end of the ulnae and the sternal ends of the clavicles are not.

   The sacrum is 4 pieced and very small. Union of the individual sacral bones is still visible.

   Surviving skeletal elements: Two mandibular fragments and two separate teeth are currently housed in the Duckworth Laboratory, The University of Cambridge (catalogue ref. NU862d). The location of the rest of the body is unknown.

   References: Anatomical recording card; Firth (1912a, 58); Firth (1912b, plan VII).

111   A disturbed female skeleton, with no age recorded.

   Original anatomical observations: All The supra orbital ridges are fairly well marked. The orbits are elliptical and horizontal.

   All of the teeth in the mandible are present and perfect. Those remaining in the maxilla are perfect.

   References: Anatomical recording card; Firth (1912a, 57); Firth (1912b, plan VII).

112A	A possible female skeleton, about 8 years old. The body was buried about 2 feet below the surface. The archaeological record does not record the presence of a child in this grave; she was however assigned the number 112A by the anatomical team.

References: Anatomical recording card; Firth (1912a, 58); Firth (1912b, Plate 4F; plan VII).

112B	A male skeleton, with no age recorded. The body was flexed on its left side. The skull was fragmentary when found. This body appears to be that numbered 58:112 in the archaeological report. There is however a discrepancy between the description here (of a partial post-cranial male skeleton) and the description provided by the anatomists.

Original anatomical observations: All of the teeth in the mandible are present, perfect and fairly well worn.

There is a facet on the anterior surface of the neck of the left femur. The left patella is notched. Both tibiae are platycnemic, the right tibia markedly so.

References: Anatomical recording card; Firth (1912b, Plate 4E; plan VII).

113	A fragmentary male, aged skeleton.

Original anatomical observations: The mandibular alveolus has been much absorbed.

There is a supracondyloid process of the right humerus.

References: Anatomical recording card; Firth (1912a, 59); Firth (1912b, plan VII).

114	The anatomists record that this grave was empty, by the archaeological report records the presence of a fragmentary skeleton, with no age or sex recorded.

References: Anatomical recording card; Firth (1912a, 59); Firth (1912b, plan VII).

115	A disturbed male skeleton, with no age recorded. The body was contracted. The mandible was found to be missing when the body was excavated.

Original anatomical observations: The coronal, lambdoid and sagittal sutures are almost obliterated. The remains of wormian bones are visible. The orbits are elliptic and slightly oblique and the nose is narrow and extremely prominent. Measurable prognathism is evident. The tori are slightly marked.

There is a manifestation of an occipital vertebrae, but the vertebrae could not be connected, as the skeleton was disturbed.

All of the teeth are present, perfect and very slightly worn in the maxilla.

The sacrum is 5 pieced and markedly curved. There is a very large facet present on the anterior surface of the neck of both femora.

There is some inflammation present around the tibio-fibula joints, both upper and lower ends.

<u>References</u>: Anatomical recording card; Firth (1912a, 59); Firth (1912b, plan VII).

New Kingdom (Dynasty 18) burials

116   A male skeleton, about 18 years old. Wavy black hair about 20mm in length is preserved. There is insect damage to the skeleton.

<u>Original anatomical observations</u>: All cranial sutures are open. There is definite prognathism.

All of the teeth are present and perfect in both jaws, including the 3rd molars which are fully erupted.

The lower epiphysis of both femora, the bones of the sacrum, the upper epiphyses of both tibiae, the head of the humerii and the sternal end of the clavicles are still separate. The proximal epiphysis of the radius is joining and the line of union on the head of the femora is still present.

<u>References</u>: Anatomical recording card; Firth (1912a, 59); Firth (1912b, plan VII).

117   A female skeleton, with no age recorded. Thick, wavy black hair 85 mm long was preserved. The body was found lying on the left, with the head to the east. The knees were slightly bent and the hands were in front of the pelvis. The body was buried with a scarab. Both sets of foot bones were recorded as missing when the body was found.

<u>Original anatomical observations</u>: All cranial sutures are open. The squamous portion of the temporal bone articulates with the frontal on both sides. There is definite measurable prognathism which is only slightly visible. The chin is moderately prominent. Orbits are elliptic and slightly oblique.

All of the teeth are present and perfect in both jaws, except the left 3rd molar in the maxilla and the right 1st and 3rd molars and the left 3rd molar in the mandible which are carious.

The manubrium is fused to the gladiolus. The sacrum is 5-pieced and much curved. There is a large facet present on the anterior surface of the neck of the right femur. Public spine elongation, with a definite bony process 8 and 8.

<u>References</u>: Anatomical recording card; Firth (1912a, 59; Fig. 17); Firth (1912b, Plate 3B; plan VII).

118   A female skeleton, with no age recorded. Long plaited black hair was preserved. The body was lying on its back, fully extended. The hands were near the pubes.

<u>Original anatomical observations</u>: The coronal and sagittal sutures are closing, the lambdoid is still open. There is marked prognathism, both visible and measurable. The orbits are elliptic and slightly oblique, and the nose is flat.

The 7th cervical vertebra with well-marked costal portion, on each side of which is a distinct facet. No cervical rib was found.

All of the teeth are present and perfect in the maxilla, except left 1st molar which has a small hole and the left 3rd molar which has a large cavity. No comments were recorded for the mandible.

The manubrium is separate from the gladiolus. The sacrum is 6-pieced (5 sacral+1 coccyx bone).

<u>References</u>: Anatomical recording card; Firth (1912a, 59); Firth (1912b, plan VII).

119   A female, aged skeleton with brown hair preserved. The body was lying on the left side with the head to the east. The knees are slightly bent.

<u>Original anatomical observations</u>: The coronal, sagittal and lambdoid sutures are almost obliterated. There is distinct visible prognathism and the chin is fairly prominent. There is a large hole involving both tables of skull and running on the left of and parallel with the sagittal suture. This sits over the coronal suture (about 20mm in front and 40mm behind it), total length 60mm, with the greatest width 27mm. Appears to be ante-mortem.

All teeth are present but very worn in both jaws, there is no caries. The left 3rd molar in the maxilla and both 3rd molars in the mandible have never appeared.

The hyoid and cuneiform cartilage is ossified. The pre-auricular groove is very marked. The manubrium is still separate from the body of the sternum, although the first rib cartilages are ossified. The ulnae, radii and hand bones are missing.

The manubrium is still separate from the body, though the first rib cartilages are ossified. The sacrum is small 5-pieced and slightly curved.

<u>Further studies</u>: A further description of the trauma to the skull in bulletin 3 by Firth (1909, 33) suggests this is an example of sharp force trauma due to the presence of slight slits at either corner of the wound.

<u>Surviving skeletal elements:</u> Two cranial fragments and broken mandible (post-mortem damage) are currently housed in the Duckworth Laboratory, The University of Cambridge (catalogue ref. NU849). The location of the rest of the body is unknown.

<u>References</u>: Anatomical recording card; Reisner (1909, 13), Firth (1909, 32-33); Firth (1912a, 60; Fig. 18), Firth (1912b, Plate 3C; plan VII).

120 A male, adult skeleton with thick wavy black hair.

Original anatomical observations: The coronal and sagittal sutures are closing, the lambdoid is open. The right lambdoid has a small wormian bone. The orbits are elliptic and slightly oblique.

All teeth are present and perfect, with little wear.

The manubrium is still separate from the gladiolus. There are facets present on the anterior surface of the neck of both femora.

References: Anatomical recording card; Firth (1912a, 60); Firth (1912b, plan VII).

121 A male, aged skeleton. The body was extended on its back, with the head to the west.

Original anatomical observations: There is no prognathism. The chin is prominent.

At the basion, there is ossification of the apical ligament of the odontoid process.

The teeth in both jaws are very worn and the alveolus has absorbed. In the maxilla the 3rd molars are high in the alveolus and the left 2nd molar is carious. The 3rd molars in the mandible have dropped out very recently.

All parts of the sternum are united.

The right ulna is fractured at the lower third.

There is spondylitis of the dorsal and lumbar vertebrae, this is severe in the lumbar region. Six dorsal vertebrae are united by inflammation of the bodies of the vertebrae.

All of the pelvic bones are ankylosed together.

References: Anatomical recording card; Firth (1912a, 60); Firth (1912b, plan VII).

122 A male, aged skeleton with straight black hair.

Original anatomical observations: All sutures are closed and obliterated except the lower lambdoid on both sides. The chin is prominent. The orbits are elliptic and slightly oblique, with thin lateral walls.

All teeth are present in the maxilla except for both 3rd molars which never erupted. The teeth in the mandible are all present and perfect. The teeth are much worn.

The sacrum is 5 pieced and slightly curved. Three pieces of the sternum are still separate. The right patella is notched.

References: Anatomical recording card; Firth (1912a, 60); Firth (1912b, plan VII).

123A   A male skeleton, about 12 years old. The body was lying on the left and partially on top of body 123B. Bodies 123A and 123B have been transposed between the original anatomical record and the later archaeological publication. The numbering used here follows the anatomists numbering system as this is what would have been marked on the skull following removal from the grave. The skeleton has suffered insect damage.

Original anatomical observations: The sagittal suture is completely obliterated, all the rest are open (Scaphocephaly). There is marked bulging of the right occipital fossa and there is a slight prognathism.

References: Anatomical recording card; Firth (1912a, 60-61); Firth (1912b, plan VII); Anatomical recording card.

123B   A male, adult skeleton, with long black slightly wavy hair.

Original anatomical observations: The sagittal and upper coronal sutures are obliterated. The lower coronal and the upper end of the lambdoids are closing. The tori are fairly prominent, and the chin is prominent. The orbits are ellipsoid, the nasal bones are narrow, and the nares are sharp and slightly rounded at lowest part.

All teeth are present and perfect in both jaws.

The sacrum is 5 pieced, wide and flat. The manubrium is not fused to the gladiolus.

References: Anatomical recording card; Firth (1912a, 60-61); Firth (1912b, plan VII).

124   A male, aged skeleton. The body has fallen over onto the face, although the body was originally placed supine in a wooden coffin which has decayed. The skull was badly broken when excavated.

Original anatomical observations: The coronal and sagittal sutures are closing, the rest are open. The tori and the chin are fairly prominent. The orbits are elliptical.

All teeth are present and perfect in both jaws.

The manubrium is separate from the gladiolus. Both femora have a facet present on the anterior surface of the neck, although this is smaller on the right.

The sacrum is fused to the left innominate bone.

References: Anatomical recording card; Firth (1912a, 61); Firth (1912b, plan VII).

125   A male, aged skeleton. The body is extended on the right, with the knees slightly bent.

Original anatomical observations: The coronal suture is closing at the lower end, the sagittal and lambdoid sutures are open. There is distinct visible and measurable prognathism. The tori are very slightly marked and the chin is prominent. The inside of the mandible and the roof of the mouth are stained a pinkish colour.

All teeth in the maxilla are present and perfect except the 2nd bicuspid and the 1st molar on the left, where there is now only a small stump with the remains of an abscess at their roots. In the mandible the 2nd molars on both sides have gone and the alveolus has been absorbed. The right 1st molar is a decayed stump.

The thyroid and 1st rib cartilage are completely ossified. The manubrium is separate, but the cuneiform cartilage is ossified and fused to gladiolus. The sacrum is 5 pieced and much curved. The transverse processes of the lumbar vertebrae are remarkably long, the 3rd lumbar transverse process measures 40 mm length.

References: Anatomical recording card; Firth (1912a, 61); Firth (1912b, plan VII).

126   A male skeleton, about 15 years old.

References: Anatomical recording card; Firth (1912a, 61; Fig. 19); Firth (1912b, plan VII).

127   A male skeleton, with no age recorded. Curly black hair is preserved.

Original anatomical observations: The coronal and sagittal sutures are closing, the rest are open. There is definite visible prognathism but this was not measurable. The mastoids are very large and the tori are fairly well marked. The chin is moderately prominent.

All teeth are present and perfect in both jaws.

The sacrum is 5 pieced, small and curved. The manubrium is separate from the gladiolus.

References: Anatomical recording card; Firth (1912a, 61); Firth (1912b, plan VII).

Cemetery 59, West bank, Kalabsha

X-group period

Cemetery 59 was discovered just north of the temple of Kalabsha (Derry 1909a, 34). There are a number of pit and end-chamber graves cut into an alluvial mound which have all previously been robbed and are now empty. Some of the graves contain the remains of extended burials that are possibly intrusive according to Firth (1912a, 36). The bodies demonstrate partial soft tissue preservation. Seven bodies were excavated from 5 graves in this cemetery, all dating to the X-group period.

All of the anatomical cards for this cemetery contain a query next to both the number of the body and the number of the cemetery. This suggests their identification as belonging to this cemetery is in some doubt.

1A   A female, adult skeleton. The grave is deep with an undercut. The anatomists noted that 'the bones apparently belonged to skull but there is nothing to show this'.

       Original anatomical observations: All cranial sutures are open. The tori are scarcely marked. There is marked visible prognathism, but this is only very slightly measurable. There is slight subnasal guttering.

       The right 2nd bicuspid in the maxilla is decayed. The teeth in the mandible are much worn. The left 2nd molar has decayed, and many teeth have dropped out.

       References: Anatomical recording card.

1B   A female, adult skeleton. The grave is deep with an undercut.

       Original anatomical observations: All cranial sutures are open. There is definite visible prognathism, but this is only very slightly measurable.

       The teeth are much worn in both jaws, with no sign on decay. On the left side of the maxilla, the 2nd bicuspid and the 1st molar have gone, and the alveolus has been absorbed.

       The sacrum is 6-pieced.

       References: Anatomical recording card.

2   A female, adult skeleton. The grave is deep with an undercut.

       Original anatomical observations: The coronal, sagittal and lambdoid sutures all closing. The squamous part of the temporal bone on the right articulates with the frontal bone. The tori are well marked, and the forehead is very low. There is a definite prognathism, both visible and measurable.

       The teeth in both jaws were much worn. The left first molar in the maxilla is decayed. The mandibular alveolus has been absorbed on both sides between the 1st bicuspid and the 2nd molar on the right and between the 2nd bicuspid and the 3rd molar on the left.

On the left of the frontal bone mm in front of the left coronal suture, is a small patch of rareifying osteitis measuring 12 x 12mm. This involves both tables of the skull.

<u>References</u>: Anatomical recording card.

3A A very small male, adult skeleton. The body is flexed in a shallow undercut tomb.

<u>Original anatomical observations</u>: All cranial sutures are open. There is marked visible prognathism, but this is only slightly measurable.

The teeth in both jaws are much worn, but in good condition.

There is a fracture in the middle of the left radius which passes obliquely downwards and inwards through the ulna. This is probably a greenstick fracture.

<u>References</u>: Anatomical recording card.

3B A possible female, adult cranium. This was the uppermost body in the tomb. The mandible was missing when excavated.

<u>Original anatomical observations</u>: All sutures are open. There is a slight prognathism.

<u>References</u>: Anatomical recording card.

4 A probable male, adult cranium. The mandible was missing when excavated.

<u>Original anatomical observations</u>: All sutures are open.

<u>References</u>: Anatomical recording card.

5 A probable female cranium, with no age recorded. The mandible was missing when excavated.

<u>Original anatomical observations</u>: The coronal suture is closing, the rest are open. The lateral orbital walls are very thin. There is marked prognathism visible, but this is only slightly measurable.

The teeth in the maxilla are perfect, but fairly worn.

<u>References</u>: Anatomical recording card.

Cemetery 62, East bank, Khor Basil

Roman-Byzantine period

A Roman-Byzantine period cemetery with no other comments provided; there is no reference to any burials in the archaeological report. On the West bank, there are two patches of Roman period burials (one group of mud-cut tombs and one group of rock cut tombs). The description of the cemetery in bulletin 3 (Reisner 1909a, 8), appears to suggest that the West bank cemetery was excavated together with that on the East bank and that they are referred to with the same cemetery number. Only a single unnumbered burial was recovered from this site.

UNKN   A male, adult skeleton. This skull, along with the rest of the skeleton, was buried with two others in a mud cut tomb at the mouth of Khor Basil. The skull was retained by the anatomists due to its 'foreign' appearance. This comment was made on the anatomical recording card by Derry. Despite this, the location of the skull is now unknown.

Original anatomical observations: All cranial sutures are open. There is a wormian bone in the left lambdoid suture.

All teeth present in both jaws are perfect and slightly worn.

References: Anatomical recording card.

Cemetery 65, East bank, Wadi Abiad

A-group/Early Dynastic period

This cemetery consisted of a single burial.

1   A skeleton, with no age or sex recorded

References: Firth (1912a, 62).

Cemetery 66, West bank, Abu Regab

New Kingdom, Roman and Christian period

A single late New Kingdom burial was reported for this cemetery (Firth 1912a, 28). A number of Roman period chamber graves and the Christian period graves are also noted, but these appear not to have been recorded.

1   A female skeleton, with no age recorded.

References: Firth (1912a, 63; Fig. 20).

Cemetery 67, West bank, Dugheish

New Kingdom period

A small plundered cemetery of just three burials located in an alluvial mud bank south of the village of Dugheish (Firth 1912a, 28).

The following grave was found to be empty upon excavation: 1 (Firth 1912a, 63-64).

2　　　A skeleton, with no age or sex recorded.

　　　References: Firth (1912a, 64).

3　　　A child skeleton, with no sex recorded.

　　　References: Firth (1912a, 64).

Cemetery 68, East bank, Moalla

C-group and New Kingdom period

A cemetery of both C-group and New Kingdom burials that has well-marked separation between the two groups (Firth 1912a, 15). A single X-group period grave was also found. The graves found in this cemetery had been completely plundered and the majority of bodies had been badly damaged (Derry 1909a, 35).

Twenty-seven graves were excavated which provided 18 burials (10 graves were either positively described as empty or no record of a body was provided for them).

C-group burials

The following graves were found to be empty upon excavation: 3, 7, 22, 29 (Firth 1912a, 65-66; Firth 1912b, plan IX).

The following graves were recorded with no clear indication of whether they contained a body; they are likely to have been empty or remained unexcavated: 14, 23 (Firth 1912a, 66; Firth 1912b, plan IX).

1   A male skeleton, with no age recorded.

   Original anatomical observations: Both tibiae and femora are platycnemic. There is spondylitis of the lumbar and thoracic vertebrae. The manubrium is separate from the sternum.

   References: Anatomical recording card; Firth (1912a, 64); Firth (1912b, plan IX).

2   A partial large male skeleton, with no age recorded. The skull was missing when the body was excavated.

   Original anatomical observations: The teeth in the mandible are much worn, with no decay.

   There is a curious backward bending at the level of upper third of the left humerus.

   References: Anatomical recording card; Firth (1912a, 64); Firth (1912b, plan IX).

4   A fragmentary male skeleton, with no age recorded.

   References: Firth (1912a, 65); Firth (1912b, plan IX).

5   A postcranial fragmentary female skeleton, with no age recorded.

   Original anatomical observations: Only the vertebral column and tibiae remain intact. The sacrum is 5-pieced. Both tibiae are platycnemic.

   References: Anatomical recording card; Firth (1912a, 65); Firth (1912b, plan IX).

6 A fragmentary post-cranial female skeleton, with no age recorded.

   <u>Original anatomical observations</u>: The pre-auricular groove is very marked.

   <u>References</u>: Anatomical recording card; Firth (1912a, 65); Firth (1912b, plan IX).

8(a) A fragmentary female, adult skeleton. Only the skull cap and the occipital bone remained of the skull when excavated.

   <u>Original anatomical observations</u>: One femur has a healed spiral fracture. The fragments are displaced, so the lower fragment lies in front and to the inner side of the upper fragment. The sacrum is 5-pieced and markedly curved. One coccyx vertebra is ossified to the sacrum.

   <u>Further studies</u>: An additional description of the femoral fracture in bulletin 3 highlights the presence of a large amount of callus, involving most of the muscles in the area of the fracture (Derry 1909a, 35)

   <u>References</u>: Derry (1909, 35); Firth (1912a, 65); Firth (1912b, plan IX); Anatomical recording card.

8(b) A child skeleton, with no sex recorded. There is no record of a second burial in this grave in the archaeological report, in contrast to the anatomical records.

   <u>References</u>: Anatomical recording card.

9 A female, very aged skeleton with grey, straight hair preserved.

   <u>Original anatomical observations</u>: The coronal and sagittal sutures are completely obliterated, the lambdoid is open. The tori are fairly well marked. The lateral walls of the orbits are thin and are perforated on the right side.

   Both alveoli are completely absorbed.

   <u>References</u>: Anatomical recording card; Firth (1912a, 65); Firth (1912b, plan IX).

15 A female skeleton, with no age recorded. The skeleton was badly damaged when excavated.

   <u>Original anatomical observations</u>: All cranial sutures are open and simple. There is right occipital bulging. The orbits are elliptical and oblique.

   The teeth remaining in both jaws are perfect with no decay.

   <u>References</u>: Anatomical recording card; Firth (1912a, 66); Firth (1912b, plan IX).

18 A female skeleton, with no age recorded.

   References: Firth (1912a, 66); Firth (1912b, plan IX).

21 A fragmentary skeleton, with no age or sex recorded.

   References: Firth (1912a, 66); Firth (1912b, plan IX).

24 A disturbed female, aged skeleton, with white straight hair preserved.

   Original anatomical observations: The coronal and sagittal sutures are closing, the lambdoid suture is open.

   There are some far worn stumps remaining in the maxilla and the rest have absorbed. In the mandible all of the teeth have gone and the alveolus has absorbed.

   The acetabular cavities are very large.

   References: Anatomical recording card; Firth (1912b, plan IX).

26 A disturbed child skeleton, with no sex recorded.

   References: Firth (1912a, 66); Firth (1912b, plan IX).

New Kingdom (Dynasty 18) burials

The following graves were found to be empty upon excavation: 27, 28 (Firth 1912a, 66; Firth 1912b, plan IX).

The following graves were recorded with no clear indication of whether they contained a body; they are likely to have been empty: 11, 13 (Firth 1912a, 65).

10 A female, aged skeleton with grey hair preserved.

   Original anatomical observations: All of the cranial sutures are open. There are epiteric bones on both sides of the head. There is definite prognathism.

   The teeth of the mandible are perfect and much worn. In the maxilla the teeth behind 1st bicuspid on both sides are absorbed except the 3rd molar on both sides.

   The bones are massive, in particular those of the pelvis. They are very masculine in type. There is spondylitis of the lumbar and thoracic spine. Both femora have a large facet on the anterior side of the neck.

12 A fragmentary female skeleton, with no age recorded.

   Original anatomical observations: There is a slight prognathism.

   The teeth are perfect.

   References: Anatomical recording card.

19 A disturbed child skeleton, with no sex recorded.

   References: Anatomical recording card; Firth (1912a, 66); Firth (1912b, plan IX).

20 A disturbed female skeleton, with no age recorded.

   Original anatomical observations: All cranial sutures are open. The tori are prominent for a female.

   All of the teeth in both jaws are perfect and fairly well worn.

   The manubrium is separate from the sternum.

   References: Anatomical recording card; Firth (1912a, 66); Firth (1912b, plan IX).

X-group burials

30 A small skeleton, with no age or sex recorded.

   References: Firth (1912a, 66); Firth (1912b, plan IX).

(References at top of page: Anatomical recording card; Firth (1912a, 65); Firth (1912b, plan IX).)

Cemetery 69/1, East bank, Moalla

A-group to New Kingdom period

This cemetery was situated on the north side of a valley that runs down to the Nile, just after the village of Moalla. There are 4 groups of burials within the cemetery: 1) a group of empty graves that were not dated, 2) C-group-New Kingdom period, 3) Early Dynastic or A-group (B-group) and 4) a 2nd patch of C-group-New Kingdom graves (Firth 1912a, 67). All of the burials had been subject to the attention of tomb robbers. There were however the remains of superstructures, at least for the C-group period burials.

Ninety-seven graves were uncovered in this cemetery, with 77 remaining skeletons (21 graves were empty and one Moslem grave remained unexcavated).

A-group burials

The following graves were found to be empty upon excavation: 29, 30, 32, 33 (Firth 1912a, 69).

The following graves were recorded with no clear indication of whether they contained a body; they are likely to have been empty: 38 (Firth 1912a, 70).

31   A fragmentary skeleton, with no age or sex recorded.

   References: Firth (1912a, 69).

34   A fragmentary skeleton, with no age or sex recorded.

   References: Firth (1912a, 69).

35   A fragmentary skeleton, with no age or sex recorded.

   References: Firth (1912a, 69).

37   A fragmentary skeleton, with no age or sex recorded.

   References: Firth (1912a, 69).

39   A partial post-cranial skeleton consisting of femora and tibiae only. No age or sex was recorded.

   References: Firth (1912a, 70).

C-group burials

The following graves were found to be empty upon excavation: 8, 10 (Firth 1912a, 67; Firth 1912b, plan IX).

The following graves were recorded with no clear indication of whether they contained a body; they are likely to have been empty: 9, 19, 47, 50, 51, 54, 56, 77 (Firth 1912a, 67-72; Firth 1912b, plan IX).

11   A male skeleton, about 15 years old.

<u>References</u>: Anatomical recording card; Firth (1912a, 67); Firth (1912b, plan IX).

16   A male skeleton, with no age recorded. Wavy black hair is preserved.

<u>Original anatomical observations</u>: The coronal and lambdoid sutures are open, the sagittal suture is closing. The chin is moderately prominent and the tori are prominent.

All teeth are present, perfect and moderately worn in the maxilla. No comments were provided on the mandible.

There is a facet present on the anterior surface of the neck of both femora. The sacrum is small, flat and 5-pieced. The tibiae are platycnemic.

<u>Surviving skeletal remains</u>: The skull was located in the Anatomical Museum, The University of Manchester when studied by Watson (prior to 1935). The current location is unknown.

<u>References</u>: Anatomical recording card; Firth (1912a, 70); Firth (1912b, plan IX); Watson (pre-1935).

18   A male, adult skeleton with black wavy hair.

<u>Original anatomical observations</u>: All cranial sutures are obliterated. The tori are very slightly marked and the chin is prominent. There is a definite slight prognathism.

All teeth are present, perfect and slightly worn in both jaws.

The manubrium is separate from the gladiolus. The sacrum is 6-pieced (5 sacral bones, plus the first coccyx), long and narrow. There are facets present on the anterior surface of the neck of both femora.

<u>References</u>: Anatomical recording card; Firth (1912a, 68); Firth (1912b, plan IX).

21 A female, aged skeleton. The skull was damaged when excavated.

Original anatomical observations: The coronal, sagittal and lambdoid sutures are all open. There is a metopic suture present. The chin is rather prominent. There is thinning of the lateral walls of the orbits. Slight subnasal guttering is observed.

The teeth are much worn, with no caries in both jaws.

Both femora are platymeric.

References: Anatomical recording card; Firth (1912a, 68); Firth (1912b, plan IX).

25 A female, young adult skeleton

Original anatomical observations: There is marked prognathism.

The maxillary teeth are perfect and a little worn. The 3rd molars are not on a level with the other teeth.

References: Anatomical recording card; Firth (1912a, 68); Firth (1912b, plan IX).

36 A female, young adult skeleton with dark brown long plaits.

Original anatomical observations: All cranial sutures are open and simple. There is an epipteric bone on the right side of the skull. The widest part of skull is between the two squamous portions of the temporal bones and above external auditory meatus on both sides. There is marked visible prognathism, but this was only slightly measurable. The lateral wall of the left orbit is perforated.

The teeth are all present and perfect in both jaws. The maxillary teeth are slightly worn and the mandibular teeth show very little wear.

The sacrum is 5-pieced and measures 99 x 100mm. Both femora are platycnemic although this is more marked on the right.

References: Anatomical recording card; Firth (1912a, 69); Firth (1912b, plan IX).

41 A female skeleton, with no age recorded. The skull was damaged when excavated. The archaeological report records only a partial post-cranial skeleton in contrast to the anatomical recording card.

Original anatomical observations: The coronal and sagittal sutures are almost obliterated, the lambdoid suture is open. There is a metopic suture present which is closing. The temporal ridges are very marked.

The teeth are all present, perfect and moderately worn in both jaws. There is an abscess at the root of the left 2nd molar in the mandible.

The sacrum is 6-pieced (5 sacral bones, plus the first coccyx) and curved.

References: Anatomical recording card; Derry (1909a, 37); Firth (1912a, 70); Firth (1912b, plan IX).

42 A partial skeleton, with no age or sex recorded.

References: Firth (1912a, 70); Firth (1912b, plan IX).

43 A child's vertebral column only.

References: Firth (1912a, 70); Firth (1912b, plan IX).

44 A male, adult skeleton.

Original anatomical observations: All sutures are open. A wormian bone is present in the right lambdoid suture. There is right occipital bulging and marked visible prognathism (not measurable).

The maxillary teeth are all present, perfect and fairly worn. No comments were recorded for the mandible.

The sacrum is 5-pieced and very flat. The manubrium is fused to the body of the sternum but joined only in the middle. The line of union on each side is gaping. The first piece of the gladiolus evidently had been attached to the second piece only by a very slight osseous union which has now broken. The bones of the lower legs are absent.

References: Anatomical recording card; Firth (1912a, 70; Fig. 23); Firth (1912b, plan IX).

45 A male skeleton, with no age recorded. The skull was damaged when excavated. There is a query over the number of this grave on the anatomical report, but the archaeological report also records a male skeleton in this grave.

Original anatomical observations: All cranial sutures are closing. The tori are well marked and the chin is prominent. There is a visible prognathism.

All teeth are present and perfect in both jaws.

References: Anatomical recording card; Firth (1912a, 70); Firth (1912b, plan IX).

48 A male skeleton, with no age recorded. Straight black hair is preserved.

Original anatomical observations: All cranial sutures are open and complicated, including a metopic suture. There is a wormian bone present in each lambdoid suture. The squamous portion of the temporal bone articulates with the parietal through a long epiteric bone 60 mm in length, and through this same bone, articulates with frontal. The condition is apparently symmetrical but has broken away on the right side. On each side of the frontal bone are deep gutters running upwards from the supra-orbital foramina for the vessels in that region. There is marked prognathism. The tori are very slightly marked and the chin is rather prominent. There is slight right occipital bulging.

All teeth are present, perfect and scarcely worn in both jaws.

The right femur has a facet on the anterior surface of the neck. The sacrum is straight and simian-like.

Surviving skeletal remains: A badly damaged skull and mandible are currently housed in the Duckworth Laboratory, The University of Cambridge (catalogue ref. NU848). The location of the rest of the body is unknown.

References: Anatomical recording card; Derry (1909a, 37); Firth (1912a, 70); Firth (1912b, plan IX).

49 A female skeleton, with no age recorded.

Original anatomical observations: There is slight occipital bulging on right and marked prognathism which is both visible and measurable.

All teeth are present and moderately well-worn in both jaws. The left 3rd molar has never appeared in either jaw.

The three parts of the sternum are separate. The sacrum is 5-pieced. There is marked torsion of the right femoral head and marked retroversion of the head of both tibiae.

References: Anatomical recording card; Firth (1912a, 70); Firth (1912b, plan IX).

52 A male skeleton, with no age recorded.

Original anatomical observations: The chin is square and prominent and the tori are very marked.

All of the teeth in the mandible are present, perfect and fairly well worn. No comments were recorded for the maxilla.

The manubrium is separate. The right femur has large facet on the anterior surface of the neck.

References: Anatomical recording card; Firth (1912a, 70); Firth (1912b, plan IX).

55 A fragmentary skeleton, with no age or sex recorded.

   References: Firth (1912a, 70); Firth (1912b, plan IX).

57 A fragmentary female skeleton, with no age recorded.

   Original anatomical observations: There is marked visible prognathism.

   The maxillary teeth are much worn, with the alveolus on both sides absorbed at the bicuspids. The 1st and 3rd molars have gone on both sides of the maxilla. The mandibular teeth are perfect. The 3rd molars never appeared on either side of the mandible.

   The manubrium is separate. The sacrum is 5-pieced. The left femur is platymeric.

   References: Anatomical recording card; Firth (1912a, 71); Firth (1912b, plan IX).

58 A partial female skeleton, with no age recorded. The skull is recorded as missing.

   Original anatomical observations: All teeth in the mandible are present, perfect and fairly well worn.

   The manubrium is separate. The sacrum is 6-pieced (5 sacral bones, plus the first coccyx).

   References: Anatomical recording card; Firth (1912a, 71); Firth (1912b, plan IX).

59 A fragmentary skeleton, with no age or sex recorded.

   References: Firth (1912a, 71); Firth (1912b, plan IX).

60 A male skeleton, with no age recorded. The skull was damaged when excavated.

   Original anatomical observations: The skull is broken. The tori are fairly well-marked and there is no apparent prognathism.

   All mandibular teeth are present, perfect and moderately worn.

   The sacrum is 5-pieced and very flat.

   References: Anatomical recording card; Firth (1912a, 71); Firth (1912b, plan IX).

63 A skeleton, with no age or sex recorded.

   References: Firth (1912a, 71); Firth (1912b, plan IX).

64   A possible female, young adult skeleton.

Original anatomical observations: All cranial sutures are open, including a metopic suture. The atlas is fused to the cranium. The skull has an unusual shape, described as having a 'curious square shaped forehead' and being 'flat-topped'.

All teeth are perfect but slightly worn in both jaws. The maxillary 3rd molars are just appearing whilst those in the mandible are level with the other teeth on both sides.

The lines of union of the epiphyses in the long bones are visible, but epiphysis of the crest of the ilium has not joined.

References: Anatomical recording card; Derry (1909a, 37); Firth (1912a, 71); Firth (1912b, plan IX).

65   A skeleton, with no age or sex recorded.

References: Firth (1912a, 71); Firth (1912b, plan IX).

71   A female, aged skeleton.

Original anatomical observations: There is fairly well marked left occipital bulging.

There are no teeth remaining, with all of the alveolus absorbed in both jaws.

The sacrum is 5-pieced. There is slight platycnemia of the right tibia.

References: Anatomical recording card; Firth (1912a, 72); Firth (1912b, plan IX).

72   A disturbed male, adult skeleton with black hair.

Original anatomical observations: All cranial sutures are open. There is marked visible prognathism which is not measurable.

All teeth are present, perfect and only slightly worn in both jaws.

The manubrium is fused to the sternum.

References: Anatomical recording card; Firth (1912a, 72); Firth (1912b, plan IX).

75   A child skeleton, with no sex recorded.

References: Firth (1912a, 72); Firth (1912b, plan IX).

78   A disturbed skeleton, with no age or sex recorded. Only the lower part of the skeleton remains in position.

<u>References:</u> Firth (1912a, 73); Firth (1912b, plan IX).

86   A fragmentary skeleton, with no age or sex recorded.

<u>References:</u> Firth (1912a, 73); Firth (1912b, plan IX).

88   A disturbed male, aged skeleton.

<u>Original anatomical observations:</u> All cranial sutures are obliterated. The occipital region is symmetrical. The tori are very prominent. There is marked visible and measurable prognathism.

The teeth in both jaws are worn stumps. A large part of the alveolus has absorbed on the right side of the mandible and the left side of the maxilla.

The manubrium is separate from the sternum, but the cartilage of the 1st rib is ossified to the sternum. There is spondylitis of the lumbar and thoracic vertebrae. The sacrum is 6-pieced comprising 1 lumbar and 5 sacral bones.

<u>References:</u> Anatomical recording card; Firth (1912a, 73); Firth (1912b, plan IX).

94   A disturbed skeleton, with no age or sex recorded.

<u>References:</u> Firth (1912a, 73).

96   A female, aged skeleton in fragmentary condition.

<u>Original anatomical observations:</u> The coronal, sagittal and lambdoid sutures are all closing. There is definite visible and measurable prognathism. The mandible is broken.

All maxillary teeth are present but very worn.

References: Anatomical recording card; Firth (1912a, 74); Firth (1912b, plan IX)..

97   A disturbed skeleton, with no age or sex recorded.

<u>References:</u> Firth (1912a, 74); Firth (1912b, plan IX).

New Kingdom burials

The following graves were found to be empty upon excavation: 13 (Firth 1912a, 68; Firth 1912b, plan IX).

The following graves were recorded with no clear indication of whether they contained a body; they are likely to have been empty: 76 (Firth 1912a, 72; Firth 1912b, plan IX).

7 A fragmentary female, aged skeleton with curly dark hair was preserved. The mandible was found to be missing when the body was excavated.

Original anatomical observations: The coronal, sagittal and lambdoid sutures are almost obliterated. There is definite prognathism. Very large and marked bilateral parietal thinning is present. The skull is perforated on the right side.

The maxillary teeth are perfect and much worn, with no caries.

There is a healed fracture of the right radius and ulna; the fracture line passes obliquely downwards and inwards through both bones, from the junction of the middle and lower third of the radius to the lower third of the ulna. There has been considerable shortening.

References: Anatomical recording card; Derry (1909a, 36-37); Firth (1912a, 67); Firth (1912b, plan IX).

12 A partial female, aged skeleton with wavy, greyish hair. The post-cranial skeleton is noted as being incomplete but there no skeletal inventory was recorded by the anatomical team.

Original anatomical observations: All of the cranial sutures are obliterated. There is marked symmetrical parietal thinning and thinning of the lateral walls of the orbits.

All of the alveolus in the maxilla has absorbed. The teeth in the mandible are much worn stumps.

There is marked platycnemia of both tibiae.

References: Anatomical recording card; Firth (1912a, 68); Firth (1912b, plan IX).

14 A male, aged skeleton.

Original anatomical observations: The coronal and sagittal sutures are closing, the lambdoid is still open. The lateral orbital walls present large gaps on both sides. The tori are fairly well marked.

The teeth are very worn with no caries in both jaws. The alveolar margin has largely absorbed in the mandible.

The manubrium is separate from the gladiolus. The sacrum is 6-pieced. There is spondylitis of the lumbar vertebrae. A large facet is present on the anterior surface of the neck of both femora. Both tibiae are platycnemic.

References: Anatomical recording card; Firth (1912a, 68); Firth (1912b, plan IX).

15   A male, adult skeleton.

Original anatomical observations: All of the cranial sutures are open. The tori are well marked and the chin is square and prominent. The mastoids are extremely large.

The teeth are perfect and moderately well-worn in both jaws, with no caries.

There is a very well-marked manifestation of an occipital vertebrae. Many of the vertebrae are missing. The sacrum is 5-pieced and markedly curved. Both tibiae are markedly platycnemic. A large facet is present on the anterior surface of the neck of both femora.

References: Anatomical recording card; Firth (1912a, 68); Firth (1912b, plan IX).

17   A female, aged skeleton.

Original anatomical observations: The coronal, sagittal and lambdoid sutures are almost obliterated. There is definite prognathism and the chin is fairly prominent.

Only stumps of teeth remain in both jaws. Parts of the alveolus are absorbed.

All three parts of the sternum are fused together. Six lumbar vertebrae are present, one of which is fused to the sacral bones. There is spondylitis of the lumbar vertebrae.

References: Anatomical recording card; Firth (1912a, 68); Firth (1912b, plan IX).

20   A female, adult skeleton.

Original anatomical observations: The coronal, lambdoid and sagittal sutures are closing. The right lambdoidal suture has a small wormian bone. There is marked visible and measurable prognathism. The chin is rather prominent.

All of the teeth in the maxilla are present and perfect, with the exception of left 3rd molar which has a carious cavity. In middle line between the two central, very large incisors is an extra small but perfect tooth. The alveolus has absorbed below the bicuspid on the right. The teeth of the mandible are normal, but the 3rd molars were never present.

The sacrum is 5-pieced and very flat. There is spondylitis of the lumbar vertebrae. Facets are present on the surface of both femora. The right tibia is platycnemic.

Further studies: The skull demonstrates a number of small lesions around the cranial sutures at the back, right side of the skull. These have been tentatively identified as evidence of multiple myeloma (Reddie 2003), but further analysis is required (Figure 5).

Surviving skeletal remains: The skull is currently located in the KNH Centre for Biomedical Egyptology at The University of Manchester (catalogue number 13675). The skull shows evidence of taphonomic damage and retention of soil deposits from the burial environment. A desiccated mass, which resembles the brain, is present in the cranial cavity (Figure 6). The location of the rest of the skeleton is unknown.

References: Anatomical recording card; Derry (1909a, 37); Firth (1912a, 68); Firth (1912b, plan IX).

Figure 5: The female skull found in cemetery 69, grave 20. There are a number of small lesions present on the back, right of the skull which appear to be pathological in nature. Earlier analysis has tentatively identified these as multiple myeloma. ©The KNH Centre for Biomedical Egyptology, The University of Manchester, 2023.

Figure 6: A desiccated mass preserved in the cranial cavity of body 69:20 which is potentially part of the brain. A significant number of skulls from the ASN excavations demonstrated evidence of preservation and retention of the brain. ©The KNH Centre for Biomedical Egyptology, The University of Manchester, 2023.

22 A child skeleton about 7 years old, with no sex recorded.

<u>References:</u> Firth (1912a, 68); Firth (1912b, plan IX).

23 A female, adult skeleton. The archaeological report describes the post-cranial remains as consisting of tibiae only, but the anatomical report describes a more complete post-cranial skeleton.

<u>Original anatomical observations</u>: All of the cranial sutures are open. The chin is moderately prominent. There is definite left occipital bulging.

The teeth are much worn in both jaws. The left 3rd molar has a small carious cavity in both the mandible and maxilla.

The sacrum is 5-pieced. There is a very marked pre-auricular groove.

<u>References:</u> Anatomical recording card; Firth (1912a, 68); Firth (1912b, plan IX).

24(a) A male, aged skeleton.

<u>Original anatomical observations</u>: All of the cranial sutures are obliterated. The tori are prominent. In the middle of the sagittal suture, lying obliquely across it is a depression in the bone measuring 32 x 19mm. This involves both tables of skull, the floor being so thin as to be actually perforated. The depression is 34.5mm behind the bregma.

The maxillary teeth are much worn, with the alveolus absorbed on both sides behind the 1st molar. The mandibular alveolus is absorbed on the left side.

The innominate bone is fused to the sacrum on the right.

<u>References:</u> Anatomical recording card; Firth (1912a, 68); Firth (1912b, plan IX).

24(b) A male skeleton, with no age recorded. The archaeological report refers to two male skeletons found in this grave but there is no anatomical record for a second body.

<u>References:</u> Firth (1912a, 68).

26 A male skeleton, with no age recorded.

<u>Original anatomical observations</u>: The coronal suture is closing, the sagittal and lambdoid sutures are still open. The skull is asymmetrical, with exaggerated left occipital bulging. The chin and tori are both prominent.

All teeth are present and perfect, although much worn, in both jaws.

The sacrum is 4-pieced, although there are apparently only 5 lumbar vertebrae. There is slight spondylitis of the lumbar vertebrae.

References: Anatomical recording card; Firth (1912a, 69); Firth (1912b, plan IX).

27   A female, adult skeleton.

Original anatomical observations: The cranial sutures are very simple. The coronal and sagittal sutures are closing, the lambdoid is open. There is marked left occipital bulging and both visible and measurable prognathism. There is slight subnasal guttering.

All teeth are present and perfect, with no caries.

The first bone of the coccyx is fused to the sacrum, which is much curved in both directions.

References: Anatomical recording card; Firth (1912a, 69); Firth (1912b, plan IX).

28   A female, adult skeleton.

Original anatomical observations: All cranial sutures are open. There is a very slight visible prognathism, but this was marked when measured.

All teeth in the maxilla are present and moderately worn, with no decay. All of the mandibular teeth have recently dropped out.

There is a healed fracture of the left femur in the upper part of shaft, just below the small trochanter. The fracture has healed with good union.

References: Anatomical recording card; Derry (1909a, 37); Firth (1912a, 69); Firth (1912b, plan IX).

UNKN   A male skeleton, with no age recorded. The body was discovered west of grave number 48, but remained unnumbered by the excavators. It appears to have been an incidental find, potentially not connected with an identifiable grave site. This may account for why only a skull and mandible appear to have been recovered (see location information below).

Original anatomical observations: All cranial sutures are open. There is a small wormian in the left lambdoid.

On lower part of the right occipital bone in position of the attachment of the complexus muscle is a large mastoid-like process of bone. The tori are fairly well marked.

The teeth are present, perfect and slightly worn in both jaws.

The left femur has a facet on the anterior surface of the neck.

Surviving skeletal remains: A partial mandible is currently housed in The Duckworth Laboratory, The University of Cambridge. The fragment forms part of the collection named 'EDN' which was transferred from UCL several decades ago but is currently uncatalogued. The location of the rest of the body is unknown.

References: Anatomical recording card

61 A female skeleton, with no age recorded. Long plaited dark brown hair had been preserved.

Original anatomical observations: The coronal and sagittal sutures are practically obliterated and the lambdoid is almost so. There is an epipteric bone present on the left side shutting out the parietal from articulating with the greater wing of the sphenoid. The occipital region is symmetrical. There is a marked visible prognathism, which was not measurable.

All teeth are perfect in both jaws.

There is a facet on the anterior surface of the neck of both femora. The tibia are platycnemic.

References: Anatomical recording card; Firth (1912a, 71; Fig. 24); Firth (1912b, plan IX).

66 A male, adult skeleton.

Original anatomical observations: The cranial sutures are very simple. The coronal suture is open, the sagittal is obliterated and the lambdoid is almost obliterated. The tori are slightly marked. There is left occipital bulging.

All teeth in the maxilla are present, perfect and little worn. No comment was provided on the mandible.

The manubrium is fused to the body of the sternum. The sacrum is 5-pieced. There is a facet on the anterior surface of the neck of both femora.

References: Anatomical recording card; Firth (1912a, 71); Firth (1912b, plan IX).

67 A partial post-cranial skeleton, with no age or sex recorded. The lower part of the skeleton only remains.

References: Firth (1912a, 71); Firth (1912b, plan IX).

68 A fragmentary skeleton, with no age or sex recorded.

References: Firth (1912a, 72); Firth (1912b, plan IX).

69   A fragmentary skeleton, with no age or sex recorded.

   References: Firth (1912a, 72); Firth (1912b, plan IX).

70   A partial male, adult skeleton. The archaeological report describes the post-cranial skeleton as consisting of femora and tibiae only, which is not consistent with the anatomical report.

   Original anatomical observations: The coronal suture is closing, the sagittal and lambdoid sutures are obliterated. There is a very slight visible prognathism. The occipital region is absolutely symmetrical.

   All teeth are present, prefect and moderately worn in both jaws.

   The manubrium is separate from the gladiolus. The sacrum is 5-pieced, long and narrow.

   References: Anatomical recording card; Firth (1912a, 72); Firth (1912b, plan IX).

74   A male, young adult skeleton.

   Original anatomical observations: All cranial sutures are open. There are wormian bones present in the lambdoid and the coronal suture is complicated. The occipital is symmetrical.

   All teeth are present, perfect and very slightly worn in both jaws.

   References: Anatomical recording card; Firth (1912b, plan IX).

79   A fragmentary skeleton, with no age or sex recorded.

   References: Firth (1912a, 72); Firth (1912b, plan IX).

80   A fragmentary skeleton, with no age or sex recorded.

   References: Firth (1912a, 72); Firth (1912b, plan IX).

81   A male, adult skeleton.

   Original anatomical observations: The cranial sutures are simple and all open. Wormian bones are present in both sides of the lambdoid. There is left occipital bulging and the tori are very prominent. There is very marked visible prognathism, but this was not measurable.

   The teeth are absolutely perfect in both jaws, with little wear.

The manubrium is separate from the gladiolus. The sacrum is 5-pieced and flat. There is a facet on the anterior surface of the neck of the right femur.

<u>References</u>: Anatomical recording card

82   A fragmentary skeleton, with no age or sex recorded.

<u>References:</u> Firth (1912a, 72); Firth (1912b, plan IX).

83   A skeleton, with no age or sex recorded.

<u>References:</u> Firth (1912a, 73); Firth (1912b, plan IX).

84   A fragmentary skeleton, with no age or sex recorded.

<u>References:</u> Firth (1912a, 73); Firth (1912b, plan IX).

85   A male, adult skeleton.

<u>Original anatomical observations</u>: The coronal suture is closing, the sagittal and lambdoid sutures closed. The tori are prominent.

The teeth are much worn with no caries in both jaws. The mandibular alveolus has absorbed on the left behind the 1st molar and on the right in position of the 1st molar.

The sacrum is very flat and 6-pieced, with the first coccyx bone fused to it. There are very large facets on the anterior surface of the neck of both femora.

<u>References:</u> Anatomical recording card; Firth (1912a, 73); Firth (1912b, plan IX.

87   A fragmentary skeleton, with no age or sex recorded.

<u>References:</u> Firth (1912a, 73); Firth (1912b, plan IX).

89   A disturbed possible male, aged skeleton.

<u>Original anatomical observations</u>: The coronal and sagittal sutures are closed, the lambdoid is closing. The skull is orthognathous.

The teeth in the maxilla are all present and much worn.

90   A disturbed female, aged skeleton.

Original anatomical observations: The coronal and sagittal sutures are beginning to close, the lambdoid is open.

The mandibular teeth are well-worn stumps, except behind the 2nd bicuspid on the left where the alveolus has absorbed. All of the maxillary alveolus has absorbed.

The sacrum is comprised of 4 sacral bones, 1 lumbar vertebra and 1 coccyx.

References: Anatomical recording card; Firth (1912a, 73); Firth (1912b, plan IX).

91A   A female skeleton, with no age recorded. Although this burial is identified with the character 'A' there is no indication of a second body in the grave.

Original anatomical observations: The cranial sutures are simple and all open. There is a very slight left occipital bulging. The skull is a small orthognathous frontal type.

All teeth in the maxilla are present, with no caries and fairly well worn. No comments were provided on the mandible.

References: Anatomical recording card; Firth (1912a, 73); Firth (1912b, plan IX).

92   A male skeleton, with no age recorded. The skull was found to be damaged when excavated.

Original anatomical observations: All cranial sutures are open. The coronal and sagittal sutures are rather simple. There is left occipital bulging and the tori are fairly prominent.

There is a facet present on the anterior surface of the neck of both femora.

References: Anatomical recording card; Firth (1912a, 73).

93   A fragmentary skeleton, with no age or sex recorded.

References: Firth (1912a, 73); Firth (1912b, plan IX).

95(a) A fragmentary post-cranial male, adult skeleton.

References: Anatomical recording card; Firth (1912a, 73).

95(b)   A fragmentary post-cranial female, adult skeleton.

References: Firth (1912a, 73).

C-group/New Kingdom burials

40   A male skeleton, with no age recorded. Very dark brown wavy hair is preserved.

Original anatomical observations: The sagittal suture is closing posteriorly, all the others are open. On the left side the temporal articulates with the frontal bone. On the right side the temporal articulates with frontal through the medium of an epipteric bone. There is right occipital bulging. Tori are well-marked.

References: Anatomical recording card.

73   A disarticulated female, adult skeleton. The skull was found to be very badly damaged when excavated.

Original anatomical observations: All cranial sutures are very simple and all are open. There is left occipital bulging. The chin is pointed.

All of the teeth in the mandible are perfect. The 3rd molars never appeared.

References: Anatomical recording card; Firth (1912a, 72).

Moslem burial

53   An unexcavated Moslem burial.

Burials of unknown date

The following graves were found to be empty upon excavation: 1, 2, 3, 5 (Firth 1912a, 67).

4   A partial skeleton consisting of a skull and part of a post-cranial skeleton. No age or sex recorded.

Surviving skeletal remains: Cranial fragments and a mandible are currently housed in the Duckworth Laboratory, The University of Cambridge (catalogue ref. NU851). The location of the rest of the body is unknown.

References: Firth (1912a, 67).

6   A partial skeleton consisting of a skull and part of a post-cranial skeleton. No age or sex recorded.

   References: Firth (1912a, 67).

UNKN A male skeleton, with no age recorded. The skull was found to be badly distorted by grave pressure. This grave not numbered; it was a single grave located on top of a high terrace, at the right bifurcation of the khor. The date is unknown.

   Original anatomical observations: All cranial sutures are open except the sagittal which is beginning to close. The sutures are very simple indeed. There are wormian bones in the lambdoid on both sides. The tori are prominent. The forehead is low and sloping and the mastoids are massive.

   All of the teeth are very much worn but perfect with no caries in both jaws.

   The manubrium is separate. The sacrum is 6-pieced (5 sacral bones, plus the first coccyx) and curved.

   References: Anatomical recording card.

Cemetery 69/100, Moalla, East bank

A-group (B-group) to C-group period

A small group of burials south-east of cemetery 69/1, dated uncertainly to the B-group to C-group periods (Firth 1912a, 74). There were five bodies found in this cemetery, with the sex of only one being recorded. A specific age estimate was only provided for the single child skeleton discovered.

100 A fragmentary skeleton, with no age or sex recorded.

   References: Firth (1912a, 74).

101 A male skeleton, with no age recorded.

   Original anatomical observations: The coronal and sagittal sutures are closing. The lambdoid is open and there is a wormian bone present on the left. On both sides there are large epipteric bones that shut out the great wing of the sphenoid from articulation with the parietal. The occipital region is symmetrical. There is very marked visible prognathism, which was only slight when measured. There are no tori.

   All teeth are present, perfect and slightly worn in both jaws.

   The vertebrae are normal (12 rib bearing, 5 lumbar vertebrae, 7 cervical). The sacrum is small, flat and 5-pieced. Only the first piece of the sacrum has fused.

   References: Anatomical recording card; Firth (1912a, 74).

102 A fragmentary skeleton, with no age or sex recorded.

   References: Firth (1912a, 74).

103 A partial skeleton, with no age or sex recorded. The lower part of the skeleton is missing.

   References: Firth (1912a, 74).

104 A child skeleton about 7 years old, with no sex recorded.

   References: Anatomical recording card.

Cemetery 69/200, Moalla, East bank

New Kingdom period

Three New Kingdom tombs cut into the alluvial bank (Firth 1912a, 75-77). Only tomb 69/200 had any remaining contents and yielded four skeletons (three male and one female).

The following graves were found to be empty upon excavation: 201, 202 (Firth 1912a, 77).

200A   A male, aged skeleton.

>Original anatomical observations: The coronal and lambdoid sutures are closing, the saggital suture is closed. The tori are very prominent and the chin is square and prominent. The occipital is symmetrical. There is definite visible and measurable prognathism. The posterior arch of the atlas has not joined, the 2 limbs overlap one another without union.
>
>The teeth in the maxilla are worn stumps and parts of the alveolus are absorbed. No comments are recorded for the mandible.
>
>The thyroid cartilage is ossified. The right ulna is fractured in lower third with good union. There is spondylitis of the lower thoracic and lumbar vertebrae. The lumbar vertebrae are badly affected. The fifth lumbar vertebra is joined to the sacrum but this is by inflammatory bone. There is a facet present on the anterior surface of the neck of both femora.
>
>References: Anatomical recording card; Firth (1912a, 74-77; Fig. 25-6); Firth (1912b, Plate 3D).

200B   A male, aged skeleton.

>Original anatomical observations: The coronal and sagittal sutures are closing, lambdoid suture is open.
>
>There is a facet on the anterior surface of neck of the left femur.
>
>References: Anatomical recording card; Firth (1912a, 74-77; Fig. 25-6); Firth (1912b, Plate 3D).

200C   A male skeleton, with no age recorded. The skull was found to be smashed when excavated.

>Original anatomical observations: The coronal and sagittal sutures are open. The tori are very prominent.
>
>The teeth are very much worn in both jaws, with no caries.
>
>The manubrium is separate from rest of the sternum. There is a large facet on the anterior surface of the neck of both femora.
>
>References: Anatomical recording card; Firth (1912a, 74-77; Fig. 25-6); Firth (1912b, Plate 3D).

200D   A female skeleton, with no age recorded. The facial bones of the skull were damaged when the body was excavated.

Original anatomical observations: All of the cranial sutures are open. There is a lambdoidal wormian bone on the right. Very slight left occipital bulging is present. The breadth of the skull is due to exaggerated parietal eminences.

References: Anatomical recording card; Firth (1912a, 74-77; Fig. 25-6); Firth (1912b, Plate 3D).

Cemetery 70, West bank, situated between Faragalla and Musa Kolei

A-group (Early Dynastic), New Kingdom and Christian period.

A range of graves and tombs cut into the clay at the foot of a sandstone bank. The majority of bodies were extended Christian period burials. The bodies were loosely wrapped in woollen cloth and sandstone slabs were placed over the burials (Firth 1912a, 77). Twenty-three bodies were recorded, although there is no record of them being studied to determine age or sex.

A-group burials

1	A skeleton, with no age or sex recorded.

	References: Firth (1912a, 77).

New Kingdom burials

3	A fragmentary skeleton, with no age or sex recorded.

	References: Firth (1912a, 77).

Christian burials

2	An extended body, with no age or sex recorded.

	References: Firth (1912a, 77).

4	An extended body, with no age or sex recorded.

	References: Firth (1912a, 77).

5	An extended body, with no age or sex recorded.

	References: Firth (1912a, 77).

6	An extended body, with no age or sex recorded.

	References: Firth (1912a, 77).

7   An extended body, with no age or sex recorded.

    References: Firth (1912a, 77).

8   An extended body, with no age or sex recorded.

    References: Firth (1912a, 77).

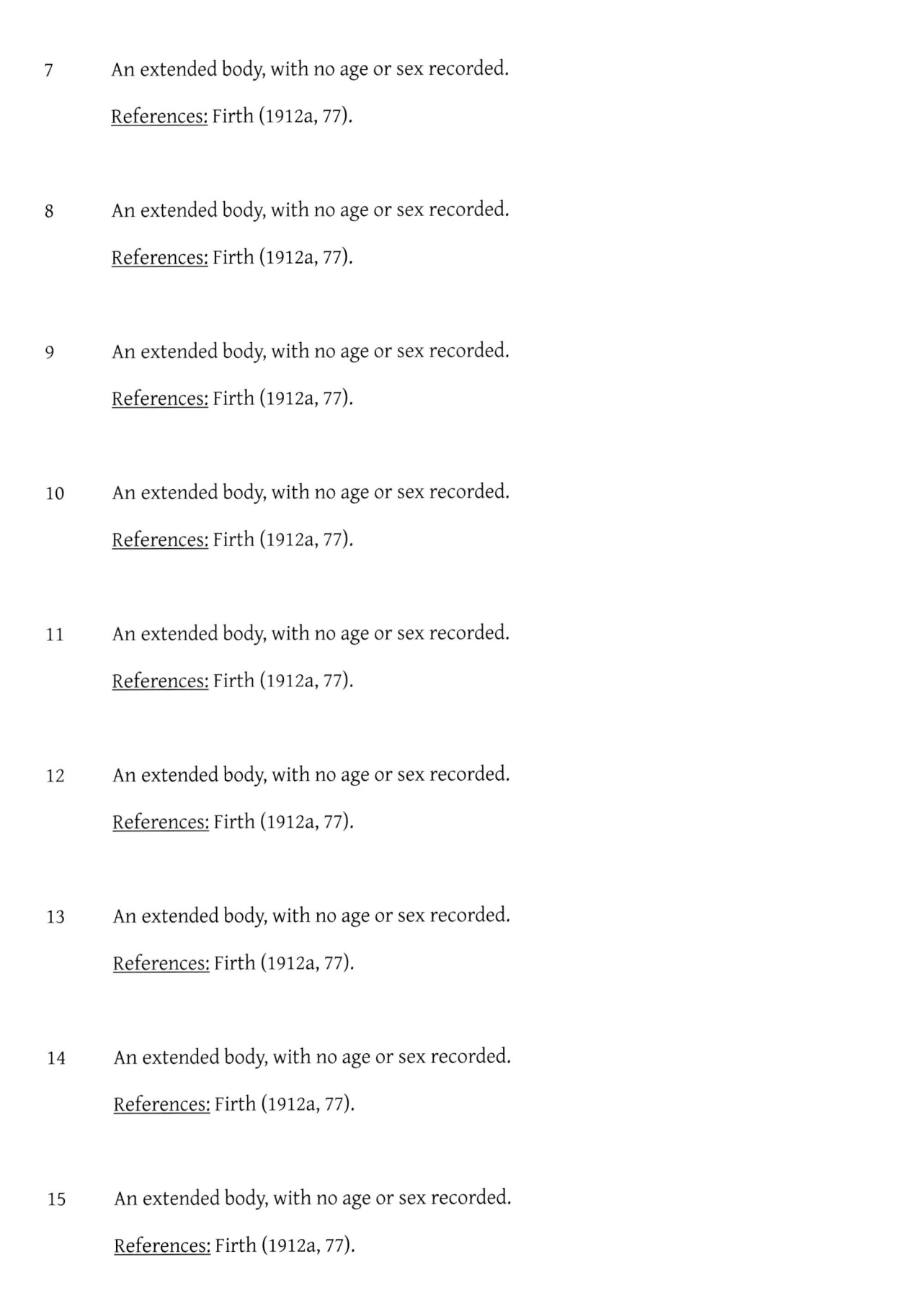

9   An extended body, with no age or sex recorded.

    References: Firth (1912a, 77).

10 An extended body, with no age or sex recorded.

    References: Firth (1912a, 77).

11 An extended body, with no age or sex recorded.

    References: Firth (1912a, 77).

12 An extended body, with no age or sex recorded.

    References: Firth (1912a, 77).

13 An extended body, with no age or sex recorded.

    References: Firth (1912a, 77).

14 An extended body, with no age or sex recorded.

    References: Firth (1912a, 77).

15 An extended body, with no age or sex recorded.

    References: Firth (1912a, 77).

16	An extended body, with no age or sex recorded.

	References: Firth (1912a, 77).

17	An extended body, with no age or sex recorded.

	References: Firth (1912a, 77).

18	An extended body, with no age or sex recorded.

	References: Firth (1912a, 77).

19	An extended body, with no age or sex recorded.

	References: Firth (1912a, 77).

20	An extended body, with no age or sex recorded.

	References: Firth (1912a, 77).

21	An extended body, with no age or sex recorded.

	References: Firth (1912a, 77).

22	An extended body, with no age or sex recorded.

	References: Firth (1912a, 77).

23	An extended body, with no age or sex recorded.

	References: Firth (1912a, 77).

Cemetery 70/100, West bank, situated between Faragalla and Musa Kolei

New Kingdom and Christian period

This cemetery consisted of 18 graves, the majority of which were extended Christian period burials. There is no record of these bodies being studied anatomically.

New Kingdom burials

The following graves were found to be empty upon excavation: 101 (Firth 1912a, 78).

100 A skeleton, with no age or sex recorded.

 References: Firth (1912a, 77-8).

Christian burials

It is not clear from the archaeological report whether any of these bodies were naturally mummified or whether they were skeletonised.

102 An extended body, with no age or sex recorded.

 References: Firth (1912a, 78).

103 An extended body, with no age or sex recorded.

 References: Firth (1912a, 78).

104 An extended body, with no age or sex recorded.

 References: Firth (1912a, 78).

105 An extended body, with no age or sex recorded.

 References: Firth (1912a, 78).

106 An extended body, with no age or sex recorded.

 References: Firth (1912a, 78).

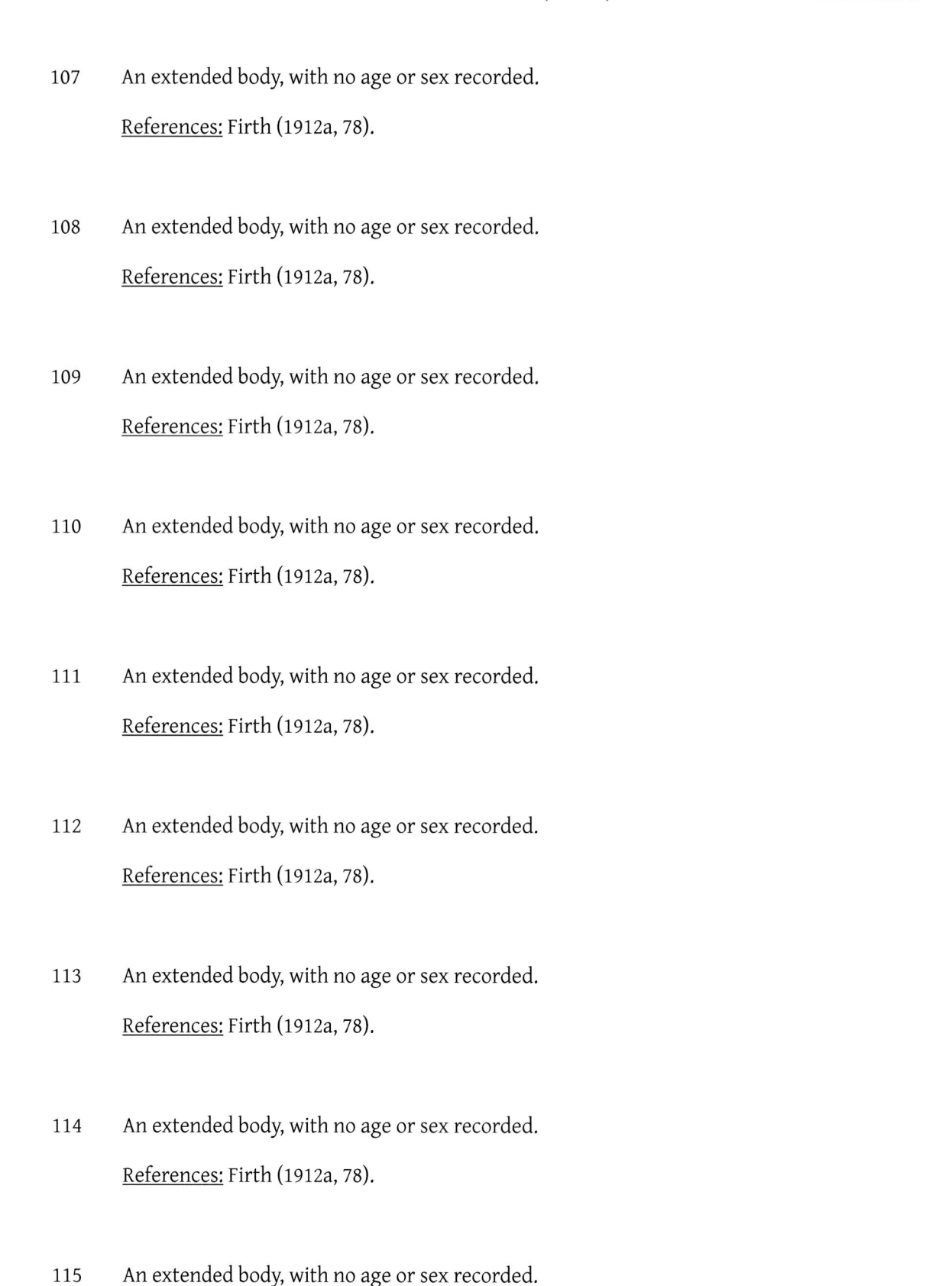

107   An extended body, with no age or sex recorded.

        References: Firth (1912a, 78).

108   An extended body, with no age or sex recorded.

        References: Firth (1912a, 78).

109   An extended body, with no age or sex recorded.

        References: Firth (1912a, 78).

110   An extended body, with no age or sex recorded.

        References: Firth (1912a, 78).

111   An extended body, with no age or sex recorded.

        References: Firth (1912a, 78).

112   An extended body, with no age or sex recorded.

        References: Firth (1912a, 78).

113   An extended body, with no age or sex recorded.

        References: Firth (1912a, 78).

114   An extended body, with no age or sex recorded.

        References: Firth (1912a, 78).

115   An extended body, with no age or sex recorded.

        References: Firth (1912a, 78).

116   An extended body, with no age or sex recorded.

References: Firth (1912a, 78).

117   An extended body, with no age or sex recorded.

References: Firth (1912a, 78).

Cemetery 71, East bank, Sharaf el Din Togog

New Kingdom period

Two deep New Kingdom tombs cut into the mud bank at the mouth of a large valley that joins the Nile. Both tombs had been largely plundered (Firth 1912a, 78).

The following graves were recorded with no clear indication of whether they contained a body; they are likely to have been empty: 2 (Firth 1912a, 78).

1   A possible male, adult skeleton. The archaeological report refers to a number of skulls found in this grave, but there is no further reference to them in the archaeological or anatomical reports.

        Original anatomical observations: There is a slight visible prognathism, which was marked when measured.

        References: Anatomical recording card; Derry (1909a, 38); Firth (1912a, 78).

Cemetery 71/100, East bank, Sharaf el Din Togog

C-group period

A small, poorly preserved group of C-group graves situated 400m inland of cemetery 71/1 (Firth 1912a, 78). Reisner (1909a, 9) records 16 graves in cemetery 71/100 (numbered 100-115) but only one is recorded in the main archaeological report, whilst human remains survive from two graves.

100   A female, adult skull and mandible. The archaeological report records this grave as empty. As no recording card for the body has survived it is impossible to know whether the skeleton was complete when excavated.

        Surviving skeletal remains: A skull and mandible are currently housed in the Duckworth Laboratory, The University of Cambridge (catalogue ref. NU852).

        References: Firth (1912a, 78).

103   A female, adult skeleton.

        Original anatomical observations: All cranial sutures are open. There is a marked visible prognathism, which was slight when measured.

        All of the teeth are present and perfect in both jaws.

        The manubrium is still separate. The sacrum is small and 5-pieced. Both patellae are notched and both tibiae are platycnemic. Both humerii are perforated.

        References: Anatomical recording card; Derry (1909a, 38); Firth (1912a, 78; Fig. 28).

Cemetery 72, West bank, Gerf Husein

C-group to New Kingdom period and X-group to Christian period

Cemetery 72 is a large cemetery which was used over several periods and situated near the Gerf Husein temple, just south of the village of Fagirdib. There were around 600 graves present in the cemetery (Derry 1909a, 39). The C-group cemetery was large but in extremely poor condition due to the activities of tomb robbers; many of the tomb contents discovered on the surface (Firth 1912a, 16). The group of New Kingdom burials was dated by Firth (1912a, 28) to the later New Kingdom period. There were a large number of X-group burials and a Christian period cemetery with long deep graves that had retained their superstructures (Firth 1912a, 37). The archaeological report refers to a group of mud-cut end chamber tombs from the Roman period but there is no further reference to these in the archaeological report or in any archival sources. Two hundred and seventy-seven graves are recorded, of which 82 were empty.

C-group burials

The following graves were recorded with no clear indication of whether they contained a body; they are likely to have been empty: 248, 261, 313, 418, 601, 619, 620, 622 (Firth 1912a, 84-86).

214   A disturbed skeleton, with no age or sex recorded.

   References: Firth (1912a, 83).

219   A female skeleton, with no age recorded.

   References: Firth (1912a, 83); Anatomical recording card.

225   A fragmentary female skeleton, with no age recorded.

   References: Firth (1912a, 83); Anatomical recording card.

226   A female, aged skeleton. The skull was fragile when excavated and the face had gone.

   Original anatomical observations: The coronal and sagittal sutures are closing, the lambdoid suture is open.

   The teeth in both the maxilla and the mandible are much worn. There is a large abscess at the root of the right 2nd incisor in the maxilla. The 3rd molars in the mandible were never present and there are the remains of a large abscess at roots of the right canine and the left 1st and 2nd molars.

   The manubrium is separate. The sacrum comprises 4 sacral bones and the first coccyx bone. There are six lumbar vertebrae. There is a facet present on the neck of both femora. The right patella is notched.

   References: Anatomical recording card; Firth (1912a, 81).

234 A fragmentary female child skeleton.

References: Anatomical recording card; Firth (1912a, 81; Fig. 30).

235 A fragmentary possible female skeleton, with no age recorded.

References: Firth (1912a, 83); Anatomical recording card.

237 A male, aged skeleton with curly brown hair preserved.

Original anatomical observations: The coronal and sagittal sutures are almost obliterated, the lambdoid suture is open. The occipital is symmetrical. There is parietal thinning especially near the pacchioman depressions. There is marked visible and measurable prognathism.

The teeth are present and perfect in both jaws.

The manubrium is separate. There is a facet present on the neck of both femora. The left tibia is slightly platycnemic.

References: Anatomical recording card

238 A fragmentary male skeleton, with no age recorded.

References: Anatomical recording card; Firth (1912a, 83).

239 A male, aged skeleton.

Original anatomical observations: All cranial sutures are obliterated. There is definite right occipital bulging. The tori are very slight. There is marked visible and measurable prognathism

The teeth are present but very much worn in both jaws.

The sacrum is 5-pieced and flat.

Surviving skeletal remains: The skull is currently located in the KNH Centre for Biomedical Egyptology at The University of Manchester (catalogue ref. 13703). The location of the rest of the skeleton is unknown.

References: Anatomical recording card

240   A child skeleton, with no sex recorded.

   References: Anatomical recording card.

241   A female, adult skeleton.

   Original anatomical observations: All cranial sutures are open. There is definite visible and measurable prognathism.

   All teeth present are perfect in both jaws. The 3rd molars never appeared in the maxilla.

   Surviving skeletal remains: The skull was located in the Anatomical Museum, The University of Manchester when studied by Watson (prior to 1935). The current location is unknown.

   References: Anatomical recording card; Watson (pre-1935).

245   A fragmentary male skeleton, with no age recorded.

   References: Anatomical recording card; Firth (1912a, 83).

249   A fragmentary female skeleton, with no age recorded.

   References: Anatomical recording card; Firth (1912a, 84).

250   A fragmentary child skeleton, with no sex recorded.

   References: Anatomical recording card; Firth (1912a, 84).

253   A female, adult skeleton contracted on the right.

   Original anatomical observations: The coronal suture is simple and open. The sagittal and lambdoid sutures are also open. On the left the squamous temporal articulates with the frontal. There is left occipital bulging. There are very well marked temporal ridges and marked visible and measurable prognathism.

   All teeth are present and perfect in both jaws. The 3rd molars are present in the mandible but there are no 3rd molars to appear in the maxilla.

   The manubrium is fused to body of sternum, which has been the subject of inflammatory action. There are very well-marked preauricular grooves. The sacrum is 5-pieced. The left humerus, at junction of lower and middle third of shaft, has a round hole on the inner side of the bone communicating with the medullary cavity, with much inflammatory reaction around it. The left humerus, left scapula, sternum, and cervical, dorsal vertebrae and the upper lumbar vertebrae have been attacked by the same inflammatory disease. The clavicles also show signs of inflammation; the left clavicle has broken at a weakened spot.

Further studies: The disease affecting this individual is described as a necrotic process in bulletin 3 and the vertebrae are considered to have been eaten away from a form of 'rarefying osteitis' (Derry 1909a, 45).

Brothwell (1967, 320-21) suggested this skeleton should be re-examined as a potential example of neoplastic disease. Unfortunately, as the location of the skeleton is unknown this is not possible.

References: Anatomical recording card; Derry (1909a, 45); Smith and Derry (1910b, 29); Firth (1912a, 81); Firth (1912b, Plate 19A), Brothwell (1967, 320-321).

257 A probable male skull only, with no age recorded.

Original anatomical observations: All cranial sutures are closed. The mastoids are large. There is marked visible and measurable prognathism. There is left occipital bulging.

Surviving skeletal remains: The skull is currently located in the KNH Centre for Biomedical Egyptology at The University of Manchester (catalogue ref. 13676).

References: Anatomical recording card.

262 A female skeleton, with no age recorded.

Original anatomical observations: All cranial sutures are open. On the left the squamous temporal articulates with the frontal bone. The occipital is symmetrical. There is definite visible and measurable prognathism.

All teeth are present and perfect in both jaws. There is a curious small peg shaped right 3rd molar in the maxilla.

References: Anatomical recording card

263 A female skeleton, with no age recorded.

Original anatomical observations: The cranial sutures are very simple and all open. There are epipteric bones on both sides of the skull. There is marked visible and measurable prognathism. The mastoids are massive. The mandible is missing.

All teeth present in the maxilla are perfect, with no caries.

The sacrum is 5-pieced. There is platycnemia of the left tibia.

References: Anatomical recording card; Firth (1912a, 84).

268　　A male, adult skeleton.

Original anatomical observations: The skull is broken at the base. All cranial sutures are open. The tori are prominent, and the mastoids are massive. There is slight right occipital bulging. The right occipital fossa is large. There is a definite visible prognathism.

All teeth are present and perfect in both jaws.

The sacrum is 6-pieced (5 sacral bones and 1 coccyx). The left patella is notched. Both tibiae are platycnemic.

References: Anatomical recording card.

269　　A female, adult skeleton.

Original anatomical observations: All cranial sutures are open. There is an epipteric bone on the left. There is slight left occipital bulging. There is no visible or measurable prognathism.

All teeth present are perfect, with no caries in both jaws.

References: Anatomical recording card.

270　　A female, adult skeleton. The skull was damaged when it was excavated.

Original anatomical observations: All cranial sutures are open. There is a definite visible prognathism, which was not measurable. The tori are prominent.

All teeth remaining are perfect in both jaws.

There is a facet present on the neck of the left femur.

References: Anatomical recording card.

271　　A male, aged skull only.

Original anatomical observations: All cranial sutures are closed. There is slight left occipital bulging. There is a definite visible and measurable prognathism. The mandible is missing.

The maxillary teeth are very much worn. There is a small abscess cavity at root of left 1st molar on each side, lingual and labial.

References: Anatomical recording card.

273   A female, adult skeleton. The skull was described as being cracked when it was discovered.

Original anatomical observations: The coronal suture is closing, the sagittal and lambdoid sutures are open.

All teeth present in the maxilla are perfect. The 2nd bicuspids on both sides have disappeared and the alveolus has absorbed. There have never been any 3rd molars. On the left side in the position that the 3rd molar should occupy is a large abscess cavity, communicating with the Antrum of Highmore. The fangs of the 2nd molar are exposed in the walls of cavity. No comments were provided for the mandible.

There is a facet present on the neck of both femora.

Surviving skeletal remains: A cranial fragment and a mandibular fragment are currently held in the Duckworth Laboratory, The University of Cambridge (catalogue ref. NU862c). The location of the rest of the skeleton is unknown. The maxillary fragment demonstrates the abscess cavity referred to in the anatomical report.

References: Anatomical recording card; Firth (1912a, 84).

275   A male skeleton, with no age recorded.

References: Anatomical recording card.

279   A male skeleton, with no age recorded.

Original anatomical observations: The left tibia is platycnemic.

References: Anatomical recording card; Firth (1912a, 84).

278   A male skeleton, with no age recorded.

References: Anatomical recording card.

280   A male skeleton, with no age recorded.

References: Anatomical recording card.

284   A female skeleton, with no age recorded.

References: Firth (1912a, 84).

287 A child skeleton, with no sex recorded.

   References: Anatomical recording card.

288 A female skeleton, with no age recorded.

   References: Anatomical recording card.

289 A female skeleton, with no age recorded.

   References: Anatomical recording card.

290 A male skeleton, with no age recorded.

   References: Anatomical recording card.

298 A child skeleton about 1 year, with no sex recorded.

   References: Anatomical recording card.

302 A male skeleton, with no age recorded.

   References: Anatomical recording card.

306 A male skeleton, with no age recorded.

   References: Anatomical recording card.

308 A probable female skeleton, with no age recorded.

   References: Anatomical recording card.

309 A female, aged skeleton.

   Original anatomical observations: All cranial sutures are closed. On the right side the temporal articulates with the frontal. There is slight left occipital bulging. A very slight visible prognathism was observed, which was marked when measured. On the right side of the cranium is an opening into the posterior wall of the external auditory meatus which apparently communicates with the mastoid cells. The anterior wall of the meatus has also got a hole through it. There has also been some inflammation in the left auditory meatus.

The maxillary teeth are much worn, with no caries. The mandibular teeth are only stumps. There is an abscess at the roots of the 1st and 2nd bicuspids on the right and the 1st bicuspid on the left. There is also an abscess at the root of the right 1st molar.

The manubrium is separate. The sacrum is 5-pieced.

References: Anatomical recording card.

310   A female, adult skeleton.

Original anatomical observations: The skull was broken. The coronal suture is closed, the sagittal suture is closing and the lambdoid suture is open.

The sacrum is 5-pieced.

References: Anatomical recording card; Firth (1912a, 84).

311   A male, adult postcranial skeleton.

Original anatomical observations: There is a facet on the neck of both femora.

References: Anatomical recording card.

312(a)   A female skeleton, with no age given. The bodies in this grave were not numbered individually.

Original anatomical observations: The only comments recorded on the dentition were 'there is an additional cusp on the lower side of the left 3rd molar'. There is no indication of whether this is in the maxilla or the mandible.

Both tibiae are platycnemic.

References: Anatomical recording card; Firth (1912a, 84.

312(b)   A female skeleton, with no age given.

References: Anatomical recording card; Firth (1912a, 84).

314   A female skeleton, with no age recorded.

   References: Anatomical recording card.

315   A female skeleton, with no age recorded.

   References: Anatomical recording card.

316   A child skeleton, with no sex recorded.

   References: Anatomical recording card.

317   A female, adult postcranial skeleton.

   Original anatomical observations: The manubrium is separate from the gladiolus.

   References: Anatomical recording card; Firth (1912a, 81).

319   A male skeleton, with no age recorded.

   References: Anatomical recording card.

320   A female skeleton, with no age recorded.

   References: Anatomical recording card.

321   A male skeleton, with no age recorded.

   References: Anatomical recording card.

322   A female, adult skeleton. The skull was found to be damaged when it was excavated.

   Original anatomical observations: All cranial sutures are open.

   All teeth that are present are well-worn and perfect in both jaws.

   The manubrium is separate. The xiphoid process is fused to the gladiolus which has a large perforation through it. The sacrum is 5-pieced and curved.

323   A male, aged skeleton. The skull was found to be badly damaged when it was excavated.

<u>Original anatomical observations</u>: The coronal suture is closing, the sagittal and lambdoid sutures are closed. There is the manifestation of an occipital vertebra.

<u>References</u>: Anatomical recording card.

324   A male, adult skeleton.

<u>References</u>: Anatomical recording card.

326   A female skeleton, with no age given recorded.

<u>Original anatomical observations</u>: The sacrum is 6-pieced (5 sacral bones + 1 coccyx).

<u>References</u>: Anatomical recording card.

327   A possible male, aged skull and mandible.

<u>Original anatomical observations</u>: All cranial sutures are closed. There is right occipital bulging. There is a marked visible and measurable prognathism. The tori are fairly well marked.

Only a few stumps of the teeth remain, the alveolus is largely absorbed.

<u>References</u>: Anatomical recording card.

328   A child skeleton, with no sex recorded.

<u>References</u>: Anatomical recording card.

329   A female skeleton, with no age recorded.

<u>References</u>: Anatomical recording card.

330 A male skeleton, with no age recorded. The body was buried with beads. The archaeological report indicates that only the leg bones remained of the skeleton.

References: Anatomical recording card; Firth (1912a, 81).

331 A child skeleton, with sex recorded.

References: Anatomical recording card; Firth (1912a, 85).

333 A male skeleton, with no age recorded.

References: Anatomical recording card.

334 A female skull and mandible, with no age recorded.

Original anatomical observations: The coronal and lambdoid sutures are closing, the sagittal suture is closed. There is slight right occipital bulging.

All teeth present are perfect and fairly well worn, with no caries in both jaws.

References: Anatomical recording card.

336 A male skeleton, with no age recorded.

References: Anatomical recording card.

337 A disturbed female skeleton, with no age recorded. The skull was found to be badly broken when excavated.

Original anatomical observations: The coronal and sagittal sutures are closing, the lambdoid is open. The occipital bone is symmetrical.

All of the mandibular teeth are present, perfect and moderately worn with no caries. Upon excavation the mandible was found to have two incisors, but there is a socket which may have held third small one. There is not sufficient room in the mandible for all the teeth and the canine on the right is crowded out by the single incisor on right side and the 1st bicuspid. There are only 14 teeth present in total, 2 incisors being absent.

The sacrum is 6-pieced (5 sacral bones and 1 coccyx).

References: Anatomical recording card; Firth (1912a, 85).

338 A male skeleton, with no age recorded.

References: Anatomical recording card; Firth (1912a, 85).

339 A male, adult skeleton. Only fragments of the skull remained when the body was excavated.

References: Anatomical recording card.

341 A male, aged skeleton. The skull was found to be broken when excavated and the facial bones had gone.

Original anatomical observations: coronal and sagittal sutures are closed, the lambdoid is closing. The tori are prominent. There is a very large cranio-pharangeal foramen. There is left occipital bulging.

The remaining mandibular teeth are much worn. There is an abscess at the root of the left 1st molar, opening onto the lingual side. No comments were provided on the maxilla.

There is a large facet on the neck of the right femur. There is severe spondylitis of the lumbar spine.

References: Anatomical recording card.

342 A male, adult skeleton with long, black straight hair preserved. The skull was found to be smashed when the body was excavated.

Original anatomical observations: All of the mandibular teeth are present, perfect and slightly worn.

References: Anatomical recording card; Firth (1912a, 85).

343 A female, adult skeleton.

Original anatomical observations: The coronal and lambdoid sutures open, the sagittal suture is closing.

The occipital bone is symmetrical.

The maxillary teeth are very much worn, with abscesses present at the roots of the right 1st bicuspid and 1st molar and the left 1st bicuspid. No comments were recorded for the mandible.

References: Anatomical recording card.

346 A male skeleton, with no age recorded.

   References: Anatomical recording card.

349 A male skeleton, with no age recorded.

   References: Anatomical recording card.

350 A child skeleton, with no sex recorded.

   References: Anatomical recording card; Firth (1912a, 85).

351 A female skeleton, with no age recorded.

   References: Anatomical recording card; Firth (1912a, 85).

352 A male skeleton, with no age recorded.

   References: Anatomical recording card.

354 A female skeleton, with no age recorded.

   References: Anatomical recording card.

356 A female skeleton, with no age recorded.

   References: Anatomical recording card.

358 A male skeleton, described as 'young'.

   References: Anatomical recording card.

360 A female, adult skeleton. The skull was found to be broken when it was excavated.

   Original anatomical observations: All cranial sutures are open. The posterior part of the sagittal suture is complicated, forming a series of wormian bones behind the parietal foramina. There is an epipteric bone present on right. On the left the squamous temporal articulates with the frontal. The occipital is symmetrical.

The teeth present in the mandible are excellent.

The sacrum is 6-pieced (5 sacral bones + 1 coccyx). There is a facet present on the neck of both femora.

References: Anatomical recording card.

361   A male skeleton, with no age recorded.

Original anatomical observations: The teeth are perfect in both jaws.

References: Anatomical recording card.

362   A male, aged skeleton.

Original anatomical observations: The coronal suture is closing, the sagittal and lambdoid sutures are closed. The tori are moderately marked. There is slight left occipital bulging. The most posterior part of the temporal ridge is exaggerated on both sides.

References: Anatomical recording card.

364   A female skeleton, with no age recorded.

References: Anatomical recording card.

365   A female skeleton, with no age recorded.

Original anatomical observations: The left tibia is platycnemic.

Surviving skeletal remains: A single damaged radius is currently located in the KNH Centre for Biomedical Egyptology at The University of Manchester (catalogue ref. 13048). The location of the rest of the skeleton is unknown.

References: Anatomical recording card.

366   A male skeleton, with no age recorded.

References: Anatomical recording card.

367 A female skeleton, with no age recorded.

Original anatomical observations: The sacrum is 5-pieced.

References: Anatomical recording card.

368 A male, adult skeleton. The archaeological report records this skeleton as post-cranial only, in contrast to the more complete anatomical report.

Original anatomical observations: The coronal and lambdoid sutures are open, the sagittal suture is closing. The mastoids are very small and the tori are fairly well-marked. There is a definite visible prognathism, which was not measurable.

All teeth present are perfect in both jaws.

The manubrium is separate. In the inter-clavicular notch is a deep eaten-at cavity which has been the seat of some inflammatory process. There is also some inflammatory process in the sacrum. There is a curious bending backwards of the head of the right humerus. Apparently, there has been a fracture at the surgical neck in early life which has healed well, but with considerable shortening.

Further studies: Smith and Derry in bulletin 6 (1910b, 29) describe the sacrum has having suffered extreme erosion, possibly due to rectal cancel.

Surviving skeletal remains: The manubrium is currently located in the Duckworth Laboratory, The University of Cambridge (catalogue ref. NU862b). The location of the rest of the skeleton is unknown.

References: Anatomical recording card; Smith and Derry (1910b, 29); Firth (1912a, 82; Figure 31).

369 A female skeleton, with no age recorded.

References: Anatomical recording card.

372 A male skeleton, with no age recorded.

Original anatomical observations: The sacrum is fused to the innominate bone on both sides.

References: Anatomical recording card; Firth (1912a, 85).

373 A child skeleton, with no sex recorded.

References: Anatomical recording card.

375   A male skeleton, with no age recorded.

References: Anatomical recording card.

377(a)   A male, aged skeleton. The skull was found to be broken when the body was excavated.

Original anatomical observations: The coronal, sagittal and lambdoid sutures are all closing. The occipital is symmetrical. The tori are moderately prominent.

All teeth present are perfect, with moderate wear in both jaws.

There is a facet present on the neck of both femora.

References: Anatomical recording card; Firth (1912a, 85).

377(b)   A child skeleton, with no sex recorded. The archaeological report did not record the presence of the child skeleton in this grave.

References: Anatomical recording card.

378   A female, adult skeleton. The skull was found to be broken when the body was excavated.

Original anatomical observations: All cranial sutures are open. There is a definite visible prognathism, which was not measurable.

References: Anatomical recording card; Firth (1912a, 85).

379   A male skeleton, with no age recorded.

References: Anatomical recording card.

380   A female, aged skeleton with brown wavy hair preserved. The skull was found to be smashed when the body was excavated.

Original anatomical observations: The coronal suture is closing, the sagittal and lambdoid sutures are both closed. There is a slight visible prognathism.

All of the maxillary teeth are present and perfect. No comments were provided for the mandible.

The sacrum is 5-pieced.

References: Anatomical recording card.

381   A child skeleton, with no sex recorded.

       References: Anatomical recording card.

382   A male, adult skeleton. The skull was found to be smashed when the body was excavated.

       Original anatomical observations: There is a marked visible prognathism.

       All teeth in the mandible are present, perfect and fairly well worn.

       The manubrium is separate. The first left rib has been fractured at an angle and repaired. There is a large facet present on the neck of both femora. The linea aspera are exaggerated on both femora.

       References: Anatomical recording card; Firth (1912a, 82; Fig. 32); Firth (1912b, Plate 19B).

383   A female, aged skeleton. The anatomical report records that the skull was found to be smashed but the archaeological report records that skull as removed.

       Original anatomical observations: The coronal suture is closing, the others are open. There are large wormian bones in both lambdoids.

       The mandibular teeth present are perfect, except for an abscess cavity at the root of the left 1st molar which opens into the lingual. The maxilla is missing.

       The manubrium is separate. There has been an injury involving all three bones of elbow joint. There has apparently been a fracture involving the lower end of the shaft of humerus and the upper end of the shaft of the ulna and radius. The trochlea of the humerus is broken right through the supra-condylar foramen and in the subsequent union a considerable amount of callus has been thrown out around the elbow joint. The sacrum is small and 5-pieced.

       References: Anatomical recording card; Firth (1912a, 82); Firth (1912b, Plate 19C).

384   A male, aged skeleton. The skull was found to be missing upon excavation, but the mandible was present.

       Original anatomical observations: The manubrium is fused to the sternum. There is a round hole through gladiolus. The left 12th rib is fused to its vertebra. There is severe spondylitis of the 5 lower dorsal and 1st lumbar vertebrae. The 5th lumbar vertebra is fused to the sacrum and also 1st coccyx.

       Further studies: A note on the anatomical recording card says that the sacrum, ankylosed vertebra and rib were given to Thomas Strangeways.

       References: Anatomical recording card.

385   A male skeleton, with no age recorded. The skull was found to be broken when the body was excavated.

Original anatomical observations: The coronal, sagittal and lambdoid sutures are all simple and closing. There is a large wormian bone between the junction of the right lambdoid and the adjacent part of the sagittal suture. There are also small wormian bones present in the left lambdoid suture. There is slight left occipital bulging.

The sacrum is 5-pieced. There is a facet present on the neck of the right femur.

References: Anatomical recording card.

387   A male, adult skeleton.

Original anatomical observations: The coronal and lambdoid sutures are open, the sagittal suture is closing. There is definite visible and measurable prognathism. There is arthritis of the right tempero-mandibular articulation.

All maxillary teeth are present and perfect, except the left 2nd molar where a large abscess cavity opens onto both lingual and labial aspects.

The sacrum is 5-pieced. All 4 parts of the coccyx are fused to each other and to the sacrum. There is spondylitis of the lumbar spine and the lumbo-sacral joint. There is a large facet present on the neck of both femora.

References: Anatomical recording card; Firth (1912a, 82).

388   A large male post-cranial skeleton, with no age recorded.

References: Anatomical recording card.

392   A male, aged skeleton.

Original anatomical observations: The coronal suture is open, the sagittal and lambdoid sutures are closing. There is a wormian bone in both lambdoid sutures. There is left occipital bulging. The tori are prominent.

The teeth are much worn in both jaws. In the maxilla, there is caries and a large abscess cavity at the root of the right 2nd molar and the left 2nd incisor. In the mandible, there is an abscess at the root of the left [...] molar.

Surviving skeletal remains: The skull was located in the Anatomical Museum, The University of Manchester when studied by Watson. The current location is unknown.

References: Anatomical recording card; Watson (pre-1935).

404   A male skeleton, with no age recorded.

         References: Anatomical recording card.

405   A male skeleton, with no age recorded.

         References: Anatomical recording card.

406   A male skeleton, with no age recorded.

         References: Anatomical recording card.

407   A female skeleton, with no age recorded.

         References: Anatomical recording card.

409   A female skeleton, with no age recorded.

         References: Anatomical recording card.

412   A disturbed male, child skeleton.

         References: Anatomical recording card; Firth (1912a, 82).

415   A male skeleton, with no age recorded.

         References: Anatomical recording card.

416   A child skeleton, with no sex recorded.

         References: Anatomical recording card.

417   A female skeleton, with no age recorded.

         References: Anatomical recording card; Firth (1912a, 85).

419 A partial child skeleton, with no sex recorded. The upper part of the skeleton only remains.

References: Anatomical recording card; Firth (1912a, 82).

421 A child skeleton, with no sex recorded.

References: Anatomical recording card.

422 A male, aged skeleton with straight brown hair preserved. The skull was found to be broken when the body was excavated.

Original anatomical observations: All cranial sutures are closed. There are epipteric bones on both sides shutting out the parietal from the great wing of the sphenoid. The occipital is symmetrical.

The sacrum is 6-pieced.

References: Anatomical recording card.

423 A child skeleton, with no sex recorded.

References: Anatomical recording card.

425 A fragmentary female skeleton, with no age recorded. Only the skull remained intact.

Original anatomical observations: The coronal, sagittal and lambdoid sutures are all closing. There are wormian bones in both lambdoid sutures. There is an epipteric bone on the right shutting out the parietal from the great wing of the sphenoid. There is a slight visible and measurable prognathism.

The teeth are all present and perfect in both jaws. Neither left 3rd molar ever appeared.

References: Anatomical recording card.

426 A male skeleton, with no age recorded.

Original anatomical observations: All cranial sutures are closed. There is marked right occipital bulging.

There is a facet present on the neck of the left femur.

References: Anatomical recording card.

427   A male skeleton, with no age recorded.

   References: Anatomical recording card.

430   A male skeleton, with no age recorded.

   Original anatomical observations: The cranial sutures are simple. The coronal suture is closing and the sagittal and lambdoid sutures are closed. There is right occipital bulging.

   The maxillary teeth are perfect and very worn. No comments were recorded for the mandible.

   References: Anatomical recording card.

433   A fragmentary male skeleton, with no age recorded. Only the skull remained intact.

   Original anatomical observations: The coronal suture is open, the sagittal and lambdoid sutures are closed. There is left occipital bulging. There is a definite visible prognathism, which was not measurable.

   The maxillary teeth are much worn. There is an abscess at the roots of the right canine and 1st molar (opening onto both sides) and the left canine and 1st molar (opening onto both sides). The left 2nd and 3rd molars have gone and the alveolus is absorbed.

   The sacrum is 6-pieced (5 sacral bones + 1 coccyx).

   References: Anatomical recording card.

445   A male skeleton, with no age recorded. The body was contracted on the right, with the hands up to the face.

   Original anatomical observations: All cranial sutures are open. There is a very large epipteric bone on the right, shutting out the parietal from articulating with the great wing of the sphenoid. There is slight right occipital bulging. No visible prognathism was observed, this was slight when measured.

   All teeth are present and perfect in both jaws.

   The manubrium is separate. The 5th rib on the right is bifurcated (anomaly). There is a large facet present on the neck of both femora.

   Surviving skeletal remains: A partial cranium and a partial mandible are currently located in the Duckworth Laboratory, The University of Cambridge (catalogue ref. NU853). The location of the rest of the skeleton is unknown.

   References: Anatomical recording card; Firth (1912a, 82).

New Kingdom burials

274   A post-cranial skeleton, with no age or sex recorded.

<u>References</u>: Firth (1912a, 86).

310   A female, adult skeleton. The skull was found to be broken when excavated.

<u>Original anatomical observations</u>: The coronal suture is closed, the sagittal suture is closing and the lambdoid is open.

The sacrum is 5-pieced.

<u>References</u>: Anatomical recording card.

394   A skeleton, with no age or sex recorded.

<u>References</u>: Anatomical recording card; Firth (1912a, 87).

440   A male, aged skeleton. The skull was found to be broken when excavated.

<u>Original anatomical observations</u>: All cranial sutures are closed. There are epipteric bones on both sides shutting out the parietal from the great wing of the sphenoid. There is right occipital bulging.

<u>References</u>: Anatomical recording card.

457   A disturbed skeleton, with no age or sex recorded.

<u>References</u>: Firth (1912a, 87).

464   A male skeleton, with no age recorded.

<u>Original anatomical observations</u>: The coronal suture is closing, the sagittal and lambdoid sutures are closed. There are two very large wormian bones in the inter-parietal part of the occipital bone. There is very slight left occipital bulging. The tori are moderately well marked. There is a slight visible and measurable prognathism.

Nearly all of the teeth in the maxilla have gone. There is an abscess at the root of the right 1st bicuspid. The alveolus on the left is mostly absorbed. No comments were recorded for the mandible.

The left femur has rheumatoid arthritis at the head of the bone, which shows great lipping especially in front.

References: Anatomical recording card.

474 A female, aged skeleton with white hair preserved.

Original anatomical observations: The coronal suture is closing, the sagittal and lambdoid sutures are closed. There is slight right occipital bulging.

Almost all of the teeth in the maxilla have gone and the alveolus has been absorbed. On the right side this is to such an extent that it is open into the Antrum of Highmore. No comments were recorded for the mandible.

The manubrium is separate. The sacrum is perfectly flat and 5-pieced. There is a Colles fracture of the left radius which has healed with a slight backward bending of the lower end. There is marked spondylitis of the lumbar and cervical spine and slight spondylitis of the thoracic spine.

References: Anatomical recording card; Firth (1912a, 87).

476 A female young adult skeleton about 21-25 years old.

Original anatomical observations: All cranial sutures are open except for the basilar suture which is closed. There is right occipital bulging. There is a definite visible prognathism, but this was found to be slight when measured.

All teeth are present and perfect in both jaws.

The manubrium is separate. The sternum has a curious division of the body passing from the middle to the lower end. A cervical rib is present.

References: Anatomical recording card; Firth (1912a, 87).

477 A child skeleton, with no sex recorded.

References: Firth (1912a, 87).

478 A skeleton, with no age or sex recorded.

References: Firth (1912a, 87).

479   A skeleton, with no age or sex recorded.

   References: Firth (1912a, 87).

480   A child skeleton, with no sex recorded.

   References: Firth (1912a, 87).

481   A skeleton, with no age or sex recorded.

   References: Firth (1912a, 87; Fig. 34).

497   A child skeleton, with sex recorded.

   References: Firth (1912a, 87).

X-group burials

The following graves were recorded with no clear indication of whether they contained a body; they are likely to have been empty: 108, 113, 174, 191 (Firth 1912b, plan XII).

41   A male, adult skeleton. The body was contracted on the right wrapped in linen and a cloak of stamped leather. Black hair with curls or waves was preserved.

   Original anatomical observations: All cranial sutures are open. There is an epipteric bone on the left side shutting out the parietal from articulating with the sphenoid. The tori are very marked and the left occipital is bulging. The base of the skull is gone through ulceration; the disease is thought to have originated in the nose and spread backwards into the pharangeal roof, the sphenoid, the antrum of Highmore, the orbital roofs and the frontal air sinuses. Both carotid arteries were also involved.

   All of the maxillary teeth are perfect and much worn. Neither 3rd molar ever appeared. All of the mandibular teeth are present and perfect, except for the right 2nd molar which is a stump with the pulp cavity exposed and abscess at root and the left 3rd molar has gone, with the alveolus absorbed.

   The manubrium is separate. The lower end of the left humerus and the upper end of the left ulna and radius have been the seat of some inflammatory process which has partly obliterated the coronoid fossa (pathological). A similar inflammatory process seems to have affected the lower ends of the bones of the forearm and the bones of the wrist. The femora are strongly curved.

Further studies: The lesion at the base of the skull was considered likely to be malignant by Smith and Derry (Derry 1909a, 41), a diagnosis supported by Brothwell (1967, 339), who thought this was likely to have been a primary carcinoma – a nasopharyngeal carcinoma (Figure 7).

Surviving skeletal remains: The cranium was originally part of the Nubian Pathological Collection at the Royal College of Surgeons. It now resides in the Natural History Museum, London (catalogue ref. NPC 188B). The location of the rest of the skeleton is unknown.

References: Anatomical recording card; Derry (1909a, 41-43); Firth (1912a, 88; Figs. 35-7); Firth (1912b, Plate 7A; Plan XII); Brothwell (1967, 339); Nubian Pathological Collection surviving record card (specimen 188B).

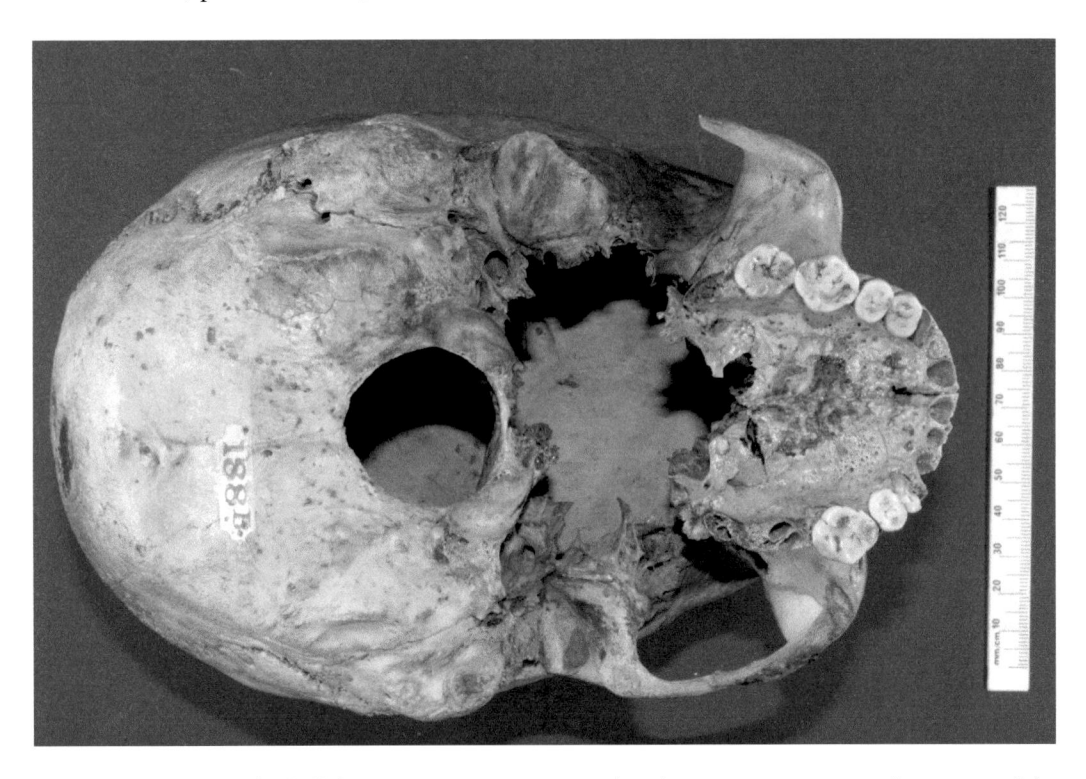

Figure 7: An adult, male skull from cemetery 72, grave 41 that demonstrates extensive destruction of the cranial base due to a nasopharyngeal carcinoma. ©The Trustees of the Natural History Museum, London, 2023.

44   A disturbed female, aged skeleton. The body was sharply contracted on the left.

Original anatomical observations: There is an epipteric bone on each side of the cranium – on the right this shuts out the parietal from articulation with the great wing of the sphenoid.

Only a few stumps remain in the maxilla, the alveolus has been absorbed. All of the alveolus has been absorbed in the mandible.

The manubrium is separate. There is rheumatoid arthritis of the right shoulder joint with lipping of the glenoid cavity and the head of the humerus. This is also slightly apparent on the left. There is a fracture of the neck of the right femur which has never healed. The separate head and the under surface of the great trocanter have formed new articular surfaces and are much eburnated. The acetabular cavity has also got adventitious articular facets. There is considerable spondylitis of the lumbar spine. The sacrum is small, curved and 5-pieced.

References: Anatomical recording card; Firth (1912b, Plate 7B; Plan XII).

45   A child skeleton, with no sex recorded.

References: Anatomical recording card; Firth (1912a, 88); Firth (1912b, Plan XII).

46   A fragmentary female, adult skeleton.

References: Firth (1912a, 88) Firth (1912b, Plan XII).

47   A disturbed child skeleton, with no sex recorded.

References: Anatomical recording card; Firth (1912a, 89) Firth (1912b, Plan XII).

48   A female, aged skeleton. The body was found outside the grave – the anatomists note that there was evidence that the original burial was removed.

Original anatomical observations: All cranial sutures are open. There is slight right occipital bulging.

All teeth are present as far as the 2nd bicuspid on both sides and much worn. The maxillary teeth are very much worn. The 3rd molars have never erupted. There is a large abscess cavity at roots of the canine and the 1st bicuspid on the right.

The sacrum is 5-pieced, curved and broken. There are large facets on the anterior surface of the neck of both femora. There is spondylitis of the lumbar vertebrae.

References: Anatomical recording card; Firth (1912a, 89); Firth (1912b, Plan XII).

49   A partially disturbed female, adult skeleton. The body was flexed on the right.

Original anatomical observations: The coronal suture is closed at the lower ends, the sagittal and lambdoid sutures are open. There is a large supra-occipital wormian bone. The occipital bones are symmetrical. There is a very marked visible prognathism, which was not measurable.

The left ulna has a fracture of the mid shaft, which has healed with good union. The sacrum is 5-pieced and slightly curved.

References: Anatomical recording card; Firth (1912a, 89; Figs. 38-40); Firth (1912b, Plate 7F; Plan XII).

50   A possible male, child skull. There is a discrepancy in the historical age assigned to this skull. Firth identifies it as X-group period, whilst Watson reported it as C-group period. Given that Watson studied the material several years after excavation, the original archaeological date has been used here.

Surviving skeletal remains: The skull was located in the Anatomical Museum, The University of Manchester when studied by Watson. The current location is unknown.

References: Firth (1912a, 89); Firth (1912b, Plan XII); Watson (pre-1935).

51   A child skeleton, with no sex recorded.

References: Firth (1912a, 90); Firth (1912b, Plate 7C; Plan XII).

52   A female juvenile naturally mummified body, about 17 years old. The body was contracted on the left, with the right knee up to the chin and the left foot against the buttock. Long brown wavy hair was preserved.

There is a discrepancy in the historical age assigned to this skull. Firth identifies it as X-group period, whilst the anatomical recording card records it as C-group period.

References: Anatomical recording card; Firth (1912a, 89); Firth (1912b, Plan XII).

59   A female skeleton, around 25 years old.

Original anatomical observations: There is a definite but slight subnasal prognathism.

References: Anatomical recording card; Firth (1912b, Plan XII).

60   A female, aged skeleton.

Original anatomical observations: All cranial sutures are closed except the lambdoid. The occipital bones are symmetrical. There is a marked visible prognathism. There is a defect in the lateral orbital wall.

The maxillary teeth are very much worn with much of the alveolus absorbed on the left. There are the remains of an abscess at the root of the 2nd bicuspid, which apparently communicates with the Antrum of Highmore. The left 2nd molar has gone. All of the mandibular teeth are present and much worn, except the molars on the right where the alveolus has absorbed.

The whole sternum is ossified. The 7th cervical vertebra is fused to the first thoracic vertebra. On the left side the small sacro-sciatic ligament is ossified and fused to spine of ischium for a distance of 31mm. The sacrum is 6-pieced (5 sacral bones + 1 coccyx).

References: Anatomical recording card; Firth (1912a, 90); Firth (1912b, Plan XII).

61   A female, young adult skeleton. The archaeological report records that only the skull and leg bones remain.

Original anatomical observations: All cranial sutures are open. There is slight right occipital bulging. There is a very pronounced prognathism, both visible and measurable. On the right side in the position of the suprameatal triangle is an abscess cavity communicating with the mastoid antrum and the mastoid cells which opens through the bony wall into the external auditory meatus. There is no direct connection with the brain or the lateral sinus but due to the extent of the abscess cavity it is thought this may have led to death through some septic process (Derry 1909a, 44).

All teeth are present and perfect in both jaws, with very slight wear.

There are facets present on the anterior surface of the neck of both femora.

References: Anatomical recording card; Derry (1909a, 43-44); Firth (1912a, 90-1); Firth (1912b, Plan XII).

64   A female skeleton, about 18 years old with long wavy brown hair. The body was contracted on the right.

Original anatomical observations: All cranial sutures are open, but in spite of her youth the basilar suture is completely closed (anomaly). There is a marked visible prognathism.

All teeth are present and perfect, except the 3rd molars which have not cut the gums, in both jaws.

The heads of the humerii, the condyles of the femora and various other secondary epiphyses are still separate. The suture between the ascending ramus of ischium and the descending ramus of pubis is not found (anomaly).

References: Firth (1912a, 91; Figs. 42-4); Firth (1912b, Plate 7D); Anatomical recording card.

65   A skeleton, with no age or sex recorded.

References: Firth (1912a, plan XII); Firth (1912b, Plan XII).

77   A disturbed female, adult skeleton.

Original anatomical observations: All cranial sutures are open. The temporal articulates with the frontal on both sides. There is marked visible and measurable prognathism. The occipital is symmetrical.

All of the maxillary teeth are present and perfect except the left 2nd molar which has a carious cavity and the left 3rd molar which never appeared. The teeth in the mandible are all present and perfect, some very worn. There is an abscess at the left 1st molar, opening on to the outer surface of the mandible (an infection from pulp cavity).

The sacrum is very curved, short and 5-pieced. Both tibiae are platycnemic. There is cartilage preserved on the right femoral head. There are very deep preauricular grooves.

References: Firth (1912a, 91-2); Firth (1912b, Plan XII); Anatomical recording card.

78   A disturbed child skeleton, with no sex recorded.

References: Anatomical recording card; Firth (1912a, 92); Firth (1912b, Plan XII).

79   A male, aged skeleton.

Original anatomical observations: The sagittal suture is beginning to close, but the rest are open. There is a complicated suture stretching across the occipital bones separating off the anterior parietal portion from the supra-orbital. On both sides at the asterion are small wormian bones. The tori are prominent. There is a well-marked manifestation of an occipital vertebra. In the middle of forehead is a shallow depression measuring 16 x 10mm.

The maxillary teeth are very much worn with abscesses at the roots of the right 2nd bicuspid, 1st and 2nd molars and the left 1st molar. No comments were recorded for the mandible.

There is considerable spondylitis in the cervical region where the 5th and 6th cervical vertebrae are fused together. Three thoracic vertebrae are fused together about the middle of the series. One of the left ribs is ankylosed to the uppermost of the fused vertebrae. There is also spondylitis of the lumbar vertebrae.

Surviving skeletal remains: The skull was located in the Anatomical Museum, The University of Manchester when studied by Watson. The current location is unknown.

References: Anatomical recording card; Firth (1912a, 92); Firth (1912b, Plan XII); Watson (pre-1935).

88   An aged skeleton, which was identified by Derry as female but was later identified as male when studied by Watson (pre 1935).

Original anatomical observations: All of the cranial sutures are open except the lowest part of the coronal suture. On both sides of the cranium the squamous articulates with the temporal through a small epipteric bone. There is a marked visible prognathism.

On the right side of the maxilla there is an abscess at root of the 1st incisor. The 2nd molar has also gone with an abscess cavity at the root and the 1st molar has slight carious cavity. On the left side of the maxilla all teeth are present and perfect, except the 2nd incisor and the canine which are carious. The 2nd molar has gone and the alveolus has absorbed. On the right side of the mandible is an abscess at the root of both bicuspids and the 1st molar, the rest of the alveolus has absorbed. On the left side the teeth are much worn and the alveolus has absorbed between the 1st bicuspid and the 2nd molar.

The left radius is fractured at the junction of the middle and lower third. This has healed with good union. There is spondylitis of the lumbar vertebrae. The sacrum is large, curved and 5-pieced. Both femora are platymeric and both tibiae are platycnemic. Small os epilepticum (identified as an anomaly).

Surviving skeletal remains: The skull was located in the Anatomical Museum, The University of Manchester when studied by Watson. The current location is unknown.

References: Anatomical recording card; Firth (1912a, 92); Firth (1912b, Plan XII); Watson (pre-1935).

90 A female, aged skeleton sharply contracted on the left, with the knees at the chin. The facial bones were damaged when excavated.

Original anatomical observations: The coronal and lambdoid sutures are open, with small wormian bones on both sides of the lambdoid suture. The sagittal suture is beginning to close.

Nearly all of the alveolus has absorbed in the maxilla. All of the alveolus has absorbed in the mandible.

The left radius is fractured about the junction of the lower middle third. This is probably a greenstick fracture; the bone is much bent. The manubrium is separate. The sacrum is 6-pieced (5 sacral bones + 1 coccyx).

References: Anatomical recording card; Firth (1912a, 92); Firth (1912b, Plan XII).

91 A female, young adult skeleton. The body was contracted on the right, with the head to the west.

Original anatomical observations: All cranial sutures are open (the basal suture is closed). There is slight left occipital bulging. There is a large symmetrical cleft in the palate, measuring 23 x 22mm.

All teeth are present and perfect in both jaws.

All parts of the sternum are separate except for 2 of the gladiolus. The left fibula has a remarkable bony groove at its upper end, beginning at the site of attachment of the soleus muscle and running across the tibia to just below the oblique line. The sacrum is 6-pieced (5 sacral bones + 1 coccyx).

Surviving skeletal remains: The cranium was originally part of the Nubian Pathological Collection at the Royal College of Surgeons. It now resides in the Natural History Museum, London (catalogue ref. NPC 210). The location of the rest of the skeleton is unknown.

References: Anatomical recording card; Derry (1909a, 43); Firth (1912a, 92; Fig. 46-7); Firth (1912b, Plate 8A; Plan XII); Nubian Pathological Collection surviving record card (specimen 210).

93 A disturbed female, aged skeleton. A sheep was also found in the grave, although no further description of this has survived.

Original anatomical observations: The coronal and sagittal sutures are almost obliterated, the lambdoid is closing. There is an epipteric bone on the right side. The tori are prominent. There is some parietal thinning. There is a very slight visible prognathism. The mastoids are very small.

The maxillary teeth comprise only stumps, with parts of the alveolus absorbed. There is an abscess at roots of both left bicuspids. The mandibular teeth are much worn, with the alveolus absorbed in places.

The manubrium is separate. The cartilage of the 1st rib is ossified. The sacrum is broad, 5-pieced and slightly curved. There are slight facets on both femora.

References: Anatomical recording card; Firth (1912a, 93-5; Fig. 48); Firth (1912b, Plate 8C; Plan XII).

103 A child skeleton, with no sex recorded.

References: Firth (1912a, 95); Firth (1912b, Plan XII).

106 A female skeleton, with no age recorded.

Original anatomical observations: The sutures are simple. The coronal suture is open, the sagittal is closing and the lambdoid is open. There is a definite visible prognathism. There is left occipital bulging.

The teeth are much worn in both jaws. There is an abscess at the root of the left canine in the maxilla and the alveolus has absorbed at the left 2nd and 3rd molars. The alveolus is absorbed on the right behind the 1st molar in the mandible.

There is slight rheumatoid arthritis of the left tibia and fibula joint. The sacrum is wide and 5-pieced. There are pronounced pre-auricular grooves.

References: Anatomical recording card; Firth (1912a, 95); Firth (1912b, Plan XII).

112   A disturbed male, adult skeleton. The body was wrapped in stamped leather.

Original anatomical observations: The coronal suture is closing, the sagittal is obliterated and the lambdoid is almost obliterated. The tori are fairly well-marked. There is slight left occipital bulging. The skull is orthognathus.

All teeth are present and perfect in both jaws. The maxillary teeth are well-worn. There is a small carious cavity in 2nd right bicuspid. The mandibular alveolus has absorbed at the left 2nd molar.

The thyroid cartilage is ossified (both the cornu and the lower border). The manubrium is separate from the xiphoid process. There is spondylitis of the lumbar and thoracic vertebrae. The sacrum is 6-pieced (5 sacral bones + 1 coccyx). There are large facets on the anterior surface of the neck of both femora.

References: Anatomical recording card; Firth (1912a, 95); Firth (1912b, Plan XII).

114   A male, aged skeleton

Original anatomical observations: All cranial sutures are open. The tori are well-marked, and the mastoids are massive. There is slight right occipital bulging.

All teeth are present, perfect and fairly well worn in both jaws.

The manubrium is fused to the gladiolus. The sacrum is 6-pieced (5 sacral bones + 1 coccyx) and very flat. There are large facets on the anterior surface of the neck of both femora.

References: Anatomical recording card; Firth (1912a, 95); Firth (1912b, Plan XII).

147   A child skull, with no sex recorded. Firth (1912a, 95) reports that another burial has been previously removed from this grave but no further information is provided.

References: Anatomical recording card; Firth (1912a, 95); Firth (1912b, Plan XII).

150   A partial possible male, aged skeleton.

Original anatomical observations: The coronal suture is closing at the lower end, the sagittal suture is beginning to close posteriorly and the lambdoid is open. There is slight left occipital bulging. The mastoids are small. There is rheumatoid arthritis in the tempero-mandibular joint on both sides. There is rarefying osteitis on both parietal bones at the junction with the squamous temporal.

The teeth are very much worn in both jaws - only stumps remain and much of the alveolus is absorbed.

References: Anatomical recording card; Firth (1912a, 95); Firth (1912b, Plan XII).

157 A naturally mummified female child, about 14 years old. Long brown hair about 90mm in length was preserved. The head was wrapped in a sheepskin, with woolly side inwards. There was also a bolster stuffed layers of hair of goat and wool.

References: Anatomical recording card; Firth (1912a, 96); Firth (1912b, Plan XII).

159 A child skeleton, with no sex recorded.

References: Anatomical recording card; Firth (1912a, 96); Firth (1912b, Plan XII).

161 A child skeleton, with no sex recorded.

References: Anatomical recording card; Firth (1912a, 96); Firth (1912b, Plan XII).

162 A naturally mummified female child, about 14 years old.

Original anatomical observations: There is a very large epipteric bone present on the left and a small one on the right of the cranium. There is a marked visible prognathism.

References: Anatomical recording card; Firth (1912a, 96; Figs. 52-3); Firth (1912b, Plan XII).

165 A male, child skeleton.

Surviving skeletal remains: The skull was located in the Anatomical Museum, The University of Manchester when studied by Watson. The current location is unknown.

References: Anatomical recording card; Firth (1912a, 96); Firth (1912b, Plan XII); Watson (pre-1935).

166 A male, aged skeleton. The body was extended on its back, hands by the sides. There was leather on the feet.

Original anatomical observations: The coronal, sagittal and lambdoid sutures are all closing. The squamous is also closing. The tori are well-marked. There are very well-marked upper temporal nodes and massive mastoids. The skull is orthognathus.

There has been an injury to the left side at root of the nose, resembling a blow with a blunt instrument.

Only stumps remain in both jaws. There is an abscess at the root of the left 1st molar in the maxilla, with parts of alveolus absorbed. On the right side of the mandible, all of the alveolus is absorbed behind the 1st bicuspid, and on the left behind the 1st molar.

The manubrium is separate, but the xiphoid process is completely ossified. The sacrum is 6-pieced. The rest of vertebral column is complete.

References: Anatomical recording card; Firth (1912a, 97; Figs. 54-5); Firth (1912b, Plate 8E; Plan XII).

171   A child skeleton, with no sex recorded.

References: Anatomical recording card; Firth (1912a, 97); Firth (1912b, Plate 8F; Plan VII).

172   A child skeleton, with no sex recorded.

References: Anatomical recording card; Firth (1912a, 97); Firth (1912b, Plan XII).

173   A partial child skeleton, with no sex recorded.

References: Anatomical recording card; Firth (1912a, 97); Firth (1912b, Plan XII).

175   A child skeleton, with no sex recorded.

References: Anatomical recording card; Firth (1912b, 97).

177   A female skeleton, about 21-25 years old.

Original anatomical observations: All cranial sutures are open. The occipital is symmetrical. There is a very slight visible prognathism, but the face is sloping.

All teeth are present and perfect in both jaws.

All epiphyses are united except the crest of ilium, ischium and the bones of the scapulae. The top of the acromion process is separate on the left scapula. The manubrium is separate. The lowest piece of the body of the sternum has a suture running through it from front to back. The sacrum is 5-pieced, large and curved. All 5 pieces of coccyx are fused.

References: Anatomical recording card; Firth (1912a, 98); Firth (1912b, Plan XII).

180   A female, aged skeleton. The archaeological report describes this body as only consisting of leg bones and pelvis, in contrast to the anatomical record.

Original anatomical observations: The coronal suture is closing, the sagittal and lambdoid sutures are open. There is marked visible prognathism. The occipital is symmetrical.

The maxillary teeth are very much worn, with an abscess present at the root of the left 3rd molar. The mandibular teeth comprise only stumps.

The sacrum is 6-pieced (5 sacral bones + 1 coccyx). There is spondylitis of the lumbar and thoracic vertebrae.

References: Anatomical recording card; Firth (1912a, 98); Firth (1912b, Plan XII).

181   A partial skeleton, with no age or sex recorded. Femora and tibiae only remain.

References: Firth (1912a, 98); Firth (1912b, Plan XII).

Christian burials

The following graves were recorded with no clear indication of whether they contained a body; they are likely to have been empty: 42, 43, 53, 55, 57, 58, 62, 66, 67, 68, 69, 70, 71, 73, 74, 75, 80, 81, 82, 83, 84, 85, 86, 87, 89, 92, 94, 95, 96, 97, 98, 99, 100, 101, 102, 104, 105, 107, 110, 111, 115, 116, 117, 118, 119, 120, 140, 143, 144, 145, 151, 152, 153, 154, 155, 156, 160, 163, 164, 167, 168, 169, 170, 176, 182, 184, 185, 186, 187, 190 (Firth 1912b, plan XII).

16A   A female, aged skeleton buried in the recess into an undercut tomb. Her legs were found outside of the recess.

Original anatomical observations: The cranial sutures are very simple. The coronal suture is beginning to close at the lower end, the sagittal suture is closing at the foramen and the lambdoidal sutures are open. There is a small epipteric bone on either side. The orbits are round and the lateral walls are deficient. The occipital region is symmetrical.

All of the mandibular teeth have gone and the alveolus absorbed, except for the right 2nd molar and the left 2nd bicuspid and 1st molar. Only the incisors and canines remain in the mandible and the alveolus is absorbed in the rest of the jaw.

The manubrium is separate. The right humerus is fractured mid shaft, close to the insertion of the deltoid muscle. There is excellent union, but with a slight bending in the bone, so that the shaft is convex forward at the level of the fracture. The right humerus is longer than the left in spite of the fracture. This was probably a greenstick fracture. The sacrum is markedly curved and 6-pieced (5 sacral bones + 1 coccyx). There is spondylitis of the lumbar vertebrae. The preauricular grooves are very marked. The left patella is notched.

References: Anatomical recording card; Derry (1909a, 40).

16B A male skeleton, with no age recorded. The body was wrapped in linen.

Original anatomical observations: All cranial sutures are open. The tori are moderately prominent.

In the mandible the 1st bicuspids, the incisors and canines are the only teeth remaining. The alveolus is absorbed elsewhere. The maxillary teeth remaining are perfect, with little wear.

The manubrium is separate. The humerus shows backward bending. The ribs are abnormally thick and long from the head to the angle, where the bend is very sharp. The bodies of the lumbar vertebrae are worn down. The sacrum is 5-pieced. There is a marked facet on the anterior surface of the neck of both femora.

References: Anatomical recording card; Derry (1909a, 40).

16C A child about 3 years old, with no sex recorded. The body was buried on top of burial 16B.

References: Anatomical recording card.

16D A child about 5 years old, with no sex recorded.

References: Anatomical recording card.

17A A male skeleton, with no age recorded.

Original anatomical observations: All cranial sutures are open. The chin is somewhat prominent but with a very sloping angle.

All mandibular teeth are present and perfect. The few maxillary teeth remaining are stumps and the alveolus is absorbed elsewhere.

The sacrum is 5-pieced. There is rheumatoid arthritis present in both femora and the upper surface of the tibiae. There is lipping of both tibiae and some eburnation. Both tibiae are platycnemic. There is a facet on the anterior surface of the right femoral neck.

References: Anatomical recording card; Derry (1909a, 40).

17B   A female, aged skeleton.

   Original anatomical observations: The coronal suture is closed, the sagittal suture is almost closed and the lambdoid is open. The skull is orthognathus.

   In the maxilla only stumps remain, with the alveolus absorbed elsewhere. All teeth in the mandible are present except the right molars, where the alveolus is absorbed. The teeth are much worn.

   The preauricular groove is broad and shallow. The sacrum is 6-pieced (5 sacral bones + 1 coccyx), large and broken.

   References: Anatomical recording card; Derry (1909a, 40).

18   A probable male, adult skeleton.

   Original anatomical observations: The skull is asymmetrical, and the right occipital bone is bulging. The coronal suture is obliterated, the sagittal and lambdoid sutures are both open. Tori are slightly marked and the mastoids are large. The skull is orthognathus.

   On the base of the skull immediately behind the jugular foramen is a perfectly round opening through the jugular process measuring 6.5 x 6.5mm, which communicates with the lateral sinus (identified as an anomaly).

   In the maxilla only stumps remain, with the alveolus absorbed elsewhere. The mandible is much worn, with the alveolus absorbed behind the canines on the right.

   References: Anatomical recording card; Derry (1909a, 40).

19A   A female, aged skeleton. The mandible was missing when the body was excavated.

   Original anatomical observations: All cranial sutures are open and simple. There is a large epipteric bone on the left side shutting out the parietal from the wing of the sphenoid. There is marked visible prognathism, which was not measurable. The occiput is symmetrical.

   The maxillary teeth are very much worn, with the alveolus absorbed in the position of the right 1st molar. There is no caries.

   The manubrium is separate. There is spondylitis of the lumbar spine. The sacrum is flat and 5-pieced. All four pieces of the coccyx are ossified and fused together (anomaly) and the little tail is curved forwards and to the right. There is a facet on the anterior surface of the neck of both femora.

   Surviving skeletal remains: The coccyx only is currently housed in the Duckworth Laboratory, The University of Cambridge (catalogue ref. NU862c). The location of the rest of the body is unknown.

   References: Anatomical recording card; Derry (1909a, 40); Firth (1912a, Plate 7E).

19B   A male, young adult skeleton

Original anatomical observations: The sutures are very complicated, and all are open. The squamous temporal articulates with the frontal on both the left and right side. The tori are exaggerated. There are well-marked temporal ridges and massive mastoids. The occipital region is symmetrical. Prognathism is apparent which is very marked (visible) and marked (measurable). The posterior arch of the atlas is not joined, but the two limbs meet.

All mandibular teeth are present and moderately worn. There is a carious cavity in the right 1st molar and an abscess cavity at its root. The left 1st and 2nd molars also contain carious cavities. All maxillary teeth are present and perfect, except the right incisors at the root of which is an abscess cavity opening on to the palate to the right of the anterior palatine foramen.

The manubrium is separate. The posterior arch of the sacrum is open all the way down except for the first piece. The sacrum is much curved. There are six lumbar vertebrae. The epiphyses of the crest of the ilium and the ramus of the pubis and the ischium are joining. The patellae are both slightly notched.

Surviving skeletal remains: The skull was located in the Anatomical Museum, The University of Manchester when studied by Watson. The current location is unknown.

References: Anatomical recording card; Derry (1909a, 40); Firth (1912b, Plate 7E); Watson (pre-1935).

19C   A male skeleton, with no age recorded.

Original anatomical observations: All cranial sutures are open. There is marked right occipital bulging and massive mastoids. There is the manifestation of an occipital vertebra.

All teeth present, perfect and moderately worn in both jaws.

Surviving skeletal remains: The skull was located in the Anatomical Museum, The University of Manchester when studied by Watson. The current location is unknown.

References: Anatomical recording card; Derry (1909a, 40); Watson (pre-1935).

19D   A female, aged skeleton. The facial bones were mostly missing when the body was excavated.

Original anatomical observations: All cranial sutures are beginning to close. There is left occipital bulging.

All of the alveolus in the mandible is absorbed. No comments were recorded for the maxilla.

References: Anatomical recording card; Derry (1909a, 40).

19E	A female, young adult skeleton

Original anatomical observations: Very visible and measurable prognathism.

References: Anatomical recording card; Derry (1909a, 40).

19F	An infant skeleton.

References: Anatomical recording card.

19G	An infant skeleton.

References: Anatomical recording card.

19H	An infant skeleton.

References: Anatomical recording card.

20	A female, aged skeleton extended on its back, with the head to the west and the hands over the pubes.

Original anatomical observations: The cranial sutures are very simple. The coronal and sagittal sutures are closing and the lambdoid is open. The squamous articulates with the frontal. There is a very marked visible prognathism which was not measurable.

The mandibular alveolus is absorbed on the right between the 1st bicuspid and the 3rd molar and on the left behind the 2nd bicuspid. The maxillary teeth are much worn. There is a large carious cavity in the right 1st molar and the alveolar margin is absorbed behind the canine.

The manubrium is separate. The body of the sternum is perforated at the second piece. The sacrum is 6-pieced. The number of vertebrae is correct or normal.

References: Anatomical recording card.

22(a)	A female, adult skeleton.

Original anatomical observations: All cranial sutures are open. There is a definite visible prognathism, which was not measurable.

All teeth in the maxilla are present and perfect. In the mandible the 1st molars have gone and the alveolus absorbed. One 2nd molar contains a small carious cavity. The remaining teeth are perfect.

The manubrium is fused to the sternum and the lowest piece of the gladiolus is perforated. The sacrum is small, curved and 5-pieced.

References: Anatomical recording card.

22(b) A child skeleton about 6-7 years old, with no sex recorded. This body was not identified as an additional burial in grave 22 in the anatomist's records.

References: Anatomical recording card.

24A A small male skeleton, with no age recorded.

Original anatomical observations: There are two lambdoidal wormian bones. There is a definite visible prognathism, which was not measurable.

Rheumatoid arthritis is present in the left elbow joint, with lipping of both the radius and ulna and eburnation. The posterior arch of the 5th lumbar vertebra has never joined. There is spondylitis of the lumbar spine.

References: Anatomical recording card.

24B A female, aged skeleton.

Original anatomical observations: The coronal suture is closing, the sagittal and lambdoidal sutures are open. There is a wormian bone present in the left lambdoid suture. There is marked left occipital bulging. The obelion is depressed.

There is an abscess cavity present at the root of the 1st bicuspid on left side of the maxilla. The teeth are well worn, with parts of the alveolus absorbed. In the mandible the right 1st molar has a large carious cavity, the rest of the teeth are much worn.

References: Anatomical recording card.

24C There is a record of a body with this number on an anatomical recording card, but no further description survives.

References: Anatomical recording card.

25A A male skeleton, with no age recorded.

Original anatomical observations: The sutures are complicated, and all are open. There is a wormian bone in the left lambdoid. There is slight left occipital bulging and the tori are slight.

All teeth are present, perfect and very slightly worn in both jaws.

The sacrum is 6-pieced (5 sacral bones + 1 coccyx).

References: Anatomical recording card.

25B A male skeleton, with no age recorded.

Original anatomical observations: There is left occipital bulging. There is a slight visible prognathism, which was not measurable.

All teeth in the mandible are present and perfect with moderate wear, except for the left 1st molar where the alveolus is absorbed. The maxillary teeth are fairly well worn. On the left the alveolus is absorbed behind the 2nd bicuspid and on the right at the 2nd molar.

References: Anatomical recording card.

54 A female skeleton, with no age recorded. The body was extended on its back. The burial was identified as belonging to the X-group by the anatomical recording card, but to the Christian period on the archaeological plans for the cemetery.

Original anatomical observations: All cranial sutures are open. There is a definite visible prognathism. There is left occipital bulging.

All teeth are present and perfect in both jaws. The 3rd molars are present in the mandible but never appeared in the maxilla.

The posterior arch of 5th vertebra is separate.

References: Anatomical recording card; Firth (1912b, plan XII).

Burials of unknown date

219 A fragmentary female skeleton, with no age recorded.

References: Anatomical recording card.

220 A fragmentary female skeleton, with no age recorded.

References: Anatomical recording card.

222(a) Fragmentary male skeletal remains, with no age recorded. Remains discovered comingled with 222(b).

References: Anatomical recording card.

222(b) Fragmentary female skeletal remains, with no age recorded. Remains discovered comingled with 222(a).

References: Anatomical recording card.

230 A fragmentary female skeleton, with no age recorded.

References: Anatomical recording card.

236 A fragmentary male skeleton, with no age recorded.

References: Anatomical recording card.

242 A fragmentary female skeleton, with no age recorded.

References: Anatomical recording card.

243 A male, aged skull only. The skull is undated but is described as 'not being C-group' on the anatomical recording card.

Original anatomical observations: The coronal and sagittal sutures are closed, the lambdoid suture is open. The tori are fairly well marked. There is slight left occipital bulging.

The teeth are very much worn and are mostly stumps. There is an abscess at the root of the right canine and the left 1st molar.

References: Anatomical recording card.

247 A fragmentary male skeleton, with no age recorded.

References: Anatomical recording card.

252   A child skeleton, with no sex recorded.

   References: Anatomical recording card.

256   A fragmentary female skeleton, with no age recorded.

   References: Anatomical recording card.

260   A fragmentary female skeleton, with no age recorded.

   References: Anatomical recording card.

443   A female skeleton, with no age recorded.

   References: Anatomical recording card.

455   A male skeleton, with no age recorded.

   References: Anatomical recording card.

Cemetery 73, West bank, Gerf Husein

A-group, C-group to New Kingdom and Ptolemaic-Roman period

A large early Dynastic (A-group) cemetery, with a small number of C-group and New Kingdom burials. The cemetery is located at the mouth of a large valley, just south of the Gerf Husein temple. The presence of Ptolemaic-Roman period graves is recorded by Reisner (1909a, 9) in bulletin 3 but there is no reference to these in the archaeological report. The cemetery has been damaged by sebakh digging and the osteological remains excavated are poorly preserved (Firth 1912a, 6). The poor condition is emphasised by the fact that 104 graves contained just 55 bodies.

A-group burials

The following graves were found to be empty upon excavation: 12, 14, 19, 23, 24, 26, 27, 30, 31, 32, 33, 34, 35, 36, 40, 41, 43, 44, 45, 53, 54, 57, 67, 68, 69, 71, 74, 75, 76, 77, 79, 82, 83, 84, 87, 89, 91, 94, 104, 105 (Firth 1912a, 99-104; Firth 1912b, plan XIII).

The following graves were recorded with no clear indication of whether they contained a body; they are likely to have been empty: 42, 78, 97 (Firth 1912a, 101-104).

3   A child skeleton, with no sex recorded.

   References: Firth (1912a, 103).

4   A female skeleton, with the bones of a foetus present in the pelvis. The age of the skeleton was not recorded.

   References: Firth (1912a, 104; Fig. 58).

6   A skeleton, with no age or sex recorded. The body is considered intrusive to the grave.

   References: Firth (1912a, 99).

15 A child skeleton, with no sex recorded.

   References: Firth (1912a, 99); Firth (1912b, Plan XIII).

16 A partial child's skeleton, with no sex recorded. The leg bones only remain.

   References: Firth (1912a, 99); Firth (1912b, Plan XIII).

17   A skeleton, with no age or sex recorded.

   References: Firth (1912a, 99); Firth (1912b, Plan XIII).

18   A fragmentary skeleton, with no age or sex recorded.

   References: Firth (1912a, 100); Firth (1912b, Plan XIII).

20A   An infant skeleton, with no age or sex recorded.

   References: Firth (1912a, 100); Firth (1912b, Plan XIII).

20B   An infant skeleton, with no sex recorded.

   References: Firth (1912a, 100); Firth (1912b, Plan XIII).

21   A post-cranial skeleton, with no age or sex recorded.

   References: Firth (1912a, 100); Firth (1912b, Plan XIII).

22A   A male skeleton, with no age recorded. This body was the earliest interment in the grave.

   References: Firth (1912a, 100; Figs. 56-7); Firth (1912b, Plan XIII).

22B   A female skeleton, with no age recorded. This body was the second interment in the grave.

   References: Firth (1912a, 100; Figs. 56-7); Firth (1912b, Plan XIII).

22C   A skeleton, with no age or sex recorded. This body was the last interment in the grave.

   References: Firth (1912a, 100; Fig. 56-7); Firth (1912b, Plan XIII).

28   An empty large jar buried on its side – possibly intended for the burial of an infant.

   References: Firth (1912a, 101); Firth (1912b, Plan XIII).

29 A fragmentary child skeleton, with no sex recorded.
References: Firth (1912a, 101).

39 An empty large jar buried on its side – possibly intended for the burial of an infant.
References: Firth (1912a, 101); Firth (1912b, Plan XIII).

46 An infant skeleton, with no sex recorded.
References: Firth (1912a, 102); Firth (1912b, Plan XIII).

47 A child skeleton, with no sex recorded.
References: Firth (1912a, 102); Firth (1912b, Plan XIII).

48 A skeleton, with no age or sex recorded.
References: Firth (1912a, 104); Firth (1912b, Plan XIII).

60 A disturbed male skeleton, with no age recorded.
References: Firth (1912a, 104); Firth (1912b, Plan XIII).

73A A child skeleton, with no sex recorded.
References: Firth (1912a, 102); Firth (1912b, Plan XIII).

73B A child skeleton, with no sex recorded.
References: Firth (1912a, 102); Firth (1912b, Plan XIII).

95 A child skeleton, with no sex recorded.
References: Firth (1912a, 103); Firth (1912b, Plan XIII).

96   A child skeleton, with no sex recorded.

        References: Firth (1912a, 103); Firth (1912b, Plan XIII).

98   Pieces of an empty large jar buried on its side – possibly intended for the burial of an infant.

        References: Firth (1912a, 103); Firth (1912b, Plan XIII).

99   A child skeleton, with no sex recorded.

        References: Firth (1912a, 104); Firth (1912b, Plan XIII).

100   A child skeleton, with no sex recorded.

        References: Firth (1912a, 104); Firth (1912b, Plan XIII).

110   A skeleton, with no age or sex recorded.

        References: Firth (1912a, 104).

111   A skeleton, with no age or sex recorded.

        References: Firth (1912a, 104).

112A   A skeleton with no age or sex recorded.

        References: Firth (1912a, 104).

112B   A skeleton, with no age or sex recorded. The grave itself for this body is numbered 73/112B – this skeleton was not found in the same grave as 112A.

        References: Firth (1912a, 105).

112B[2] A skeleton, with no age or sex recorded. This skeleton was found in the same grave as 73/112B and was given the same character in the archaeological report.

        References: Firth (1912a, 105).

113(a)   A disturbed skeleton, with no age or sex recorded.

References: Firth (1912a, 105).

113(b)   A disturbed skeleton, with no age or sex recorded.

References: Firth (1912a, 105).

114   A child skeleton, with no sex recorded.

References: Firth (1912a, 105).

C-group burials

The following graves were found to be empty upon excavation: 11, 58, 59, 64, 70, 81, 85, 86, 93, 101 (Firth 1912a, 105-107; Firth 1912b, plan XIII).

The following graves were recorded with no clear indication of whether they contained a body; they are likely to have been empty: 106 (Firth 1912a, 107; Firth 1912b, plan XIII).

5   A fragmentary female skeleton, with no age recorded. The burial was originally dated to the B-group (A-group) but following excavation and subsequent study was positively dated to the C-group.

Original anatomical observations: The coronal suture is closing, the sagittal suture is closed and the lambdoid is open. There is left occipital bulging. There is a marked visible prognathism.

All teeth are present and perfect, but well-worn in both jaws.

References: Anatomical recording card; Firth (1912a, 104).

7   A skeleton, with no age or sex recorded.

References: Firth (1912a, 105); Firth (1912b, Plan XIII).

8   A partial post-cranial male skeleton, with no age recorded.

Original anatomical observations: The sacrum is 6-pieced (5 sacral bones and 1 coccyx). There are facets present on the neck of both femora.

References: Anatomical recording card; Firth (1912a, 105); Firth (1912b, Plan XIII).

9   A child skeleton, with no sex recorded.

   <u>References</u>: Firth (1912a, 105); Firth (1912b, Plan XIII).

10 A possible female, adult skeleton.

   <u>Original anatomical observations</u>: The coronal and sagittal sutures are obliterated. The occipital is symmetrical. The tori are well marked.

   In the maxilla, there is an abscess at the roots of the 1st and 2nd bicuspids and 1st molar on the right and another abscess at the root of the left 1st bicuspid. The 1st molar on the left has gone and the alveolus is absorbed. No comments were recorded for the mandible.

   <u>References</u>: Anatomical recording card; Firth (1912a, 105; Fig. 59); Firth (1912b, Plan XIII).

25 A very fragile male skeleton, with no age recorded. The body was flexed on the right.

   <u>Original anatomical observations</u>: There is a marked visible prognathism.

   <u>References</u>: Anatomical recording card; Firth (1912a, 101); Firth (1912b, Plan XIII).

37 A disturbed partial post-cranial male skeleton, with no age recorded. The archaeological report records the presence of the femora and tibiae only, although the anatomical recording card indicates the presence of additional skeletal elements.

   <u>Original anatomical observations</u>: The sacrum is 5-pieced and absolutely straight. There is a facet present on the neck of both femora.

   <u>References</u>: Anatomical recording card; Firth (1912a, 106); Firth (1912b, Plan XIII).

38 A disturbed post-cranial male skeleton, with no age recorded.

   <u>Original anatomical observations</u>: There is a facet present on the neck of both femora.

   <u>References</u>: Anatomical recording card; Firth (1912a, 106) Firth (1912b, Plan XIII).

60 A male, adult skeleton.

   <u>Original anatomical observations</u>: All cranial sutures are open. There is a large wormian bone present in the posterior part of the sagittal suture. The tori are fairly well marked. There is left occipital bulging.

The maxillary teeth are all present and perfect, with very little wear. There is an abscess at the root of the left 1st bicuspid which possibly communicates with the Antrum of Highmore. No comments were recorded for the mandible.

The sacrum is 6-pieced and very flat.

<u>References</u>: Anatomical recording card; Firth (1912b, Plan XIII).

66 A disturbed partial skeleton, with no age or sex recorded.

<u>References</u>: Firth (1912a, 106); Firth (1912b, Plan XIII).

72 A female skeleton, with no age recorded.

<u>Original anatomical observations</u>: All sutures are closed. There is an epipteric bone present on both sides of the skull. There is left occipital bulging. There is a marked visible and measurable prognathism.

All of the maxillary teeth are present and perfect, but much worn. In the mandible abscesses are present at the roots of the right 1st molar and both bicuspids and the 1st molar on the left. The 3rd molar on both sides has gone and the alveolus is absorbed.

<u>References</u>: Anatomical recording card; Firth (1912a, 106); Firth (1912b, Plan XIII).

80 A partial post-cranial skeleton, with no age or sex recorded. Only the pelvis and a humerus remain.

<u>References</u>: Firth (1912a, 106); Firth (1912b, Plan XIII).

88 A male, adult skeleton. The archaeological report indicates the presence of only the pelvis and leg bones of a post-cranial skeleton, in contrast to the anatomical records.

<u>Original anatomical observations</u>: The sagittal and coronal sutures are closed, but the lambdoid is open. The tori are moderately prominent.

All teeth are present and perfect in both jaws.

The manubrium is separate. There is a facet present on the neck of both femora.

<u>References</u>: Anatomical recording card; Firth (1912a, 106); Firth (1912b, Plan XIII).

90 A male post-cranial skeleton, with no age recorded.

Original anatomical observations: The sacrum is 5-pieced. There is a facet present on the neck of both femora.

References: Anatomical recording card; Firth (1912a, 106); Firth (1912b, Plan XIII).

102 A disturbed male, aged skeleton.

Original anatomical observations: All cranial sutures are closing. There is an epipteric bone on the left side of the skull, the right side is destroyed. There is right occipital bulging. The tori are prominent.

All teeth present are perfect, but much worn in both jaws.

Surviving skeletal remains: A partial, fragmentary cranium is currently located in the Duckworth Laboratory at The University of Cambridge (catalogue ref. NU854). The location of the rest of the skeleton is unknown.

References: Anatomical recording card; Firth (1912a, 107); Firth (1912b, Plan XIII).

103 A partial post-cranial skeleton, with no age or sex recorded.

References: Firth (1912a, 107).

107 A female, adult skeleton. It was noted that upon excavation the skull was found to have been deliberately moved in the grave.

Original anatomical observations: All cranial sutures are open. There is a distinct visible prognathism, which was not measurable.

All teeth are present, perfect and very slightly worn in both jaws.

The manubrium is separate. The sacrum is 5-pieced.

References: Anatomical recording card; Firth (1912a, 107; Fig. 60); Firth (1912b, Plate 19D; Plan XIII).

108 A female skeleton, under 21 years.

Original anatomical observations: All cranial sutures are open except the basilar. There are wormian bones in the lambdoids and the posterior part of sagittal. A metopic suture is present which is completely open. There is definite alveolar (visible) prognathism. The occipital is symmetrical.

All teeth present are perfect in both jaws. The 3rd molars are not yet cut.

<u>Surviving skeletal remains</u>: A skull and mandible are currently housed in the Duckworth Laboratory, The University of Cambridge (catalogue ref. NU486). The location of the rest of the body is unknown.

<u>References</u>: Anatomical recording card; Firth (1912a, 107); Firth (1912b, Plan XIII).

109   An infant skeleton, with no sex recorded.

<u>References</u>: Firth (1912a, 107); Firth (1912b, Plan XIII).

New Kingdom burials

1   A child skeleton, with no sex recorded.

<u>References</u>: Firth (1912a, 107-8).

2   A skeleton, with no age or sex recorded.

<u>References</u>: Firth (1912a, 108).

Ptolemaic burials

The following graves were found to be empty upon excavation: 13, 49, 50, 51, 52, 55, 56, 61, 62, 63, 65 (Firth 1912b, plan XIII).

Cemetery 74, West bank, Gedekol, Gerf Husein

C-group, Roman period, X-group and Christian periods

Cemetery 74 is a cemetery with multiple periods of occupation – C-group, Ptolemaic-Roman period, X-group and Christian period burials were located. There are a number of Ptolemaic period rock-cut tombs, located in the cliff on the south side of a valley just beyond Gedekol village. The tombs were reused in the Christian period for extended communal burials (Firth 1912a, 32). There are two groups of Christian period burials – one group on the north side of the valley, which have surviving superstructures and a second group further south which is a mixture of Christian and late X-group period graves (Firth 1912a, 43). Many of the bodies, especially from the Christian period, had been badly affected by water damage (Derry 1909a, 46).

Ninety-seven graves were excavated containing 99 bodies; unfortunately, the anatomical records for this cemetery are poor and the recording of age and/or sex is frequently absent.

C-group burials

The following graves were recorded with no clear indication of whether they contained a body; they are likely to have been empty: 501, 503 (Firth 1912a, 109).

504   A child skeleton, with no sex recorded.

         References: Anatomical recording card; Firth (1912a, 109).

505   A male skeleton, with no age recorded.

         References: Anatomical recording card; Firth (1912a, 109).

506   A male, young adult skeleton. The skull was found to be broken when the body was excavated.

         Original anatomical observations: All cranial sutures are open. There are epipteric bones on both sides on the skull, on the right this shuts out the parietal from the great wing of the sphenoid. The mastoids are attenuated. The occipital is symmetrical. The skull is orthognathus. Tori [...] marked.

         All of the teeth that are present are perfect in both jaws. The 3rd molars are just appearing.

         The sacrum is 5-pieced.

         References: Anatomical recording card; Firth (1912a, 109).

507   A male, adult skeleton. According to the archaeological report, the lower leg bones only remain – this is not consistent with the anatomical record.

Original anatomical observations: The coronal and sagittal sutures are closing, the lambdoid suture is open. The occipital is symmetrical. The tori are slightly marked. The mastoids are very small.

All teeth have gone, fallen out. There is no sign of decay.

The manubrium is separate from the gladiolus. The sacrum is very flat and 6-pieced.

References: Anatomical recording card; Firth (1912a, 109; Fig. 62).

509   A child skeleton, with no sex recorded.

References: Anatomical recording card; Firth (1912a, 109).

510   A partial female skeleton, with no age or sex recorded.

References: Anatomical recording card; Firth (1912a, 109).

511   A female skeleton, with no age recorded.

Original anatomical observations: All cranial sutures are closed. The occipital is symmetrical.

All teeth present are perfect but much worn in both jaws.

The manubrium is separate from the gladiolus. There is small facet on the neck of the right femur.

References: Anatomical recording card; Firth (1912a, 109; Fig.63).

512   A female skeleton, with no age recorded.

References: Anatomical recording card.

514   A female, adult skeleton.

Original anatomical observations: The coronal suture is beginning to close, the sagittal, lambdoid and metopic sutures are all open. There is a slight left occipital bulging.

There is no sign of decay in the maxilla, but the teeth are broken. All mandibular teeth are present and perfect, but much worn.

The manubrium is separate from the body of the sternum. The sacrum is wide, flat and 5-pieced. There is a slight facet on the neck of the left femur.

References: Anatomical recording card; Firth (1912a, 109).

515   A male skeleton, with no age recorded.

References: Anatomical recording card.

516   A male skeleton, with no age recorded.

References: Anatomical recording card.

518   A female skeleton, with no age recorded.

References: Anatomical recording card; Firth (1912a, 109).

519   A female skeleton, with no age recorded.

References: Anatomical recording card; Firth (1912a, 108).

520   A partial male skeleton, with no age recorded.

References: Anatomical recording card; Firth (1912a, 109).

524   A female skeleton, with no age recorded.

References: Anatomical recording card.

Roman-Christian burials

101   A male skeleton, with no age recorded.

References: Anatomical recording card.

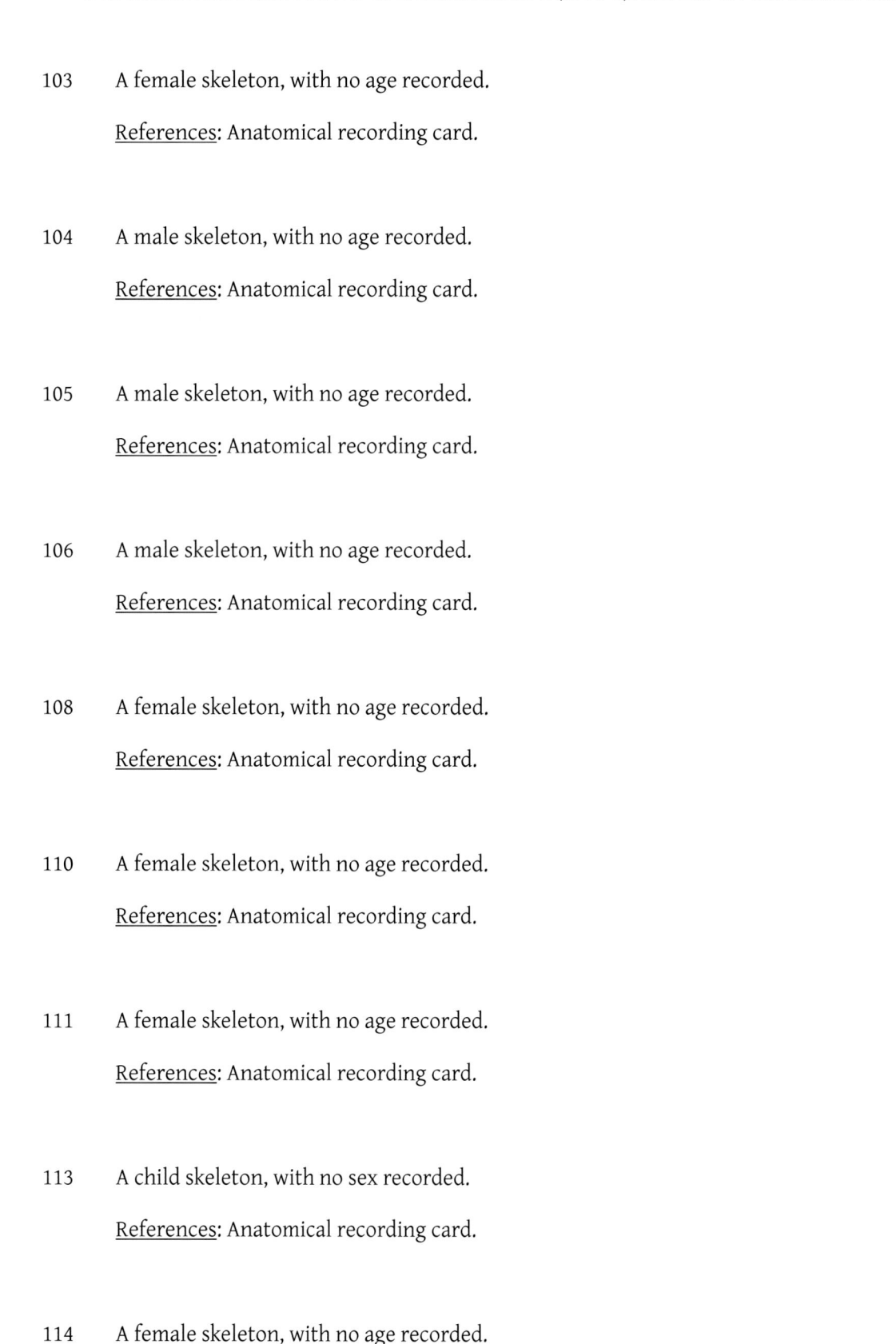

103 A female skeleton, with no age recorded.

References: Anatomical recording card.

104 A male skeleton, with no age recorded.

References: Anatomical recording card.

105 A male skeleton, with no age recorded.

References: Anatomical recording card.

106 A male skeleton, with no age recorded.

References: Anatomical recording card.

108 A female skeleton, with no age recorded.

References: Anatomical recording card.

110 A female skeleton, with no age recorded.

References: Anatomical recording card.

111 A female skeleton, with no age recorded.

References: Anatomical recording card.

113 A child skeleton, with no sex recorded.

References: Anatomical recording card.

114 A female skeleton, with no age recorded.

References: Anatomical recording card.

118 A female skeleton, with no age recorded.

References: Anatomical recording card.

119 A child skeleton, with no sex recorded.

References: Anatomical recording card.

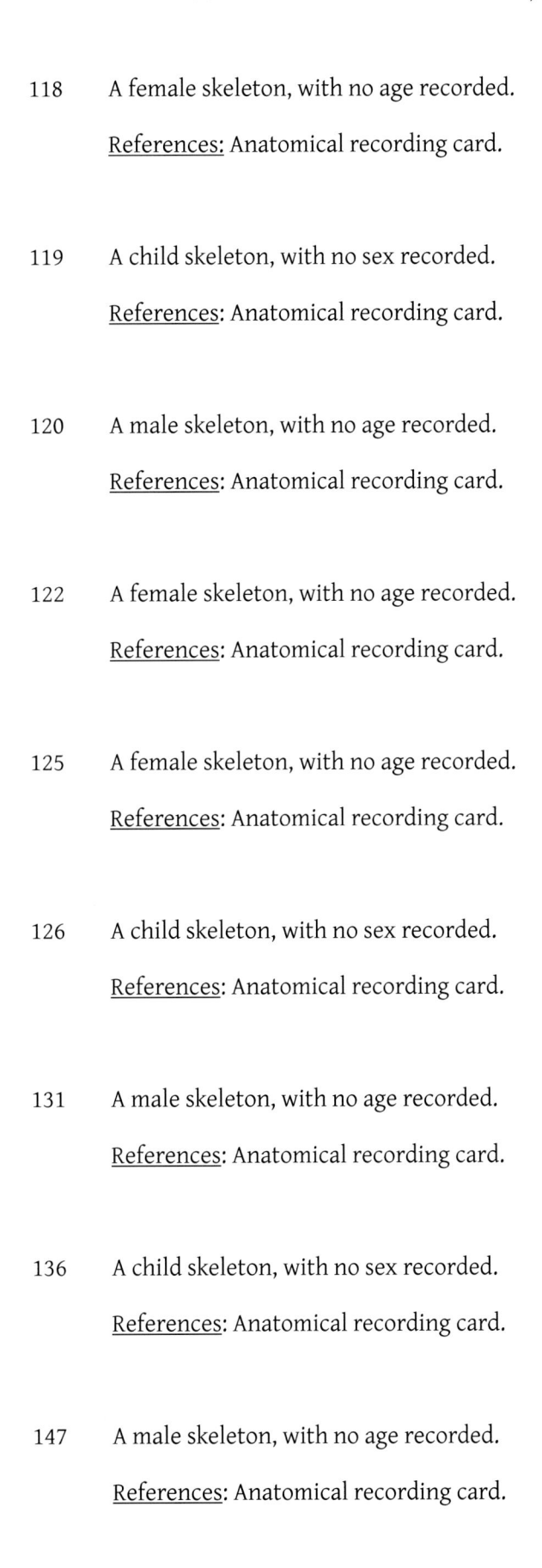

120 A male skeleton, with no age recorded.

References: Anatomical recording card.

122 A female skeleton, with no age recorded.

References: Anatomical recording card.

125 A female skeleton, with no age recorded.

References: Anatomical recording card.

126 A child skeleton, with no sex recorded.

References: Anatomical recording card.

131 A male skeleton, with no age recorded.

References: Anatomical recording card.

136 A child skeleton, with no sex recorded.

References: Anatomical recording card.

147 A male skeleton, with no age recorded.

References: Anatomical recording card.

148   A female skeleton, with no age recorded.

        References: Anatomical recording card.

149   A male skeleton, with no age recorded.

        References: Anatomical recording card.

151   A child skeleton, with no sex recorded.

        References: Anatomical recording card.

152   A male skeleton, with no age recorded.

        References: Anatomical recording card.

154   A female skeleton, with no age recorded.

        References: Anatomical recording card.

157   A child skeleton, with no sex recorded.

        References: Anatomical recording card.

158   A male skeleton, with no age recorded.

        References: Anatomical recording card.

160   A female skeleton, with no age recorded. Originally recorded as a male skeleton, the innominate has been subsequently identified as female.

        Surviving skeletal remains: A left innominate is currently housed in the Duckworth Laboratory, The University of Cambridge (uncatalogued). The location of the rest of the skeleton is unknown.

        References: Anatomical recording card.

166 A child skeleton, with no sex recorded.

References: Anatomical recording card.

167 A female skeleton, with no age recorded.

References: Anatomical recording card.

171 A female skeleton, with no age recorded.

References: Anatomical recording card.

174 A child skeleton, with no sex recorded.

References: Anatomical recording card.

178 A male child skeleton.

References: Anatomical recording card.

180 A female skeleton, with no age recorded.

References: Anatomical recording card.

181 A child skeleton, with no sex recorded.

References: Anatomical recording card.

182 A male skeleton, with no age recorded.

References: Anatomical recording card.

183 A male skeleton, with no age recorded.

References: Anatomical recording card.

184 A child skeleton, with no sex recorded.

References: Anatomical recording card.

185 A child skeleton, with no sex recorded.

References: Anatomical recording card.

186 A child skeleton, with no sex recorded.

References: Anatomical recording card.

188(a) A female skeleton, with no age recorded.

References: Anatomical recording card.

188(b) A male skeleton, with no age recorded.

References: Anatomical recording card.

190 A male skeleton, with no age recorded.

References: Anatomical recording card.

191 A child skeleton, with no sex recorded.

References: Anatomical recording card.

192 A female skeleton, with no age recorded.

References: Anatomical recording card.

193(a) A child skeleton, with no sex recorded.

References: Anatomical recording card.

193(b) A male skeleton, with no age recorded.

  References: Anatomical recording card.

193(c) A male skeleton, with no age recorded.

  References: Anatomical recording card.

198(a) A female skeleton, with no age recorded.

  References: Anatomical recording card.

198(b) A female skeleton, with no age recorded.

  References: Anatomical recording card.

199 A child skeleton, with no sex recorded.

  References: Anatomical recording card.

X-group burials

3 A male, aged skeleton.

  Original anatomical observations: The coronal and lambdoid sutures are open, the sagittal suture is closing. There is right occipital bulging. The tori are well-marked.

  The maxillary teeth are very much worn. The right 1st molar has a large abscess cavity, and the alveolus is absorbed at the incisors on both sides. All of the teeth present in the mandible are not carious.

  References: Anatomical recording card.

13 A male, adult skeleton.

  Original anatomical observations: All cranial sutures are open. The occipital is symmetrical. The mastoids are long and attenuated. There is a well-marked manifestation of an occipital vertebra. The skull is orthognathus.

  All teeth present in both jaws are perfect and fairly well worn.

The manubrium is separate. There is a large facet present on both femora.

References: Anatomical recording card.

25 A female, aged skeleton.

Original anatomical observations: All cranial sutures are closed. There is left occipital bulging. There are hardly any mastoids.

Those teeth present in the maxilla are much worn and alveolus is much absorbed on both sides. No comments were recorded for the mandible.

The sacrum is 5-pieced and rather curved.

References: Anatomical recording card.

34 A female skeleton, with no age recorded.

References: Anatomical recording card.

Christian burials

5 A female, adult skeleton with wavy brown hair. The body was lying on its back, head to the west with the hands on the pubes.

Original anatomical observations: All cranial sutures are open. The lambdoid is very complicated. There is an epipteric bone on the right shutting out the parietal from the great wing of the sphenoid. On the left, the squamous just touches the frontal. There is slight right occipital bulging. There is a very marked visible prognathism, which was slightly measurable.

All of the maxillary teeth are present and perfect except the right 1st bicuspid which has a cavity and an abscess at its root and the left 3rd molar of which only a stump remains with an abscess at the root. Those mandibular teeth present are perfect. The 1st and 3rd molars have gone and the alveolus absorbed on both sides. The alveolus is also absorbed at the left 1st incisor. There was apparently no room in the mandible for the right 2nd incisor as this is absent.

All pieces of the sternum are separate. The sacrum is 5-pieced and slightly curved.

References: Anatomical recording card.

6 A female, adult skeleton. The body was extended on its back, arms straight at the sides and hands on the pubes.

Original anatomical observations: All cranial sutures are open. The occiput is symmetrical. There is a definite visible prognathism.

All maxillary teeth present are perfect except the right 2nd molar and the left 2nd molar and 2nd bicuspid which have disappeared and the alveolus is absorbed. There are small carious cavities in the right 3rd molar and the left 1st molar. In the mandible the alveolus has absorbed behind the 1st bicuspid on the right and, except for the 3rd molar, behind the 2nd bicuspid on the left.

The sacrum is 5-pieced. The line of union of the epiphyses of the ilium and the ramus of the ischium are still visible. The woman is evidently over 40 years.

References: Anatomical recording card.

12   A male, aged skeleton.

Original anatomical observations: All cranial sutures are closed. There is left occipital bulging. The mastoids are long and thin. There is a depression measuring 21 x 18mm which has almost completely absorbed. There are thin spicules of bone only being left.

In the maxilla all of the alveolus is absorbed except at the right canine and 1st bicuspid. In the mandible this is all absorbed behind canines.

There is a fracture of the right clavicle in middle with good union, but much shortening. There is a fracture of the right ulna at the junction with the lower middle third. This has healed with good union. The head of the right humerus has altered to adapt itself to a sub-coracoid dislocation. The glenoid cavity is almost completely worn away and there is eburnation on the head of the bone and on the central surface of the scapula below the coracoid. There is a probable fracture of the neck of the right femur, with the head loose in the acetabular cavity. A facet is present on the neck of the left femur. The sacrum is 6-pieced (5 sacral bones + 1 coccyx). There is slight lumbar spondylitis.

Surviving skeletal remains: Several skeletal elements with different catalogue numbers are currently located in the Duckworth Laboratory, The University of Cambridge. The skull, demonstrating the depressed fracture (Figure 8) and the mandible are catalogued as NU855. The right ulna, radius, humerus and femur discussed in the anatomical report are present in the collection but are currently uncatalogued. The right scapula is located separately and is catalogued as NU862a. The location of the rest of the skeleton is unknown.

References: Anatomical recording card; Derry (1909a, 47).

15   A male, adult skeleton. Curly brown hair is preserved.

Original anatomical observations: The coronal and sagittal sutures are closed, the lambdoid suture is closing. There is definite right occipital bulging and a definite visible prognathism.

All maxillary teeth are perfect except the right 1st molar which has a small carious cavity and the left 1st molar which is a carious stump with an abscess at the root. The third molars never appeared. All mandibular teeth are present and perfect. There is a rudimentary tooth between the right 1st and 2nd bicuspids on the lingual side.

All the cartilages of the larynx are ossified, including the thyroid and cricoids (Figure 9). The right clavicle is fractured about its middle and in uniting the two ends have overlapped with much shortening and widening of the bone. The manubrium is separate but the xiphoid process is completely fused to the body and has long oval hole through it. The sacrum is 5-pieced. There is a facet on the neck of both femora.

Surviving skeletal remains: The cranium and mandible are located at the Duckworth Laboratory, The University of Cambridge (catalogue ref. NU856). The larynx, right clavicle and fragments of the sternum are catalogued separately as NU861d. The location of the rest of the skeleton is unknown.

References: Anatomical recording card; Derry (1909a, 47).

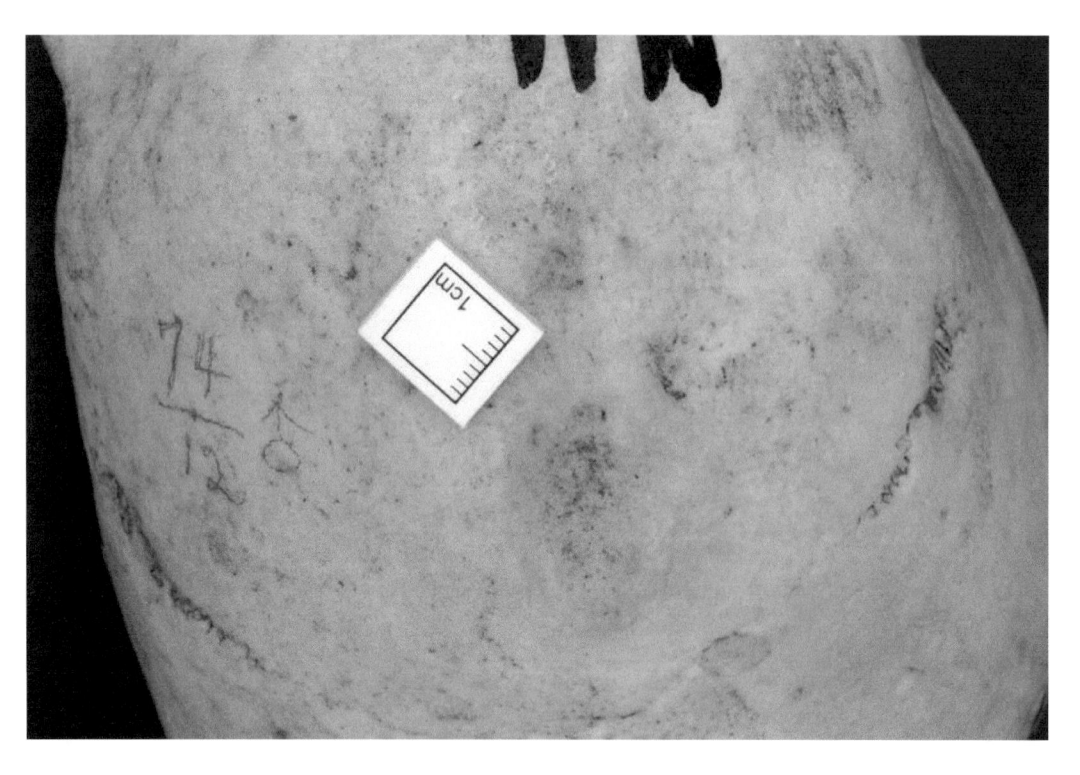

Figure 8: The skull of an adult, male found in cemetery 74, grave 12. The frontal bone shows signs of a well-healed depressed fracture measuring 23.6 x 20.9 mm. ©The Duckworth Laboratory, The University of Cambridge, 2023.

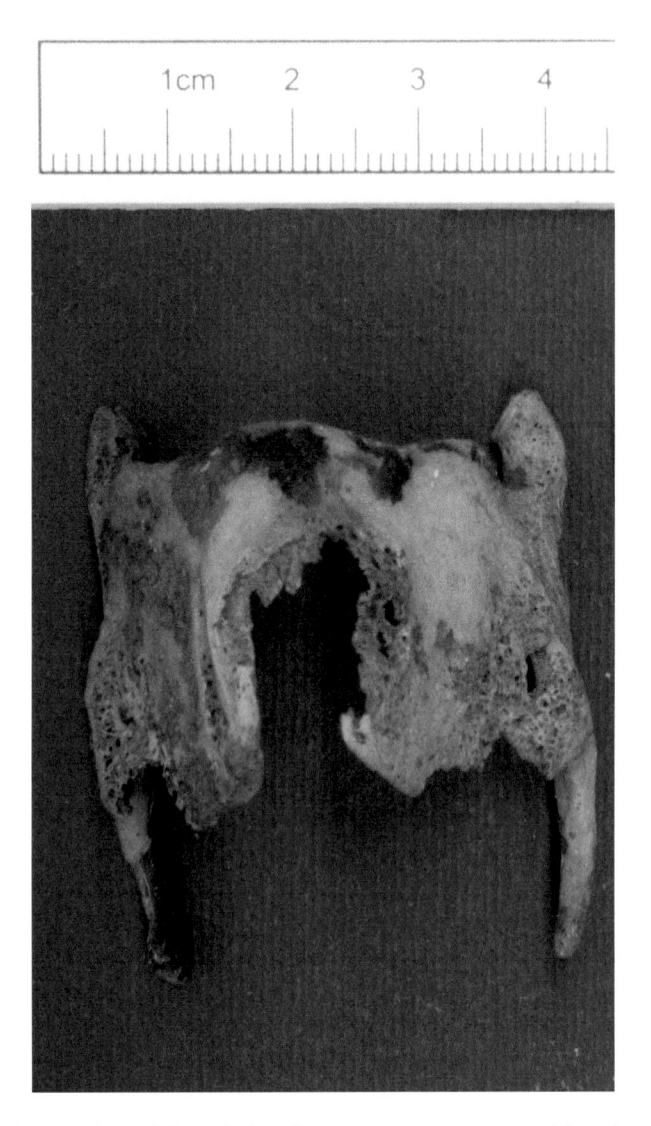

Figure 9: The ossified larynx of an adult, male found in cemetery 74, grave 15. Although a number of examples were found during the ASN, this is the only example currently known to survive. ©The Duckworth Laboratory, The University of Cambridge, 2023.

19 A male, adult skeleton. The body was extended on its back, with the hands over the pubes.

<u>Original anatomical observations</u>: All cranial sutures are open. There are no tori.

All teeth present are perfect and fairly well-worn in both jaws. There is a carious cavity in the right 2nd molar in the maxilla.

The manubrium is separate from the gladiolus. The posterior arches of the 4th and 5th lumbar vertebrae are separate from the body. The sacrum is 5-pieced, very flat and narrow.

<u>References</u>: Anatomical recording card.

23   A male skeleton, under 17 years old.

Original anatomical observations: There are many wormian bones in the lambdoid suture.

The maxillary teeth are all present and the 3rd molars are fully erupted. The right 2nd molar has large abscess cavity at the roots, the right 3rd molar is also carious and the left 1st molar is carious with inflammation at the root. In the mandible the right 2nd bicuspid is carious and the right 1st and 2nd molars have gone and the alveolus has absorbed. The left 2nd molar is also carious, only a stump remains.

None of the secondary epiphyses are united. The internal condyle of the humerus is still separate, placing the age under 17 but the teeth are all present.

References: Anatomical recording card; Derry (1909a, 48).

53   A male, adult skeleton. The body was on its back with the hands on the thighs and the head to the west.

Original anatomical observations: The sagittal suture is closing, the coronal and lambdoid sutures are still open. The occipital is symmetrical. There is a definite visible prognathism.

All maxillary teeth present are perfect except the left 3rd molar which is a carious stump with an abscess at the root. The milk canine on the right is still present; the permanent canine is visible though in the alveolus. In the mandible the right 2nd bicuspid is carious and the left 1st molar has disappeared and the alveolus has absorbed. The rest of the teeth are perfect.

The manubrium is still separate. There is a hole in the lower end of the gladiolus. The sacrum is 5-pieced. There is a facet present on the neck of both femora.

References: Anatomical recording card.

58   A male, aged skeleton lying on its back, with the head to the west.

Original anatomical observations: The coronal suture is closed in the lowest part, the sagittal and lambdoid sutures are closing. The squamous temporal articulates with the frontal on both sides. There is a slight left occipital bulging.

All of the alveolus is absorbed in both jaws, except for the parts of the mandible containing the incisors and canines.

Some of the rib cartilages are ossified to the sternum. One rib has a bifurcated extremity. The manubrium is separate, but the xiphoid process is partly ossified and fused. The sacrum is 6-pieced (5 sacral bones + 1 coccyx), long and rounded (broken). Both patellae have large notches.

References: Anatomical recording card.

61 A female, aged skeleton with wavy grey hair.

<u>Original anatomical observations</u>: The coronal and sagittal sutures are closed, the lambdoid suture is closing. There is left occipital bulging.

All of the alveolus has completely absorbed except for one or two stumps in both jaws.

There is spondylitis of the lumbar spine. The sacrum is fused to the right innominate bone (due to spondylitis).

<u>References</u>: Anatomical recording card.

68 A male, aged skeleton. White hair, a beard and moustache were preserved.

<u>Original anatomical observations</u>: The coronal, sagittal and lambdoid sutures are all closing. The tori are prominent. The occipital is symmetrical. Above the right orbit, extending from orbital margin for 26mm upwards, there is a narrow, deep gutter looking as if caused by a sharp instrument, one of the edges being apparently undercut.

The maxillary teeth are worn to stumps. There is an abscess at the roots of the right 2nd molar and the left 1st incisor, both bicuspids and the 1st molar. The mandibular teeth are also much worn. The right 2nd molar has gone and the alveolus has absorbed. There is an abscess at the root of the left 2nd incisor and the alveolus has absorbed behind the 1st bicuspid.

The manubrium is separate from the gladiolus. The xiphoid process is completely ossified and is fused to body of sternum. It is also bifurcated. There is a fracture of the neck of the left femur, without subsequent union, so that a false joint has been formed between the great trocanter and the separated head. There is much inflammatory adventitious bone around the acetabulum and eburnation of broken surfaces. There is a fracture at the junction of the middle and lower third of the right fibula and tibia. Union is good, but there is much thickening of the lower end of the tibia and both bones are joined by an osseous bar. There is a large facet present on the neck of the right femur.

<u>Further studies</u>: In addition to the fractures identified on the anatomical recording card, Derry (1909a, 48) describes four ribs about the middle of the series on the right side that are fractured and healed with good union.

<u>Surviving skeletal remains</u>: The skull was located in the Anatomical Museum, The University of Manchester when studied by Watson. The current location is unknown.

<u>References</u>: Anatomical recording card; Derry (1909a, 47-48); Watson (pre-1935).

70 A female, adult skeleton with brown curly hair preserved.

<u>Original anatomical observations</u>: The coronal and sagittal sutures are quite closed, the lambdoid suture is closing. There is slight left occipital bulging. There is a slight visible prognathism.

There has been suppuration in the right auditory meatus, causing a large round abscess cavity destroying both anterior and posterior walls of the meatus and opening up the middle ear.

The maxillary teeth are all present but stumps only remain. There are cavities in the right canine and at the root of the right 2nd incisor opening onto both sides. Tartar is present. The alveolus on the right side of the mandible is absorbed behind the 1st bicuspid and on the left at the 2nd bicuspid and the 2nd molar. The left 3rd molar has a carious cavity.

The manubrium is fused to the body of the sternum. The sacrum is very flat and 5-pieced.

References: Anatomical recording card; Derry (1909a, 48).

81   A female, adult skeleton.

Original anatomical observations: All cranial sutures are open and very complicated. There is a wormian bone in the right coronal suture. A large epipteric bone on both sides shuts out the parietal from the great wing of the sphenoid. On the left the squamous also articulates with the temporal. There is marked visible prognathism. There is a slight left occipital bulging.

All maxillary teeth are present, perfect and little worn. In the mandible the right 2nd incisor, canine and 1st molar and the left 1st and 2nd incisors and 1st molar all have carious cavities.

References: Anatomical recording card.

84   A female, adult skeleton.

Original anatomical observations: All cranial sutures are open. The occipital is symmetrical. There is very marked visible prognathism.

In the maxilla, the right 1st molar has gone and the alveolus is absorbed. The left 2nd and 3rd molars are carious stumps, the rest of the teeth present are perfect. The right 2nd molar and the left 3rd molar in the mandible are carious. Tartar is present.

References: Anatomical recording card.

169 A female, young adult skeleton. The body was lying on its back, thighs widely apart, knees slightly flexed.

Original anatomical observations: There is marked visible prognathism.

The pubic portion of the pelvis has disappeared. Low down in the pelvic cavity is the head of a full-term foetus, with the occiput on a level with the ischial tuberosities. The head is lying in the ROA (Right Occiput Anterior) position, with the chin against the left sacro-iliac articulation. This, in the unmoved portion of the bones, is gaping to the extent of 22mm; but on the right side the sacrum is found ossified to the innominate bone. The left parietal bone of the foetus has [...]

upon the right to the extent of nearly an inch (23mm), and the same has happened, but to a less degree in the case of the two frontal bones. The vertebral column is normal.

References: Anatomical recording card.

Burials of uncertain date (Christian/X-group)

4   A female child skeleton, about 6 years old.

References: Anatomical recording card.

7   A child skeleton, with no sex recorded.

References: Anatomical recording card.

8   A child skeleton, with no sex recorded.

References: Anatomical recording card.

9   A child skeleton, with no sex recorded.

References: Anatomical recording card.

22   A male child skeleton.

References: Anatomical recording card.

31   A child skeleton, with no sex recorded.

References: Anatomical recording card.

45   A child skeleton, with no sex recorded.

References: Anatomical recording card.

46 A child skeleton, with no sex recorded.

References: Anatomical recording card.

47 A female skeleton, with no age recorded.

References: Anatomical recording card.

51 A child skeleton, with no sex recorded.

References: Anatomical recording card.

52 A child skeleton, with no sex recorded.

Surviving skeletal remains: A sacrum is currently located in the Duckworth Laboratory, The University of Cambridge identified as belonging to this body (uncatalogued). The sacrum demonstrates sacralisation of the 5th lumbar vertebra and a sacral hiatus. The degree of fusion exhibited suggests the sacrum belongs to an adult, suggesting the cemetery/grave number on the sacrum may be erroneous.

55 A child skeleton, with no sex recorded.

References: Anatomical recording card.

69 A child skeleton, with no sex recorded.

References: Anatomical recording card.

71 A child skeleton, with no sex recorded.

References: Anatomical recording card.

78 A child skeleton, with no sex recorded.

References: Anatomical recording card.

79 A female skeleton, with no age recorded.

References: Anatomical recording card.

Cemetery 75, East bank, Shalub Batha

X-group period and Roman-Byzantine period

Although given a cemetery number, there is no record of any burials from this cemetery in the archaeological reports or on the surviving anatomical recording cards. The graves had been extensively damaged by sebakh digging (Firth 1912a, 38).

88   Skeletal remains of unknown age or sex. Only the presence of skeletal remains in the Duckworth collection has demonstrated that any bodies were excavated from this cemetery. It is a possibility that these bones were isolated finds recovered from damaged graves.

   <u>Surviving skeletal remains</u>: A partial, fractured femur and a section of fused lumbar vertebra are currently housed in the Duckworth Laboratory, The University of Cambridge (uncatalogued).

Cemetery 76, West bank, Gedekol, Gerf Husein

A-group period and C-group-early New Kingdom period

Cemetery 76 was located in the alluvial mud banks on the south side of a khor near Gedekol village. The earliest Predynastic/A-group burials are located towards the southern end of the cemetery, with the later Early Dynastic burials situated towards the north. The C-group-New Kingdom burials are located in the centre of the cemetery (Firth 1912a, 6-7). There are also a small number of isolated later burials dated to the X-group and the Roman-Moslem period. One hundred and twenty-one bodies from 165 graves were uncovered.

A-group burials

The following graves were found to be empty upon excavation: 100, 101, 103, 120, 137, 138 (Firth 1912a, 114-120; Firth 1912b, plan XIII).

The following graves were recorded with no clear indication of whether they contained a body; they are likely to have been empty: 1, 2, 20, 85, 86, 92, 121, 123, 129, 140 (Firth 1912a, 115-123; Firth 1912b, Plan XIII).

8   A fragmentary skeleton, with no age or sex recorded.

   References: Firth (1912a, 123).

59   A child skeleton, with no sex recorded

   References: Firth (1912a, 111); Firth (1912b, Plan XIII).

60   A partial post-cranial skeleton, with no age or sex recorded. The leg bones only remain.

   References: Firth (1912a, 111); Firth (1912b, Plan XIII).

61   A skeleton, with no age or sex recorded.

   References: Firth (1912a, 111); Firth (1912b, Plan XIII).

62   A skeleton, with no age or sex recorded.

   References: Firth (1912a, 111); Firth (1912b, Plan XIII).

63 A fragmentary infant skeleton, with no sex recorded.

References: Firth (1912a, 111); Firth (1912b, Plan XIII).

64 An infant skeleton, with no sex recorded.

References: Firth (1912a, 112; Figs. 64-5); Firth (1912b, Plan XIII).

65 A skeleton, with no age or sex recorded.

References: Firth (1912a, 112; Figs. 65-6); Firth (1912b, Plan XIII).

66 A male skeleton, with no age recorded.

References: Anatomical recording card; Firth (1912a, 112); Firth (1912b, Plan XIII).

67A A male skeleton, with no age recorded.

References: Anatomical recording card; Firth (1912a, 112; Figs. 68-9); Firth (1912b, Plan XIII).

67B A skeleton, with no age or sex recorded.

References: Firth (1912a, 112-13; Figs. 68-9); Firth (1912b, Plan XIII).

70 A male skeleton, with no age recorded.

References: Anatomical recording card; Firth (1912a, 113; Figs. 70-1); Firth (1912b, Plan XIII).

72 A male skeleton, with no age recorded.

Original anatomical observations: The coronal and sagittal sutures are closing, the lambdoid suture is still open. The mastoids are very small. There is slight right occipital bulging.

All teeth present are perfect and well-worn in both jaws.

References: Anatomical recording card; Firth (1912a, 119); Firth (1912b, Plan XIII).

89   A disturbed female, aged skeleton.

Original anatomical observations: All cranial sutures are closed. There is a definite visible prognathism. Parietal thinning is commencing on both sides.

All teeth present are perfect in both jaws.

The manubrium is fused to the body of the sternum through which there is a hole. The 2nd and 3rd phalanges of one of the fingers are fused. There is spondylitis of the lumbar spine. The sacrum is 5-pieced and slightly curved.

References: Anatomical recording card; Firth (1912a, 120); Firth (1912b, Plan XIII).

93   A male, young adult skeleton.

References: Anatomical recording card; Firth (1912a, 113); Firth (1912b, Plan XIII).

96   A skeleton, with no age or sex recorded.

References: Firth (1912a, 113); Firth (1912b, Plan XIII).

98   A male skeleton, with no age recorded.

References: Anatomical recording card; Firth (1912a, 113); Firth (1912b, Plan XIII).

99   A female skeleton, with no age recorded. Long wavy hair is preserved.

Original anatomical observations: All cranial sutures are open. There are wormian bones in the posterior sagittal and both lambdoid sutures. There is slight left occipital bulging. There is a marked visible prognathism.

All teeth present are perfect and slightly worn in both jaws, with the exception of the right 3rd molar in the mandible which is carious.

The manubrium is separate from the gladiolus. The sacrum is 5-pieced and slightly curved.

References: Anatomical recording card; Firth (1912b, Plan XIII).

105   A skeleton, with no age or sex recorded. The grave is cut into by 76/107.

References: Firth (1912a, 114; Figs. 72-3); Firth (1912b, Plan XIII).

107(a)　A male skeleton, with no age recorded. This grave is described as being empty in the archaeological report, which does not match the anatomical record.

References: Anatomical recording card; Firth (1912a, 114; Figs. 72-3); Firth (1912b, Plan XIII).

107(b)　A female skeleton, with no age recorded. This grave is described as being empty in the archaeological report, which does not match the anatomical record.

References: Anatomical recording card; Firth (1912a, 114; Figs. 72-3); Firth (1912b, Plan XIII).

109　A female skeleton, with no age recorded.

References: Anatomical recording card; Firth (1912a, 114; Figs. 74-5); Firth (1912b, Plan XIII).

111　An infant skeleton, with no sex recorded.

References: Firth (1912a, 114); Firth (1912b, Plan XIII).

112　A female skeleton, with no age recorded.

References: Anatomical recording card; Firth (1912a, 114; Figs. 76-7); Firth (1912b, Plan XIII).

113　An empty large jar buried on its side – possibly intended for the burial of an infant.

References: Firth (1912a, 115; Fig. 78); Firth (1912b, Plan XIII).

114　A fragmentary skeleton, with no age or sex recorded.

References: Firth (1912a, 115); Firth (1912b, Plan XIII).

119　A skull, with no age or sex recorded.

References: Firth (1912a, 115); Firth (1912b, Plan XIII).

122　A partial male skeleton, with no age recorded. The upper part of the skeleton only remains.

References: Anatomical recording card; Firth (1912a, 115); Firth (1912b, Plan XIII).

124A   A male, adult skeleton.

       Original anatomical observations: Tori are very slightly marked. The mastoids are small.

       References: Anatomical recording card; Firth (1912a, 115); Firth (1912b, Plan XIII).

124B   A child skeleton, with no sex recorded.

       References: Firth (1912a, 115); Firth (1912b, Plan XIII).

125   A female skeleton, with no age recorded. The skull was found to be broken when the body was excavated.

       Original anatomical observations: The sagittal suture is closing, all of the others are open. There is a wormian bone in the lambdoid. There is distinct visible prognathism.

       All teeth are present, perfect and worn in both jaws except the right 1st molar in the mandible which is carious and the alveolus behind it is absorbed.

       The sacrum is 5-pieced and slightly curved.

       References: Anatomical recording card; Firth (1912a, 116; Figs. 79-80); Firth (1912b, Plan XIII).

126   A partial post-cranial skeleton, with no age or sex recorded. The lower part of the skeleton only remains.

       References: Firth (1912a, 116); Firth (1912b, Plan XIII).

127   A male, adult skeleton.

       Original anatomical observations: All cranial sutures are open. There is an epipteric bone on the left side of the skull. The tori are very slightly marked. The mastoids are very small.

       All teeth are present, perfect and much worn in both jaws.

       The sacrum is 4-pieced and flat. The 6th lumbar vertebra articulates with the sacrum [...] transverse process. There are 6 lumbar vertebrae and 11 rib-bearing vertebrae present (the correct number).

       References: Anatomical recording card; Firth (1912a, 116); Firth (1912b, Plan XIII).

130 A male skeleton, with no age recorded.

Original anatomical observations: All cranial sutures are closed. There is slight right occipital bulging.

All teeth are present and perfect in both jaws.

References: Anatomical recording card; Firth (1912a, 116); Firth (1912b, Plan XIII).

131 A partial post-cranial skeleton, with no age or sex recorded. The lower part of the skeleton only remains.

References: Firth (1912a, 116); Firth (1912b, Plan XIII).

132 A child skeleton, with no sex recorded.

References: Firth (1912a, 116); Firth (1912b, Plan XIII).

133 A female skeleton, with no age recorded.

Original anatomical observations: There is a definite visible prognathism.

References: Anatomical recording card; Firth (1912a, 116-17; Figs. 81-2); Firth (1912b, Plan XIII).

134 A male, aged skeleton

Original anatomical observations: All cranial sutures are closed. There are epipteric bones on both sides, shutting out the parietal from the great wing of the sphenoid. The tori are very slightly marked. The mastoids are very small. The occipital is symmetrical. There is a depression on the left parietal bone, close to the sagittal suture and about 12mm in front of parietal foramina, measuring 26.5 x 20mm. There is a slight manifestation of an occipital vertebra. The groove on the posterior arch of the atlas for the vertebral artery is bridged over on both sides.

All teeth present are perfect and much worn in both jaws. The alveolus is absorbed on both sides at the 1st bicuspid and the 1st molar in the maxilla.

References: Anatomical recording card; Firth (1912a, 117).

135 A child skeleton, with no sex recorded.

References: Anatomical recording card; Firth (1912a, 117); Firth (1912b, Plan XIII).

139   A male skeleton, with no age recorded. Black curly hair is preserved.

   Original anatomical observations: The tori are very slight and the mastoids are small. There is a definite visible prognathism. The mandible is rather square, and the chin is not prominent with a long deeply sloping ramus.

   In the maxilla all teeth are present and perfect, except for abscesses at the roots of both central incisors due to infection through the pulp cavity. In the mandible all teeth present are perfect and slightly worn. The mandible is too small for the number of teeth, consequently the right 2nd incisor and the left 3rd molar are somewhat crowded out.

   References: Anatomical recording card; Firth (1912a, 118; Fig. 85); Firth (1912b, Plan XIII).

141   A child skeleton, with no sex recorded.

   References: Anatomical recording card; Firth (1912a, 118); Firth (1912b, Plan XIII).

142   A male, adult skeleton.

   Original anatomical observations: All cranial sutures closing. The tori are faintly marked. The obelion is flattened. There is slight left occipital bulging.

   All teeth present are perfect and very much worn in both jaws.

   The manubrium is separate from the gladiolus. The cartilage of the left 1st rib is ossified. The sacrum is 6-pieced (5 sacral bones + 1 coccyx). There is a facet on the neck of the right femur.

   References: Anatomical recording card; Firth (1912a, 118; Figs. 86-7); Firth (1912b, Plan XIII).

143   A male, adult skeleton. The skull was found to be broken when the body was excavated.

   Original anatomical observations: All cranial sutures are open. There is a very large epipteric bone on the left shutting out the parietal from the great wing of the sphenoid.

   All teeth are present, perfect and much worn in both jaws.

   All parts of the sternum are separate, except for two parts of the gladiolus. There is a facet present on the neck of both femora.

   References: Anatomical recording card; Firth (1912a, 118; Fig. 88); Firth (1912b, Plan XIII).

144   A child skeleton, with no sex recorded.

   References: Anatomical recording card; Firth (1912a, 118); Firth (1912b, Plan XIII).

146   A child skeleton, with no sex recorded.

        References: Firth (1912a, 119); Firth (1912b, Plan XIII).

Burials of uncertain date (A to C-group)

The following graves were recorded with no clear indication of whether they contained a body; they are likely to have been empty: 75, 91 (Firth 1912a, 119).

58   A female, adult skeleton.

        Original anatomical observations: The coronal, sagittal and lambdoid sutures are all closing. An epipteric bone is shutting out the parietal from the great wing of the sphenoid on the right. On the left the squamous temporal articulates with the frontal. There is right occipital bulging.

        Both femora are platymeric but there is no platycnemia present in the tibiae.

        References: Anatomical recording card.

94   A male, adolescent skeleton.

        Original anatomical observations: There is a fracture of the right femur at the junction of the upper and middle third. Union has taken place with much forward convexity of the shaft.

        References: Anatomical recording card.

C-group burials

The following graves were found to be empty upon excavation: 80, 104 (Firth 1912a, Figs. 90-91), 117, 118 (Firth 1912a, 119; Firth 1912b, Plan XIII).

The following graves were recorded with no clear indication of whether they contained a body; they are likely to have been empty: 71, 73, 88, 102, 110 (Firth 1912a, 119-120; Firth 1912b, Plan XIII).

68   A child, with no sex recorded.

        References: Anatomical recording card; Firth (1912a, 119); Firth (1912b, Plan XIII).

69   A child, with no sex recorded.

        References: Anatomical recording card; Firth (1912a, 119); Firth (1912b, Plan XIII).

74 A female, adult skeleton.

Original anatomical observations: All cranial sutures are closed. There is slight right occipital bulging. There is a marked visible prognathism.

All teeth are present, perfect and well-worn in both jaws, except the left 3rd molar in the maxilla which is carious.

References: Anatomical recording card; Firth (1912a, 119); Firth (1912b, Plan XIII).

76 A disturbed female, adult skeleton.

Original anatomical observations: The coronal and sagittal sutures are closed, the lambdoid suture is closing. There is slight left occipital bulging. There is a marked visible prognathism. The roofs of both orbits are very much thinned and posteriorly completely absorbed. There is a well-marked third condyle on the anterior margin of the foramen magnum. The mandible is missing.

All teeth are present and perfect but much worn in the maxilla.

The sacrum is 6-pieced and acutely flexed at level of junction of 3rd and 4th pieces. There is a facet present on the neck of the right femur.

References: Anatomical recording card; Firth (1912a, 119); Firth (1912b, Plan XIII).

77 A female, adult skeleton. The archaeological report indicates the presence of only the pelvis and femora which does not match the anatomical report.

Original anatomical observations: All cranial sutures are closed. There is slight left occipital bulging. There is a marked visible prognathism. There are two large parietal thinnings. Immediately behind the two parietal foramina there is a depressed fracture of the skull, measuring 15mm x 15mm which involves both tables and communicates with the interior by a long narrow cleft. There seems to have been some suppuration in the nasal air-sinuses which has caused absorption and thinning of the internal lateral orbital walls on both sides. This has spread to the antrum of Highmore and caused bulging of the posterior wall.

All teeth present are perfect and well-worn in both jaws. There is tartar present on the maxillary teeth. The left alveolus is partially absorbed at the 2nd and 3rd molars in the mandible.

The sacrum is 6-pieced (5 sacral bones + 1 coccyx). The left tibia is platycnemic.

References: Anatomical recording card; Firth (1912a, 119); Firth (1912b, Plan XIII).

79 A skeleton, with no age or sex recorded.

References: Firth (1912a, 119); Firth (1912b, Plan XIII).

83   A disturbed male, aged skeleton.

Original anatomical observations: The coronal and sagittal sutures are closing, the lambdoid suture is still open. There is pronounced visible prognathism. Some ulcerative process, probably commencing in the middle ear, has caused destruction of the anterior wall of the left external auditory meatus and tympanic plate and has involved the tempero-mandibular articulation, the condyle of the mandible being destroyed by the inflammation. It has spread backwards into the antrum and has opened into lateral sinus. The antrum communicates with the exterior by several apertures at the site of the suprameatal triangle. Further, the pus has found its way downwards behind jugular foramen and has made its way into the jugular process and from there beneath the condyle both forwards and backwards. The posterior part of the condyle has given way and has flattened out into post condylar foramen. The carotid canal and Eustachian tube are both opened up and the pus has also escaped at the lower inner part of the mastoid process. There are curious supramastoid osseous projections.

The maxillary teeth are much worn. There are abscesses at the root of the 1st bicuspid and the 1st molar on the right side and on left at the roots of the 1st and 2nd molars. The alveolus is absorbed at the 3rd molar. All teeth present in the mandible are perfect and much worn, except the right 3rd molar which projects forwards and is much worn. This has a facet where the upper 3rd molar [...] it.

There is a fracture at the junction of the mid lower third of the right ulna. This has healed with perfect union. There is a facet present on the neck of the right femur.

References: Anatomical recording card; Derry (1909a, 51); Firth (1912a, 119); Firth (1912b, Plan XIII); McKenzie & Brothwell (1967, 470).

84   A disturbed skeleton, with no age or sex recorded.

References: Firth (1912a, 120); Firth (1912b, Plan XIII).

87   A disturbed female, adult skeleton.

Original anatomical observations: The coronal and lambdoid sutures are open and the sagittal suture is closing. There is an epipteric bone on the right and a small one on the left. There is marked visible prognathism and slight left occipital bulging.

All teeth are present, perfect and not much worn in both jaws, except for both 1st molars in the mandible which are carious.

There has been disease in the acromial end of the left clavicle, causing eating away of the bone. Apparently, the same disease has affected both scapulae in the spinous process. The sacrum is 5-pieced and slightly curved. There is a facet present on the neck of both femora.

Further studies: There are some small lesions present in the frontal bone which were not commented upon during the initial study. Further investigation is required to allow for a differential diagnosis (see Figure 10).

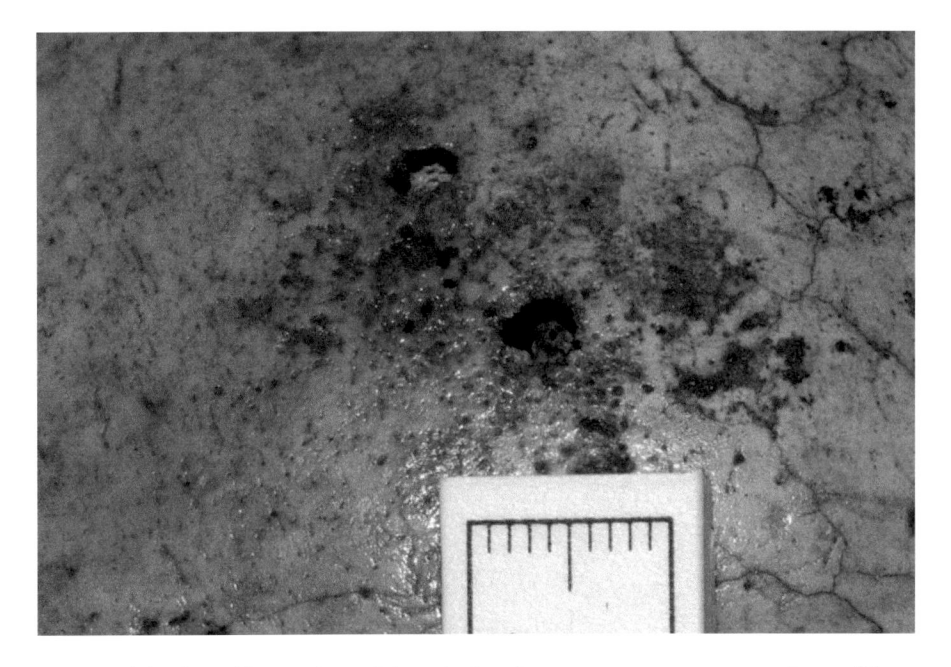

Figure 10: Part of the frontal bone of an adult male found in cemetery 76, grave 87. The small lesions were not reported by Smith and Derry and require further study to allow for a differential diagnosis. This suggests that intensive study of some material excavated during season 2 was not subject to the same scrutiny seen in season 1, resulting in some less obvious pathological changes being missed. ©The Duckworth Laboratory, The University of Cambridge, 2023.

Surviving skeletal remains: A damaged cranium and complete mandible are located in the Duckworth Laboratory, The University of Cambridge (catalogue ref. NU487).

References: Anatomical recording card; Firth (1912a, 120); Firth (1912b, Plan XIII).

90   A female skeleton, with no age recorded.

References: Anatomical recording card; Firth (1912a, 120); Firth (1912b, Plan XIII).

106   A disturbed female, young adult skeleton with brown curly hair.

Original anatomical observations: The skull is slightly sprung. On the left, the squamous temporal almost articulates with the frontal. On the right side it does so through an epipteric bone. There is slight right occipital bulging.

All teeth present are perfect and little worn in both jaws, except the right 1st and 2nd molars and the left 2nd molar in the mandible which are carious.

The sacrum is 5-pieced and very flat. There is a facet present on the neck of both femora.

Surviving skeletal remains: A single innominate bone is located in the KNH Centre for Biomedical Egyptology, The University of Manchester (catalogue ref. 13263). The location of the rest of the body is unknown.

References: Anatomical recording card; Firth (1912a, 120); Firth (1912b, Plan XIII).

108(a) A female, adult skeleton. The anatomical card describes this body as male, but the later publication (bulletin 3) refers to the body as female.

Original anatomical observations: All cranial sutures are open. The mastoids are very large. There is slight left occipital bulging. There has apparently been some suppuration in the antrum of Highmore as the wall posteriorly are thin and discoloured, and the antra are swollen, and the disease has also spread into the sphenoid air-sinuses. There has possibly been suppuration in the mastoid antra which on the right side may have communicated with the sigmoid sinus (the whole skull kept). There is a depressed fracture between the parietal foramina, measuring 15 x 15mm. This involved both tables of the skull (Derry 1909a, 52).

All maxillary teeth are present, perfect and slightly worn. No comments were recorded for the mandible.

References: Anatomical recording card; Derry (1909a, 52); Firth (1912a, 120); Firth (1912b, Plan XIII).

108(b) A child skeleton about 12 years old, with no sex recorded. The archaeological report only records the presence of one body in the grave, unlike the anatomical record.

References: Anatomical recording card.

116 A male, adult skeleton. The grave cuts through 76/117. The archaeological report records this grave as being empty in contrast to the anatomical records.

Original anatomical observations: All cranial sutures are open. There is a wormian bone present in the right lambdoid. There is slight right occipital bulging and marked visible prognathism.

All teeth are present and perfect in both jaws.

References: Anatomical recording card; Firth (1912a, 120).

New Kingdom burials

The following graves were found to be empty upon excavation: 15, 17, 21, 22, 23, 30, 136 (Firth 1912a, 117-121).

The following graves were recorded with no clear indication of whether they contained a body; they are likely to have been empty: 3, 25, 32, 33, 43 (Firth 1912a, 121-122).

5   A male, adult skeleton. The archaeological report indicates there may have been more than one body present in the grave, but no further information is given.

Original anatomical observations: The coronal, sagittal and lambdoid sutures are all closing. The occipital is symmetrical. The tori are prominent.

All teeth present are perfect and much worn in both jaws.

Manubrium is separate from the gladiolus, but the xiphoid process has ossified and fused to it. There is a large hole through the lower point of the gladiolus. The sacrum is 5-pieced, very large and slightly curved.

References: Anatomical recording card; Firth (1912a, 121).

6   A child skeleton, with no sex recorded.

References: Firth (1912a, 121).

7   A child skeleton, with no sex recorded.

References: Firth (1912a, 121).

9   A child skeleton, with no sex recorded.

References: Firth (1912a, 121).

10 A child skeleton, with no sex recorded.

References: Firth (1912a, 121).

11 A child skeleton, with no sex recorded.

References: Anatomical recording card; Firth (1912a, 121).

12 A child skeleton, with no sex recorded.

References: Anatomical recording card; Firth (1912a, 121).

13   A child skeleton, with no sex recorded.

References: Anatomical recording card; Firth (1912a, 121).

14A   A possible male, adult skeleton.

Original anatomical observations: The coronal, sagittal and lambdoid sutures are all closing. There is slight right occipital bulging. The tori are fairly well marked. There is no visible prognathism.

All teeth present in the maxilla are perfect and much worn. No comments were recorded for the mandible.

References: Anatomical recording card; Firth (1912a, 121).

14B   A male, adult skeleton. Wavy hair that was going grey was preserved.

Original anatomical observations: The coronal, sagittal and lambdoid sutures are all closing. There is slight right occipital bulging. The tori are fairly prominent. There is visible, perhaps only alveolar, prognathism.

All teeth are present, perfect and much worn in both jaws.

References: Anatomical recording card; Firth (1912a, 121).

14C   A possible female, adult skeleton.

Original anatomical observations: All cranial sutures are open. There are epipteric bones on the left, separating the parietal from the great wing of the sphenoid. There is also an epipteric bone on the right. There is left occipital bulging. No prognathism is visible.

All maxillary teeth are present and much worn. The right 3rd molar is a carious stump and the left 2nd molar has a carious cavity. Tartar is present. No comments were recorded for the mandible.

References: Anatomical recording card; Firth (1912a, 121).

14D   A female, adult skeleton.

Original anatomical observations: There is a large epipteric bone on the right shutting out the parietal from the great wing of the sphenoid. The os japonicum on the left is not complete, but it is on the right. All cranial sutures are open and complicated. There is a wormian bone in the lambdoid suture. There is slight right occipital bulging

All teeth in the maxilla are present and perfect, except the 3rd molars which never appeared. No comments were recorded for the mandible.

Surviving skeletal remains: The cranium is currently housed in the Duckworth Laboratory, The University of Cambridge (catalogue ref. NU857). The location of the rest of the body is unknown.

References: Anatomical recording card; Firth (1912a, 121).

14E   A female, adult skeleton.

Original anatomical observations: The coronal and sagittal sutures are closing, the lambdoid suture is open. There is slight right occipital bulging.

All of the alveolus is absorbed in both jaws.

References: Anatomical recording card; Firth (1912a, 121).

14F   A female, aged skeleton.

Original anatomical observations: The coronal and sagittal sutures are closing, the lambdoid suture is open. The sutures are very simple. The occipital is symmetrical. The mandible is missing.

On the right the canine, 1st, 2nd and 3rd molars all have abscesses at the root. On the left the canine, 2nd incisor, 1st and 2nd bicuspids and 1st molar have abscesses at the root.

References: Anatomical recording card; Firth (1912a, 121).

14G   A female, aged skeleton.

Original anatomical observations: The coronal, sagittal and lambdoid sutures are all closing. There is an epipteric bone on the left separating the parietal from the great wing of the sphenoid. There is also an epipteric bone on the right. The occipital is symmetrical.

The maxillary teeth are much worn. The right 1st bicuspid and 1st molar and the left 1st molar have abscesses at the root. No comments were recorded for the mandible.

References: Anatomical recording card; Firth (1912a, 121).

14H   A female skeleton, with no age recorded. This body was given the same number as the child below (14H²).

References: Anatomical recording card; Firth (1912a, 121).

14I   A child skeleton, with no sex recorded.

References: Firth (1912a, 121).

18   A female, aged skeleton.

Original anatomical observations: All cranial sutures are open. There is slight left occipital bulging.

In the maxilla, the alveolus has almost absorbed on the right side. On the left there are abscesses at the roots of the left canine and 1st bicuspid and the alveolus has absorbed except at the 2nd and 3rd molars. All teeth present in the mandible are perfect, but much worn.

The sacrum is 5-pieced. It has been distorted by non-fusion of the first piece on the left side. There is a large facet present on the neck of both femora.

References: Anatomical recording card.

19   A child skeleton, with no sex recorded. The archaeological report records this grave as being empty in contrast to the anatomical records.

References: Anatomical recording card; Firth (1912a, 121).

24   A disturbed male, aged skeleton.

Original anatomical observations: The coronal and sagittal sutures are closing, the lambdoid suture is open. The occipital is symmetrical. The tori are well marked. Supraorbital vessels perforate the frontal bone on the right side 7mm above the orbital margin and on the left side 17mm above the orbital margin.

All teeth are present, perfect and very much worn in both jaws except the 3rd molars in the maxilla which has an abscess cavity at the root. In the mandible the alveolus is absorbed on the right behind the 1st bicuspid and on the left behind the 2nd bicuspid.

References: Anatomical recording card; Firth (1912a, 121).

26A   A female, aged skeleton with grey curly hair.

Original anatomical observations: The coronal and sagittal sutures are closed, lambdoid suture is still open. There is an epipteric bone on the left. The tori are well marked. There is slight left occipital bulging. The left occipitomastoid suture is slightly sprung. There is a manifestation of an occipital vertebra, with a well-marked para-mastoid process which almost meets an upward projection on the transverse process of the atlas.

The maxillary alveolus on the right is absorbed, on the left the teeth have gone except the 3rd molar which is carious. The alveolus is absorbed in the mandible.

There is spondylitis of the lower lumbar spine.

References: Anatomical recording card; Firth (1912a, 121).

26B A male skeleton, with no age recorded. The archaeological report indicates the presence of only a single burial in this grave, in contrast to the anatomical records.

References: Anatomical recording card; Firth (1912a, 121).

27A A male, adult skeleton with straight brown hair.

Original anatomical observations: coronal and sagittal sutures are closing, the lambdoid suture is open. The occipital is symmetrical. There is no visible prognathism.

All teeth present are perfect and much worn in both jaws. The right 1st incisor in the maxilla has gone, apparently due to an abscess at the root.

References: Anatomical recording card; Firth (1912a, 121).

27B A male, aged skeleton with grey hair. The archaeological report indicates the presence of only a single burial in this grave, in contrast to the anatomical records.

Original anatomical observations: The coronal and sagittal sutures are closed, the lambdoid suture is closing. There is left occipital bulging.

In the maxilla, the right side is largely absorbed, only the 1st and 2nd molars remain. There is an abscess at the root of the 1st molar. The left side has an immense abscess cavity at the roots of the incisors and the canine, opening onto the face and palate, but not perforating the mucous membrane of the palate which is still in situ. The rest of the teeth have gone, except the 1st molar and the alveolus has absorbed. In the mandible, the alveolus has absorbed behind the 1st bicuspid on both sides. At the roots of the 1st and 2nd incisors on the left are abscess cavities.

References: Anatomical recording card; Firth (1912a, 121).

28 A skeleton, with no age or sex recorded.

References: Firth (1912a, 121).

29	A female skeleton, with no age recorded.

	References: Anatomical recording card; Firth (1912a, 121).

31	A male skeleton, with no age recorded. The skull was recorded as having been deliberately moved from its anatomical position when discovered.

	Original anatomical observations: There is a persistent interparietal suture.

	References: Anatomical recording card; Firth (1912a, 121).

35	A male, adult skeleton.

	Original anatomical observations: All cranial sutures are open. The tori are very prominent. There is left occipital bulging. No prognathism is visible.

	All teeth present are perfect and slightly worn. There is a rudimentary 3rd left bicuspid present in the mandible.

	The sacrum is 5-pieced, flat and slightly curved. There is a facet present on the neck of both femora.

	Surviving skeletal remains: The skull was located in the Anatomical Museum, The University of Manchester when studied by Watson. The current location is unknown.

	References: Anatomical recording card; Firth (1912a, 122); Watson (pre-1935).

36A	A female, adult skeleton.

	Original anatomical observations: All cranial sutures are open. There is an epipteric bone on the left. There is slight left occipital bulging. There is a visible prognathism.

	All teeth present are perfect in both jaws.

	References: Anatomical recording card; Firth (1912a, 122).

36B	A female, aged skeleton. The archaeological report records the presence of only a single burial in this grave in contrast to the anatomical record. Bodies were not however assigned individual characters.

	Original anatomical observations: All cranial sutures are open and very simple. There is left occipital bulging.

	The alveolus of the mandible is absorbed. No comments were recorded for the maxilla.

36(c)   A skeleton with no age or sex recorded.

   References: Anatomical recording card.

37   A male skeleton, with no age recorded.

   References: Anatomical recording card.

38   A child skeleton, with no sex recorded.

   References: Firth (1912a, 122).

39   A child skeleton, with no sex recorded.

   References: Firth (1912a, 122).

40   A child skeleton, with no sex recorded.

   References: Anatomical recording card; Firth (1912a, 122).

41   A child skeleton, with no sex recorded.

   References: Anatomical recording card; Firth (1912a, 122).

42   A child skeleton, with no sex recorded.

   References: Firth (1912a, 122).

44A   A female, aged skeleton with white hair.

   Original anatomical observations: The coronal and sagittal sutures are closing, the lambdoid suture is open. There is left occipital bulging.

All teeth in the maxilla have gone, the alveolus is absorbed and there are signs of caries. The mandibular alveolus is absorbed on both sides behind the 1st molars. There are abscess cavities in the right 1st bicuspid and 1st molar and the left 1st and 2nd bicuspid and 2nd incisor.

References: Anatomical recording card; Firth (1912a, 122).

44B A child skeleton, with no sex recorded.

References: Anatomical recording card; Firth (1912a, 122).

45 An infant skeleton, with no sex recorded.

References: Firth (1912a, 122).

46 A post-cranial child skeleton, with no sex recorded.

References: Anatomical recording card; Firth (1912a, 122).

47 A disturbed skeleton, with no age or sex recorded.

References: Firth (1912a, 122).

48 A grave with no record of the presence of a body.

References: Firth (1912a, 122).

51 The partially mummified body of a child, with no sex recorded. This child appears to have been naturally mummified but the archaeological record does not explicit say this.

References: Firth (1912a, 122).

52A A partial female, adult skeleton.

Original anatomical observations: All cranial sutures are open. An epipteric bone on the right shuts out the parietal from the great wing of the sphenoid. There is also an epipteric bone on the left. There is slight right occipital bulging.

All teeth present are perfect and slightly worn, except right 2nd molar and the left 1st molar in the maxilla which are carious.

References: Anatomical recording card; Firth (1912a, 122).

52B A female skeleton, with no age recorded. The archaeological report records the presence of only a single burial in this grave in contrast to the anatomical record.

References: Anatomical recording card.

52C A male skeleton, with no age recorded.

References: Anatomical recording card.

52(d) A female skeleton, with no age recorded. The presence of a fourth body was recorded by the anatomists, but it was not assigned an individual character.

Original anatomical observations: All cranial sutures are open. There is an epipteric bone on the right shutting out the parietal from the sphenoid. There is right occipital bulging. There is a definite visible prognathism.

The right 2nd molar and the left 1st molar in the maxilla are carious. No comments were recorded for the mandible.

References: Anatomical recording card.

53 A child skeleton, with no sex recorded.

References: Anatomical recording card.

54 A partial post-cranial skeleton, with no age or sex recorded. Only the femoral heads were present.

References: Firth (1912a, 122).

55 A male, young adult skeleton whose burial can be dated to Dynasty 18. Brown hair was preserved.

Original anatomical observations: All cranial sutures are open. There is left occipital bulging.

All teeth present are perfect and slightly worn in both jaws.

The sacrum is 5-pieced and curved.

References: Anatomical recording card.

78 A male skeleton, with no age recorded.

References: Anatomical recording card.

81 A male skeleton, about 20 years with curly brown hair.

Original anatomical observations: All cranial sutures are open including the metopic suture. There is an epipteric bone on the left side. Wormian bones are present in the posterior parietal, both lambdoids and the posterior parietal squamous suture. [...] of secondary sutures are still open. There is slight left occipital bulging. The mastoids are very small.

All teeth present are perfect and very slightly worn in both jaws.

All parts of the sternum are still separate. The sacrum is 6-pieced (5 sacral bones + 1 coccyx), long and narrow.

Surviving skeletal remains: A largely complete skeleton is currently housed in the Duckworth Laboratory, The University of Cambridge (catalogued in part as catalogue ref. LXX).

References: Anatomical recording card; Firth (1912a, 119).

82 A female, adult skeleton with curly brown hair.

Original anatomical observations: The coronal and sagittal sutures are closing, the lambdoid suture is open. On the right, the squamous temporal articulates with the frontal. There is slight left occipital bulging.

All teeth present are perfect and very much worn in both jaws.

The manubrium is separate. There is a large facet present on the neck of both femora.

References: Anatomical recording card.

141 A child skeleton, with no sex recorded.

References: Firth (1912b, Plan XIII)

X-group burials

23 A possible male skeleton, with no age recorded.

<u>Original anatomical observations</u>: All cranial sutures are open. There is left occipital bulging. There is a definite visible prognathism.

All teeth are present in the maxilla but are much worn. The left 2nd bicuspid and 1st molar are carious. In the mandible, the right 1st molar is carious with an abscess cavity at the root. There is also an abscess at the root of the left 2nd bicuspid.

The manubrium is separate. The sacrum is 5-pieced and flat.

<u>References</u>: Anatomical recording card.

Roman-Moslem burials

16 A skeleton, with no age or sex recorded.

<u>References</u>: Firth (1912a, 123).

18 A disturbed skeleton, with no age or sex recorded.

<u>References</u>: Firth (1912a, 123).

34 A sheep burial.

<u>References</u>: Firth (1912a, 123).

37 A Moslem burial

<u>References</u>: Firth (1912a, 123).

55 A disturbed skeleton, with no age or sex recorded, possibly a Moslem burial.

<u>References</u>: Firth (1912a, 123).

Burials of unknown date

181   A female skeleton, with no age recorded.

   References: Anatomical recording card.

Cemetery 77/1, West bank, Gedekol South, Gerf Husein

A-group to C-group period

A cemetery containing about 70 graves: C-group burials are found to the north of the cemetery and circular A-group graves to the south (Reisner 1909a, 9). Archaeological records have only been preserved for 35 of the graves and only two of which contained bodies.

A-group burials

The following graves were found to be empty upon excavation: 2, 14, 21, 22, 23, 24, 27, 30, 31, 33, 24 (Firth 1912a, 126-127; Firth 1912b, Plan XIII).

1   A female, adult skeleton. The archaeological report records this body as that of an infant, in contrast to the anatomical records (Firth 1912a, 126).

   <u>Original anatomical observations</u>: All cranial sutures are open. There are wormian bones in left lambdoidal suture. There are two small epipteric bones shutting out the parietal from great wing of the sphenoid on left and another epipteric bone on the right. There is left occipital bulging. There is a definite visible prognathism.

   All teeth present are perfect and not much worn in both jaws.

   The manubrium is separate from the gladiolus. The posterior arch of the 5th lumbar vertebra is separate. The sacrum is 5-pieced and rather curved.

   <u>References</u>: Anatomical recording card; Firth (1912a, 126); Firth (1912b, Plan XIII).

13   A male, adult skeleton.

   <u>References</u>: Derry (1909a, 52); Firth (1912a, 126; Fig. 95); Firth (1912b, Plan XIII).

Burials of uncertain date (A to C-group)

The following graves were found to be empty upon excavation: 26 (Firth 1912a, 126; Firth 1912b, plan XIII).

C-group burials

The following graves were found to be empty upon excavation: 3, 4, 5, 6, 7, 8, 9, 10, 11, 15, 16, 17, 18, 19, 20, 25, 28, 29, 32, 35 (Firth 1912a, 126; Firth 1912b, Plan XIII).

Cemetery 77/100, West bank, Gedekol South, Gerf Husein

A-group and Christian periods

A small cemetery containing 23 graves and 10 surviving skeletons.

A-group burials

The following graves were found to be empty upon excavation: 101, 102, 103, 104, 105 (Firth 1912a, 124).

The following graves were recorded with no clear indication of whether they contained a body; they are likely to have been empty: 107, 108, 109, 110, 111, 112, 118, 119, 120 (Firth 1912a, 124-125).

106　A skeleton, with no age or sex recorded.

References: Firth (1912a, 124).

113　A male skeleton, with no age recorded.

Surviving skeletal remains: The skull was located in the Anatomical Museum, The University of Manchester when studied by Watson. The current location is unknown.

References: Firth (1912a, 124); Watson (pre-1935).

114　A disturbed skeleton, with no age or sex recorded.

References: Firth (1912a, 124).

115(a)　A male, aged skeleton. The head was resting on the left hand, with the body flexed on the left side. The body was not assigned an individual character in the anatomical records.

Original anatomical observations: The coronal, sagittal and lambdoid sutures are all closing. There is slight left occipital bulging. The tori are well marked.

All of the alveolus in the maxilla has been absorbed behind the canines on both sides. There has been an abscess at the root of the right 2nd incisor. In the mandible all teeth present are perfect and very much worn. There are abscesses at the roots of both canines and the left 1st and 2nd bicuspids.

The manubrium is separate from the gladiolus. The sacrum is 5-pieced and curved. Both patellae are notched. There is a facet present on the neck of the left femur.

References: Anatomical recording card; Firth (1912a, 124-5; Figs. 92-3).

115(b) An infant skeleton, with no sex recorded.

References: Firth (1912a, 124-5; Figs. 92-3).

116 A skeleton, with no age or sex recorded.

References: Firth (1912a, 125; Fig. 94).

117 A skeleton, with no age or sex recorded.

References: Firth (1912a, 125).

Christian burials

125 A skeleton, with no age or sex recorded. The body was wrapped in coarse woollen cloth.

References: Firth (1912a, 126).

Burials of unknown date

126 A child skeleton, with no age or sex recorded.

References: Firth (1912a, 126).

127 A child skeleton, with no age or sex recorded.

References: Firth (1912a, 126).

Cemetery 78, West bank, Mediq, Gerf Husein

A-group (Late Predynastic/Dynasty 1) period

Cemetery 78 is situated on a small mound at the mouth of a valley near Mediq. It has been completely plundered by tomb robbers. There is little reference to this cemetery in the archaeological report or any of the archival documents.

18 A fragile male, adult skeleton.

    Original anatomical observations: The tori are small and the mastoids are very small.

    All teeth present in the maxilla are perfect. The maxillary 3rd molars never appeared. There is an abscess at the root of the right 1st molar (the pulp cavity is exposed). All mandibular teeth are present, perfect and very much worn, except the right 3rd molar which never appeared.

    All parts of sternum are united. Both patellae are notched. The tibiae are very platycnemic.

    References: Anatomical recording card; Derry (1909a, 52).

Cemetery 79, West bank, Mediq, Gerf Husein

A-group and Christian period

Cemetery 79 is thought to be a continuation of cemetery 78, although the burials are considered to be dated to later in the A-group period. Social stratification is visible within this cemetery; the largest graves are located at the end of the cemetery facing the river. These particular graves have received the most attention from tomb robbers (Firth 1912a, 7-8). There is no description of the Christian period area of this cemetery.

There are 155 bodies from 207 graves; a considerable number of graves no longer contained bodies, particularly as a number of intact graves contained evidence of multiple burials. As with previous cemeteries, in around half the bodies found age and/or sex has not been identified or recorded.

A-group burials

The following graves were found to be empty upon excavation: 1, 4, 5, 6, 8, 16, 21, 24, 26, 27, 28, 31 (Firth 1912a, Figs. 102-103), 38, 43, 47, 50, 51, 56, 59, 60, 63, 64, 69, 71, 72, 74, 75, 77, 78, 81, 82, 83, 84, 87, 94, 95, 99, 102, 103, 105, 106, 107, 108, 109, 110, 114, 115, 116, 118, 123, 125, 126, 127, 128, 129, 131, 132, 140, 145, 146, 151, 153, 154, 155, 156, 158, 174, 181, 182, 183, 184, 186, 187, 188, 191, 192, 193, 194, 195, 196, 197, 198, 199, 200, 203, 204, 206, 207, 208, 209, 210, 211, 212, 213, 214, 215, 216, 217, 218, 219, 220, 221, 222, 223 (Firth 1912a, 129-151; Firth 1912b, Plan XIV).

2   A male skeleton, with no age recorded.

Original anatomical observations: All cranial sutures are closed. The tori are slightly marked. There is slight right occipital bulging. The mastoids are long and pointed.

All teeth that are present are perfect in both jaws. No 3rd molars ever appeared.

The manubrium is separate. The sacrum is 6-pieced (5 sacral bones + 1 coccyx). There is spondylitis of the lumbar and dorsal spine. There is a facet present on the neck of both femora.

References: Anatomical recording card; Firth (1912a, 127; Figs. 96-7); Firth (1912b, Plan XIV).

3   A male, adult skeleton. Leather and matting were present in the grave.

Original anatomical observations: One side of the head is so caked with hard mud that accurate measurements are impossible. The coronal suture is closed at the lower end, the sagittal is open (at the visible part) and the lambdoid is open. The tori and mastoids are small. There is slight left occipital bulging. The nasal spine is prominent. The skull is orthognathus.

All teeth are present, perfect and much worn in both jaws.

The manubrium is separate. There is slight spondylitis of the 5th lumbar vertebra. The sacrum is 5-pieced and very flat. Both patellae are notched.

References: Anatomical recording card; Firth (1912a, 127; Figs. 98-9); Firth (1912b, Plate 14A; Plan XIV).

7	A female, adult skeleton. The skull was smashed when the body was excavated.

Original anatomical observations: The sternum is ossified.

References: Anatomical recording card; Firth (1912a, 128); Firth (1912b, Plan XIV).

9	A female, adult skeleton.

Original anatomical observations: The sternum is ossified. There is spondylitis of the lumbar spine.

References: Anatomical recording card; Firth (1912a, 128); Firth (1912b, Plan XIV).

10A	A male, adult skeleton.

Original anatomical observations: All teeth present are perfect, but much worn in both jaws. The right 1st molar and the left 1st and 3rd molars have gone, and the alveolus has absorbed in the mandible.

The clavicular ends are greatly enlarged.

References: Anatomical recording card; Firth (1912a, 128); Firth (1912b, Plan XIV).

10B	A child skeleton about 7 years old, with no sex recorded.

References: Anatomical recording card; Firth (1912a, 128); Firth (1912b, Plan XIV).

11	A male skeleton about 10 years old.

Original anatomical observations: A metopic suture is present.

References: Anatomical recording card; Firth (1912a, 128; Figs. 100-101); Firth (1912b, Plan XIV).

12	A male, adult skeleton. The skull was badly distorted by grave pressure; the anatomists note that it was not possible to make any osteological measurements.

Original anatomical observations: The nasal spine is very prominent.

Teeth are perfect and only slightly worn in both jaws.

All parts of the sternum are separate except the last 2 pieces of the body, which are united, but the suture is still visible both anteriorly and posteriorly. The 4th piece is completely divided into 2 by a longitudinal suture. The spinal column is normal. The lamina of the 1st lumbar vertebra on the right side is not joined to the pedicle.

References: Anatomical recording card; Firth (1912a, 128); Firth (1912b, Plan XIV).

13   A male, adult skeleton. The skull was found to be broken when the body was excavated.

Original anatomical observations: The sagittal suture is closed, the rest are open. On the left side of the skull a process from the atlas proceeds upwards to articulate with the paraoccipital.

The teeth are considerably worn, but healthy in both jaws.

The thyroid is partly ossified. The manubrium is separate from the body of the sternum which is very large. There is a vertical fracture of the right patella which has perfectly healed. There is a large riders bone present.

References: Anatomical recording card; Firth (1912a, 128); Firth (1912b, Plan XIV).

14   A partial probable male, young adult skeleton. Only the upper part of the skeleton is present.

Original anatomical observations: The teeth are practically unworn and perfectly healthy in both jaws.

References: Anatomical recording card; Firth (1912a, 128); Firth (1912b, Plan XIV).

15   A fragmentary skeleton, with no age or sex recorded.

References: Firth (1912a, 129); Firth (1912b, Plan XIV).

20(a)   A male skeleton, with no age recorded. The archaeological report records this grave as empty, in contrast to the anatomical report.

References: Anatomical recording card; Firth (1912a, 151); Firth (1912b, Plan XIV).

20(b)   A child skeleton, with no sex recorded.

References: Anatomical recording card; Firth (1912a, 151); Firth (1912b, Plan XIV).

22 A fragmentary skeleton, with no age or sex recorded.

   References: Firth (1912a, 129); Firth (1912b, Plan XIV).

23 A fragmentary male skeleton, with no age recorded. There are well marked muscular prominences.

   References: Anatomical recording card; Firth (1912a, 129); Firth (1912b, Plan XIV).

25 A disturbed male, adult skeleton.

   Original anatomical observations: There is a deep groove along the lambdoid sutures and a very deep occipital fossa, especially on the left side. The occiput is projecting.

   The teeth are only slightly worn and healthy in both jaws.

   The xiphoid process is ossified and fused to the gladiolus.

   References: Anatomical recording card; Firth (1912a, 129); Firth (1912b, Plan XIV).

29(a) A male skeleton, with no age recorded. The archaeological report records only two bodies in this grave (one male, one female), in contrast to the anatomical records.

   References: Anatomical recording card; Firth (1912a, 129); Firth (1912b, Plan XIV).

29(b) A male skeleton, with no age recorded.

   References: Anatomical recording card; Firth (1912a, 129); Firth (1912b, Plan XIV).

29(c) A male skeleton, with no age recorded.

   References: Anatomical recording card.

29(d) A female skeleton, with no age recorded.

   References: Anatomical recording card.

30   An infant skeleton, with no sex recorded.

   References: Firth (1912a, 129); Firth (1912b, Plan XIV).

32   A sheep burial.

   References: Firth (1912a, 151); Firth (1912b, Plan XIV).

33   A male, adult skeleton. The anatomists record that the burial is intrusive; however, this is not indicated in the archaeological report.

   Original anatomical observations: The skull is scaphocephalic. There are prominent frontal tori. There is very marked subnasal prognathism and well-marked subnasal gutters.

   The teeth are only slightly worn and perfect in both jaws.

   There is marked torsion on the tibia.

   References: Anatomical recording card; Firth (1912a, 130); Firth (1912b, Plan XIV).

34   A male, adult skeleton. The archaeological report records the presence of only the vertebrae in the grave, in contrast to the anatomical records.

   Original anatomical observations: The teeth are good and slightly worn in both jaws.

   References: Anatomical recording card; Firth (1912a, 130); Firth (1912b, Plan XIV).

35   An infant skeleton, with no sex recorded.

   References: Firth (1912a, 130); Firth (1912b, Plan XIV).

36   A partial male, adult post-cranial skeleton. The archaeological report records that only the lower vertebrae remain.

   References: Anatomical recording card; Firth (1912a, 130-1); Firth (1912b, Plan XIV).

37   A disturbed child skeleton, with no sex recorded.

   References: Firth (1912a, 131); Firth (1912b, Plan XIV).

39   A skeleton, with no record of age or sex

References: Firth (1912b, Plan XIV).

40(a)   A partial post-cranial skeleton, with no age or sex recorded. The leg bones only remain.

References: Firth (1912a, 131); Firth (1912b, Plan XIV).

40(b)   A partial post-cranial skeleton, with no age or sex recorded. The leg bones only remain.

References: Firth (1912a, 131); Firth (1912b, Plan XIV).

41A   A partial infant skeleton, with no sex recorded. The long bones only remain.

References: Firth (1912a, 131); Firth (1912b, Plan XIV).

41(b)   A male skeleton, about 16 years old.

Original anatomical observations: All cranial sutures are open except the basilar suture which is completely obliterated. A typical Egyptian skull, face and jaw.

The upper wisdom teeth are cutting, whilst the lower are cut.

The lower epiphyses of the tibia are beginning to join. The upper epiphysis of the radius has joined, but the lower has not.

References: Anatomical recording card; Firth (1912a, 131); Firth (1912b, Plan XIV).

42   A partial post-cranial skeleton, with no age or sex recorded. The right femur and tibia and the pelvis only remain.

References: Firth (1912a, 131); Firth (1912b, Plan XIV).

44A   A child skeleton, with no sex recorded.

References: Firth (1912a, 131-2); Firth (1912b, Plan XIV).

44B   A partial post-cranial skeleton, with no age or sex recorded. The leg bones only remain.

References: Firth (1912a, 132); Firth (1912b, Plan XIV).

45A   A young adult skeleton, with no sex recorded.

References: Firth (1912a, 132); Firth (1912b, Plan XIV).

45B   An infant skeleton, with no sex recorded.

References: Firth (1912a, 132); Firth (1912b, Plan XIV).

46A   A partial adult post-cranial skeleton, with no sex recorded. The lower part of the skeleton only remains.

References: Reisner (1909a, 19); Firth (1912a, 132; Fig. 104); Firth (1912b, Plate 12C; Plan XIV).

48(a)   A partial post-cranial large male, adult skeleton. The lower part of the skeleton only remains. The archaeological report records only the presence of a single male skeleton in this grave, in contrast to the anatomical records.

References: Anatomical recording card; Firth (1912a, 132-3; Figs. 105-6); Firth (1912b, Plate 14B; Plan XIV).

48(b)   A large male, adult skeleton.

References: Anatomical recording card.

48(c)   A disturbed small female, adult skeleton.

References: Anatomical recording card.

49(a)   A partial fragmentary post-cranial male, adult skeleton. The lower part of the skeleton only remains.

References: Anatomical recording card; Firth (1912a, 133); Firth (1912b, Plan XIV).

49(b) A fragmentary female, adult skeleton.

References: Anatomical recording card; Firth (1912a, 133); Firth (1912b, Plan XIV).

52(a) A partial post-cranial skeleton with no age or sex recorded. The lower part of the skeleton only remains.

References: Firth (1912a, 133); Firth (1912b, Plan XIV).

52(b) A disturbed skeleton, with no age or sex recorded.

References: Firth (1912a, 133); Firth (1912b, Plan XIV).

52(c) A dog skeleton.

References: Firth (1912a, 133); Firth (1912b, Plan XIV).

53 A fragmentary skeleton, with no age or sex recorded.

References: Firth (1912a, 134); Firth (1912b, Plan XIV).

54 A fragmentary skeleton, with no age or sex recorded.

References: Firth (1912a, 134); Firth (1912b, Plan XIV).

55 A male, adult skeleton.

Original anatomical observations: The teeth are healthy and only slightly worn in both jaws.

References: Anatomical recording card; Firth (1912a, 134); Firth (1912b, Plan XIV).

57 A fragmentary skeleton, with no age or sex recorded.

References: Firth (1912a, 134); Firth (1912b, Plan XIV).

58	An infant skeleton, with no sex recorded.

	References: Firth (1912a, 134); Firth (1912b, Plan XIV).

62	A fragmentary skeleton, with no age or sex recorded.

	References: Firth (1912a, 134); Firth (1912b, Plan XIV).

65(a)	A male, adult skeleton. Only fragments of the skull survive. The archaeological report records the presence of the lower limbs only, in contrast with the anatomical records for all bodies in grave 65.

	Original anatomical observations: The humerii are unperforated.

	References: Anatomical recording card; Firth (1912a, 135); Firth (1912b, Plan XIV).

65(b)	A male, adult skeleton. Only fragments of the skull survive.

	Original anatomical observations: The humerii are unperforated.

	References: Anatomical recording card; Firth (1912a, 135); Firth (1912b, Plan XIV).

65(c)	A female, adult skeleton. Only fragments of the skull survive. The archaeological report records the presence of only one female body in the grave, in contrast to the anatomical records.

	Original anatomical observations: The humerii have large perforations.

	References: Anatomical recording card; Firth (1912a, 135); Firth (1912b, Plan XIV).

65(d)	A female, adult skeleton. Only fragments of the skull survive.

	Original anatomical observations: The humerii have large perforations.

	References: Anatomical recording card.

66A	A female, young adult skeleton. The bones of this skeleton have been pushed aside. They are thought to be those of the original occupant of the tomb. Her physical characters (the shape of the skull and limb bones) were recorded as being very similar to those of 66B.

<u>Original anatomical observations</u>: All cranial sutures are open. There is an epipteric bone on the right. There is slight subnasal guttering. There is a definite subnasal prognathism. The nasal spine is almost suppressed.

All teeth that are present are perfect but very slightly worn in both jaws.

The skeleton is very slenderly built. There are large humeral perforations.

<u>References</u>: Anatomical recording card; Firth (1912a, 135; Figs. 107-8); Firth (1912b, Plate 12B, Plan XIV).

66B   A male skeleton, aged 18 years. The burial is intrusive to this grave.

<u>Original anatomical observations</u>: The skull is a small ovoid.

There are large humeral perforations.

<u>References</u>: Anatomical recording card; Firth (1912a, 135; Figs. 107-8); Firth (1912b, Plate 12B, Plan XIV).

67   A fragmentary skeleton, with no age or sex recorded.

<u>References</u>: Firth (1912a, 135); Firth (1912b, Plan XIV).

68   A skeleton, with no age or sex recorded.

<u>References</u>: Firth (1912a, 135); Firth (1912b, Plan XIV).

70   A disturbed massive skeleton, with no age or sex recorded.

<u>References</u>: Firth (1912a, 135); Firth (1912b, Plan XIV).

73   A fragmentary skeleton, with no age or sex recorded.

<u>References</u>: Firth (1912a, 136); Firth (1912b, Plan XIV).

76   A fragmentary skeleton, with no age or sex recorded.

<u>References</u>: Firth (1912a, 136); Firth (1912b, Plan XIV).

79   A partial post-cranial skeleton, with no age or sex recorded. The lower part of the skeleton only remains.

   References: Firth (1912a, 136); Firth (1912b, Plan XIV).

80   A skeleton, with no age or sex recorded.

   References: Firth (1912a, 136); Firth (1912b, Plan XIV).

85   A child skeleton, with no sex recorded. This grave is listed as empty in the archaeological report, in contrast to the anatomical record.

   References: Anatomical recording card; Firth (1912a, 151); Firth (1912b, Plan XIV).

86   A fragmentary female skeleton, aged under 30 years.

   Original anatomical observations: The teeth are healthy, moderately worn and encrusted with tartar which shows distinct impressions of some instrument pushed between adjacent teeth.

   References: Anatomical recording card; Firth (1912a, 137; Figs. 109-10); Firth (1912b, Plan XIV).

88   A male skull, with no age recorded.

   Original anatomical observations: A moderately broad ovoid skull.

   References: Anatomical recording card; Firth (1912a, 137; Figs. 111-12); Firth (1912b, Plan XIV).

89   A male skeleton, about 17 years old. This grave is listed as empty in the archaeological report, in contrast to the anatomical record.

   Original anatomical observations: The cranium is ovoid.

   The wisdom teeth are on the same level as the other molars.

   The upper epiphyses of the femora have just joined. The upper epiphyses of humerii are unjoined. There are large humeral perforations.

   References: Anatomical recording card; Firth (1912a, 151); Firth (1912b, Plan XIV).

90A A skeleton, with no age or sex recorded.

References: Firth (1912a, 137-8); Firth (1912b, Plan XIV).

90B A skeleton, with no age or sex recorded.

References: Firth (1912a, 137-8); Firth (1912b, Plan XIV).

92A A skeleton, with no age or sex recorded.

References: Firth (1912a, 138; Figs. 113-14); Firth (1912b, Plate 13D; Plan XIV).

92B A skeleton, with no age or sex recorded.

References: Firth (1912a, 138; Figs. 113-14); Firth (1912b, Plate 13D; Plan XIV).

92C A skeleton, with no age or sex recorded.

References: Firth (1912a, 138; Figs. 113-14); Firth (1912b, Plate 13D; Plan XIV).

93A A skeleton, with no age or sex recorded.

References: Firth (1912a, 138).

93B A skeleton, with no age or sex recorded. This burial is a later interment.

References: Firth (1912a, 138); Firth (1912b, Plan XIV).

96 An infant skeleton, with no sex recorded.

References: Firth (1912a, 138-9); Firth (1912b, Plan XIV).

97 A male, adult skeleton. The skull was caked in hardened mud when it was excavated. A large amount of *Durra sefi* (sorghum) was found in the grave.

Original anatomical observations: A very large powerful skull, with definite subnasal prognathism. The coronal and lambdoid sutures are open, whilst the sagittal suture is covered with hard mud. The tori are well marked. The mastoids are very small and there is no nasal spine.

The teeth are healthy, moderately worn and perfect in both jaws.

References: Anatomical recording card; Firth (1912a, 139; Figs. 115-6); Firth (1912b, Plan XIV).

98A   A skeleton, with no age or sex recorded.

References: Firth (1912a, 139); Firth (1912b, Plan XIV).

98B   A skeleton, with no age or sex recorded.

References: Firth (1912a, 139); Firth (1912b, Plan XIV).

98C   A skeleton, with no age or sex recorded.

References: Firth (1912a, 139); Firth (1912b, Plan XIV).

100   An infant skeleton, with no sex recorded.

References: Firth (1912a, 139); Firth (1912b, Plan XIV).

104   A fragmentary infant skeleton, with no sex recorded.

References: Anatomical recording card; Firth (1912a, 139); Firth (1912b, Plan XIV).

111   A male, young adult skeleton, with no sex recorded. The skull has been distorted by grave pressure.

Original anatomical observations: All cranial sutures are open, including the metopic suture. There is an epipteric bone on the left. There is a very slight subnasal prognathism.

The teeth are perfect and scarcely worn in both jaws.

References: Anatomical recording card; Firth (1912a, 139); Firth (1912b, Plan XIV).

113   An adult skeleton, with no sex recorded. This grave is listed as empty in the archaeological report, in contrast to the anatomical record.

References: Anatomical recording card; Firth (1912a, 151); Firth (1912b, Plan XIV).

117A   A child skeleton, with no sex recorded.

References: Firth (1912a, 139-40; Fig. 117); Firth (1912b, Plate 13C; Plan XIV).

117B   A female skeleton, about 15 years old.

Original anatomical observations: The basilar suture is open.

The wisdom teeth are cutting.

All epiphyses of the long bones are separate. The ilium is not joined to the rest of the innominate.

References: Anatomical recording card; Firth (1912a, 139-40; Fig. 117); Firth (1912b, Plate 13C; Plan XIV).

119   An infant skeleton, with no sex recorded.

References: Firth (1912a, 140); Firth (1912b, Plan XIV).

120   A skeleton, with no age or sex recorded.

References: Firth (1912a, 140); Firth (1912b, Plan XIV).

121   A sheep burial

References: Firth (1912a, 151); Firth (1912b, Plan XIV).

122(a)   A disturbed male skeleton, with no age recorded.

Original anatomical observations: The bones are large and there are well-marked muscular attachments.

References: Anatomical recording card; Firth (1912a, 140; Fig. 118); Firth (1912b, Plan XIV).

122(b)   A disturbed female skeleton, with no age recorded.

   Original anatomical observations: The bones are large and there are well-marked muscular attachments.

   References: Anatomical recording card; Firth (1912a, 140; Fig. 118); Firth (1912b, Plan XIV).

122(c)   A disturbed male skeleton, with no age recorded. The archaeological report records the presence of only one male skeleton in this grave, in contrast to the anatomical record.

   Original anatomical observations: The bones are large and there are well-marked muscular attachments.

   References: Anatomical recording card.

124(a)   A male skeleton, with no age recorded.

   Original anatomical observations: There are facets present on the neck of both femora. One femur is broken.

   References: Anatomical recording card; Firth (1912a, 140); Firth (1912b, Plan XIV).

124(b)   A female skeleton, with no age recorded. This individual was not identified using an individual character.

   Original anatomical observations: There are facets present on the neck of both femora.

   References: Anatomical recording card; Firth (1912a, 140); Firth (1912b, Plan XIV).

124(c)   A male skeleton, with no age recorded. The archaeological report records the presence of only one male skeleton in this grave, in contrast to the anatomical record.

   Original anatomical observations: There are facets present on the neck of both femora.

   References: Anatomical recording card.

130(a)   A female, adult skeleton.

   Original anatomical observations: The coronal suture is closing, the sagittal and lambdoid sutures are open. There is a marked visible prognathism and the nasal spine is suppressed.

   References: Anatomical recording card; Firth (1912a, 141); Firth (1912b, Plan XIV).

130(b) A child skeleton, with no sex recorded.

References: Anatomical recording card; Firth (1912a, 141); Firth (1912b, Plan XIV).

130(c) A skeleton, with no age or sex recorded. This burial is a later addition to the grave.

References: Firth (1912a, 141); Firth (1912b, Plan XIV).

133 A skeleton, with no age or sex recorded.

References: Firth (1912a, 151); Firth (1912b, Plan XIV).

134 A skeleton, with no age or sex recorded.

References: Firth (1912a, 141); Firth (1912b, Plan XIV).

135A A male, adult skeleton.

Original anatomical observations: The tori are well-marked, and the mastoids are massive. There are well-marked remains of the canaliculus chordae.

The teeth are healthy and well-worn in both jaws.

The vertebral column is normal.

References: Anatomical recording card; Firth (1912a, 141-43; Figs. 119-20); Firth (1912b, Plan XIV).

135A[2] A male, adult skeleton. This individual has the same numbering as the body above but from the descriptions preserved on the two anatomical cards, they are different bodies. This second body cannot be positively matched to the archaeological report description, but it is possible that it should be body 135D which is identified as a male skeleton. There is no other surviving anatomical card for body 135D.

Original anatomical observations: The coronal suture is open, the sagittal is closing posteriorly and the lambdoid is closing. The tori are well-marked. The mastoids are very small. There is definite subnasal prognathism. The zygomata are almost straight. There is a depression measuring 25.5 x 16mm on the right parietal bone. There is inflammatory reaction in and around the injured part.

The teeth are very much worn in both jaws. In the maxilla there are pulp cavity abscesses and the pulp cavity is exposed in the mandible.

135B A fragmentary male, adult skeleton. This body is identified as an infant in the archaeological report, in contrast to the anatomical records.

Original anatomical observations: The bones are very large and powerfully developed.

References: Anatomical recording card; Firth (1912a, 141-43; Figs. 119-20); Firth (1912b, Plan XIV).

135C A fragmentary female, young adult skeleton. This body is identified as a male in the archaeological report, in contrast to the anatomical report.

Original anatomical observations: The bones of the woman present most extensive periostitis, involving the femora, the tibiae, the os calcis and the radii, the fibulae. The clavicles are quite free from this process. The os innominate is only slightly affected.

References: Anatomical recording card; Firth (1912a, 141-43; Figs. 119-20); Firth (1912b, Plan XIV).

136 A female skeleton, with no age recorded.

Original anatomical observations: All cranial sutures are open. There is a very slight subnasal prognathism. The nasal spine is small.

The teeth are only very slightly worn in both jaws.

The sternal end of the left 5th rib is bifurcated. The sternal epiphyses of the clavicle are just joining. The epiphyses of the os innominatum have recently joined.

References: Anatomical recording card; Firth (1912a, 143); Firth (1912b, Plan XIV).

137 A skeleton, with no age or sex recorded. The burial is apparently intrusive.

References: Firth (1912a, 143; Fig. 121); Firth (1912b, Plan XIV).

138 A skeleton, with no age or sex recorded.

References: Firth (1912a, 143; Fig. 122); Firth (1912b, Plan XIV).

139	A disturbed infant skeleton, with no sex recorded.

	References: Firth (1912a, 144; Fig. 124); Firth (1912b, Plan XIV).

141	A much disturbed skeleton, with no age or sex recorded.

	References: Firth (1912a, 144); Firth (1912b, Plan XIV).

142	An infant skeleton, with no sex recorded.

	References: Firth (1912a, 144; Fig. 125); Firth (1912b, Plan XIV).

143	A skeleton, with no age or sex recorded.

	References: Firth (1912a, 144; Figs. 126-7); Firth (1912b, Plan XIV).

144(a)	A male skeleton, with no age recorded.

	Original anatomical observations: The upper extremity of the left radius has been dislocated and was found ankylosed in a position of supination. The same condition was found on the right side. There is a fracture of the left pubic ramus immediately below the symphysis.

	References: Anatomical recording card; Firth (1912a, 144); Firth (1912b, Plan XIV).

144(b)	A dog skeleton.

	References: Firth (1912a, 144); Firth (1912b, Plan XIV).

147(a)	A fragmentary female, young adult skeleton. The archaeological report only records the presence of a single female skeleton in this grave.

	Original anatomical observations: There are only 11 dorsal vertebrae.

	References: Anatomical recording card; Firth (1912a, 145; Figs. 128-9); Firth (1912b, Plate 13B; Plan XIV).

147(b)	A female skeleton, with no age recorded.

	References: Anatomical recording card.

148   A male skeleton, with no age recorded.

        Original anatomical observations: Extreme platycnemia in both tibiae.

        References: Anatomical recording card; Firth (1912a, 145); Firth (1912b, Plan XIV).

149   An infant skeleton, with no sex recorded.

        References: Firth (1912a, 145); Firth (1912b, Plan XIV).

150   A child skeleton, with no sex recorded.

        References: Firth (1912a, 145); Firth (1912b, Plan XIV).

152   A female, adult skeleton.

        Original anatomical observations: The frontal bones are extremely thick.

        All teeth that are present are perfect in both jaws.

        The sacrum is very flat and 5-pieced.

        References: Anatomical recording card; Firth (1912a, 145); Firth (1912b, Plan XIV).

157   A male, adult skeleton.

        Original anatomical observations: The coronal and sagittal sutures are closing, the lambdoid suture is open. There is a slight suggestion of subnasal prognathism. The mastoids and tori are well-marked. The nasal spine is moderately well marked.

        The teeth are health but worn in both jaws.

        The sternum is markedly asymmetrical, with the manubrium bent towards the left.

        References: Anatomical recording card; Firth (1912a, 145-6); Firth (1912b, Plan XIV).

159(a) A male skeleton, with no age recorded.

        Original anatomical observations: There are facets present on the neck of both femora. The body has well marked muscular ridges.

        References: Anatomical recording card; Firth (1912b, Plan XIV).

159(b)　A male skeleton, with no age recorded.

 Original anatomical observations: There are facets present on the neck of both femora. The body has well marked muscular ridges.

 References: Anatomical recording card; Firth (1912b, Plan XIV).

159(c)　A male skeleton, with no age recorded.

 Original anatomical observations: The body has well marked muscular ridges.

 References: Anatomical recording card; Firth (1912b, Plan XIV).

160　A male, adult skeleton.

 Original anatomical observations: The coronal and lambdoid sutures are open, the sagittal suture is closing. On the left, the squamous temporal articulates with the frontal. The tori are prominent, and the mastoids are fairly large.

 References: Anatomical recording card; Firth (1912a, 146); Firth (1912b, Plan XIV).

161　A male, adult skeleton.

 Original anatomical observations: The mastoids are well-marked.

 References: Anatomical recording card; Firth (1912a, 146); Firth (1912b, Plan XIV).

162　A skeleton, with no age or sex recorded.

 References: Firth (1912a, 146); Firth (1912b, Plan XIV).

163　An infant skeleton, with no sex recorded.

 References: Firth (1912a, 146-7); Firth (1912b, Plan XIV).

164　A male skeleton, with no age recorded.

 Original anatomical observations: The teeth are slightly worn in both jaws. In the maxilla, the left 2nd incisor is worn down to the pulp cavity and a small abscess opens into the palate from the root.

The sternum is completely ossified.

<u>References</u>: Anatomical recording card; Firth (1912a, 147); Firth (1912b, Plan XIV).

165(a)   A male, adult skeleton.

<u>Original anatomical observations</u>: The sagittal suture is closed, the coronal and lambdoid sutures are closing. The metopic suture is closing. The tori are well-marked fairly. There is some visible prognathism.

All teeth are present and perfect in both jaws, except the 1st molar is worn down on both sides. There is an abscess at the root of both 1st molars in the maxilla. There is no 3rd molar on the right in the mandible.

<u>References</u>: Anatomical recording card; Firth (1912a, 147; Figs. 132-3); Firth (1912b, Plan XIV).

165(b)   A child skeleton, with no sex recorded. The body was found under 165(a).

<u>References</u>: Firth (1912a, 147; Figs. 132-3); Firth (1912b, Plan XIV).

166A   A male, adult skeleton.

<u>Original anatomical observations</u>: All cranial sutures are open. There are very large wormian bones in the lambdoid suture. A metopic suture is present. The tori are prominent, and the mastoids are large.

All teeth are well worn and perfect in both jaws.

<u>Surviving skeletal remains</u>: There is a single sacrum labelled 79:166 currently in the KNH Centre for Biomedical Egyptology (catalogue ref. 13081). This cannot currently be identified as belonging to body A or B.

<u>References</u>: Anatomical recording card; Firth (1912a, 147; Fig. 135); Firth (1912b, Plate 14; Plan XIV).

166(b)   A male, adult skeleton. This body was not assigned an individual character – the recording card lists it as just body 166, unlike the first body recorded (166A).

<u>Original anatomical observations</u>: The coronal suture is open, the sagittal suture is closed and the lambdoid suture is closing. A metopic suture is apparent in whole length, but this is closing. The tori are moderately prominent, and the nasal spine is prominent. The mastoids are well-marked.

All teeth are present and perfect in both jaws.

The manubrium is separate from the gladiolus. The left tibia is platycnemic.

References: Anatomical recording card; Firth (1912a, 147; Fig. 135); Firth (1912b, Plate 14; Plan XIV).

167 A male, adult skeleton.

Original anatomical observations: The tori are well-marked. The mastoids are very large.

The teeth are very much worn but perfect with the exception of abscesses present at the roots of several teeth in the maxilla and at the roots of canines in the mandible, with the pulp cavities exposed.

There is considerable spondylitis of the lumbar and thoracic spine.

References: Firth (1912a, 147); Firth (1912b, Plan XIV).

168 A male, adult skeleton. The skull was found to be smashed when the body was excavated.

Original anatomical observations: All of the teeth present are perfect and much worn in both jaws.

The manubrium is fused to body of the sternum. There is a large facet present on the neck of both femora.

References: Anatomical recording card; Firth (1912a, 148); Firth (1912b, Plan XIV).

169 An infant skeleton, with no sex recorded.

References: Firth (1912a, 148); Firth (1912b, Plan XIV).

170 A partially fragmentary female skeleton, with no age recorded.

Original anatomical observations: The teeth are only slightly worn in both jaws.

References: Anatomical recording card; Firth (1912a, 148; Fig. 138); Firth (1912b, Plan XIV).

171 An infant skeleton, with no sex recorded.

References: Firth (1912a, 148); Firth (1912b, Plan XIV).

172 A skeleton, with no age or sex recorded.

References: Firth (1912a, 148); Firth (1912b, Plan XIV).

173 A skeleton, with no age or sex recorded.

References: Firth (1912a, 149); Firth (1912b, Plan XIV).

176 An infant skeleton, with no sex recorded.

References: Firth (1912a, 149); Firth (1912b, Plan XIV).

177 An adult skeleton, with no sex recorded. This is one of two skeletons buried in this grave, but it is not clear whether this is 177A or 177B.

Original anatomical observations: The head is distorted in the grave. There are no tori. The mastoids are very small. There is a marked visible prognathism.

References: Anatomical recording card; Firth (1912a, 149); Firth (1912b, Plan XIV).

177^2 A skeleton, with no age or sex recorded.

References: Firth (1912a, 149); Firth (1912b, Plan XIV).

178 A skeleton, with no age or sex recorded.

References: Firth (1912a, 149; Fig. 142); Firth (1912b, Plan XIV).

179 A skeleton, with no age or sex recorded.

References: Firth (1912a, 149); Firth (1912b, Plan XIV).

180 An infant skeleton, with no sex recorded.

References: Firth (1912a, 149-50); Firth (1912b, Plan XIV).

185   A skeleton, with no age or sex recorded.

References: Firth (1912a, 150); Firth (1912b, Plan XIV).

187   A child skeleton, with no sex recorded.

References: Firth (1912a, 150); Firth (1912b, Plan XIV).

189   A partial infant skeleton, with no sex recorded.

References: Firth (1912a, 150); Firth (1912b, Plan XIV).

190   An infant skeleton, with no sex recorded.

References: Firth (1912a, 150); Firth (1912b, Plan XIV).

193   A skeleton, with no age or sex recorded.

References: Firth (1912a, 150); Firth (1912b, Plan XIV).

198   A skeleton, with no age or sex recorded.

References: Firth (1912a, 150); Firth (1912b, Plan XIV).

201   A male skeleton, with no age recorded.

Original anatomical observations: The tori are fairly prominent. The mastoids are fairly well-marked.

The teeth are very much worn, but perfect in both jaws.

References: Anatomical recording card; Firth (1912a, 150); Firth (1912b, Plan XIV).

202   An infant skeleton, with no sex recorded.

References: Firth (1912a, 150); Firth (1912b, Plan XIV).

205	A male skeleton, about 7 years old.

	References: Firth (1912a, 151); Firth (1912b, Plan XIV).

227	A fragmentary adult skeleton, with no sex recorded.

	References: Anatomical recording card.

Christian burials

The following graves were recorded with no clear indication of whether they contained a body; they are likely to have been empty: 18, 19 (Firth 1912a, 151; Firth 1912b, Plan XIV).

17(a)	A skeleton, with no age or sex recorded.

	References: Firth (1912a, 151); Firth (1912b, Plan XIV).

17(b)	A skeleton, with no age or sex recorded.

	References: Firth (1912a, 151); Firth (1912b, Plan XIV).

46	A skeleton, with no age or sex recorded. The lower body is wrapped in cloth and the legs are tied together at the ankles with cord.

	References: Firth (1912a, 132); Firth (1912b, Plan XIV).

91	A body (possibly mummified or partially mummified) with no age or sex recorded.

	References: Firth (1912a, 151); Firth (1912b, Plan XIV).

175	A body (possibly mummified or partially mummified) with no age or sex recorded.

	References: Firth (1912a, 151); Firth (1912b, Plan XIV).

Cemetery 80, West bank, Mediq, Gerf Husein

A-group period

Cemetery 80 is situated on a mud knoll just south of cemetery 79 (Reisner 1909a, 9). Of the 23 bodies located, 3 were identified as children and 1 as an infant - the rest are unidentified. There are no indications that sex was determined for any of these bodies.

The following grave was found to be empty upon excavation: 11 (Firth 1912b, Plan XV).

1 A skeleton, with no age or sex recorded.

   References: Firth (1912a, 151); Firth (1912b, Plan XV).

2 A skeleton, with no age or sex recorded.

   References: Firth (1912a, 151); Firth (1912b, Plan XV).

3 A child skeleton, with no sex recorded.

   References: Firth (1912a, 152); Firth (1912b, Plan XV).

4 A child skeleton, with no sex recorded.

   References: Firth (1912a, 152); Firth (1912b, Plan XV).

5 A skeleton, with no age or sex recorded.

   References: Firth (1912a, 152); Firth (1912b, Plan XV).

6 A skeleton, with no age or sex recorded.

   References: Firth (1912a, 152); Firth (1912b, Plan XV).

7 A skeleton, with no age or sex recorded.

   References: Firth (1912a, 152; Fig. 144); Firth (1912b, Plan XV).

8   A skeleton, with no age or sex recorded.

    References: Firth (1912a, 152); Firth (1912b, Plan XV).

9   A skeleton, with no age or sex recorded.

    References: Firth (1912a, 152); Firth (1912b, Plan XV).

10 A skeleton, with no age or sex recorded.

    References: Firth (1912a, 152); Firth (1912b, Plan XV).

12 A fragmentary skeleton, with no age or sex recorded.

    References: Firth (1912a, 153); Firth (1912b, Plan XV).

13 A skeleton, with no age or sex recorded.

    References: Firth (1912a, 153; Fig. 146); Firth (1912b, Plan XV).

14 An infant skeleton, with no sex recorded.

    References: Firth (1912a, 153); Firth (1912b, Plan XV).

15 A skeleton, with no age or sex recorded.

    References: Firth (1912a, 153; Fig. 148); Firth (1912b, Plan XV).

16 A skeleton, with no age or sex recorded.

    References: Firth (1912a, 153); Firth (1912b, Plan XV).

17 A skeleton, with no age or sex recorded.

    References: Firth (1912a, 154; Fig. 150); Firth (1912b, Plan XV).

18	A skeleton, with no age or sex recorded.

	References: Firth (1912a, 154); Firth (1912b, Plan XV).

19	A skeleton, with no age or sex recorded.

	References: Firth (1912a, 154); Firth (1912b, Plan XV).

20	A skeleton, with no age or sex recorded.

	References: Firth (1912a, 154); Firth (1912b, Plan XV).

21	A skeleton, with no age or sex recorded.

	References: Firth (1912a, 154); Firth (1912b, Plan XV).

22	A skeleton, with no age or sex recorded.

	References: Firth (1912a, 154); Firth (1912b, Plan XV).

23A	A skeleton, with no age or sex recorded.

	References: Firth (1912a, 154-5); Firth (1912b, Plan XV).

23B	A child skeleton, with sex recorded.

	References: Firth (1912a, 154-5); Firth (1912b, Plan XV).

Cemetery 81, Mediq South, Gerf Husein

C-group period

A small patch of C-group burials, found alongside the possible remains of a settlement from the same period (Firth 1912a, 16). The burials are largely those of infants as they comprise 6 of the 7 burials found.

1   A fragmentary infant skeleton, with no sex recorded.

    References: Firth (1912a, 155).

2   A fragmentary infant skeleton, with no sex recorded.

    References: Firth (1912a, 155).

4   A grave with no record of the presence of a body.

    References: Firth (1912a, 155).

6   An infant skeleton, with no sex recorded.

    References: Firth (1912a, 155).

7   A fragmentary infant skeleton, with no sex recorded.

    References: Firth (1912a, 155).

8   A skeleton, with no age or sex recorded.

    References: Firth (1912a, 155; Fig. 152); Firth (1912b, Plate 19E).

9(a)   A new-born infant skeleton, with no sex recorded.

    References: Firth (1912a, 155).

9(b)   A new-born infant skeleton, with no sex recorded.

    References: Firth (1912a, 155).

Cemetery 82, Gerf Husein

A-group period

A small group of contracted burials located on the edge of the high desert (Firth 1909, 17). Only two graves retained a body, at least one of which was in a poor condition.

The following graves were recorded with no clear indication of whether they contained a body; they are likely to have been empty: 2, 4 (Firth 1912a, 156).

Graves 5, 7 and 8 contained only empty broken urns, which may originally have held skeletal remains (Firth 1912a, 156)

1   A skeleton, with no age or sex recorded.

           References: Firth (1912a, 155).

9   A fragmentary skeleton, with no age or sex recorded.

           References: Firth (1912a, 156).

Cemetery 83, Gerf Husein

A-group (B-group) and C-group period

Cemetery 83 consists of a small patch of graves, some of which are cut very deeply (Firth 1909, 17). The superstructures had largely gone, and the tombs had been plundered; eleven graves were actually excavated.

A-group burials

1   A male skeleton, with no age recorded.

          References: Firth (1912a, 156).

2   A disturbed male skeleton, with no age recorded.

          References: Firth (1912a, 156).

5   A fragmentary skeleton, with no age or sex recorded.

          References: Firth (1912a, 156).

7   A child skeleton, with no sex recorded.

          References: Firth (1912a, 156).

C-group burials

The following graves were recorded with no clear indication of whether they contained a body; they are likely to have been empty: 6, 8, 9, 10, 12, 13, 14 (Firth 1912a, 156).

Cemetery 85, Koshtamna

A group (B-group), Ptolemaic-Roman and Christian period

he descriptions of this cemetery refer to a number of Ptolemaic-Roman period burials and a late Christian period cemetery (Firth 1912a, 32; 41). There is also a small group of A-group burials on the top of a knoll in the cemetery; these were completely examined and measured (Derry 1909b, 22). Only a small number of the Ptolemaic-Roman period tombs were opened, and the bodies discovered were studied according to Derry (1909b) – the records of this have not however survived to the present day.

A-group burials

The following grave was recorded with no clear indication of whether it contained a body; it is likely to have been empty: 60 (Firth 1912a, 157).

29 A male skeleton, with no age recorded.

Original anatomical observations: There is spondylitis of the lumbar spine. There is a facet present on the neck of the left femur. Grafton Elliot Smith originally recorded the presence of rheumatoid arthritis at the head of the metacarpals of the right hand, lipping and at the head of 2nd right metatarsal, with marked lipping and eburnation.

Further studies: A later note added to the anatomical recording card re-classifies the pathology seen in the right hand as a case of true gout. The diagnosis was made by the British pathologist Thomas Strangeways.

References: Anatomical recording card; Firth (1912a, 157).

31A A female, adult skeleton with curly black hair preserved.

Original anatomical observations: All of the cranial sutures are open. There are no tori and no nasal spine. The mastoids are very small. The zygomata are straight. There is a very marked visible prognathism.

All teeth are present, perfect and little worn in both jaws.

The sacrum is 5-pieced and flat.

References: Anatomical recording card.

31B A male skeleton, with no age recorded.

Original anatomical observations: All of the cranial sutures are open. The tori are well-marked. The mastoids are fairly large. There is a well-marked prognathism. There is no nasal spine.

The teeth are worn but perfect in both jaws. The left 1st molar and 2nd bicuspid in the maxilla and the right 1st molar in the mandible have disappeared and the alveolus has absorbed.

36 A male skeleton, about 16 years old.

Original anatomical observations: All of the cranial sutures are open, including the basilar suture. The lambdoid suture is very complicated. An almost complete interparietal bone is present. There is a distinct visible subnasal prognathism. The nasal spine is small.

All present, perfect and very little worn in both jaws, except the 3rd molars which have dropped out. No caries.

References: Anatomical recording card.

37 A female, adult skeleton.

Original anatomical observations: There is a simulation of an interparietal bone.

References: Anatomical recording card.

38 A male, adult skeleton.

Original anatomical observations: The coronal, sagittal and lambdoid sutures are closing. There is a simulation of an interparietal bone. The tori are moderately prominent. The mastoids are medium. The nasal spine is sharp. The roofs and lateral walls of the orbits are deficient.

All of the teeth present are perfect but much worn in both jaws. The 1st molar has gone on both sides of the maxilla and the alveolus has absorbed. The 2nd molar has gone on both sides of the mandible and the alveolus has absorbed.

The manubrium is separate from the body of the sternum.

References: Anatomical recording card.

43A A female, adult skeleton with black very curly hair.

Original anatomical observations: All cranial sutures are open. The tori are well-marked. The mastoids are very small. The zygomata are slightly curved. There is a very marked visible prognathism. The nasal bones are very small and the nasal spine is supressed.

All teeth are present and perfect, except the right 3rd molar in the maxilla is peg-like and the left 1st molar in the mandible is carious with an abscess.

References: Anatomical recording card.

43B A female, adult skeleton.

Original anatomical observations: All cranial sutures are open. The tori are slight and the mastoids are very small. There is a definite visible prognathism. The nasal spine is suppressed.

All teeth present are perfect and much worn in both jaws. The left 1st molar in the maxilla has gone.

References: Anatomical recording card.

56 A male, young adult skeleton. This body was dated to the C-group period in the anatomical records but the archaeological record places it in the A-group.

Original anatomical observations: All cranial sutures are open. The tori are fairly marked. The mastoids are large. There is left occipital bulging.

All teeth are present, perfect and little worn in both jaws.

The manubrium is separate from the body of the sternum. The sacrum is slightly curved and 6-pieced. There is a facet present on the neck of both femora.

References: Anatomical recording card; Firth (1912a, 157).

58 A male, child skeleton.

References: Anatomical recording card; Firth (1912a, 157).

59 A fragmentary skeleton, with no age or sex recorded.

References: Firth (1912a, 157).

62 A female, adult skeleton.

Original anatomical observations: All cranial sutures are open. There are no tori and the mastoids are small. The nasal spine is small. There is a very marked visible prognathism.

All teeth are present, perfect and little worn in both jaws. The left 3rd molar was apparently never cut in the maxilla. The right 1st molar has disappeared in the mandible.

References: Anatomical recording card.

Cemetery 86, Hamadab, Koshtamna

Ptolemaic to X-group period

A cemetery containing end chamber and side chamber tombs with extended burials dating to the Ptolemaic to X-group periods (Firth 1912a, 32). Many of the bodies were artificially mummified and were found inside mud maghraras. The bodies dating to the X-group however showed no sign of artificial mummification (Derry 1909b, 22-23). All of the graves have been affected by denudation (Reisner 1909b, 8). The numbering system indicates many more tombs, if not bodies should have been recorded for this cemetery. The anatomical records follow a pattern established earlier in the sequence of cemeteries – determination of sex was carried out consistently, but the recording of age is much poorer.

Ptolemaic-Roman burials

277A   A female, artificially mummified body (dissected). No age is recorded.

   Original anatomical observations: There is no opening into the brain.

   References: Anatomical recording card.

277B   A male, artificially mummified body (dissected). No age is recorded.

   Original anatomical observations: There is no opening into the brain.

   References: Anatomical recording card.

291   A male, possibly mummified body. No age is recorded and there is no record of any dissection/study.

   References: Anatomical recording card.

Roman burials

266A   A female, artificially mummified body (dissected). No age is recorded.

   Original anatomical observations: All cranial sutures are open. The tori and mastoids are small. The nasal bones and spine are very small.

   There is a hole through the ethmoid and partly through the sphenoid to remove the brain.

   The teeth are perfect and very small in size. No 3rd molars ever appeared.

   The chest and abdomen were stuffed with linen. The sacrum is very flat and 6-pieced (5 sacral bones + 1 coccyx).

   References: Anatomical recording card.

266B A male, artificially mummified body (dissected). No age recorded.

Original anatomical observations: The coronal suture is closing, the rest are open. The tori are very pronounced. The mastoids are small. The nasal spine is suppressed. The roof of the nose has been broken to remove the brain. The walls of both orbits are also broken.

The teeth much resemble those of 266A, being very small. All are present and perfect in both jaws, except the right 3rd molars which appear as carious stumps. The upper right 2nd molar is slightly affected by it. There are no other 3rd molars present.

References: Anatomical recording card.

X-group period

208 A female skeleton, with no age recorded.

Original anatomical observations: All cranial sutures are open. The tori are scarcely marked. The mastoids are large. The nasal spine is suppressed.

All teeth are present, perfect and a little worn in both jaws except both 2nd molars in the maxilla, of which only carious stumps remains. Neither 3rd molar in the mandible ever appeared.

The manubrium is separate from the sternum. The sacrum is 6-pieced (5 sacral bones + 1 coccyx). The left hip joint has been partially dislocated; this is partly congenital. This has resulted in a flattening of the femoral head and a widening and flattening of the acetabular cavity. A small crest of the ilium has not developed. There is shortening of the femur.

References: Anatomical recording card.

Burials of unknown date

34 A male, adult skeleton.

Original anatomical observations: The coronal, sagittal and lambdoid sutures are all closing. There are no tori. The mastoids are rather small. There is very marked visible prognathism. The anterior palatine foramen opens into a large abscess cavity in anterior part of the nasal floor, which again has opened up the alveolus around the nasal spine.

All teeth are perfect and moderately worn in both jaws, except the right 1st molar in the maxilla is carious.

References: Anatomical recording card.

52 A male, aged skeleton.

Original anatomical observations: All cranial sutures are closed. The tori are well-marked, and the mastoids are moderate. The nasal spine is pronounced.

The teeth are much worn down in both jaws. There are pulp cavity abscesses in the maxilla. In the mandible, the left 1st molar is carious and the left 2nd bicuspid and right 2nd molar have gone.

References: Anatomical recording card.

205 A male skeleton, with no age recorded. Straight white hair is preserved.

Original anatomical observations: The coronal, sagittal and lambdoid sutures are closing. There are epipteric bones on both sides.

All of the teeth have gone in both jaws and the alveolus is completely absorbed.

The manubrium is separate from the gladiolus. There are very marked bony projections on the axillary bodies at the site of the teres major attachments. There is spondylitis of the lumbar spine. The sacrum is 6-pieced (5 sacral bones + 1 coccyx).

References: Anatomical recording card.

206 A male, adult skeleton with straight hair that is going grey.

Original anatomical observations: All cranial sutures are open. The tori are small. The mastoids are very large.

The teeth are very much worn in both jaws. There are several abscesses, the alveolus has absorbed in some places and there are pulp cavity abscesses.

All parts of the sternum are fused together and the xiphoid process is ossified to the rest. The lower extremity of the right radius shows signs of osteitis. There is spondylitis of the lumbar and thoracic spine. The left sacro-iliac ligaments are ossified. On the anterior surface of the right pubic bone are osseous inflammatory processes.

References: Anatomical recording card.

267 A female skeleton, with no age recorded.

Original anatomical observations: All cranial sutures are open. The tori are small. The mastoids are medium. The nasal bones and nasal spine are very small.

The teeth are well worn in both jaws. The 1st molar in the maxilla has gone on both sides. The right 2nd molar and the left 1st and 2nd bicuspids in the mandible are carious and there are abscess cavities at the roots of the latter two teeth.

The sacrum is 6-pieced (5 sacral bones + 1 coccyx).

References: Anatomical recording card.

295   A female, aged skeleton.

Original anatomical observations: The coronal, sagittal and lambdoid sutures are all open. The mastoids are very small and there are no tori. The nasal spine is small.

The teeth are much worn in both jaws. In the maxilla, the left 1st bicuspid has a carious cavity and an abscess. On the right side of the mandible all of the teeth behind the 1st bicuspid have gone and the alveolus has absorbed, except for the 3rd molar. On the left side the alveolus is absorbed behind the 1st molar which has large carious cavity.

References: Anatomical recording card.

305   A female, adult skeleton.

Original anatomical observations: The coronal suture is beginning to close below on the left, the rest of others are open. The tori are small. The mastoids are fairly large. There is a distinct visible prognathism. The zygomata are almost straight. The nasal bones are very small and the nasal spine is suppressed.

In the maxilla, the 2nd bicuspid and 1st molar on both sides are carious stumps. The 3rd molars have both disappeared. All of the teeth present in the mandible are perfect. The right 2nd molar has gone and the alveolus has absorbed.

The sacrum is 6-pieced (5 sacral bones + 1 coccyx).

References: Anatomical recording card.

Cemetery 86/500, Koshtamna

A-group to C-group period

There is no description of the burials in cemetery 86/500 in the archaeological report. The presence of just one body was recorded.

A-group burials

The following graves were recorded with no clear indication of whether they contained a body; they are likely to have been empty: 501, 503, 505 (Firth 1912a, 157).

A to C-group burials

504   A skeleton, with no age or sex recorded. The body is intrusive to an earlier A-group period grave.

References: Firth (1912a, 158).

Cemetery 87, Koshtamna

A-group and C-group period

The best preserved C-group cemetery excavated during the 1908-09 season despite being damaged by the activities of tomb robbers. The cemetery is large and in general, the superstructures are well preserved (Firth 1912a, 16-21). The southern end of the cemetery had been destroyed previously and the edges of the cemetery had been affected by the work of sebakh diggers (Reisner 1909b, 8).

A-group burials

The following graves were found to be empty upon excavation: 34 (Firth 1912a, 165; Firth 1912b, Plan XVIII).

The following graves were recorded with no clear indication of whether they contained a body; they are likely to have been empty: 91, 129 (Firth 1912a, 176-183; Firth 1912b, Plan XVIII).

54   A fragmentary male skeleton, with no age recorded.

         <u>References</u>: Firth (1912a, 167); Firth (1912b, Plan XVIII).

132   A child skeleton, with no sex recorded.

         <u>References</u>: Firth (1912a, 183).

C-group burials

The following graves were found to be empty upon excavation: 11, 23, 26, 27, 30, 31, 32, 37, 43, 49, 51, 53, 92, 118, 122, 134, 136, 139, 140, 141, 142, 143, 144, 145, 146, 147, 148, 149, 150, 151, 159, 160, 161, 164 (Firth 1912a, 162-185; Firth 1912b, Plan XVIII).

The following graves were recorded with no clear indication of whether they contained a body; they are likely to have been empty: 55, 128, 137, 165 (Firth 1912a, 168-187; Firth 1912b, Plan XVIII).

1   A fragmentary male skeleton, with no age recorded. The archaeological report records this body as female, in contrast to the anatomical records.

         <u>References</u>: Anatomical recording card; Firth (1912a, 159); Firth (1912b, Plan XVIII).

2   A fragmentary female skeleton, with no age recorded.

         <u>References</u>: Anatomical recording card; Firth (1912a, 159); Firth (1912b, Plan XVIII).

3   A fragmentary female skeleton, with no age recorded.

       <u>References</u>: Anatomical recording card; Firth (1912a, 159); Firth (1912b, Plan XVIII).

4   A partial fragmentary female skeleton, with no age recorded.

       <u>References</u>: Anatomical recording card; Firth (1912a, 159); Firth (1912b, Plan XVIII).

5   A partial fragmentary male skeleton, with no age recorded.

       <u>Original anatomical observations</u>: There is spondylitis of the thoracic spine.

       <u>References</u>: Anatomical recording card; Firth (1912a, 159); Firth (1912b, Plan XVIII).

6   A fragmentary male skeleton, with no age recorded.

       <u>References:</u> Firth (1912a, 159); Firth (1912b, Plan XVIII).

7   A fragmentary skeleton, with no age or sex recorded.

       <u>References:</u> Firth (1912a, 160); Firth (1912b, Plan XVIII).

8   A partial fragmentary male skeleton, with no age recorded.

       <u>References</u>: Anatomical recording card; Firth (1912a, 160); Firth (1912b, Plan XVIII).

9   A fragmentary male skeleton, with no age recorded.

       <u>References</u>: Anatomical recording card; Firth (1912a, 160); Firth (1912b, Plan XVIII).

10   A male, adult skeleton. The skull was found to be damaged when the body was excavated.

       <u>Original anatomical observations</u>: The tori are well-marked. The mastoids are large.

       On the left side of the sternum the cartilage of the 7th and 8th ribs are ossified and fused. There is a transverse fracture of the left radius and ulna at the junction of the lower and middle third. There is a double fracture of the right femur: the upper fracture is in the middle of the shaft, the other at the junction of the lower and middle third. In both cases, the lower fragments have been drawn up behind the upper and united in that position. There is very much shortening.

References: Anatomical recording card; Derry (1909b, 24); Firth (1912a, 160); Firth (1912b, Plan XVIII).

12   A partial fragmentary male skeleton, with no age recorded.

Original anatomical observations: There is spondylitis of the lumbar and thoracic spine. The sacrum is 6-pieced (5 sacral bones + 1 coccyx).

References: Anatomical recording card; Firth (1912a, 160); Firth (1912b, Plan XVIII).

13   A fragmentary probable female skeleton, with no age recorded.

References: Firth (1912a, 160); Firth (1912b, Plan XVIII).

14   A fragmentary female skeleton, with no age recorded. The skull was found to be smashed when the body was excavated.

Original anatomical observations: The mandible is pointed. The ramus is low and sloping.

References: Anatomical recording card; Firth (1912a, 160; Figure 154); Firth (1912b, Plate 20A; Plan XVIII).

15   A fragmentary male, adult skeleton.

Original anatomical observations: All cranial sutures are open, except the left lambdoid suture which is commencing to close. There is an epipteric bone on the left shutting out the parietal from the sphenoid. The tori are well-marked. The mastoids are medium. The occiput is symmetrical.

All of the maxillary teeth that are present are perfect. The permanent right canine has never been cut and the socket of the milk canine has been recently occupied. No comments were recorded for the mandible.

References: Anatomical recording card; Firth (1912a, 161); Firth (1912b, Plan XVIII).

16   A fragmentary post-cranial male, adult skeleton. The leg bones only remain according to the archaeological report.

References: Anatomical recording card; Firth (1912a, 161; Figure 155); Firth (1912b, Plate 20B; Plan XVIII).

16A A skeleton, with no age or sex recorded. The body belongs to a grave numbered 16A, which cuts through grave 16.

References: Firth (1912a, 161; Figure 155).

16A² A disturbed sheep burial, found along with body 16A but not numbered separately.

References: Firth (1912a, 161; Figure 155).

17 A fragmentary post-cranial male skeleton, with no age recorded.

Original anatomical observations: There is a facet present on both femora.

References: Anatomical recording card; Firth (1912a, 161); Firth (1912b, Plan XVIII).

18 A fragmentary male skeleton, with no age recorded.

References: Anatomical recording card; Firth (1912a, 161); Firth (1912b, Plan XVIII).

19 A fragmentary female skeleton, with no age recorded.

References: Anatomical recording card; Firth (1912a, 161); Firth (1912b, Plan XVIII).

20 A fragmentary female child skeleton. The archaeological report does not record that this skeleton is a child, in contrast to the anatomical record.

References: Firth (1912a, 161); Firth (1912b, Plan XVIII).

21(a) A partial post-cranial skeleton, with no age or sex recorded. The lower part of the skeleton only remains.

References: Firth (1912a, 161-62; Figure 156); Firth (1912b, Plan XVIII).

21(b) A goat or gazelle burial.

References: Firth (1912a, 161-62; Figure 156); Firth (1912b, Plan XVIII).

22   A child skeleton, with no age or sex recorded.

References: Firth (1912a, 162).

24   A partial post-cranial skeleton, with no age or sex recorded. The tibiae only remain.

References: Firth (1912a, 162-63); Firth (1912b, Plan XVIII).

25   A male skeleton, with no age recorded. The archaeological report records the skull as missing in contrast to the anatomical records.

Original anatomical observations: The coronal and sagittal sutures are closing, the lambdoid suture is open. There is an epipteric bone on the left, shutting out the squamous temporal from the frontal. The tori are well-marked. The mastoids are small.

All teeth present are perfect and moderately worn in both jaws.

The 5th lumbar vertebra is fused to the sacrum.

References: Anatomical recording card; Firth (1912a, 163-64; Fig. 157); Firth (1912b, Plate 20D; Plan XVIII).

28   A disturbed female, adult skeleton.

Original anatomical observations: All cranial sutures are open. The squamous temporal articulates with the frontal on both sides. There are no tori and the mastoids are small. There is a definite subnasal prognathism. The nasal spine is very small.

All of the teeth present are good with no caries, but much worn. There is an abscess at the root of the 1st incisor in the maxilla; this probably affects the pulp cavity.

The sacrum is very wide, 5-pieced and rather flat.

References: Anatomical recording card; Firth (1912a, 164); Firth (1912b, Plan XVIII).

29   A skeleton, with no age or sex recorded.

References: Firth (1912a, 164); Firth (1912b, Plan XVIII).

33   A disturbed female, adult skeleton.

Original anatomical observations: All cranial sutures are open. There is an epipteric bone on both sides shutting out the parietal from the great wing of the sphenoid. The tori are fairly well-marked. The mastoids are very small. There is definite left occipital bulging. The zygomata are slightly arched. The nasal spine is very prominent.

All of the teeth present are perfect and well-worn in both jaws.

The manubrium is separate from the gladiolus.

Surviving skeletal remains: A cranium is currently located in the KNH Centre for Biomedical Egyptology, The University of Manchester (no reference no.) The location of the rest of the body is unknown.

References: Anatomical recording card; Firth (1912a, 165); Firth (1912b, Plan XVIII).

35 A fragmentary female skeleton, with no age recorded.

References: Firth (1912a, 165); Firth (1912b, Plan XVIII).

36 A female, aged skeleton.

Original anatomical observations: All cranial sutures are closed. There is a definite visible prognathism.

The teeth are much worn in both jaws, with several pulp cavity abscesses.

There is severe lumbar and slight thoracic spondylitis.

References: Anatomical recording card; Firth (1912a, 165); Firth (1912b, Plan XVIII).

38 A fragmentary male, child skeleton.

References: Anatomical recording card; Firth (1912a, 165); Firth (1912b, Plan XVIII).

39 A fragmentary child skeleton, with no sex recorded. Both the archaeological and anatomical records list this as a child burial. However, a female, adult cranium is currently located in the Duckworth Laboratory, The University of Cambridge (catalogue ref. NU488) that carries this grave/cemetery number.

References: Anatomical recording card; Firth (1912a, 165); Firth (1912b, Plan XVIII).

40 A fragmentary male skeleton, with no age recorded.

References: Anatomical recording card; Firth (1912a, 165-66); Firth (1912b, Plan XVIII).

41 A fragmentary female skeleton, with no age recorded.

References: Anatomical recording card; Firth (1912a, 166); Firth (1912b, Plan XVIII).

42 A disturbed female, adult skeleton.

Original anatomical observations: The coronal suture is closing and the sagittal and lambdoid sutures are open. The mastoids are small. There is curious bulging of the glabella. There is very slight occipital bulging. The zygomata are almost straight. The nasal spine is fairly prominent.

All teeth are present, perfect and very slightly worn in both jaws.

The sacrum is very wide, short, flat and 5-pieced. There is a facet present on the neck of both femora.

Surviving skeletal remains: The skull was located in the Anatomical Museum, The University of Manchester when studied by Watson. The current location is unknown.

References: Anatomical recording card; Firth (1912a, 166); Firth (1912b, Plan XVIII); Watson (pre-1935).

44 A fragmentary female skeleton, with no age recorded.

References: Anatomical recording card; Firth (1912a, 166); Firth (1912b, Plan XVIII).

45 A fragmentary probable female skeleton, with no age recorded.

References: Anatomical recording card; Firth (1912a, 166); Firth (1912b, Plan XVIII).

46 A male, adult skeleton.

Original anatomical observations: The mandibular teeth are slightly worn and perfect. No comments were recorded for the maxilla.

The sacrum is flat, wide and 5-pieced.

References: Anatomical recording card; Firth (1912a, 166); Firth (1912b, Plan XVIII).

47 A disturbed female skeleton, with no age recorded.

   References: Firth (1912a, 166); Firth (1912b, Plan XVIII).

48 A fragmentary female skeleton, with no age recorded.

   Original anatomical observations: There is spondylitis of the lumbar and thoracic spine. The sacrum is 6-pieced (5 sacral bones + 1 coccyx).

   References: Anatomical recording card; Firth (1912a, 166-67); Firth (1912b, Plan XVIII).

50 A fragmentary female skeleton, with no age recorded.

   References: Anatomical recording card; Firth (1912a, 167); Firth (1912b, Plan XVIII).

52 A fragmentary female skeleton, with no age recorded.

   References: Anatomical recording card; Firth (1912a, 167); Firth (1912b, Plan XVIII).

54 A female skeleton, with no age recorded.

   References: Anatomical recording card.

56 A fragmentary skeleton, with no age or sex recorded.

   References: Firth (1912a, 168).

57 A fragmentary male skeleton, with no age recorded.

   Original anatomical observations: The sacrum is 6-pieced (5 sacral bones + 1 coccyx).

   References: Anatomical recording card; Firth (1912a, 168); Firth (1912b, Plan XVIII).

58 A fragmentary male skeleton, with no age recorded.

   Original anatomical observations: There is very severe spondylitis of the lumbar and thoracic spine. The sacrum is 6-pieced (5 sacral bones + 1 coccyx).

   References: Anatomical recording card; Firth (1912a, 168); Firth (1912b, Plan XVIII).

59   A fragmentary male skeleton, with no age recorded.

References: Anatomical recording card; Firth (1912a, 168); Firth (1912b, Plan XVIII).

60   A fragmentary post-cranial male skeleton, with no age recorded. The leg bones only remain.

References: Anatomical recording card; Firth (1912a, 168); Firth (1912b, Plan XVIII).

61   A fragmentary post-cranial male skeleton, with no age recorded. The lower part of the skeleton only remains.

References: Anatomical recording card; Reisner (1909b, 9); Firth (1912a, 168-69; Figure 159); Firth (1912b, Plan XVIII).

62   A fragmentary skeleton, with no age or sex recorded.

References: Firth (1912a, 169); Firth (1912b, Plan XVIII).

63   A fragmentary female skeleton, with no age recorded.

Original anatomical observations: There is spondylitis of the lumbar spine.

References: Anatomical recording card; Firth (1912a, 169); Firth (1912b, Plan XVIII).

64   A fragmentary male skeleton, with no age recorded.

References: Anatomical recording card; Firth (1912a, 169-70); Firth (1912b, Plan XVIII).

65   A fragmentary female, child skeleton.

References: Anatomical recording card; Firth (1912a, 169); Firth (1912b, Plan XVIII).

66   A fragmentary child skeleton, with no sex recorded.

References: Anatomical recording card; Firth (1912a, 169; Figure 160); Firth (1912b, Plate 20E and 20F; Plan XVIII).

67 A fragmentary male skeleton, with no age recorded.

   References: Anatomical recording card; Firth (1912a, 169); Firth (1912b, Plan XVIII).

68 A fragmentary female, infant skeleton.

   References: Anatomical recording card; Firth (1912a, 169); Firth (1912b, Plan XVIII).

69 A disturbed female, adult skeleton.

   Original anatomical observations: All cranial sutures are closed. The tori and mastoids are very small. The zygomata are straight. The cranio-pharangeal fossa is deep. The nasal spine is moderately prominent. There is marked left occipital bulging.

   The teeth are much worn in both jaws. In the maxilla, the right 3rd molar has gone and the alveolus is absorbed. In the mandible, the left 2nd incisor has gone and the alveolus is absorbed.

   References: Anatomical recording card; Firth (1912a, 169); Firth (1912b, Plan XVIII).

70 A female skeleton, with no age recorded.

   References: Firth (1912a, 171); Firth (1912b, Plan XVIII).

71 A fragmentary probable male skeleton, with no age recorded.

   Original anatomical observations: There is spondylitis of the lumbar spine.

   References: Anatomical recording card; Firth (1912a, 171); Firth (1912b, Plan XVIII).

72 A male, adult skeleton. The skull was found to be broken when the body was excavated.

   Original anatomical observations: All cranial sutures are open. The tori are fairly well marked. There is a marked visible prognathism. The nasal spine is suppressed.

   All teeth are present and perfect in both jaws.

   The manubrium is separate from the gladiolus.

   References: Anatomical recording card; Firth (1912a, 171); Firth (1912b, Plan XVIII).

73   A female, adult skeleton.

Original anatomical observations: The coronal suture is closed, whilst the sagittal and lambdoid sutures are closing. The zygomata are practically straight. There is no nasal spine.

References: Anatomical recording card; Firth (1912a, 171); Firth (1912b, Plan XVIII).

74   A partial post-cranial female, adult skeleton. The lower part of the skeleton only remains.

References: Anatomical recording card; Firth (1912a, 171); Firth (1912b, Plan XVIII).

75   A fragmentary child skeleton, with no sex recorded.

References: Anatomical recording card; Firth (1912a, 171); Firth (1912b, Plan XVIII).

76   A fragmentary female, aged skeleton

Original anatomical observations: The teeth are much worn and the alveolus is very much absorbed.

The right patella is slightly notched.

References: Anatomical recording card; Firth (1912a, 171-72); Firth (1912b, Plan XVIII).

77   A disturbed female, adult skeleton

Original anatomical observations: All cranial sutures are open. There is a definite visible prognathism. The nasal spine is suppressed.

The teeth are very much worn and perfect in both jaws.

The sacrum is very flat and 5-pieced.

References: Anatomical recording card; Firth (1912a, 172-73); Firth (1912b, Plan XVIII).

78   A male, adult partial skeleton. The skull was found to be missing when the body was excavated.

Original anatomical observations: The mandibular teeth are perfect and very little worn.

The lower part of the skeleton only remains.

References: Anatomical recording card; Firth (1912a, 173); Firth (1912b, Plan XVIII).

79   A partial post-cranial male skeleton, with no age recorded.

Original anatomical observations: The manubrium is fused to the gladiolus. The left humerus has a large osseous projection at the site of the insertion of the teres minor muscle. The sacrum is 6-pieced; there are five lumbar vertebrae.

Surviving skeletal remains: A single radius is currently located in the KNH Centre for Biomedical Egyptology, the University of Manchester (catalogue ref. 13022). The location of the rest of the body is unknown.

References: Anatomical recording card; Firth (1912a, 173); Firth (1912b, Plan XVIII).

79[2]   A male, adult skeleton. The anatomical recording card for this body originally read 87:97 but was amended. There is no additional card for the body in grave 97. The archaeological report does not record the presence of a body in grave 79, so this may be a recording error. Grave 79 cuts through an earlier circular burial, numbered 79A.

Original anatomical observations: The coronal and sagittal sutures are closing, the lambdoid suture is open. The tori are moderate. The mastoids are small.

All teeth are present, perfect and well-worn in both jaws. There is no room on the left side of the maxilla for the 2nd incisor which is pushed back into the palate. In the mandible, the left canine is crowded out into the labial side of the jaw. There is a large cavity which it occupied, but the tooth has fallen out.

References: Anatomical recording card.

80   A fragmentary male skeleton, with no age recorded.

References: Anatomical recording card; Firth (1912a, 173-74); Firth (1912b, Plan XVIII).

81   A fragmentary male skeleton, with no age recorded.

References: Anatomical recording card; Firth (1912a, 173-74); Firth (1912b, Plan XVIII).

82   A fragmentary child skeleton, with no sex recorded.

References: Anatomical recording card; Firth (1912a, 173-74); Firth (1912b, Plan XVIII).

83   A male post-cranial skeleton, with no age recorded. The archaeological report records that only the lower partial of the post-cranial skeleton remains, in contrast to the anatomical records.

Original anatomical observations: All of the mandibular teeth are perfect.

The sacrum is 6-pieced (5 sacral bones, plus 1st coccyx); there are 5 lumbar vertebrae present. There is a facet present on the neck of both femora. The right tibia is platycnemic.

References: Anatomical recording card; Firth (1912a, 174); Firth (1912b, Plan XVIII).

84 A male, adult skeleton.

Original anatomical observations: The coronal and lambdoid sutures are closing, the sagittal is closed. There is a small epipteric bone on the right. The tori are slightly marked. The mastoids are small. There is a slight visible prognathism.

The teeth are much worn, with no cavities in both jaws. There are no 3rd molars in the maxilla. There are large pulp cavity abscesses at the root of each 1st molar in the mandible.

The manubrium is separate from the gladiolus. The sacrum is very flat and 5-pieced. The right patella is slightly notched. The left tibia is fractured in the middle of shaft, with the lower fragment pulled upward and inwards behind the upper fragment. Union has taken place in that position.

References: Anatomical recording card; Derry (1909b, 24); Firth (1912a, 174-75); Firth (1912b, Plan XVIII).

85 A male, adult skeleton. The skull was found to be broken when the body was excavated.

Original anatomical observations: All cranial sutures are closed.

The sacrum is very small, 5-pieced and flat. There is a large facet present on the back and front of the neck of both femora. The manubrium is separate from the gladiolus.

References: Anatomical recording card; Firth (1912a, 175); Firth (1912b, Plan XVIII).

86 A fragmentary male, young adult skeleton.

References: Anatomical recording card; Firth (1912a, 175); Firth (1912b, Plan XVIII).

87 A disturbed male skeleton, with no age recorded.

References: Firth (1912a, 175); Firth (1912b, Plan XVIII).

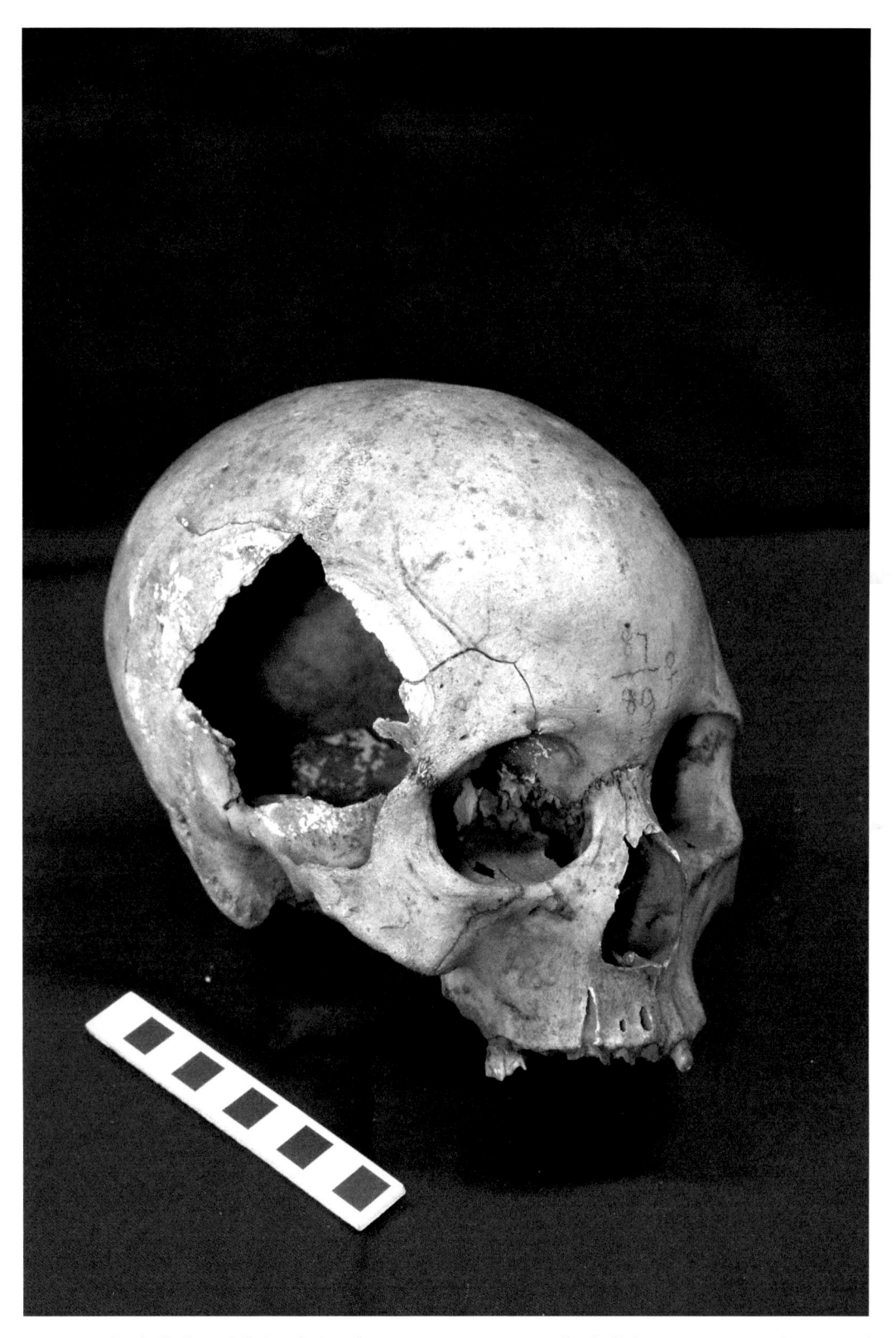

Figure 11: The skull of an adult female found in cemetery 87, grave 89. The skull shows post-mortem damage and evidence of attempts to reattach the section of skull that is missing (the white patches visible around the edge of the damaged area). The skull was used for the anatomy demonstrations for many years which is probably when the damage occurred. ©The KNH Centre for Biomedical Egyptology, The University of Manchester, 2023.

89   A female, adult skeleton.

Original anatomical observations: The coronal and lambdoid sutures are closing, the sagittal suture is open. The tori are very slight. The mastoids are very small. There is a definite visible prognathism. The nasal spine is prominent.

All teeth are present, perfect and slightly worn in both jaws.

The manubrium is separate from the gladiolus. There is spondylitis of the lumbar and thoracic spine. Eleven dorsal vertebrae are rib bearing, 2 being fused together due to spondylitis. The sacrum is 5-pieced and very flat.

Surviving skeletal remains: A cranium is currently located in the KNH Centre for Biomedical Egyptology, the University of Manchester (catalogue ref. 13702). This has been damaged post-mortem and attempted repair, most likely during handling by anatomy students (Figure 11). The location of the rest of the body is unknown.

References: Anatomical recording card; Firth (1912a, 175-76; Fig. 163); Firth (1912b, Plan XVIII).

90   A disturbed male, adult skeleton.

Original anatomical observations: The coronal suture is commencing to close, the sagittal is closed and the lambdoid is open. The tori are fairly well marked. The mastoids are small. The occipital is symmetrical. There is a distinct visible prognathism. The nasal spine is prominent.

The teeth are perfect, but much worn in both jaws.

The sacrum is long and 5-pieced.

Surviving skeletal remains: The skull was located in the Anatomical Museum, The University of Manchester when studied by Watson (pre 1935). The current location is unknown.

References: Anatomical recording card; Firth (1912a, 176); Firth (1912b, Plan XVIII); Watson (pre-1935).

93   A large male, adult skeleton.

Original anatomical observations: All cranial sutures are closed. The mastoids and tori are described as 'massive'. The nasal spine is moderately prominent.

The teeth in the maxilla are very much worn. There are pulp cavity abscesses. Some teeth have completely gone and the alveolus has absorbed. No comments were recorded for the mandible.

All parts of the sternum, xiphoid process and manubrium have fused together. The sacrum is 5-pieced and moderately curved. There is a very large facet on the neck of both femora.

References: Anatomical recording card; Firth (1912a, 177); Firth (1912b, Plan XVIII).

94 A female, adult skeleton.

<u>Original anatomical observations</u>: All cranial sutures are open. The tori are scarcely visible and the mastoids are very small. There is a distinct visible prognathism. The occipital is symmetrical.

All teeth are present, perfect and very little worn in both jaws.

The sacrum is 5-pieced and slightly curved. Both patellae are notched. The manubrium is separate from the gladiolus.

<u>References</u>: Anatomical recording card; Firth (1912a, 177); Firth (1912b, Plan XVIII).

95 A disturbed female, adult skeleton.

<u>Original anatomical observations</u>: The coronal suture is open, the sagittal is closed and the lambdoid is almost closed. The tori and the mastoids are small. The zygomata are nearly straight. The nasal spine is prominent.

All teeth present are perfect and much worn in both jaws.

The manubrium is fused to the body of the sternum.

<u>References</u>: Anatomical recording card; Firth (1912a, 177).

96A A female, adult skeleton. There is some confusion over the numbering of bodies in this grave – the archaeological report records two bodies as 87/96 (female, child) and 87/96A (female, adult) in contrast to the anatomical records.

<u>Original anatomical observations</u>: All cranial sutures are open. On the left an epipteric bone shuts out the parietal from the great wing of the sphenoid. On the right the squamous temporal articulates with the frontal. The zygomata are arched.

The teeth are very much worn, but perfect with no caries in both jaws.

The manubrium is separate. There is a hole through the lowest part of the body of the sternum. There is spondylitis of the thoracic spine. The sacrum is 6-pieced (5 sacral bones + 1 coccyx).

<u>References</u>: Anatomical recording card; Firth (1912a, 177; Fig. 164); Firth (1912b, Plan XVIII).

96B A female, aged skeleton.

<u>Original anatomical observations</u>: The coronal suture is closing, the sagittal is closed and the lambdoid is open. There is a very large epipteric bone on the left. The mastoids and tori are very small. There is inflammation of the tempero-mandibular articulation on both sides due to arthritis.

The right radius has had a colles fracture and the left radius and ulna have been fractured at the lower extremity. The lower end of the ulna has been pushed outwards and united in an angular fashion, such that it lies behind the lower end of the radius, which now articulates with it by a false joint. There is spondylitis of the cervical, thoracic and lumbar spine. The sacrum is very short, wide and 5-pieced. Both patellae are notched.

References: Anatomical recording card; Derry (1909b, 24-25); Firth (1912a, 177; Fig. 164); Firth (1912b, Plan XVIII).

97   A disturbed skeleton, with no age or sex recorded.

References: Firth (1912a, 177).

98   A disturbed male, adult skeleton.

Original anatomical observations: The coronal, sagittal and lambdoid sutures are all closing. The tori are prominent. The mastoids are medium. There is a definite visible prognathism. There is left occipital bulging. The nasal spine is suppressed.

All teeth present are perfect and very slightly worn in the maxilla. No comments were recorded for the mandible.

The manubrium is separate from the gladiolus. There is a facet present on the neck of both femora. The right patella is notched.

Surviving skeletal remains: The skull was located in the Anatomical Museum, The University of Manchester when studied by Watson - the current location is unknown. The KNH Centre for Biomedical Egyptology does however retain both humerii, a radius, a tibia and an ulna (catalogue refs. respectively 13404, 13405, KNH002, 13659, 13061). The location of the rest of the body is unknown but it may form part of the small unprovenanced skeletal collection present in the KNH Centre.

References: Anatomical recording card; Firth (1912a, 178); Firth (1912b, Plan XVIII); Watson (pre-1935).

99   A male, adult post-cranial skeleton. The archaeological report records the presence of a skull in this burial, in contrast to the anatomical report.

Original anatomical observations: The manubrium is fused to the body of the sternum. The sacrum is very short, wide and 5-pieced. There is a facet present on the neck of the right femur.

Surviving skeletal remains: A single humerus and a pelvis are currently located in the KNH Centre for Biomedical Egyptology, The University of Manchester (catalogue refs. 13411, 13629). The location of the rest of the body is unknown.

References: Anatomical recording card; Firth (1912a, 178); Firth (1912b, Plan XVIII).

100   A disturbed male, adult skeleton with 'peppercorn' hair preserved.

Original anatomical observations: All cranial sutures are open. On both sides the squamous temporal articulates with the frontal. The tori are very prominent. The mastoids are large. There is a definite visible prognathism. The zygomata are arched. The occiput is symmetrical. The nasal spine is prominent.

All teeth are present, perfect and slightly worn in both jaws.

All parts of the sternum are fused together. The sacrum is very wide, flat and 5-pieced. There is a facet present on the neck on both femora. Both patellae are notched. The left tibia is slight platycnemic.

Surviving skeletal remains: Both tibia and a femur are currently located in the KNH Centre for Biomedical Egyptology, The University of Manchester (catalogue refs. 13118, 13641, 13646) (Figure 4). The location of the rest of the body is unknown.

References: Anatomical recording card; Firth (1912a, 178); Firth (1912b, Plan XVIII).

101   A disturbed male skeleton, with no age recorded.

References: Anatomical recording card; Firth (1912a, 178); Firth (1912b, Plan XVIII).

102   A female, adult skeleton with straight black hair.

Original anatomical observations: All cranial sutures are open. The mastoids are very small and there are no tori. There is very slight left occipital bulging. The zygomata are arched. The nasal spine is very small. The obelion is flattened.

All teeth present are perfect and very much worn in both jaws. In the maxilla, the right 1st molar appears to have an abscess at the root. The right 2nd molar has gone in mandible and the alveolus has absorbed.

The manubrium is separate from the gladiolus. The sacrum is flat and 5-pieced. There is a facet present on the neck of both femora.

Surviving skeletal remains: The skull was located in the Anatomical Museum, The University of Manchester when studied by Watson. The current location is unknown.

References: Anatomical recording card; Firth (1912a, 178); Firth (1912b, Plan XVIII); Watson (pre-1935).

103   A female, adult skeleton.

Original anatomical observations: All cranial sutures are open. There are wormian bones in the posterior part of the sagittal suture. The tori are very small. The mastoids are small. There is slight left occipital bulging. The zygomata are nearly straight. The nasal spine is very small.

The maxillary teeth are very much worn. There are pulp cavity abscesses at both right bicuspids and the right 1st molar, the left 1st incisor, both left bicuspids and the left 1st molar. All of the mandibular teeth present are perfect and very much worn. The left canine has gone and the alveolus has absorbed. There are the remains of an abscess at the root.

The manubrium is separate from the gladiolus. There is severe spondylitis of the lumbar spine and slight spondylitis of the thoracic spine. There is slight platycnemia of the right tibia.

References: Anatomical recording card; Firth (1912a, 179); Firth (1912b, Plate 20C; Plan XVIII).

104   A male adult, skeleton with wavy black hair preserved.

Original anatomical observations: The coronal and sagittal sutures are closing, the lambdoid suture is open. The mastoids are large. There is a marked visible prognathism. There is right occipital bulging. The zygomata are arched. The nasal spine is suppressed.

All teeth are present and perfect in both jaws.

The manubrium is separate from the gladiolus. The sacrum is 7-pieced (6 sacral bones + 1 coccyx). The vertebrae are complete. There is a facet present on the neck of the right femur. There is marked backwards curvature in both tibiae.

Surviving skeletal remains: Both humerii and a radius are currently located in the KNH Centre for Biomedical Egyptology, The University of Manchester (catalogue refs. 13398, 13410, KNH003). The location of the rest of the body is unknown.

References: Anatomical recording card; Firth (1912a, 179); Firth (1912b, Plan XVIII).

105   A female skeleton, with no age recorded. The archaeological report records this body as a disturbed male skeleton.

Original anatomical observations: There is a facet present on the neck of both femora.

References: Anatomical recording card; Firth (1912a, 179); Firth (1912b, Plan XVIII).

106   A female, adult skeleton.

Original anatomical observations: The coronal suture is closing, the sagittal suture is closed and the lambdoid is almost closed. The mastoids are very small. The glabella is prominent. The zygomata are almost straight. The nasal spine is small.

The teeth are extremely worn, with no caries in both jaws.

The manubrium is separate from the gladiolus. There is marked spondylitis of the lumbar spine. The sacrum is very large and 6-pieced (5 sacral bones + 1 coccyx). There are five lumbar vertebrae present.

References: Anatomical recording card; Firth (1912a, 179; Fig.165); Firth (1912b, Plan XVIII).

107   A disturbed female, adult post-cranial skeleton

Original anatomical observations: The femora are much bent backwards and inwards.

References: Anatomical recording card; Firth (1912a, 179); Firth (1912b, Plan XVIII).

108   A child skeleton, with no sex recorded.

References: Anatomical recording card; Firth (1912a, 179); Firth (1912b, Plan XVIII).

109   A child skeleton, with no sex recorded.

References: Anatomical recording card; Firth (1912a, 179); Firth (1912b, Plan XVIII).

110   A female, young adult skeleton.

Original anatomical observations: All cranial sutures are open. There are no tori. The mastoids are very large and curiously flattened. The zygomata are slightly arched. There is slight right occipital bulging. There is a definite visible prognathism. The nasal spine is fairly prominent.

All teeth are present, perfect and very slightly worn in both jaws. There are no 3rd molars, but the right 3rd molar can be seen buried in maxilla and both 3rd molars are buried in the mandible.

The sacrum is very small and 5-pieced. The patellae are both notched.

References: Anatomical recording card; Firth (1912a, 180); Firth (1912b, Plan XVIII).

111   A disturbed skeleton, with no age or sex recorded.

References: Firth (1912a, 180); Firth (1912b, Plan XVIII).

112   A child skeleton, with no sex recorded.

References: Anatomical recording card; Firth (1912a, 180); Firth (1912b, Plan XVIII).

113   A female, child skeleton.

References: Anatomical recording card; Firth (1912a, 180); Firth (1912b, Plan XVIII).

114   A female skeleton, with no age recorded.

References: Anatomical recording card; Firth (1912a, 180); Firth (1912b, Plan XVIII).

115   A fragmentary child skeleton, with no sex recorded.

References: Anatomical recording card; Firth (1912a, 180); Firth (1912b, Plan XVIII).

116   A partial post-cranial male, adult skeleton. The lower part of the skeleton only remains.

Original anatomical observations: The sacrum is 5-pieced and flat.

References: Anatomical recording card; Firth (1912a, 180); Firth (1912b, Plan XVIII).

117   A male, adult skeleton.

Original anatomical observations: The coronal and sagittal sutures are closing, the lambdoid suture is open. The tori are prominent. The mastoids are large. The occipital is symmetrical. The zygomata are arched. There is a definite visible prognathism.

All teeth are present and very much worn in both jaws. There are pulp cavity abscesses at the root of the left 2nd bicuspid and 1st molar in the maxilla and the right 1st molar in the mandible.

The manubrium is separate from the gladiolus. The posterior arch of the 5th lumbar vertebra is separate. The 1st and 2nd lumbar vertebrae are united from spondylitis. The sacrum is rather flat and 5-pieced. There is union of the phalanx to the 2nd right metacarpal. There is a facet present on the neck of the left femur. There is arthritis of the left knee joint and the right shoulder joint.

Further studies: Smith and Derry originally diagnosed rheumatoid arthritis of the knee and shoulder joints. Thomas Strangeways later reclassified this this as septic arthritis according to an additional note on the anatomical recording card.

Surviving skeletal remains: A sacrum and an ulna are currently located in the KNH Centre for Biomedical Egyptology, The University of Manchester (catalogue refs. 13275, 13085). The location of the rest of the body is unknown.

References: Anatomical recording card; Firth (1912a, 180-81); Firth (1912b, Plan XVIII).

119 A male, child skeleton.

References: Anatomical recording card; Firth (1912a, 181); Firth (1912b, Plan XVIII).

120A A child skeleton, with no sex recorded.

References: Anatomical recording card; Firth (1912a, 181-82; Fig. 166); Firth (1912b, Plan XVIII).

120B A disturbed male skeleton, with no age recorded. The femora have been displaced.

References: Anatomical recording card; Firth (1912a, 181-82; Fig. 166); Firth (1912b, Plan XVIII).

121 A male, adult skeleton. The skull was found to be smashed when the body was excavated.

Original anatomical observations: All teeth present are perfect and moderately worn in both jaws.

The sacrum is very flat and 5-pieced.

References: Anatomical recording card; Firth (1912a, 182); Firth (1912b, Plan XVIII).

123 A disturbed probable male skeleton, with no age recorded.

References: Anatomical recording card; Firth (1912a, 182); Firth (1912b, Plan XVIII).

124 A skeleton, with no age or sex recorded.

References: Firth (1912a, 182); Firth (1912b, Plan XVIII).

125 A male, adult skeleton.

Original anatomical observations: All cranial sutures have been obliterated. The tori are slightly prominent.

The mastoids are small and flattened. There is a definite visible prognathism. There is right occipital bulging. The zygomata are slightly arched.

All teeth present are perfect and slightly worn in both jaws.

The manubrium is separate, but the xiphoid process has fused to the body of the sternum. There is a large hole through the lowest part of the sternum. The sacrum is 5-pieced and rather flat. There is a large facet present on the neck of both femora.

<u>References</u>: Anatomical recording card; Firth (1912a, 182); Firth (1912b, Plan XVIII).

126   A fragmentary skeleton, with no age or sex recorded.

<u>References</u>: Firth (1912a, 182-83); Firth (1912b, Plan XVIII).

127   A male, child skeleton.

<u>References</u>: Anatomical recording card; Firth (1912a, 183); Firth (1912b, Plan XVIII).

130   An infant skeleton, with no age or sex recorded.

<u>References</u>: Firth (1912a, 183); Firth (1912b, Plan XVIII).

131   A disturbed female, adult skeleton.

<u>Original anatomical observations</u>: The zygomata are almost straight.

The teeth are much worn, with no caries in both jaws. There are pulp cavity abscesses in the maxilla.

<u>References</u>: Anatomical recording card; Firth (1912a, 183); Firth (1912b, Plan XVIII).

133   A disturbed partial post-cranial skeleton, with no age or sex recorded. Only the pelvis and leg bones remain.

<u>References</u>: Firth (1912a, 183); Firth (1912b, Plan XVIII).

135   An infant skeleton, with no sex recorded.

<u>References</u>: Firth (1912a, 183); Firth (1912b, Plan XVIII).

138   A partial post-cranial skeleton, with no age or sex recorded. Only the lower part of the skeleton remains.

<u>References</u>: Firth (1912a, 184); Firth (1912b, Plan XVIII).

152   A female, infant skeleton.

<u>References</u>: Firth (1912a, 185-86); Firth (1912b, Plan XVIII).

153   A female, adult skeleton.

<u>Original anatomical observations</u>: The coronal and sagittal sutures are closing, the lambdoid suture is open. There is a large epipteric bone on the right shutting out the parietal from the great wing of the sphenoid and another large epipteric bone on the left. The mastoids and tori are very small.

The teeth are much worn, but perfect in both jaws.

<u>References</u>: Anatomical recording card; Firth (1912a, 186); Firth (1912b, Plan XVIII).

154   A skeleton, with no age or sex recorded.

<u>References</u>: Firth (1912a, 186); Firth (1912b, Plan XVIII).

155   A disturbed skeleton, with no age or sex recorded.

<u>References</u>: Firth (1912a, 186); Firth (1912b, Plan XVIII).

156   A skeleton, with no age or sex recorded.

<u>References</u>: Firth (1912a, 186); Firth (1912b, Plan XVIII).

157   A female, adult skeleton. The archaeological report records the presence of only the leg bones, in contrast to the anatomical records.

<u>Original anatomical observations</u>: The tori are well-marked. The mastoids are small. The zygomata are almost straight. The nasal bones are very small and the nasal spine is fairly well-marked.

The teeth are very much worn. There are pulp cavity abscesses on the right 2nd bicuspid and 1st molar and the left 2nd molar in the maxilla. In the mandible there is a pulp cavity abscess on the left 1st molar. The alveolus is absorbed and the right 1st molar has gone.

The manubrium is separate from the gladiolus. The sacrum is small, 5-pieced and markedly curved.

Surviving skeletal remains: The skull was located in the Anatomical Museum, The University of Manchester when studied by Watson. The current location is unknown.

References: Anatomical recording card; Firth (1912a, 186); Firth (1912b, Plan XVIII); Watson (pre-1935).

158   A child skeleton, with no sex recorded.

References: Firth (1912a, 186); Firth (1912b, Plan XVIII).

162   A partial post-cranial male skeleton, with no age recorded. The femora and tibiae only remain.

References: Firth (1912a, 187).

163   A female, adult skeleton. The skull was badly distorted by grave pressure and the bones were broken when excavated.

Original anatomical observations: There is an extreme visible prognathism.

The sacrum is small and slightly curved.

References: Anatomical recording card; Firth (1912a, 187); Firth (1912b, Plan XVIII).

166   A skeleton, with no age or sex recorded.

References: Firth (1912a, 187).

167   A male, child skeleton.

Original anatomical observations: There is a definite prognathism.

References: Anatomical recording card; Firth (1912a, 187).

169   A female, adult skeleton which is slightly distorted by grave pressure. The skull was fragile and the facial bones were broken during excavation (Derry 1909b, 25).

Original anatomical observations: There is a suture running from the nasal margin to the lower margin of the orbit, cutting off the nasal processes from the body (anomaly). The condition is present on both sides. There is a marked visible prognathism. The zygomata are perfectly straight. The nasal spine suppressed.

The sacrum is small, 5-pieced and slightly curved.

References: Anatomical recording card; Derry (1909b, 25); Firth (1912a, 187); Firth (1912b, Plan XVIII).

170   A child skeleton, with no sex recorded.

References: Anatomical recording card; Firth (1912a, 187).

171   A child skeleton, with no sex recorded.

References: Anatomical recording card; Firth (1912a, 187).

172   A male skeleton, with no age recorded.

References: Anatomical recording card; Firth (1912a, 187); Firth (1912b, Plan XVIII).

173   A male, young adult skeleton.

Original anatomical observations: All cranial sutures are open. There is an epipteric bone on the left shutting out the parietal from the great wing of the sphenoid. The tori are small. The mastoids are medium. The zygomata are slightly arched. There is some visible prognathism. There is no nasal spine.

All teeth present are perfect and slightly worn in both jaws. The 3rd molars have not yet appeared in the maxilla.

The clavicular ends are not united. The manubrium is separate from the body of the sternum and the first piece of the body is also separate. The sacrum is very flat and wide.

References: Anatomical recording card; Firth (1912a, 187); Firth (1912b, Plan XVIII).

Cemetery 88, Koshtamna

A-group period

A small denuded cemetery on a mud mound (Reisner 1909b, 13). The ten graves excavated contained seven skeletons (2 child burials, 1 adult male skeleton and 4 further burials about which no further information has been located)

The following graves were recorded with no clear indication of whether they contained a body; they are likely to have been empty: 5, 6 (Firth 1912a, 158).

1   A partial post-cranial child skeleton, with no sex recorded. Only the lower part of the skeleton remains.

    References: Firth (1912a, 158).

2   A female, child skeleton. The archaeological report does not indicate that this burial is that of a child.

    References: Anatomical recording card; Firth (1912a, 158).

3   A skeleton, with no age or sex recorded.

    References: Firth (1912a, 158).

7   A disturbed skeleton, with no age or sex recorded.

    References: Firth (1912a, 158).

8   A male, young adult skeleton. This body is recorded as being intrusive to the grave.

    References: Anatomical recording card; Firth (1912a, 158).

9   A disturbed skeleton, with no age or sex recorded.

    References: Firth (1912a, 158).

10   A skeleton, with no age or sex recorded.

    References: Firth (1912a, 158).

Cemetery 89/1, Awam, Koshtamna

A-group, New Kingdom and Ptolemaic-Roman period

Cemetery 89 is a large cemetery containing burials from the A-group, New Kingdom and Ptolemaic-Roman periods. The cemetery is divided into two sections divided by a gully. The northern most graves are those of the A-group, with a number of further graves mixed in with the Ptolemaic burials (Firth 1912a, 9). The archaeological report records just two later New Kingdom period graves in this cemetery, although bodies from three graves are recorded (Firth 1912a, 28). The second half of the graves (numbering from 500) belong to further A-group burials and a large number of chamber tombs that contained wrapped mummies (Firth 1912a, 32-34).

A-group burials

The following graves were recorded with no clear indication of whether they contained a body; they are likely to have been empty: 2, 18, 24, 28, 30, 33, 60, 69, 70, 72, 74, 77 (Firth 1912a, 188-189).

1A   A female skeleton, with no age recorded. The archaeological report records this body as male.

   Original anatomical observations: The coronal and lambdoid sutures are open, the sagittal suture is closed. The tori are medium and the mastoids are small. The zygomata are almost straight. The occipital is symmetrical. There is a very marked visible prognathism. There is no nasal spine.

   References: Anatomical recording card; Firth (1912a, 188).

1B   A male, probably young skeleton.

   Original anatomical observations: There is a visible and measurable prognathism.

   References: Anatomical recording card; Firth (1912a, 188).

17   A partial post-cranial skeleton, with no age or sex recorded. The vertebrae only remain.

   References: Firth (1912a, 188).

23   A fragmentary massive male skeleton, with no age recorded.

   References: Firth (1912a, 188).

25   A skeleton, with no age or sex recorded.

   References: Firth (1912a, 188-89).

26(a)   A skeleton, with no age or sex recorded.

References: Firth (1912a, 189).

26(b)   A skeleton, with no age or sex recorded.

References: Firth (1912a, 189).

75A   A male, adult skeleton.

Original anatomical observations: All cranial sutures are open. The tori are prominent. The mastoids are massive. The zygomata are arched. The nasal spine is suppressed.

References: Anatomical recording card; Firth (1912a, 189).

75B   A fragmentary female skeleton, with no age recorded.

References: Firth (1912a, 189).

New Kingdom burials

173   A female, adult skeleton.

Original anatomical observations: All cranial sutures are open. The zygomata are slightly arched. The nasal spine is small.

All maxillary teeth present are perfect, except the right 2nd bicuspid which has a carious cavity. The mandible is broken.

References: Anatomical recording card.

174   A female, child skeleton.

References: Anatomical recording card.

175   A skeleton, with no age or sex recorded.

References: Firth (1912a, 189).

Cemetery 89/500, Koshtamna

A-group burials

The following graves were found to be empty upon excavation: 670, 760 (Firth 1912a, 192-194; Firth 1912b, Plan XV).

546   A partial post-cranial female, adult skeleton. The lower part of the skeleton only remains.

Original anatomical observations: The sacrum is very flat and 5-pieced.

References: Anatomical recording card; Firth (1912a, 190); Firth (1912b, Plan XV).

549   A male, child skeleton.

References: Anatomical recording card; Firth (1912a, 190); Firth (1912b, Plan XV).

570   A male, adult post-cranial skeleton. All bones are much damaged by insects. The archaeological report does not indicate the absence of the skull in contrast to the anatomical record.

Original anatomical observations: The posterior arch of the atlas is not joined. The sternal epiphyses of the clavicles are not completely united. The sternal end of the left clavicle has a large inflammatory bony process probably due to some injury at the joint. The inflammation has spread on to the sides and back of the manubrium. There is a perforation through the last piece of the body of the sternum. There is a large abscess cavity in the bodies of the 11th and 12th dorsal vertebrae. The 11th vertebra is almost completely collapsed and has fallen forward onto the 12th dorsal vertebra.

Further studies: A diagnosis of Pott's disease was later made for this individual by Derry (1909b, 26).

References: Anatomical recording card; Derry (1909b, 26); Firth (1912a, 190); Firth (1912b, Plan XV).

575   A female, adult skeleton.

References: Firth (1912a, 190); Firth (1912b, Plan XV).

576(a)   A partial post-cranial skeleton, with no age or sex recorded. The femora and tibiae only remain (they were destroyed by the later addition of a goat burial).

References: Firth (1912a, 190); Firth (1912b, Plan XV).

576(b) A goat burial.

References: Firth (1912a, 190); Firth (1912b, Plan XV).

577 A male, aged skeleton. The facial bones were found to be damaged when the body was excavated.

Original anatomical observations: All of the cranial sutures have been obliterated. There are epipteric bones on the left side. The tori and mastoids are small. The nasal spine is large.

The teeth are very worn and most of the alveolus is absorbed in both jaws.

References: Anatomical recording card; Firth (1912a, 190); Firth (1912b, Plan XV).

583 A female, adult skeleton. The archaeological report records the presence of female tibiae only.

Original anatomical observations: All cranial sutures are open including a metopic suture. There is a large wormian bone in the lambdoid. The zygomata are almost straight. The nasal spine is suppressed. The mandible is missing.

All of the maxillary teeth present are perfect.

The sacrum is small and 5-pieced.

References: Anatomical recording card; Firth (1912a, 190).

601A A female, adult skeleton.

Original anatomical observations: of the cranial sutures are closed. There are no tori. The mastoids are small. The right zygoma is straight and the left zygoma is slightly curved. The nasal spine is suppressed. The occipital is symmetrical. There is a marked visible prognathism.

All teeth are present and perfect in both jaws.

References: Anatomical recording card; Firth (1912a, 190-91; Fig. 167); Firth (1912b, Plan XV).

601B A male, adult skeleton.

Original anatomical observations: coronal and sagittal sutures are closed, the lambdoid suture is closing. The mastoids and tori are small. There is left occipital bulging. The zygomata are almost straight. The nasal spine is small.

All of the teeth present are perfect and much worn in both jaws. The right 3rd molar in the maxilla has gone and the alveolus is absorbed.

The manubrium is separate from the gladiolus. The humerii are curiously bent. There is severe spondylitis of the lumbar spine.

References: Anatomical recording card; Firth (1912a, 190-91; Fig. 167); Firth (1912b, Plan XV).

614 A male, adult skeleton.

Original anatomical observations: The skull and face are smashed. All cranial sutures are open. The tori are very small. The mastoids are medium.

All teeth are present, perfect and not much worn in both jaws. The 3rd molars never appeared. There are two milk 2nd molars present in the mandible.

The manubrium is separate from the gladiolus. There is a facet present on the neck of both femora.

References: Anatomical recording card; Firth (1912a, 191); Firth (1912b, Plan XV).

618 A child skeleton, with no sex recorded.

References: Firth (1912a, 191); Firth (1912b, Plan XV).

622 A female, adult skeleton.

Original anatomical observations: All cranial sutures are open. The mastoids are very small and there are no tori. There is a definite visible prognathism. The nasal spine is small.

All teeth present are perfect and very worn in both jaws.

The manubrium is separate from the gladiolus. The sacrum is flat and 5-pieced. The 2nd lumbar vertebra on the right and the 3rd lumbar vertebra on the left have the laminae fissured.

References: Anatomical recording card; Firth (1912a, 191); Firth (1912b, Plan XV).

627 A male, adult skeleton.

Original anatomical observations: The coronal suture is closing, the sagittal is obliterated and the lambdoid is still open. There is a very marked visible prognathism. The zygomata are arched. The nasal spine is suppressed.

All teeth are present, perfect and slightly worn.

On the right side, the sacrum is fused to the right innominate bone. The left tibia and fibula are fused together at the junction of the inter-osseous membrane. The bones of ankle joint are fused together, and to the tibia and fibula.

References: Anatomical recording card.

633 A partial male skeleton, with no age recorded.

References: Firth (1912a, 191); Firth (1912b, Plan XV).

638 A female skeleton, with no age recorded.

References: Firth (1912a, 191); Firth (1912b, Plan XV).

639 A male skeleton, with no age recorded.

References: Anatomical recording card; Firth (1912a, 191); Firth (1912b, Plan XV).

647 A male skeleton, with no age recorded.

Original anatomical observations: All cranial sutures are open. The tori are small. The mastoids are large. The zygomata are nearly straight. The nasal spine is small.

The maxillary teeth are absolutely perfect and not much worn. No comments were recorded for the mandible.

The sacrum is flat and 5-pieced.

References: Anatomical recording card; Firth (1912a, 191-92; Fig. 169); Firth (1912b, Plate 21F; Plan XV).

655(a) A male skeleton, with no age recorded.

References: Anatomical recording card; Firth (1912a, 192); Firth (1912b, Plan XV).

655(b) A female skeleton, with no age recorded.

References: Anatomical recording card; Firth (1912a, 192); Firth (1912b, Plan XV).

673A   A male, adult skeleton

Original anatomical observations: The coronal and sagittal sutures are closing, the lambdoid suture is open. The tori are small. The mastoids are large. There is a definite visible prognathism. The nasal bones are extremely small. The nasal spine is prominent.

The teeth are all present, perfect and much worn in both jaws. However, on the left side of the maxilla the canine has come down in an abnormal position on the labial side and between the two bicuspids, pushing them apart, so that the 1st bicuspid is nearer the 2nd incisor than the canine. In the position of the canine there is a socket, now gaping. It has apparently once held a tooth, possibly a persistent milk canine.

The sacrum is flat and 5-pieced. Both tibiae are platycnemic.

References: Anatomical recording card; Derry (1909b, 27); Firth (1912a, 192); Firth (1912b, Plan XV).

673B   A male, adult skeleton.

Original anatomical observations: All cranial sutures are closing. The tori are medium. The mastoids are large. There are very well marked temporal ridges. There is a definite visible prognathism. The nasal spine is suppressed.

All teeth are present, perfect and well-worn in both jaws.

The manubrium is separate from the gladiolus. The sacrum is 6-pieced (5 sacral bones, plus 1st coccyx). There is a facet present on the neck of both femora. The 3rd metatarsal of the left foot is fractured and has mended with good union.

References: Anatomical recording card; Firth (1912a, 192); Firth (1912b, Plan XV).

678   A skeleton, with no age or sex recorded.

References: Firth (1912a, 192); Firth (1912b, Plan XV).

683A   A female, adult skeleton.

Original anatomical observations: All cranial sutures are open. There are no tori and the mastoids are small. The glabella is bulging. There is a definite visible prognathism. The nasal spine is fairly prominent.

All of the teeth are present, perfect and very little worn in both jaws.

The epiphyses of the clavicles are not joined. The manubrium is separate from the gladiolus. The sacrum is 6-pieced (5 sacral bones, plus 1st coccyx), flat and wide. Both tibiae are platycnemic.

References: Anatomical recording card; Firth (1912a, 193; Fig. 171); Firth (1912b, Plate 21A; Plan XV).

683B   A female skeleton, with no age recorded. The skull was recorded as being distorted by grave pressure when excavated.

Original anatomical observations: All cranial sutures are open. The tori are very small. The glabella are prominent. There is a definite subnasal visible prognathism. The nasal spine is small.

All of the teeth are present, perfect and fairly well worn in both jaws.

The manubrium is separate from the gladiolus. The sacrum is wide, fairly curved and 5-pieced.

References: Anatomical recording card; Firth (1912a, 193; Fig. 171); Firth (1912b, Plates 21A and 21B; Plan XV).

683C   A newly born infant skeleton, with no sex recorded. The infant was found under the pelvis of 683B.

References: Firth (1912a, 193; Fig. 171); Firth (1912b, Plan XV).

684   A male skeleton, about 12 years old.

References: Anatomical recording card; Firth (1912a, 193); Firth (1912b, Plan XV).

686   A male, adult skeleton.

Original anatomical observations: The coronal suture is open, the sagittal is beginning to close and the lambdoid is open. The tori and mastoids are small.

All of the maxillary teeth are present, except the right 2nd bicuspid. There are no caries. All of the mandibular teeth are present and fairly worn, with no caries.

The right humerus has an unusual and fusiform swelling at the junction of the upper and middle third of the shaft. The head of the left humerus is enormously swollen, measuring 75.5mm from side to side and appears to be composed of solid bone judging from weight. The inflammatory process has involved the glenoid cavity of the scapula and the corachoid and acromion processes as well as the adnomial end of the clavicle. A false joint has been formed between the glenoid cavity and the mass forming the head of the humerus. Little or no movement would have possible. The manubrium has fused to the body of sternum and there is a hole through the lower piece of the body. There is a facet present on the neck and lipping of the lower articular surfaces of both femora. The left patella on the outer side has a roughened semi-lunar surface due to some inflammation. The upper end of the right tibia shows lipping of the articular surface.

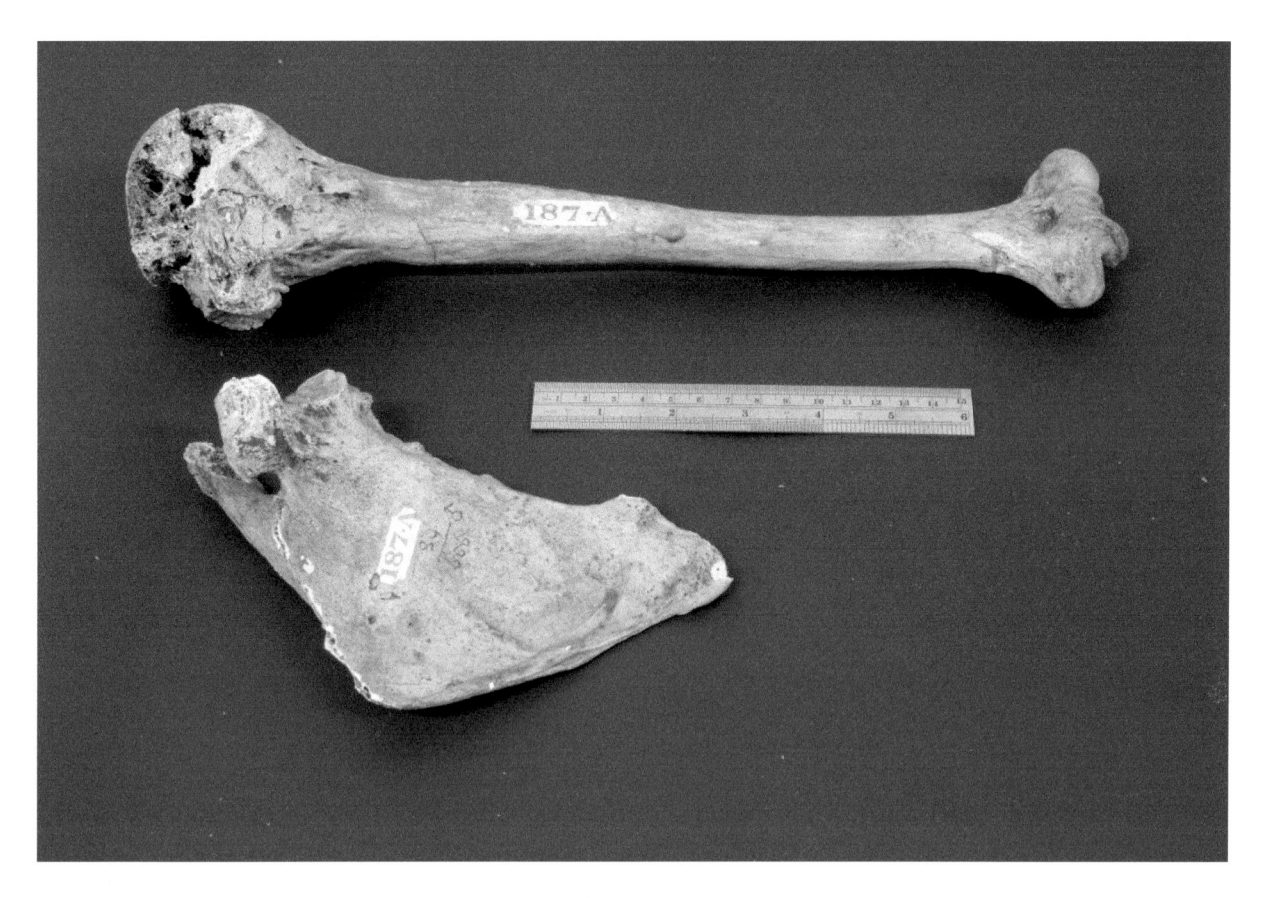

Figure 12: The humeral head and scapula of an adult male from cemetery 89, grave 686 with a benign bony tumour. This has been identified as a chondroblastic or giant cell tumour. The scapula shows signs of modification due to the presence of the tumour. ©The Trustees of the Natural History Museum, London, 2023.

Further studies: Brothwell (1967, 324) described the left humeral head of this individual and suggested a benign chondroblastic tumour or a giant cell tumour as the most likely diagnoses.

Surviving skeletal remains: The left humerus and scapula were originally part of the Nubian Pathological Collection at the Royal College of Surgeons. Both bones now reside in the Natural History Museum, London (catalogue ref. NPC 187A) (Figure 12). The location of the rest of the body is unknown.

References: Anatomical recording card; Derry (1909b, 26-27); Firth (1912a, 193; Figure 172); Firth (1912b, Plate 21D; Plan XV); Brothwell (1967, 324-5).

687A   A male, adult skeleton. The facial bones were found to be broken when the body was excavated.

Original anatomical observations: All cranial sutures are open. The mastoids are medium.

The teeth are perfect and very slightly worn in both jaws.

References: Anatomical recording card; Firth (1912a, 194); Firth (1912b, Plan XV).

687B   A male, adult skeleton.

Original anatomical observations: The tori and mastoids are small.

The teeth are perfect and very slightly worn in both jaws.

The manubrium is fused to the body of the sternum (the man is quite young). There is a very large hole in the lowest piece of the body, measuring 16 x 14mm.

The sacrum is 6-pieced (1 lumbar vertebra plus 5 sacral bones). There are four lumbar vertebrae. There is a facet present on the neck of the right femur. This is markedly pilastered. The patellae are notched.

References: Anatomical recording card; Firth (1912a, 194); Firth (1912b, Plan XV).

688   A male skeleton, with no age recorded.

References: Anatomical recording card.

754   A fragmentary male, adult skeleton.

Original anatomical observations: All cranial sutures are closed. The tori are small. The mastoids are fairly large. There is arthritis of both tempero-mandibular joints.

All of the teeth that remain are much worn in both jaws. Abscesses are present.

There is very severe rheumatoid arthritis in both shoulder joints. On the left side, the head of the humerus has collapsed.

Further studies: Thomas Strangeways added the following comment to the anatomical recording card following his study of the humerii after they were brought to the UK: 'The left humerus shows an intracapsular fracture (impacted) with dislocation and the other also appears to have been injured'.

Surviving skeletal remains: The left humerus was originally part of the Nubian Pathological Collection at the Royal College of Surgeons. It now resides in the Natural History Museum, London in two pieces (catalogue ref. NPC 64A and 64B). The location of the rest of the body is unknown.

References: Anatomical recording card; Firth (1912a, 194); Firth (1912b, Plan XV).

763   A fragmentary skeleton, with no age or sex recorded.

References: Firth (1912a, 194); Firth (1912b, Plan XV).

764 A partial post-cranial male skeleton, with no age recorded. The lower part of the skeleton only remains.

References: Anatomical recording card; Firth (1912a, 194); Firth (1912b, Plan XV).

765 A male skeleton, with no age recorded.

References: Anatomical recording card; Firth (1912a, 194); Firth (1912b, Plan XV).

766 A female skeleton, with no age recorded.

References: Firth (1912a, 194); Firth (1912b, Plan XV).

768 A partial post-cranial male skeleton, with no age recorded.

References: Anatomical recording card; Firth (1912a, 195; Figure 174); Firth (1912b, Plan XV).

807 A male, adult skeleton.

Original anatomical observations: The coronal and sagittal sutures are closing, the lambdoid suture is open. The tori are small. The mastoids are moderately large. The occipital is symmetrical. The nasal spine is small.

All of the maxillary teeth are present, perfect and moderately worn. No comments were recorded for the mandible.

References: Anatomical recording card.

810 A female, adult skeleton.

Original anatomical observations: The coronal and sagittal sutures are closed, the lambdoid suture is closing. The tori are fairly marked. The mastoids are medium. There is a slight visible prognathism. The zygomata are almost straight. There is slight left occipital bulging. The nasal spine is moderately prominent.

The maxillary teeth are much worn. No 3rd molars ever appeared on the right - otherwise the teeth are perfect. In the mandible those teeth present are perfect, except the right 1st molar which is a carious stump with an abscess cavity at the root.

The manubrium is separate from the gladiolus. The sacrum is 6-pieced (5 sacral bones, plus 1st coccyx).

References: Anatomical recording card; Firth (1912a, 195); Firth (1912b, Plan XV).

812A A male, adult skeleton.

Original anatomical observations: The coronal and sagittal sutures are closed, the lambdoid suture is closing. The tori are small. The mastoids are large and long. The occipital is symmetrical. The nasal spine is very prominent.

The teeth are very much worn in both jaws. There are signs of abscesses in the positions of the right 2nd molar and the left 1st molar, communicating with antrum of Highmore in the maxilla and at the roots of the left canine and 1st molar in the mandible.

The manubrium and the body of the sternum are fused together. The sacrum is 6-pieced and the vertebrae are all correct.

References: Anatomical recording card; Firth (1912a, 195); Firth (1912b, Plate 21E; Plan XV).

812B A female, adult skeleton. The archaeological report records the presence of only a single body in this grave, unlike the anatomical record.

Original anatomical observations: All cranial sutures are closed. There is a large epipteric on the right shutting out the parietal from the great wing of the sphenoid. There is a small epipteric on the left. The tori are faint. The mastoids are large. The occipital is symmetrical. There is no nasal spine.

The maxillary teeth are very much worn. The left 2nd molar is carious. The left 3rd molar is a curious peg-shape and no right 3rd molar ever appeared. No comments were recorded for the mandible.

The sacrum is 6-pieced (5 sacral bones, plus 1st coccyx).

References: Anatomical recording card; Firth (1912b, Plan XV).

819 A male, adult skeleton. The body is considered to be intrusive.

Original anatomical observations: All cranial sutures are open. The tori are moderate. The mastoids are small. The occipital is symmetrical. There is a definite visible prognathism. The nasal spine is small.

All teeth present are perfect and not much worn, with no caries in both jaws.

The manubrium is separate from the gladiolus. There is very severe spondylitis in the 3rd and 4th lumbar vertebrae which has eaten away part of the body of the 4th lumbar vertebrae.

References: Anatomical recording card; Firth (1912a, 195); Firth (1912b, Plan XV).

823 A partial post-cranial skeleton, with no age recorded. The lower part of the skeleton only remains.

References: Firth (1912a, 196); Firth (1912b, Plan XV).

825 A partial male, adult skeleton. The skull and humerii only remain.

Original anatomical observations: All cranial sutures are closed. The tori are prominent. The mastoids are large.

References: Anatomical recording card; Firth (1912a, 196); Firth (1912b, Plan XV).

855 A male, adult skeleton.

Original anatomical observations: All cranial sutures are open. On the left side the squamous temporal articulates with the frontal. The tori are slight. The mastoids are fairly large. The occipital is symmetrical. There is a slight visible prognathism. There appears to have been some injury to the ramus of mandible in the neighbourhood of the left tempero-articulation, causing elongation of the ramus and the neck of the bone.

All of the teeth present and perfect and much worn in both jaws.

The manubrium is separate from the gladiolus. There is a small pit in the bend of the elbow of the left arm. There has apparently been an abscess cavity affecting the lower dorsal and upper lumbar vertebrae. The body of the 2nd lumbar and most of the 1st and 3rd lumbar vertebrae have been destroyed. The 2nd, 3rd and 4th lumber vertebrae are fused together and there is an acute kyphosis at the dorso-lumber junction. The left femur has been fractured in the middle of the shaft. The upper fragment has united in front of the lower fragment which has been pulled upwards, but apparently without much shortening.

Further studies: Derry (1909b, 26) later identified the vertebral lesions as Pott's disease.

References: Anatomical recording card; Derry (1909b, 26); Firth (1912a, 196); Firth (1912b, Plan XV).

858 A male, adult skeleton.

Original anatomical observations: All cranial sutures open. The tori are well marked and the mastoids are attenuated. The occipital is symmetrical. There is a marked visible prognathism. The nasal spine is suppressed.

All teeth are present, perfect and slightly worn in both jaws. In the mandible, the right 1st incisor has an abscess cavity at the root (pulp). There is also no 3rd molar on the left and on the right, this is a peg.

All parts of the sternum are fused except the xiphoid process. Both tibiae are platycnemic.

References: Anatomical recording card; Firth (1912a, 196); Firth (1912b, Plan XV).

861 A male, adult skeleton.

Original anatomical observations: All cranial sutures are open. There are epipteric bones on the right. The tori are well marked. The mastoids are fairly large. There is a very marked visible prognathism. The occipital is symmetrical. The nasal spine is fairly prominent.

All teeth are present, perfect and very slight worn in both jaws. The right 1st molar in the maxilla has a pulp cavity abscess.

The right tibia is very platycnemic.

References: Anatomical recording card; Firth (1912a, 196); Firth (1912b, Plan XV).

871 A fragmentary child skeleton, with no sex recorded.

References: Firth (1912a, 196); Firth (1912b, Plan XV).

880 A male, adult skeleton.

Original anatomical observations: The coronal and lambdoid sutures are open, the sagittal suture is closed. The tori are fairly well-marked. The mastoids are medium. The zygomata are very slightly curved. The nasal spine is very prominent.

All maxillary teeth present are perfect and fairly worn. No comments were recorded for the mandible.

References: Anatomical recording card; Firth (1912a, 196); Firth (1912b, Plan XV).

882 A partial post-cranial skeleton, with no age or sex recorded. The lower part of the skeleton only remains.

References: Firth (1912a, 196); Firth (1912b, Plan XV).

917 A female, adult skeleton.

Original anatomical observations: All cranial sutures are open. The mastoids are small. The zygomata are almost straight. There is very marked visible prognathism. The glabella is prominent. The nasal spine is moderately prominent.

The teeth are perfect and moderately worn in both jaws.

The manubrium is separate from the gladiolus. The sacrum is very small and 5-pieced. The patellae are notched.

References: Anatomical recording card; Firth (1912a, 196); Firth (1912b, Plate 21C; Plan XV).

1161A   A male, adult partial skeleton. The skull was missing when the body was excavated.

Original anatomical observations: The mandibular teeth are fairly well-worn and perfect.

The manubrium is separate from the gladiolus. There is a facet present on the neck of both femora.

References: Anatomical recording card; Firth (1912a, 196); Firth (1912b, Plan XV).

1161B   A male, adult skeleton.

Original anatomical observations: All cranial sutures are open. The tori and mastoids are small. The occipital is symmetrical. There is a slight visible prognathism. There is no nasal spine.

All that are present are perfect and very little worn in both jaws.

References: Anatomical recording card; Firth (1912a, 196); Firth (1912b, Plan XV).

Ptolemaic-Roman burials

129   A wrapped, artificially mummified body with a cartonnage head mask, chest, leg and foot cartonnage pieces. There is no evidence that the body was dissected.

References: Firth (1912b, Plate 30C).

252   An artificially mummified body with cartonnage foot piece (it is possible the body had been provided with a cartonnage head piece, chest and leg cover as well but this cannot be determined from the photographic record. The mummy was placed in a stone or pottery coffin.

References: Firth (1912b, Plate 30B).

283   An artificially mummified body wrapped in bandages. The body was discovered lying on a string bedstead. There is no evidence the mummy was dissected.

References: Firth (1912b, Plate 30A).

286 A mummified gazelle. This tomb also contained two rectangular stone coffins although the contents of these have not been recorded.

References: Firth (1912b, Plate 25C).

393 An artificially mummified body wrapped in bandages. There is no evidence the mummy was dissected.

References: A contact prints from a glass photography plate survives in the George Andrew Reisner Archive, Museum of Fine Arts, Boston, US.

677 A male, aged artificially mummified body (dissected). A white chin beard, slight whiskers and long curly black hair are preserved. The body was covered from head to foot with cloth, which had been loosely thrown on. Covering his forehead down to the top of the orbits was a strip of cloth with a fringe falling over his hair and another strip round the lower part of the face, leaving the middle part of the face exposed. The hands were in front of the pubes. The head was away from the river (to the west?). No resin was used in the preparation of the mummy.

Original anatomical observations: The skull is very massive. All cranial sutures are open. The tori are prominent. The mastoids are large. The zygomata are almost straight. The nasal spine is moderately prominent. There was no perforation of the ethmoid.

The maxillary teeth are very much worn and carious. There are abscess cavities at the roots of the right 2nd incisor and 1st molar and the left 2nd bicuspid and 1st molar. On the right side of the mandible the alveolus is absorbed behind the 1st bicuspid and on the left, except for the left 2nd molar which is still there.

There was no stuffing of the body cavities. He was possibly circumcised.

References: Anatomical recording card.

711A A male, adult artificially mummified body (dissected). Wavy black hair is preserved. The body was wrapped in linen and no resin was used.

Original anatomical observations: All cranial sutures are open including a metopic suture. The tori are prominent and the mastoids are very large. The zygomata are almost straight. The nasal spine is small. There is distinct right occipital bulging. The ethmoid has been perforated and the skull is empty.

All of the maxillary teeth are present and perfect. In the mandible the alveolus is absorbed behind the 1st bicuspids on both sides.

The manubrium is separate from the gladiolus. There is union of the semilunar and cuneiform bones of both hands. The sacrum is 6-pieced (5 sacral bones, plus the 5th lumbar vertebra). There are four lumbar vertebrae present.

References: Anatomical recording card; Derry (1909b, 28).

711B   A female, adult artificially mummified body (dissected). The body was wrapped in linen and no resin was used.

Original anatomical observations: All cranial sutures are open including a metopic suture. The tori are very slight. The mastoids are small. The zygomata are quite straight. The nasal spine is small. There is slight right occipital bulging.

All teeth are present, perfect and slightly worn in both jaws. There are no 3rd molars in either jaw. The right 1st molar in the mandible has a carious cavity and the right 2nd molar has gone and the alveolus has absorbed.

The manubrium is separate from the gladiolus. The sacrum is large, wide and 5-pieced.

References: Anatomical recording card.

711C   A male, adult artificially mummified body (dissected). The body was wrapped and covered with resin.

Original anatomical observations: The individual was circumcised.

References: Anatomical recording card.

711D   A male, adult artificially mummified body (skull only studied anatomically). The body was wrapped in linen and was hardened by resin.

Original anatomical observations: All cranial sutures are open. The tori are slightly marked. The mastoids are very long.

All of the maxillary teeth are present, perfect and slightly worn. All of the teeth present in the mandible are prefect. The right molar has gone and the alveolus is absorbed and there is no 3rd molar.

References: Anatomical recording card.

722   A male, adult body showing signs of soft tissue preservation. The body is recorded only as a photograph in the archive collections in both London, UK and Boston, US (see below). It is not clear whether the man was artificially or naturally mummified. The image shows an extended, unwrapped body that had not been dissected. There are a small number of loose linen strips around his arms and chest. The notation on the photograph in London identifies that the man suffered from leprosy.

References: Contact prints from a glass photography plate survives in the George Andrew Reisner Archive, Museum of Fine Arts, Boston, US and in the Institute of Archaeology Library, UCL, UK.

731 A male, aged skeleton. Wavy black hair is preserved.

Original anatomical observations: The coronal suture is closed, the sagittal is closing and the lambdoid is commencing to close. The tori and mastoids are massive. The zygomata are straight. The occipital is symmetrical. The nasal bones are very small and the nasal spine is very prominent.

The teeth are very much worn in both jaws. In the maxilla all teeth except the incisors and canines have gone and the alveolus has absorbed. In the mandible the 1st molars have gone on both sides and the alveolus has absorbed. There is an abscess at the root of the right 1st incisor and a carious cavity in the left 2nd molar.

The scapulae are immensely wide. The manubrium and the 1st piece of the body are separate. At the inner edge of each clavicular facet is a small bony process about size of a split pea and on the right side the inter-articular fibre cartilage is attached to this small bone. On the left side the 1st rib has a curious semi-lunar shaped bony process which has articulated with a cervical rib. The sacrum is 7-pieced (5 sacral bones, plus 2 coccyx) and is much curved. There is a facet present on the neck of both femora.

References: Anatomical recording card.

733 A male, adult artificially mummified body (dissected).

Original anatomical observations: The skull and all muscular attachments are described as 'massive'. The cranial sutures are all open. There is a large wormian bone in the upper part of the supra-occipital. The tori and mastoids are massive. The nasal spine is small. The zygomata are very slightly arched. The occipital is symmetrical. An aperture is broken through the body of the sphenoid and the skull is empty.

All teeth are present, perfect and slightly worn in both jaws.

The manubrium is separate from the gladiolus. The sacrum is 5-pieced and slightly curved. There is a facet present on the neck of both femora.

References: Anatomical recording card.

735 A wrapped artificially mummified body with a cartonnage head mask, chest, leg and foot cartonnage pieces. The mummy was found shrouded in a large linen sheet and placed inside a stone coffin. There is no evidence that the body was dissected.

References: Firth (1912b, Plates 26B, 26C and 26D).

736 A wrapped artificially mummified body with a cartonnage head mask, chest, leg and foot cartonnage pieces. The mummy was found inside a stone coffin. There is no evidence that the body was dissected.

References: Firth (1912b, Plate 27A and 27C).

752 A female skeleton, with no age recorded.

Original anatomical observations: The coronal suture is closing, the sagittal and lambdoid sutures are open. The metopic is closed, but still visible. The tori are slight. The mastoids are large. There is very slight left occipital bulging. The zygomata are very slightly arched. There is a distinct visible prognathism. The nasal spine is very small.

The maxillary teeth are in very poor condition. On both sides behind the 2nd bicuspid the alveolus has absorbed. The right 2nd incisor, canine and 1st bicuspid and the left 2nd incisor and both bicuspids are all carious. The mandibular teeth are much worn. The right 1st bicuspid is carious and the alveolus has absorbed behind the right 2nd bicuspid. The left 1st bicuspid is also carious and there is an abscess cavity at the root. The left 1st molar has gone and the alveolus has absorbed.

References: Anatomical recording card.

772 A male, adult artificially mummified body (dissected). No resin was used to prepare the body.

Original anatomical observations: The coronal suture is open, the sagittal is closed and the lambdoid is beginning to close. There is an epipteric bone on both sides shutting out the parietal from the great wing of the sphenoid. The tori are prominent and the mastoids are large. The nasal spine is prominent. The zygomata are very slightly curved. There is left occipital bulging. The ethmoid has been perforated. There is the remains of an old wound on the right parietal bone just behind the coronal suture.

The teeth are small and even. In the maxilla all teeth are perfect except the left 1st incisor which is carious and has a large abscess cavity at its root. All of the teeth present in the mandible are perfect. Both 1st molars are missing and the alveolus has absorbed.

The humerii both have well-marked muscle attachments. The sacrum is small, curved and 4-pieced. There is a facet present on the neck of both femora. The body cavity is stuffed with linen.

References: Anatomical recording card.

785 A male skeleton, with no age recorded.

Original anatomical observations: The coronal suture is beginning to close, the sagittal is closed and the lambdoid is closing. The sphenoid articulates with the frontal on both sides. The tori are very prominent. The mastoids are large. The zygomata are slightly arched. The nasal spine is suppressed.

The teeth are perfect but slightly worn in both jaws.

The manubrium is separate from the gladiolus. The sacrum is 6-pieced.

References: Anatomical recording card.

794 An artificially mummified body wrapped in bandages; there is a large linen sheet wrapping the entire body and the head and feet are bound separately. There was no coffin found with this burial and there is no evidence the mummy was dissected.

Surviving mummified remains: This mummy is thought to be located in the South Australia Museum, Adelaide. The identification of tomb number is not completely certain but archival documents do suggest this mummy came from the ASN excavations during season 2. If correctly identified the body is that of an adult male.

References: Anatomical recording card; Firth (1912b, Plate 22B).

797A A poorly preserved male, adult artificially mummified body (dissected). The body was wrapped on palm sticks.

Original anatomical observations: All cranial sutures are open. The tori are moderately prominent. The mastoids are large. The zygomata are slightly arched. The ethmoid bone is perforated.

All of those teeth present are perfect and little worn, except the left 1st molar in the maxilla which has a large carious cavity.

The sacrum is 6-pieced (5 sacral bones, plus 1st coccyx) and very curved. Only 3 lumbar vertebrae and 1 thoracic vertebra were found in the wrappings or the tomb. The tibia and fibula were found broken beneath the wrappings; the lower parts of the bones are missing. This was the site of an old fracture.

References: Anatomical recording card.

797B A female, adult artificially mummified body (dissected).

Original anatomical observations: All cranial sutures are open. The tori and mastoids are medium. The zygomata are almost straight. There is a slight visible prognathism. The nasal spine is prominent. The body of the sphenoid is perforated. The skull is empty except for the remains of flowers.

The teeth are perfect and very slightly worn in both jaws, except for the right 1st incisor in the mandible which has a pulp cavity abscess. Both 1st molars in the mandible have also gone and the alveolus has absorbed.

The last 3 coccygeal vertebrae are ossified and fused together. There is a facet present on the neck of both femora.

References: Anatomical recording card.

797C   A female, aged skeleton.

Original anatomical observations: All cranial sutures are open and very simple, yet there is no doubt that the skeleton is aged. The tori and mastoids are both very small. There is definite left occipital bulging. The zygomata are nearly straight. The nasal bones are very small and the nasal spine is small.

The teeth are nearly all gone and the alveolus has absorbed in both jaws. In the mandible all teeth have gone behind the 1st bicuspids. There are pulp cavity abscesses in both jaws.

The manubrium is separate from the gladiolus. The sacrum is 6-pieced (5 sacral bones, plus 1st coccyx) and much curved.

References: Anatomical recording card.

798   A wrapped artificially mummified child with a cartonnage head mask, chest, leg and foot cartonnage pieces. There is no evidence that the body was dissected.

References: Firth (1912b, Plate 32A).

802   A male, adult artificially mummified body (skull only studied anatomically). The body was found alone in a large maghragha. The mummy was cartonnaged and resined.

Original anatomical observations: All cranial sutures are open, including a metopic suture. The tori are pronounced. The zygomata are slightly arched. The nasal spine is very small.

The teeth are rather small and regular. They are all present and perfect in both jaws.

References: Anatomical recording card.

803   A male artificially mummified body, with no age recorded (unwrapped but no evidence of dissection). The body was wrapped in linen. A red cloth was found over the head and down the front of the body, gummed to, but not covering the back. Resin was applied to the body.

Original anatomical observations: There is evidence of circumcision.

References: Anatomical recording card.

806   A wrapped artificial mummy, photographed covered in debris. The body was buried with a number of amulets outside the wrapping; these were in situ when the tomb was excavated. There is no evidence the body was dissected.

   References: Firth (1912b, Plate 30E).

848(a)   A wrapped artificially mummified child with a cartonnage head mask, chest, leg and foot cartonnage pieces. There are broad strips of bandages running horizontally across the mummy, over the cartonnage pieces. There is no evidence that the body was dissected.

   References: A contact print from a glass photography plate survives in the George Andrew Reisner Archive, Museum of Fine Arts, Boston, US.

848(b)   A wrapped artificial mummy with a cartonnage head mask, chest, leg and foot cartonnage pieces. There are broad strips of bandages running horizontally across the mummy, over the cartonnage pieces. There is no evidence that the body was dissected.

   References: A contact print from a glass photography plate survives in the George Andrew Reisner Archive, Museum of Fine Arts, Boston, US.

852   A female, adult skeleton.

   Original anatomical observations: All cranial sutures are open. On the left the temporal articulates with the frontal. On the right a large epipteric bone is shutting out the parietal from the great wing of the sphenoid. The tori are slight. The mastoids are moderate. The occipital is symmetrical. The zygomata are straight. There is a distinct visible prognathism. The nasal spine is suppressed.

   All of the teeth present are perfect and moderately worn in both jaws. The right 1st molar in the mandible is missing and the alveolus has absorbed.

   References: Anatomical recording card.

888   A wrapped artificially mummified child with a cartonnage head mask, chest, leg and foot cartonnage pieces. There are broad strips of bandages running horizontally across the mummy, over the cartonnage pieces. The mummy was found inside a much larger painted anthropoid pottery coffin. There is no evidence that the body was dissected.

   References: Firth (1912b, Plate 31B and 31C).

890   A wrapped artificially mummified child with a cartonnage head mask, chest, leg and foot cartonnage pieces. There are broad strips of bandages running horizontally across the mummy, over the cartonnage pieces. The mummy was found inside a much larger painted anthropoid pottery coffin. There is no evidence that the body was dissected.

         References: A contact print from a glass photography plate survives in the George Andrew Reisner Archive, Museum of Fine Arts, Boston, US.

897(a)   An artificially mummified body in an anthropoid cartonnage coffin. The inner coffin was nested inside a wooden coffin and a stone rectangular coffin. The body was not dissected.

         References: Firth (1912b, Plate 22B and 22C).

897(b)   An artificially mummified body wrapped in bandages. There was no coffin found with this burial and there is no evidence the mummy was dissected.

         References: Firth (1912b, Plate 22B).

900(a)   An artificially mummified body in an anthropoid cartonnage coffin. The inner coffin was nested inside an outer wooden anthropoid coffin. The body was not dissected.

         References: Firth (1912b, Plate 23A).

900(b)   An artificially mummified body in an anthropoid cartonnage coffin. The inner coffin was nested inside an outer wooden anthropoid coffin. The body was not dissected.

         References: Firth (1912b, Plate 23B).

900(c)   An artificially mummified body in an anthropoid cartonnage coffin. The inner coffin was nested inside an outer wooden anthropoid coffin. The body was not dissected.

         References: Firth (1912b, Plate 23C).

928   A wrapped artificially mummified body which was wrapped in large sheets of linen, with thinner bandages criss-crossing the body overlying these. There is no evidence the body was dissected.

         References: Firth (1912b, Plate 32D).

953 A wrapped artificially mummified body with a cartonnage head mask, chest, leg and foot cartonnage pieces. There are criss-crossed bandages beneath the cartonnage pieces. The mummy was found inside an anthropoid pottery coffin. There is no evidence that the body was dissected.

References: Firth (1912b, Plate 28B and 28C).

1114 A wrapped artificially mummified body with a cartonnage head mask, chest, leg and foot cartonnage pieces. There are thin strips of bandages running horizontally and across the mummy, over the cartonnage pieces. The mummy was found inside an anthropoid clay coffin. There is no evidence that the body was dissected.

References: A contact print from a glass photography plate survives in the George Andrew Reisner Archive, Museum of Fine Arts, Boston, US.

1152 A female, adult artificially mummified body (skull only studied anatomically). The body is wrapped in painted cartonnage.

Original anatomical observations: All cranial sutures are open. There is an epipteric bone on both sides shutting out the parietal from the great wing of the sphenoid. There are practically no tori. The mastoids are very large. The occipital is symmetrical. The zygomata are very slightly curved. The nasal spine is prominent.

References: Anatomical recording card.

1154 A female, aged artificially mummified body (dissected).

Original anatomical observations: All cranial sutures are open in spite of evident age of the body. The tori are well-marked. The mastoids are large. There is slight left occipital bulging. The zygomata are almost straight. The nasal spine is prominent.

The maxillary teeth are very much worn and decayed. Only carious stumps of the incisors and canines are left, the rest of the alveolus has absorbed. In the mandible both right incisors and the right canine have gone and the alveolus has absorbed. The left 1st incisor, 1st molar and 3rd molar have also gone and the alveolus has absorbed.

The manubrium is separate from the gladiolus. The 12th rib has faeces adhering to it, showing that the colon was full at the time of death. The sacrum is 6-pieced (5 sacral bones, plus 1st coccyx) and much curved. There is a facet present on the neck of both femora. There is very marked rheumatoid arthritis in the knee joints, hip joints, shoulder joints and sterno-clavicular joints. There is severe spondylitis of the lumbar, thoracic and cervical vertebrae and also in both ossa calcium.

References: Anatomical recording card.

1205   An artificially mummified body wrapped in bandages. There is no record of a coffin found with this burial and there is no evidence the mummy was dissected.

References: Firth (1912b, Plate 25A and 25B).

1215   A wrapped artificially mummified body with a cartonnage head mask, chest, leg and foot cartonnage pieces. There are thin strips of bandages running horizontally and across the mummy, over the cartonnage pieces. The mummy was found inside an anthropoid clay coffin. There is no evidence that the body was dissected.

References: Firth (1912b, Plate 32B and 32C).

1278   A poorly preserved, wrapped artificially mummified body with a cartonnage head mask, chest, leg and foot cartonnage pieces. There are thin strips of bandages running horizontally and across the mummy, over the cartonnage pieces. The mummy was found inside an anthropoid clay coffin. There is no evidence that the body was dissected.

References: A contact print from a glass photography plate survives in the George Andrew Reisner Archive, Museum of Fine Arts, Boston, US.

1377A   A male, adult artificially mummified body (skull only studied anatomically). The body was covered in resin, then wrapped in cloth.

Original anatomical observations: All cranial sutures are closed. The tori are very prominent and the mastoids are large. The zygomata are arched. There is left occipital bulging. The nasal spine is suppressed. The ethmoid is unperforated and the loose brain remains in the skull. Resin was poured into the mouth.

All teeth present are perfect in both jaws. The maxillary left 1st molar has disappeared and the alveolus is slightly absorbed. In the mandible both 2nd molars have disappeared and the alveolus is absorbed. There were never any 3rd molars.

References: Anatomical recording card.

1377B   A male, adult artificially mummified body (dissected). The body was wrapped in cloth.

Original anatomical observations: All cranial sutures are open. The tori and mastoids are small. The zygomata are nearly straight. The nasal spine is small. The ethmoid is perforated but there is no resin in the skull.

All teeth are present, perfect and little worn in both jaws, except the right 2nd bicuspid has gone in maxilla and the left 2nd molar has gone in the mandible. The alveolus is absorbed in both. There were never any 3rd molars.

The manubrium is separate from the gladiolus. The sacrum is 5-pieced, very narrow and very curved. The patellae are very small and notched.

References: Anatomical recording card.

Cemetery 90/500, Kuri

New Kingdom period

A small number of New Kingdom graves, with just 1 skeleton remaining in situ.

The following graves were found to be empty upon excavation: 2 (Firth 1912a, 197).

The following grave was recorded with no clear indication of whether it contained a body; it is likely to have been empty: 3 (Firth 1912a, 197).

1   A female skeleton, with no age recorded.

    References: Firth (1912a, 197).

Cemetery 91, Kuri

A-group period

A small A-group period cemetery which had previously been excavated by Prof John Garstang in 1900 (Firth 1912a, 9). Four bodies were recovered in 1909.

1   A skeleton, with no age or sex recorded.

    References: Firth (1912a, 198).

2   A skeleton, with no age or sex recorded.

    References: Firth (1912a, 198).

3   A skeleton, with no age or sex recorded.

    References: Firth (1912a, 198).

4   A skeleton, with no age or sex recorded.

    References: Firth (1912a, 198).

Cemetery 92, Aman Daud

A-group and X-group period

The small number of A-group burials in this cemetery have been denuded and disturbed by the X-group period burials that also occupy the cemetery (Firth 1912a, 9). The X-group burials had been largely plundered although there were a few intact graves. A single New Kingdom grave was also discovered in the cemetery.

The osteological material was well preserved and provided a considerable number of skulls and pathological examples according to Firth (1912a, 38). This is not however reflected in the surviving anatomical records for this cemetery which are unfortunately sparse. Forty-nine graves appear to have been excavated and only 22 still contained human remains.

A-group burials

The following graves were found to be empty upon excavation: 7, 8, 10, 11, 12, 14, 15, 16, 18, 20, 22, 27, 31, 32, 34, 35, 36, 37, 39, 40, 42, 44, 46, 51, 53, 58, 59, 60, 61, 62, 64, 73, 74, 76A, 93 (Firth 1912a, 199-201; Firth 1912b, Plan XIX).

The following graves were recorded with no clear indication of whether they contained a body; they are likely to have been empty: 1, 79 (Firth 1912a, 199-200).

3A A skeleton, with no age or sex recorded.

References: Firth (1912a, 199); Firth (1912b, Plan XIX).

3B A partial post-cranial skeleton, with no age or sex recorded. A tibia and foot only remain.

References: Firth (1912a, 199); Firth (1912b, Plan XIX).

9 A skeleton, with no age or sex recorded.

References: Firth (1912a, 199); Firth (1912b, Plan XIX).

80 A skeleton, with no age or sex recorded.

References: Firth (1912a, 200); Firth (1912b, Plan XIX).

83A A partial post-cranial skeleton, with no age or sex recorded. A femur and tibia only remain. The grave was cut through by 92:83 during the Christian period.

References: Firth (1912a, 200); Firth (1912b, Plan XIX).

95	A fragmentary skeleton, with no age or sex recorded.

	References: Firth (1912a, 201); Firth (1912b, Plan XIX).

96	A partial post-cranial skeleton, with no age or sex recorded. The legs only remain.

	References: Firth (1912a, 201); Firth (1912b, Plan XIX).

New Kingdom burials

2	A male skeleton, with no age recorded.

	References: Firth (1912a, 198-99); Firth (1912b, Plan XIX).

X-group burials

The following graves were found to be empty upon excavation: 5, 6, 17, 19, 21, 23, 24, 28, 29, 30, 41, 43, 45, 47, 50, 56, 68, 75, 76, 77, 82, 86, 87, 91, 98, 102 (Firth 1912b, XIX).

13	A disturbed infant skeleton, with no sex recorded.

	References: Firth (1912a, 201); Firth (1912b, Plan XIX).

26	A skeleton, with no age or sex recorded.

	References: Firth (1912a, 202); Firth (1912b, Plan XIX).

33	A child skeleton, with no sex recorded.

	References: Firth (1912a, 202); Firth (1912b, Plan XIX).

38	A child skeleton, with no sex recorded.

	References: Firth (1912a, 202); Firth (1912b, Plan XIX).

48	A male skeleton, with no age recorded.

	References: Firth (1912a, 202); Firth (1912b, Plan XIX).

49   A skeleton, with no age or sex recorded.

  References: Firth (1912b, Plan XIX).

52   A female skeleton, with no age recorded.

  References: Firth (1912b, Plan XIX); Watson (pre-1935).

  Body location: The skull was located in the Anatomical Museum, The University of Manchester when studied by Watson. The current location is unknown.

63   A child skeleton, with no sex recorded.

  References: Firth (1912a, 202); Firth (1912b, Plan XIX).

70   A disturbed skeleton, described as a 'young person'. No sex was recorded.

  References: Firth (1912a, 202); Firth (1912b, Plan XIX).

78   A skeleton, with no age or sex recorded.

  References: Firth (1912a, 202); Firth (1912b, Plan XIX).

97   A skeleton, with no age or sex recorded.

  References: Firth (1912a, 202-3); Firth (1912b, Plan XIX).

103   A skeleton, with no age or sex recorded.

  References: Firth (1912a, 203).

114   A male, aged skeleton.

  Original anatomical observations: There is a large depression of the frontal bone, measuring 37 x 18mm. There is a 'clean-cut' oval groove encircling the depression which has the appearance of having been produced artificially (a trephination).

  Further studies: The skull lesion was identified as an example of trauma and not trephination in subsequent publication (Derry 1909b, 15; Plate VII) (Figure 13).

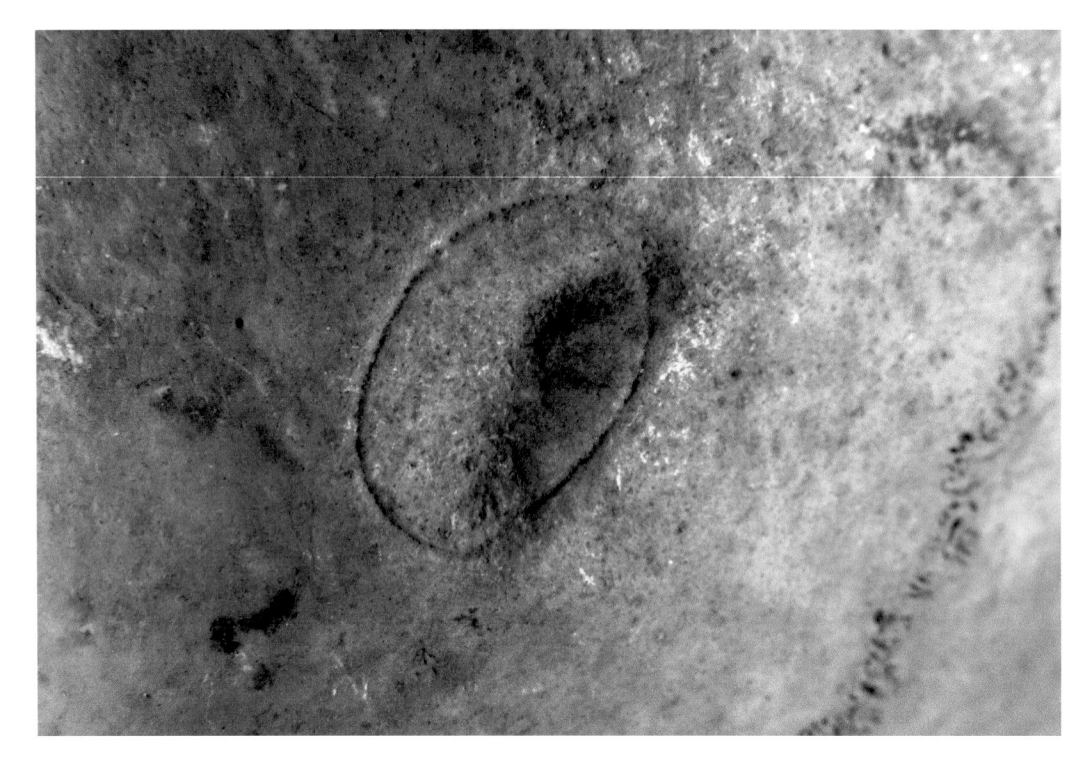

Figure 13: A healed depressed fracture identified by Smith and Derry in an adult male from cemetery 92, grave 114. The original publication of this fracture points out the potential for this to be mistakenly identified as evidence of trepanation. ©The Trustees of the Natural History Museum, London, 2023.

Surviving skeletal remains: The skull was originally part of the Nubian Pathological Collection at the Royal College of Surgeons. It now resides in the Natural History Museum, London (catalogue ref. NPC 13A). The location of the rest of the body is unknown.

References: Anatomical recording card; Smith and Derry (1910a, 15; Plate VII, Figure 4); Smith and Derry (1910b, 29); Nubian Pathological Collection surviving record card (specimen 13A).

121   A male, young adult skeleton.

Original anatomical observations: There are three sword cuts to the cranium – a blow to the left side of the frontal bone (A), a slicing blow to the left parietal (B) and a slicing cut through both parietal bones (C). The wounds were not afflicted at the same time.

Further studies: After consideration, Smith and Derry (1910b, 30) concluded that wound B was inflicted first, and that wounds A and C were likely to have been received at the same time (Figure 14). Both later wounds were thought to show signs of healing indicating that the man survived his injuries for several days or weeks.

Brothwell (1967, 67) briefly refers to this skull, discussing the severe damage experienced by this individual to the prefrontal region of their cerebral hemisphere during life.

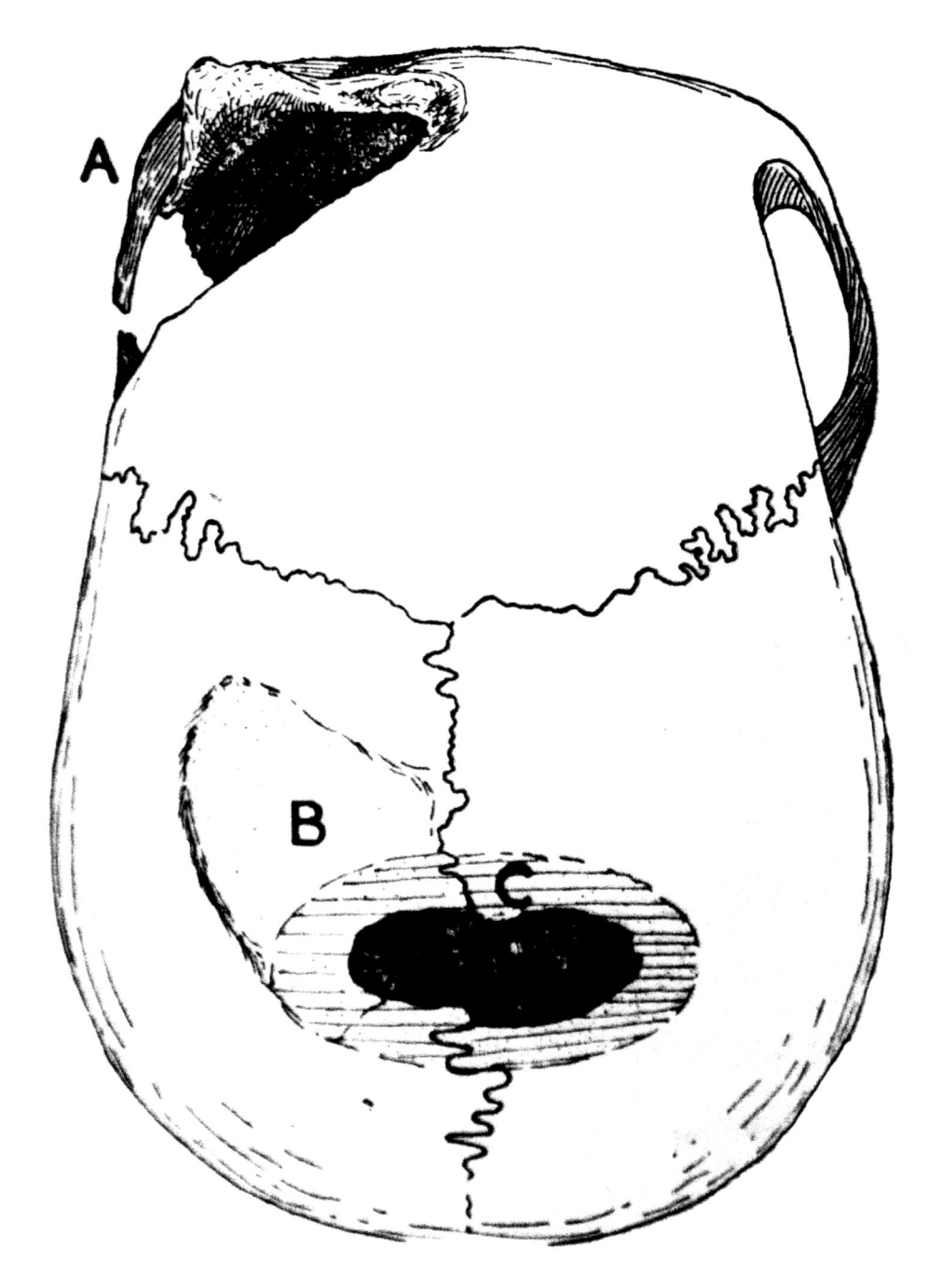

Figure 14: One of the original line diagrams produced by Smith and Derry, detailing three cranial injuries experienced by this adult male (cemetery 92, grave 121) (Adapted from Smith and Derry 1910a, Figure 1, 13).

Surviving skeletal remains: The skull and mandible were originally part of the Nubian Pathological Collection at the Royal College of Surgeons. They both now reside in the Natural History Museum, London (catalogue ref. NPC 15A). The location of the rest of the body is unknown.

References: Anatomical recording card; Smith and Derry (1910a, 13-14); Smith and Derry (1910b, 30); Brothwell (1967, 67), Nubian Pathological Collection surviving record card (specimen 15A)

137   A skeleton, with no age or sex recorded.

References: Firth (1912a, 203; Fig. 177).

Christian period burials

The following graves were found to be empty upon excavation: 25, 65, 66, 67, 69, 71, 72, 81, 83, 85 (Firth 1912a, 199; Firth 1912b, Plan XIX).

84   A skeleton, with no age or sex recorded.

References: Firth (1912b, Plan XIX).

90   A child skeleton, with no sex recorded.

References: Firth (1912a, 200); Firth (1912b, Plan XIX).

92   A skeleton, with no age or sex recorded.

References: Firth (1912a, 200); Firth (1912b, Plan XIX).

Cemeteries with no surviving human remains

Although the following cemeteries were given a number, there is no record of any burials being excavated from them:

Cemetery 60, East bank, Aqabaten - Roman period

No surviving description

Cemetery 61, East bank, Nagi-koleh - Roman period

No surviving description

Cemetery 63, West bank, Dendur - X-group and Christian period

Traces of X-group burials, along with extended Christian period burials were located 1 kilometre north of Dendur temple (Firth 1912a, 37). On the East bank directly opposite cemetery 63, there are circular pits of A-group (or possibly C-group period) and empty Roman period burials (one group of mud-cut tombs and one group of rock cut tombs). The description of the cemetery in bulletin 3 (Reisner 1909a, 8), appears to suggest that the East bank cemetery was excavated together with that on the West bank and that they are referred to with the same cemetery number.

There is no surviving information regarding the numbering of any of these graves or tombs. Firth's archaeological report records nothing for this cemetery and the surviving anatomical recording cards do not report any bodies from cemetery 63. Reisner's report (1908a) indicates that most, if not all of these were empty.

Cemetery 64, West bank, Metardul - New Kingdom (early Dynasty 18) period

An early New Kingdom cemetery that has been subject to considerable plundering. Firth (1912a, 28) thought this was likely to have been the cemetery for a small Egyptian colony or expedition, based on the discovery of a cowroid seal of the pharaoh Ahmose. Four graves numbered 1 to 4 were excavated but these were all devoid of human remains Firth (1912a, 62).

Cemetery 71/200, East bank, Sharaf el Din Togog - A-group to C-group period

Cemetery 71/200 is a poorly preserved cemetery containing 30 graves from the Early Dynastic (A-group) and C-group periods. It is situated on the south side of the same khor as cemetery 71/100. Firth (1912a, 79) does not describe any of the graves in detail and the short description provided indicates all of the graves (numbered 200 to 229 consecutively) were empty.

Area 84, the fortified town of Sabagura, East bank - Byzantine period

There are no burials from the area as the number was assigned to the fortress and surrounding structures (Firth 1909, 17).

References

Aufderheide, A. (2003). *The Scientific Study of Mummies.* Cambridge: Cambridge University Press.

Baker, B.J. and Judd, M.A. (2012). Development of Paleopathology in the Nile Valley. In: J. Buikstra and C. Roberts (eds). *The Global History of Paleopathology.* Oxford: Oxford University Press, 209-234.

Batrawi, A. (1945). The Racial History of Egypt and Nubia. *The Journal of the Royal Anthropological Institute of Great Britain and Ireland* 75(1/2), 81-101.

Berman, L.M. (2018). *Unearthing Ancient Nubia*, Boston: MFA Publications.

Brothwell, D. (1967). The Biocultural Background to Disease. In: D. Brothwell and A.T. Sandison (eds) *Diseases in Antiquity: A Survey of the Diseases, Injuries, and Surgery of Early Populations.* Springfield, Illinois: Charles C. Thomas, 56-68.

Brothwell, D. (1967). The Evidence for Neoplasms. In: D. Brothwell and A.T. Sandison (eds) *Diseases in Antiquity: A Survey of the Diseases, Injuries, and Surgery of Early Populations.* Springfield, Illinois: Charles C. Thomas, 320-345.

Carruthers, W., Niala, J.C., Davis, S., Challis, D., Schiappacasse, P.A., Dixon, S., Milosavljević, M., Moore, L., Nevell, R., Fitzpatrick, A., Abd el Gawad, H. and Stevenson, A. (2021). Special Issue: Inequality and Race in the Histories of Archaeology. *Bulletin of the History of Archaeology* 31(1), 1–19.

Challis, D. (2013). *The Archaeology of Race. The Eugenic Ideas of Francis Galton and Flinders Petrie.* London: Bloomsbury.

Cockitt, J. (2014). Whose body? The human remains from the 1908-09 season of the Archaeological Survey of Nubia. In Metcalfe, R et al. (eds). *Palaeopathology in Egypt and Nubia: A Century in Review.* Oxford: Archaeopress Egyptology 6, 9-22.

Derry, D.E. (1909a). Anatomical Report (B). In: G.A. Reisner, G.E. Smith and D.E. Derry, eds. *The Archaeological Survey of Nubia. Bulletin III.* Cairo: National Printing Department, 29-52.

Derry, D.E. (1909b). Field Notes. In: C.M. Firth, G.A. Reisner, G.E. Smith and D.E. Derry, eds. *The Archaeological Survey of Nubia. Bulletin IV.* Cairo: National Printing Department, 22-28.

Derry, D.E. (1911a). Damage done to Skulls and Bones by Termites. *Nature* 86, 45-46.

Derry, D.E. (1911b). Note on Accessory Articular Facets between the Sacrum and Ilium, and their Significance. *Journal of Anatomy* 45(3), 202-10.

Firth, C.M. (1910). Description of Cemeteries Nos. 81-84 and 90-92. In: C.M. Firth, G.A. Reisner, G.E. Smith and D.E. Derry, (eds). *The Archaeological Survey of Nubia. Bulletin V.* Cairo: National Printing Department, 11-25.

Firth, C.M. (1912a). *The Archaeological Survey of Nubia. Report for 1908-1909 Vol. I.* Cairo: Government Press.

Firth, C.M. (1912b). *The Archaeological Survey of Nubia. Report for 1908-1909 Vol. II. Plates and Plans accompanying Vol. 1.* Cairo: Government Press.

Jones, F.W. (1910). Anatomical Variations and the Determination of the Age and Sex of Skeletons. In: G.E. Smith and F.W. Jones (eds). *The Archaeological Survey of Nubia Report for 1907-1908. Volume II.* Cairo: National Printing Dept, 221-262.

McKenzie, W. and Brothwell, D. (1967). Diseases in the Ear Region. In D. Brothwell and A.T. Sandison (eds) *Diseases in Antiquity: A Survey of the Diseases, Injuries, and Surgery of Early Populations.* Springfield, Illinois; Charles C. Thomas, 464-473.

Molleson, T. (1993). The Nubian Pathological Collection in the Natural History Museum, London. In W.V. Davies and R. Walker (eds). *Biological Anthropology and the Study of Ancient Egypt.* London: British Museum Press, 136-143.

Morse, D. (1967) Tuberculosis. In D. Brothwell and A.T. Sandison (eds) *Diseases in Antiquity: A Survey of the Diseases, Injuries, and Surgery of Early Populations.* Springfield, Illinois; Charles C. Thomas, 249-271.

Pettigrew, T.J. (1834). *A History of Egyptian Mummies.* London: Longman, Rees, Orme, Brown, Green & Longman

Quickel, A.T. and Williams, G. (2016). In Search of Sibakh: Digging Up Egypt from Antiquity to the Present Day. *Journal of Islamic Archaeology* 3(1), 89–108.

Reddie, L.C.R. (2003). *An Osteological and Palaeopathological Analysis of the Elliot Smith Human Skeletal Collection housed at the Manchester Museum.* Manchester: University of Manchester, Unpublished MSc Dissertation.

Reisner, G.A. (1909a). The Archaeological Survey of Nubia. In: G.A. Reisner, G.E. Smith and D.E. Derry, eds. *The Archaeological Survey of Nubia. Bulletin III.* Cairo: National Printing Department, 5-20.

Reisner, G.A. (1909b). The Archaeological Survey of Nubia. In: C.M. Firth, G.A. Reisner, G.E. Smith and D.E. Derry, eds. *The Archaeological Survey of Nubia. Bulletin III.* Cairo: National Printing Department, 7-16.

Smith, G.E. (1909) Anatomical Report A. In: G.A. Reisner, G.E. Smith and D.E. Derry (eds) *The Archaeological Survey of Nubia. Bulletin III.* Cairo: National Printing Department, 21-27.

Smith, G.E. (1910). Introduction. In Smith, G.E. and Jones, F.W. (eds). *The Archaeological Survey of Nubia 1907-08 Vol II. Report on the Human Remains.* Cairo: Government Press, 7-14.

Smith, G.E. and Derry, D.E. (1910a). Anatomical Report. In: C.M. Firth, G.A. Reisner, G.E. Smith and D.E. Derry, eds. *The Archaeological Survey of Nubia. Bulletin V.* Cairo: National Printing Department, 11-25.

Smith, G.E. and Derry, D.E. (1910b). Anatomical Report. In: C.M. Firth, G.E. Smith and D.E. Derry, eds. *The Archaeological Survey of Nubia. Bulletin VI.* Cairo: National Printing Department, 9-30.

Smith, G.E. and Jones, F.W. (1910). *The Archaeological Survey of Nubia 1907-08 Vol II. Report on the Human Remains.* Cairo: Government Press.

Watson, J.V., (pre1935). *Osteometrical Data* [Workbook]. RCS-MUS/7/8/13. Royal College of Surgeons Archive, London.

Index: Pathology, trauma, non-metric traits and minor anatomical variations

This index provides a quick reference guide to the examples of pathology, trauma, non-metric traits and minor anatomical variations recorded for the ASN season two bodies. The index is divided into individual body parts or bones in alphabetical order to make referencing easier. Body numbers are referred to in brackets as they were in the ASN reports, bulletins and other publications – (cemetery:grave).

Clavicle:

Fracture: (74:12), (74:15), (89:570)

Unspecified necrotic process: (72:253)

Undefined pathological condition: (76:87)

Coccyx:

Sacral-coccygeal fusion: (58:7), (58:18), (58:100), (58:109), (58:118), (58:120), (68:8), (69:17), (69:27), (69:41), (69:85), (69:88), (69:90), (69:UNKN), (72:16A), (72:17B), (72:25A), (72:60), (72:90), (72:91), (72:112), (72:114), (72:180), (72:268), (72:226), (72:326), (72:360), (72:384), (72:422), (72:337), (72:387), (72:433), (74:12), (74:58), (74:507), (76:76), (76:77), (76:81), (76:142), (79:2), (86:205), (86:208), (86:266A), (86:267), (86:305), (87:12), (87:48), (87:57), (87:58), (87:79), (87:83), (87:96A), (87:104), (87:106), (89:673B), (89:683A), (89:731), (89:775), (89:797A), (89:797C), (89:810), (89:812B), (89:1154)

Cranium:

Cleft palate: (72:91)

Epipteric bones: (68:10), (69:36), (69:40), (69:48), (69:61), (69:101), (72:16A), (72:41), (72:44), (72:88), (73:72), (73:102), (72:93), (72:162), (72:263), (72:269), (72:360), (72:440), (72:445), (72:422), (72:425), (74:5), (74:81), (74:506), (76:81), (76:87), (76:14C), (76:14D), (76:14G), (76:26A), (76:36A), (76:52), (76:52A), (76:58), (76:81), (76:106), (76:127), (76:134), (77:1), (79:66A), (79:111), (87:15), (87:25), (87:33), (87:84), (87:96A), (87:96B), (87:153), (89:577), (89:772), (89:812B), (89:852), (89:1152)

Fracture: (58:9), (58:119), (69:24(A)), (72:79), (74:12), (74:68), (76:77), (76:134), (79:135A[2]), (89:772)

Mastoiditis: (72:61), (72:309), (74:70), (76:83), (76:108)

Metopic suture: (58:17), (69:21), (69:41), (69:48), (69:64), (73:108), (76:81), (74:514), (76:81), (79:11), (79:111), (79:165), (79:166A), (79:166), (89:583), (89:711A), (89:711B), (89:752), (89:802)

Nasal bone fracture: (72:166)

Nasopharangeal carcinoma: (72:41)

Occipital plagiocephaly: (69:26), (69:27), (69:40), (69:44), (69:48), (69:66), (69:71), (69:73), (69:81), (69:91A), (69:92), (69:200D), (72:18), (72:19C), (72:19D), (72:24B), (72:25A), (72:25B), (72:41), (72:48), (72:54), (72:61), (73:5), (73:60), (73:72), (73:102), (72:91), (72:113), (72:114), (72:150), (72:239), (72:243), (72:253), (72:268), (72:269), (72:271), (72:309), (72:327), (72:334), (72:341), (72:362),

267

(72:392), (72:426), (72:420), (72:433), (72:440), (72:445), (72:464), (72:474), (72:476), (74:3), (74:5), (74:12), (74:15), (74:25), (74:58), (74:61), (74:70), (74:81), (76:14A), (76:14B), (76:14D), (76:14E), (76:18), (76:23), (76:26A), (76:27B), (76:35), (76:36A), (76:36B), (76:44B), (76:52), (76:52A), (76:55), (76:72), (76:74), (76:76), (76:77), (76:81), (76:82), (76:87), (76:99), (76:106), (76:108), (76:116), (76:130), (76:142), (77:1), (77:115), (79:2), (79:3), (85:56), (87:33), (87:42), (87:98), (87:102), (87:103), (87:110), (87:125), (89:601B), (89:711), (89:772), (89:810), (89:1154), (89:1377A).

Osteitis: (72:150)

Osteoarthritis, tempero-mandibular articulation: (72:387), (87:96B), (72:150)

Parietal thinning: (72:93), (72:237), (76:77), (76:89)

Sinusitis: (76:77)

Third occipital condyle: (76:76)

Unspecified craniosynostosis: (72:64)

Wormian bones: (58:120), (59:1A), (69:20), (69:44), (69:48), (69:UNKN (west of 48)), (69:74), (69:81), (69:101), (69:200D), (69:UNKN), (72:24A), (72:24B), (72:25A), (72:49), (72:79), (72:90), (73:108), (72:360), (72:383), (72:385), (72:392), (72:425), (72:464), (73:60), (74:23), (74:81), (76:81), (76:99), (76:116), (76:125), (77:1), (79:166A), (85:36), (85:37), (85:38), (87:103), (89:583), (89:733)

Dentition:

Ante-mortem tooth loss: (58:5), (58:8), (58:13), (58:18), (58:102), (58:109), (58:113), (58:121), (58:125), (59:1A), (59:1B), (59:2), (68:9), (68:10), (68:12), (68:14), (68:17), (68:24), (68:24(A)), (68:28), (68:57), (68:85), (68:88), (72:16A), (72:16B), (72:17A), (72:18), (72:19A), (72:19D), (72:20), (72:22), (72:24B), (72:25B), (72:27B), (72:41), (72:44), (72:60), (72:88), (72:90), (72:93), (72:106), (72:112), (72:150), (72:166), (72:273), (72:433), (72:464), (72:474), (73:10), (73:72), (74:3), (74:5), (74:6), (74:12), (74:23), (74:25), (74:53), (74:58), (74:61), (74:68), (74:70), (74:84), (74:507), (76:18), (76:24), (76:26A), (76:27A), (76:27B), (76:36B), (76:44A), (76:125), (77:115(A)), (79:10A), (85:31B), (85:38), (85:62), (86:52), (86:205), (86:206), (86:295), (86:305), (87:69), (87:76), (87:93), (87:102), (87:103), (87:157), (89:577), (89:601B), (89:673), (89:711A), (89:711B), (89:731), (89:752), (89:772), (89:797B), (89:797C), (89:1154), (89:1377A), (89:1377B)

Caries: (58:106B), (58:117), (58:118), (58:121), (58:125), (59:1A), (59:2), (69:20), (69:23), (72:19B), (72:88), (72:112), (72:392), (74:5), (74:6), (74:15), (74:19), (74:23), (74:53), (74:70), (74:81), (74:84), (76:14C), (76:23), (76:26A), (76:44A), (76:52), (76:52A), (76:74), (76:87), (76:99), (76:106), (76:125), (85:43A), (86:34), (86:52), (86:208), (86:266B), (86:267), (86:295), (86:305), (89:173), (89:677), (89:711B), (89:731), (89:752), (89:772), (89:797A), (89:810), (89:812B), (89:1154).

Dental abscesses: (58:8), (58:19), (58:125), (69:41), (72:19B), (72:20), (72:22), (72:24B), (72:41), (72:48), (72:60), (72:77), (72:79), (72:88), (73:10), (73:60), (73:72), (72:93), (72:106), (72:166), (72:180), (72:226), (72:243), (72:271), (72:273), (72:309), (72:341), (72:343), (72:383), (72:387), (72:392), (72:433), (72:464), (74:3), (74:5), (74:6), (74:15), (74:23), (74:53), (76:14F), (76:14G), (76:18), (76:23), (76:24), (76:26A), (76:27A), (76:27B), (76:44A), (76:139), (76:83), (77:115), (78:18), (79:135A^2), (79:164), (79:165), (79:167), (86:34), (85:43A), (86:52), (86:206), (86:267), (86:295), (87:28), (87:36), (87:84), (87:93), (87:103), (87:117), (87:131), (87:157), (89:677), (89:731), (89:752), (89:772), (89:797A), (89:797B), (89:797C), (89:810), (89:812A), (89:858), (89:861).

Dental calculus: (74:70), (74:84), (76:14C), (76:77)

INDEX: PATHOLOGY, TRAUMA, NON-METRIC TRAITS AND MINOR ANATOMICAL VARIATIONS

Retained deciduous tooth: (74:53), (87:15), (89:614), (89:673A)

Supernumerary tooth: (58:110), (69:20), (72:262), (72:337), (74:15), (76:35), (85:43A), (89:858)

Third molar agenesis: (69:20), (69:49), (69:57), (69:73), (72:226), (72:241), (72:253), (72:273), (72:425), (74:15), (76:14D), (78:18), (79:2), (79:165), (85:62), (86:208), (89:614), (89:810), (89:1377A), (89:1377B)

Elbow joint:

Rheumatoid arthritis: (72:24A)

Femur:

Femoral neck facet: (58:9), (58:10), (58:18), (58:112B), (58:115), (58:117), (58:120), (58:123B), (58:124), (69:14), (69:15), (69:16), (69:18), (69:48), (69:UNKN, west of 48), (69:52), (69:61), (69:66), (69:81), (69:85), (69:92), (69:200A), (69:200B), (69:200C), (72:16B), (72:17A), (72:19A), (72:48), (72:61), (73:37), (73:38), (73:88), (73:90), (72:93), (72:112), (72:114), (72:226), (72:237), (72:270), (72:311),(72:341), (72:360), (72:377), (72:382), (72:385), (72:387), (72:426), (72:445), (74:12), (74:13), (74:15), (74:53), (74:68), (74:511), (74:514), (76:18), (76:35), (76:76), (76:82), (76:83), (76:87), (76:106), (76:142), (76:143), (77:115), (79:2), (79:124), (79:159), (79:168), (85:29), (85:56), (87:17), (87:83), (87:85), (87:93), (87:98), (87:99), (87:100), (87:105), (87:102), (87:104), (87:117), (87:125), (89:614), (89:673B), (89:686), (89:687B), (89:731), (89:733), (89:772), (89:797B), (89:1161A), (89:1154)

Femoral torsion: (58:4), (58:9), (58:9), (58:10), (58:14), (69:49)

Fracture: (68:8), (69:28), (72:44), (74:12), (74:68), (76:94), (79:124(A)), (87:10), (89:855)

Osteophytic lipping: (89:686)

Periostitis: (79:136C)

Platymeria: (69:36), (69:57), (72:88), (76:58)

Rheumatoid arthritis: (72:17A), (72:464),

Fibula:

Fracture: (74:68), (89:797A)

Tibiofibula synostosis – see under Tibia

Foot:

Metatarsal fracture: (89:673B)

Periostitis: - see under Femur

Semi-lunar and cuneiform fusion: (89:711A)

Gout: (85:29)

269

Hand:

Gout – see under Foot

Hip joint:

Dislocation: (86:208)

Humerus:

Fracture: (72:16A), (72:368), (72:383), (89:754)

Humeral septal apertures: (71:10B), (79:65), (79:66A), (79:66B), (79:89)

Giant cell tumour: (89:686)

Unspecified necrotic process – see under Clavicle

Supracondyloid process: (58:113)

Knee joint:

Septic arthritis: (87:117)

Rheumatoid arthritis: (72:106)

Mandible:

Fracture: (89:855)

Osteoarthritis, tempero-mandibular articulation – see under Cranium

Patella:

Fracture: (79:13)

Notched patella: (58: 2), (58:3), (58:4), (58:9), (58:13), (58:14), (58:105), (58:112B), (58:122), (71:10B), (72:16A), (72:19B), (72:226), (72:268), (74:58), (77:115), (78:18), (79:3), (87:76), (87:84), (87:94), (87:96B), (87:98), (87:100), (87:110), (89:687B), (89:917), (89:1377B)

Rheumatoid arthritis: (89:1154)

Pelvis:

Fracture: (79:144(A))

Sacroiliac fusion: (69:24(A)), (72:60), (72:372), (74:61), (74:169), (89:627)

Rider's bone: (79:13)

Rheumatoid arthritis: (89:1154)

Phalanges:

Fusion, 2nd and 3rd phalanges: (76:89)

Radius:

Fracture: (59:3A), (69:7), (72:88), (72:90), (72:383), (72:474), (79:144(A)), (87:10), (87:96B)

Osteitis: (86:206)

Periostitis: - see under Femur

Ribs:

Bifid rib: (72:445), (74:58), (79:136)

Cervical rib: (72:476), (89:731), (58:118), (58:18)

Fracture: (72:382), (74:68)

Sacrum:

Possible rectal cancer: (72: 368)

Possible partial sacral agenesis: (69:26), (69:90), (89:772)

Sacral-coccygeal fusion – see under Coccyx

Sacroiliac fusion – see under Pelvis

Sacralisation: (69:17), (69:18), (69:58), (69:90), (69:200A), (72:384), (73:60), (87:25), (89:687B), (89:711A)

Tuberculosis (Potts Disease) - see under Vertebrae

Spina bifida occulta: (72:19B)

Unilateral sacral fusion: (76:18)

Scapula:

Separate acromion process: (72:177)

Undefined pathological condition – see under Clavicle

Unspecified necrotic process – see under Clavicle

Shoulder joint:

Septic arthritis – see under Knee

Sub-coracoid dislocation: (74:12)

Rheumatoid arthritis: (89:1154), (72:44)

Sterno-clavicular joint:

Rheumatoid arthritis: (89:1154)

Sternum:

Bifid xiphoid process: (74:68)

Undefined inflammatory process, interclavicular notch: (72:368)

Unspecified necrotic process – see under Clavicle

Sternal foramen: (72:20), (72:384), (74:53), (74:15), (76:5), (76:89), (87:96A), (87:125), (89:570), (89:687B)

Tibia:

Fracture: (87:84), (74:68), (89:797A)

Osteophytic lipping: (89:686), (72:17A)

Periostitis: - see under Femur

Platycnemia: (58:3), (58:10), (58:105), (58:112B), (68:5), (69:14), (69:15), (69:16), (69:21), (71:10B), (72:17A), (72:77), (72:88), (72:237), (72:268), (72:279), (76:77), (78:18), (79:148), (79:166), (87:83), (87:100), (87:103), (89:673A), (89:683A), (89:858), (89:861)

Retroversion, tibial head: (69:49)

Rheumatoid arthritis: (72:17A)

Tibiofibula synostosis: (89:627)

Ulna:

Fracture: (58:121), (59:3A), (69:7), (69:200A), (72:49), (72:383), (76:83), (87:10), (87:96B)

Periostitis: - see under Femur

Vertebrae:

Additional sacral bone: (72:166), (89:812A)

Laminae fissure, lumbar: (89:622)

Lumbarisation: (72:226), (76:127)

Occipitalization: (58:3), (58:115), (69:15), (69:65), (72:19C), (72:79), (72:323), (74:13), (76:26A), (76:134)

Sacralisation: see under Sacrum

Index: Pathology, trauma, non-metric traits and minor anatomical variations

Sixth lumbar vertebra: (69:17), (72:19B)

Spondylitis: (58:5), (58:16), (58:18), (58:102), (58:121), (68:10), (69:14), (69:17), (69:20), (69:26), (69:88), (69:200A), (72:16A), (72:19A), (72:24A), (72:44), (72:48), (72:79), (72:88), (72:112), (72:180), (72:341), (72:384), (72:387), (72:474), (74:12), (74:61), (76:26A), (76:89), (79:2), (79:3), (79:9), (79:167), (86:205), (86:206), (87:5), (87:12), (87:48), (87:58), (87:63), (87:71), (87:36), (87:89), (87:96A), (87:96B), (87:103), (87:106), (87:117), (89:601B), (89:819), (89:1154).

Tuberculosis (Potts disease): (58: 100), (89:570), (89:855)

Unfused posterior arch, atlas: (69:200A), (72:19B), (89:570)

Unfused posterior arch, lumbar: (58:19), (72:24A), (72:54), (74:19), (77:1), (87:117)

Unspecified necrotic process – see under Clavicle

Unspecified wear, lumbar vertebrae: (72:16B)

Appendix I

List of surviving skeletal elements identified from season 2

ASN no.	Sex	Period	Bone(s)	Location
58:03	Male	C-group	Skull, mandible	The University of Cambridge
58:14	Female	C-group	Skull	The University of Cambridge
58:110	Male	C-group	Skull	The University of Cambridge
58:119	Female	New Kingdom	Skull, mandible	The University of Cambridge
58:##	Unknown	C-group	Vertebrae	Natural History Museum, London
58:##	Unknown	C-group	Vertebrae	Natural History Museum, London
60:##	Unknown	Unknown	Skull	The University of Cambridge
62:##	Male	Unknown	Skull, mandible	The University of Cambridge
69:04	Unknown	Unknown	Skull, mandible	The University of Cambridge
69:20	Female	C-group	Skull	The University of Manchester
69:48	Male	C-group	Skull	The University of Cambridge
71:100	Unknown	Unknown	Skull, mandible	The University of Cambridge
72:19A	Female	Christian	Coccyx	The University of Cambridge
72:41	Male	X-group	Skull	Natural History Museum, London
72:91	Female	X-group	Skull	Natural History Museum, London
72:239	Male	C-group	Skull	The University of Manchester

APPENDIX I

ASN no.	Sex	Period	Bone(s)	Location
72:257	Male	C-group	Skull	The University of Manchester
72:273	Female	C-group	Skull, mandible	The University of Cambridge
72:365	Female	C-group	Radius	The University of Manchester
72:368	Male	C-group	Sternum	The University of Cambridge
72:445	Male	C-group	Skull, mandible	The University of Cambridge
73:102	Female	C-group	Skull, mandible	The University of Cambridge
73:108	Female	C-group	Skull, mandible	The University of Cambridge
74:12	Male	Christian	Partial skeleton	The University of Cambridge
74:15	Male	Christian	Skull, mandible, ossified larynx	The University of Cambridge
75:88	Unknown	Unknown	Post-cranial skeleton	The University of Cambridge
76:15D	Female	Unknown	Skull	The University of Cambridge
76:81	Male	Unknown	Partial skeleton	The University of Cambridge
76:87	Female	Unknown	Skull, mandible	The University of Cambridge
76:106	Female	C-group	Innominate	The University of Manchester
76:##	Unknown	Unknown	Radius	The University of Manchester
79:166	Male	A-group	Sacrum	The University of Manchester
83:107	Unknown	C-group	Post-cranial skeleton	The University of Cambridge
87:33	Female	C-group	Skull	The University of Manchester
87:39	Unknown	C-group	Skull, pelvis	The University of Cambridge

ASN no.	Sex	Period	Bone(s)	Location
87:79	Male	C-group	Radius	The University of Manchester
87:89	Female	C-group	Skull	The University of Manchester
87:98	Male	C-group	Tibia, radius, ulna and both humerii	The University of Manchester
87:99	Male	C-group	Innominate, humerus	The University of Manchester
87:100	Male	C-group	Femur, both tibiae	The University of Manchester
87:104	Male	C-group	Both humerii, radius	The University of Manchester
87:117	Male	C-group	Sacrum, ulna	The University of Manchester
87:##	Unknown	Unknown	Femur	The University of Manchester
87:##	Unknown	Unknown	Humerus	The University of Manchester
87:##	Unknown	Unknown	Ulna	The University of Manchester
89:686	Male	A-group	Left humerus, left scapula	Natural History Museum, London
89:754	Male	A-group	Left humerus	Natural History Museum, London
89:794	Male	Roman	Wrapped mummy	South Australia Museum, Adelaide
89:##	Unknown	Unknown	Fibula	The University of Manchester
89:##	Unknown	Unknown	Radius	The University of Manchester
89:##	Unknown	Unknown	Sacrum	The University of Manchester
92:114	Male	X-group	Skull, mandible	Natural History Museum, London
92:121	Male	X-group	Skull	Natural History Museum, London

Appendix IIa

Cranial measurements from anatomical recording cards produced by Douglas Derry and Sir Grafton Elliot Smith (part 1)

Facial base	91	88	98	99	102	93	94	103	97	90	101	94	99	111	103
Cranial base	92	91	100	103	103	105	95	89	100	97	108	91	100	100	99
Upper facial height	61.5		70	67	64	64	65.5		66	68	60	61	62	65	66
Total facial height	103.5		110	113	117	108.5	102		114	113	102	104	107.5	113	117.5
Bizygomatic breadth	115	114	123	120	120	125.5	118.5		123	120.5	126	113	130	124	121
Auricular height					118	112		110.5	111.5	112	106	108		102	
Bas. Height	125	128	129	132	144	140.5	133		136	127	148	125	129	~128	126	134
Front. Breadth	87.5	88	92	87	94	95	86		90	87	91	85	90.5	90	95	87
Max. breadth	128	134	133.5	128	130	137	126		134	132	135.5	127	131.5		132	128
Max. length	179	182	175	183	188	189	175		185	171	186	170	181.5		185	182
Length-breadth index																
Nasal index	57.47	57.14	54	44.44	54.09	48	53.06		50.96	46.6	63.53	62.65	57.61	55.81	48	
Grave	106A	106B	106C	106D	106E	774	775	832	835	840	846	848	875	2	3	5
Cemetery	55	55	55	55	55	55	55	55	55	55	55	55	55	58	58	58

The Archaeological Survey of Nubia Season 2 (1908-9). Report on the Human Remains

Facial base		99			100	100	89	99			102		98	91	103			
Cranial base		98			104	104	102	100			102		94	91	105		110	
Upper facial height		69			66	68	66	65			64		67	63	71			
Total facial height		123			114	111	108	114			110		110.5					
Bizygomatic breadth		127			120	~114		126					121		124		127	
Auricular height		116			100	107	122	97		100	106	114	113	104	110		116	
Bas. Height		131			129.5	133	140	132		127	124		125	129	136		136.5	
Front. Breadth	93	98			90	95	90	89		88	90	88	86	82.5	92		91	
Max. breadth		134			123.5	130	134	139		125	129	131	132	134.5	131		134	
Max. length		179		167.5	174	177	185	187		172	186	188	187	172	186		192	
Length-breadth index																		
Nasal index		49.06		42.31	56.38	46.94	50	49.02			47.82		57.14	57.77	57.77			
Grave	8	9	12	13	14	17	18	19	20	100	101	102	105	106A	106B	108	109	110
Cemetery	58	58	58	58	58	58	58	58	58	58	58	58	58	58	58	58	58	58

Appendix IIa

	Grave 111	Grave 112B	Grave 113	Grave 115	Grave 116	Grave 117	Grave 118	Grave 119	Grave 120	Grave 121	Grave 122	Grave 123A	Grave 123B	Grave 124	Grave 125	Grave 126	Grave 127	Grave 1A
Facial base				106	104	96.5	102	93	97	100	106		93	98		94	102	
Cranial base				104	103	91	98	94	103	102	109		99	103	100		100	101
Upper facial height				70	65	63	61	72	63.5	71			69		74		68	65
Total facial height				117	112	113	101	120	107.5	112			120		125		120	111
Bizygomatic breadth					120	116	118		124.5	~127			126.5	126			122	124
Auricular height				108	112	104	106	107	113	115	113.5		112	114.5	107.5		111.5	108
Bas. Height				129	133	120	132	128	131	131	130.5		135.5	132	130.5		137	136
Front. Breadth				88	95	89	93.5	89	91	90	91.5		89		93		93	94
Max. breadth				137	135	131	131	132	~126	133	135		~137	137	133		137	132
Max. length				188	182	171	173	179	179	184	191	189	184	184	188.5		180	184
Length-breadth index																		71.74
Nasal index				50	52.08	53.33	48.93	60.46	57.77	46.29	43.75		49.05		51.96		48.08	69.05
Grave	111	112B	113	115	116	117	118	119	120	121	122	123A	123B	124	125	126	127	1A
Cemetery	58	58	58	58	58	58	58	58	58	58	58	58	58	58	58	58	58	59

Facial base	98	105	95	94	100	92.5	99		93.5	102			90.5	~91	93		97	99
Cranial base	97	102	95	94	104.5	92.5	103		100	102			95.5	100	92	92	101	100
Upper facial height	61	63	64	56.5			65.5		60				60.5	66.5	67		65	68.5
Total facial height	105.5	104.5	109				105.5		105				103	99.5			111	118.5
Bizygomatic breadth	115	120	115	119	122	122			121.5	121			114	115	122		133	139
Auricular height	110	110	113	105	112	112	117.5			109			110	115	104		111.5	112
Bas. Height	126	128	132	120.5	130.5	126.5	132		126	135		125	126.5	132	128	121	133.5	135
Front. Breadth	91	87	90	87	97	88	97		88	89			85.5	90	90.5	91	92	98
Max. breadth	131	129	122	124	130.5	138.5	146.5		130	137.5		122	124	132.5	129	128	138.5	136.5
Max. length	179	183.5	177	172.5	184	183	172		175	189		167	177	175	178	172	186	180
Length-breadth index	73.18	70.30	68.92	71.88	70.92	75.68	85.1		74.2	72.2		73.05	70.06	75.7	72.47	74.42	74.4	75.8
Nasal index	56.7	57.95	63.95	56.10	45.19	52.87	51.5		53	46			57.14	48.4	53.33	45.2	50	47.2
Grave	1B	2	3A	3B	4	5	UNKN	2	9	10	12	15	20	24	7	12	14	15
Cemetery	59	59	59	59	59	59	62	68	68	68	68	68	68	68	69	69	69	69

Appendix IIa

Facial base	103.5	102	96	102	92	95	94	96.5	98	96	98.5	96.5	94	104.5	103		102	96
Cranial base	105	99	99	98	95	100	100.5	96	104.5	93	94.5	96.5	97	97	104		99	98
Upper facial height	70	75	68	69		66.5	65		74	65	58	68	58	71	73	69	73	69
Total facial height	119.5	122	113	115.5		~114	118		124	~115	~95	115	105	118.5		117.5	125	114
Bizygomatic breadth		125	128	122		~122	132		129	117.5	126	120	125	129		129	124
Auricular height	115	111.5	108	110	102		106.5	105.5	113	106	107.5	110		111	110		116	112.5
Bas. Height	136	129	129	129	125	130	126.5	130.5	132.5	126.5	118.5	131.5	129	129	132		135.5	132
Front. Breadth	89	96	93	92	96	84	92	94	92	94.5	86	90	95	97	90		100	89
Max. breadth	130.5	132.5	~136	133		136	140	133	139	137.5	131.5	128	140		132		141	133
Max. length	177	176	184	183		180	182	169	186	172	176	178	184.5	178	184	176	175	181
Length-breadth index	73.7	75.2	73.9	72.68		75.56	76.9	78.7	74.7	79.9	74.7	71.91	75.8		71.7		80.5	73.4
Nasal index	50	51.5	55.7	50.98	57.1	54.6	47.1	49.4	44.5	55.3	50	51.02	63.1	58.3	44.4	42.45	52.8	41.7
Grave	16	17	18	20	21	23	24	25	26	27	28	36	40	41	44	45	48	west of 48
Cemetery	69	69	69	69	69	69	69	69	69	69	69	69	69	69	69	69	69	69

Facial base	105					91	96	~92	90	~82	102.5		98	102	102	101	92	~90
Cranial base	99					92	89	100	94	98	105		98	102	102	99	99	91
Upper facial height	67		65		70	60.5	62	60	66		63		67	71	70	70	~66	
Total facial height	112		~113		114	109	101		105.5		112		118	123	118			
Bizygomatic breadth	113					115	116	121	125	119	125		135	129	125.5	133	117	
Auricular height	115					107	97	112	113		105	113	113.5	117	116	105.5	110.5	
Bas. Height	130					126	111	125	133	134	139	119	132.5	135	136	134	128	126
Front. Breadth	91					90	95	95	85	88	94	94	84	92	84	91	93	86
Max. breadth	125.5					129	126	128	124	129	137	130.5	128	138	129	130	129	131
Max. length	183	200				173	170	190	176	180	182.5	180	183	184	176	178	184	176
Length-breadth index	68.7					74.5	74.1	67.3	70.4	71.6	78.3	72.5	69.9	75	73.3	73.03	70.1	74.4
Nasal index	53.1		53.7		44.2	57.8	46.1	58.7	60.4	46.1	51.06		47.9	50.9	50	50.9	45.1	67.4
Grave	49	52	57	58	60	61	64	66	70	71	72	73	74	81	85	88	89	90
Cemetery	69	69	69	69	69	69	69	69	69	69	69	69	69	69	69	69	69	69

Appendix IIa

Cemetery	Grave	Nasal index	Length-breadth index	Max. length	Max. breadth	Front. Breadth	Bas. Height	Auricular height	Bizygomatic breadth	Total facial height	Upper facial height	Cranial base	Facial base
69	91A	50.5	74.1	178	132	84	122	105	113		57.5	88	86
69	92		69.01	192	132.5	89							
69	96	52	74.6	189	141	92.5	131	114	~124		67	103	107
69	101	44	75.4	173	130.5	93	133.5	115	124	~111.5	66	95	95
69	200A	47.1		190		93	134			~116	70	106	107.5
69	200B		74.05	185	137	86	136						
69	200C												
69	200D		77.8	183.5	143	89	131						
69	UNKN	49	74.7	178	133	82	140	109	122	~107.5	63	100	97
71	1	58.2	78.2	179	140	93	132	122	116	115	67.5	96	99
71	103		69.8	169	118	80	119	116	119	106.5	60	99	100
72	16A	55.5	74.16	178	132	89	127	122	138	104	~56	92	~81
72	16B	50.8	78.8	189	149	101	138	120	125	~112	70	101	94
72	17A	55.2	70.2	178	125	89	128.5	116	132	110	~61	~97	101
72	17B	50	77.9	172	134	98	128	122	126.5	100	69	103	96
72	18	47.6	84.2	165	139	92	130	120	128.5		~62	94	81
72	19A	89.7	65.3	183	119.5	94	131	111.5			67	99.5	99.5
72	19B	62.06	73.1	179	131	84	124	106	120	112	65	97	100

283

Facial base	106.5		87	100	92	97	96.5	105	104	99	90.5	93	97	95	94	98	94	101.5
Cranial base	113		91	103	92.5	100	97	108.5	108.5	99	92	92	97	98.5	101.5	98	91	102
Upper facial height	71			65	59		56.5	66	67	69	62.5	61	64	62	67	65	59	61.5
Total facial height	125			104	101		~90	120	118	124	~92.5	108	111	105	81	113	106	103.5
Bizygomatic breadth	139			124	115		125	125.5	135		115	116		120	119	120.5	121.5	124.5
Auricular height	114.5			111	113		108	111	117.5	110	104	111.5	109	107		106	108	109
Bas. Height	135	130		130	128	129	118.5	131.5	136.5	131	118.5	126	125	124	125	120	123.5	125.5
Front. Breadth	103	86		90	88	92	100	97	100.5	85	86	85	90	90	90	93	91	94
Max. breadth	133	127		130.5	128.5	123	134	131	132.5	140	125	129	123	127	124	~129.5	132.5	125
Max. length	194	167		185	175	172	169	197	187	196	178	181	180	174	187.5	190	170	185
Length-breadth index	68.5	76.05		70.5	73.4	71.5	79.2	66.5	76.3	71.4	70.2	71.2	68.3	72.9	66.1	68.1	77.9	67.5
Nasal index	51.9			53.1	60.2		52.2	48.5	55.1	44	47.2	55.8	59.09	56.04	52	56.5	51.1	59.3
Grave	19C	19D	19E	20	22	24A	24B	25A	25B	41	44	48	49	54	59	60	61	64
Cemetery	72	72	72	72	72	72	72	72	72	72	72	72	72	72	72	72	72	72

Appendix IIa

Facial base	96.5	101	97		86	107	100	94.5	96	98	85	91.5	101	103		105	102	92.5
Cranial base	91	102	100	95	92	108	102	97.5	100	101	85	99	99	104.5	91	99	97	90
Upper facial height	59	66	65		62	70	62.5	69	67	75		68.5	61	73		66	62	62
Total facial height	107		109.5		104	~116.5	111.5	118	~115	121		120.5	105	~118.5		115	~106	104
Bizygomatic breadth	119	119	120	125	120	~129	114	125	137	126		129.5	121	124		126	115	115
Auricular height	116	115.5	108	115		121	111	114	116	115		117	104	116	111.5	112.5	113	108
Bas. Height	121	131.5	129.5	131	127	134	130.5	130.5	138	128.5		130.5	122	130	128.5	129	129.5	126
Front. Breadth	87	99	90	95	91	99	91.5	88	96	92		96.5	90	95.5	87.5	88	92	90
Max. breadth	127	133	130	134.5	129	140.5	133	132	139	132		135.5	122.5	135	126	134	126	134
Max. length	175	185	179	182	176	187.5	186	176.5	191.5	187		180.5	168	186	174	179	182	171
Length-breadth index	72.5	71.8	72.6	73.9	73.3	74.9	71.51	74.7	72.5	70.5		75.06	71.1	72.5	72.4	74.8	69.2	78.3
Nasal index	54.7	50	54.3	42.8	46	52.04	52.2	45.1	51.5	47.2		54.4	51.6	46		56.1	63.3	59.7
Grave	77	79	88	90	91	93	106	112	114	150	162	166	177	180	226	237	239	241
Cemetery	72	72	72	72	72	72	72	72	72	72	72	72	72	72	72	72	72	72

Facial base	98	101	106.5	98.5	97		103	92.5	104	96	100			104	93.5	
Cranial base	105	98	104.5	95	93.5		104.5	97.5	103	97	94	95	97	104	93.5	104
Upper facial height	61.5	66.5	69.5	65.5	64	68.5	68	61	66.5	62	67			69.5	69.5	
Total facial height		111		116		116	~114		111		106.5			~100	116	
Bizygomatic breadth		111	122	119	113	129			122	116	117.5			117		
Auricular height		118	113	117	120		110.5	104	114	111	115.5	109	110	125.5	119.5	114	118.5	118
Bas. Height	146	135	137.5	135	135		133	125.5	136	136.5	127.5	131	126	142.5	143	127	133	132
Front. Breadth	96.5	82	91	88	86	90	85.5	82	94	90	86.5		93	98	96	93	95	95
Max. breadth	139	123	133	136	127	139.5	125	123.5	136	131.5	128.5	~128.5	125	144	135	129.5	135	136.5
Max. length	188	174	188	177.5	170	182	183.5	175	180	173.5	186	174	168	185	188	179	193	188.5
Length-breadth index	73.9	70.6	70.7	76.6	74.7	76.6	68.1	70.5	75.5	75.7	69.08	73.8	74.4	77.8	71.8	72.3	69.9	72.4
Nasal index	51.6	57.7	52.6	57.4	45.1	51	58.1		57.4	59.09	54.8			56.2	48.08		
Grave	243	253	257	262	263	268	269	270	271	273	309	310	322	323	327	334	337	341
Cemetery	72	72	72	72	72	72	72	72	72	72	72	72	72	72	72	72	72	72

Appendix IIa

Facial base		95			96	106	98						101.5	97		95	102	
Cranial base		96	92	108	106	108	101					101	101	100	101	93	103.5	98
Upper facial height		65			74.5	68	61.5						68.5	67.5		66.5		
Total facial height					125								118	103.5				
Bizygomatic breadth		119			125								126	129.5	~112	128		
Auricular height		113.5	122.5	117.5	108.5	122	109					113	118	108	120	111	115	122
Bas. Height		129.5	138.5	140	131.5	137.5	132.5	113		133		133	136.5	130	139.5	127.5	138	140
Front. Breadth		89	91.5	93	96	105	86	87				94.5	89	93	95	91	87	~80
Max. breadth		133.5	134.5	133	127	138	~126			131		126.5	131	131	127	128	129.5	130
Max. length		174.5	166	187	182	195	178	183				181	179	180.5	182	176.5	179	178
Length-breadth index		76.4	81.02	71.1	69.7	70.7	70.7					69.8	73.1	72.5	69.7	72.5	72.3	
Nasal index		52.04			45.6	50.5	49.5						53.1	54		49.4		
Grave	342	343	360	362	368	377	378	380	382	383	384	385	387	392	422	425	426	430
Cemetery	72	72	72	72	72	72	72	72	72	72	72	72	72	72	72	72	72	72

Facial base	~99		99	102	95	92	92		103	~98	105	98			95	92.5	91	~92
Cranial base	102	100	97.5	100	100	91.5	96		106	~106	110.5	97			100	94.5	92	~101
Upper facial height	~66		57	69	66	62.5	64		62	56	69	67	69		63.5	64	62.5	~63.5
Total facial height			98	114	~99	105.5	109		113.5	104		113.5	119		115	115.5	105	92
Bizygomatic breadth	121		125	128	122	119.5	118			126.5	130				119.5	119	129	
Auricular height	119	110	112	114	111	108	107			118	111				115	108.5	112	115
Bas. Height	140.5	140	128	127	126	128	128.5		~131.5	144	133				136.5	130	133	131
Front. Breadth	86		87	92.5	93	85	96			92	93.5		96		92	93	90	94
Max. breadth	127.5	133.5	131	130	131	128	127	139		121	136				139	137	135	130
Max. length	174	179	167	188	176	168	177.5	143	193.5	~191	188	178.5			177	166.5	170	183
Length-breadth index	73.2	74.5	78.4	69.1	74.4	76.1	71.5	97.2		64.3	76.1				78.5	82.2	79.4	71.04
Nasal index	57.7		55.6	46.1	56.2	53.4	51.6		49.02	50	55.3	45.8			48.4	52.8	45.3	52.1
Grave	433	440	445	464	474	476	5	8	10	25	60	72	88	90	102	107	108	3
Cemetery	72	72	72	72	72	72	73	73	73	73	73	73	73	73	73	73	73	74

Appendix IIa

Facial base	97	94	97	100.5	97.5	103	97	108	96.5	89	105	92.5	90	105.5	95.5	94.5	~91.5	94
Cranial base	96	94	98.5	104.5	104	104.5	94	106.5	102	92	111	97	93	95	90	102	104.5	97.5
Upper facial height	91.5	68.5	~58	65	74	71	65	70		59	74.5	58.5	59	67		60		57
Total facial height	108.5	119	~92.5	119	121.5	120		116		125	95.5	104.5	113		106.5		102	
Bizygomatic breadth	120.5	113	121.5	130	129	133		128.5	126	125.5	136.5	120	115	120.5		119.5		
Auricular height	111	108.5	113	109	106.5	115.5	105	112	114	110.5	116	101	107	104			115	
Bas. Height	129	123.5	127.5	132	133	135	125.5	135	137	127.5	134.5	122.5	132	116.5	131		138.5	133
Front. Breadth	89	85	90	95.5	95.5	95	89.5	94	93	95	92	90	85.5	94	87.5	90	91	89.5
Max. breadth	127	127.5	132.5	134	125.5	131.5	121.5	136.5	126	135	137.5	135	127.5	132	130.5		131.5	~123
Max. length	180	173	184	190	177	188	181.5	187	175	182.5	191.5	175	182	185	167		184	168
Length-breadth index	70.5	73.6	72.01	70.5	71.2	69.9	66.09	72.9	77.7	73.9	71.8	77.1	70.05	71.3	78.1		71.4	73.2
Nasal index	49.4	52.7	56.8	44.7	53.3	56	52.7	51	52	59.5	59.6	55.5	49.4	65.9		44.6		56.3
Grave	5	6	12	13	15	19	25	53	58	61	68	70	81	84	169	506	507	511
Cemetery	74	74	74	74	74	74	74	74	74	74	74	74	74	74	74	74	74	74

Facial base	92.5	101.5	97	100	87.5	93	~93	90	93	103	95	95	93.5	96	99.5	103	99.5	96.5
Cranial base	102	102.5	99	105	97	95.5	96.5	96.5	93	101	94	103.5	98.5	97.5	100	97	100	94.5
Upper facial height	69	65.5	64.5	63	72.5	67		65.5	65	66.5	65	70		64	~67.5	63	58	
Total facial height	118.5	113								107.5	111.5	117.5		105.5	~106	111		
Bizygomatic breadth	122	131	123.5	128	124	119.5		121	117.5	123.5	126	132	126.5	125	122	124.5	122	123
Auricular height	110	108	109	116	111.5	108	112	113	106	111	116	113.5	114.5	107	111	106	113	107
Bas. Height	136.5	136.5	135	130.5	132	125	127	130	125	131	135	137	136.5	123.5	129	127	139	129
Front. Breadth	86.5	94	89.5	95	88	89	92	92	89.5	90	92	96	93	87	79	84	84.5	89
Max. breadth	134	138	135	129	134.6	128	132	137	131	123.5	132	146	139.5	129.5	136	131.5	132.5	133
Max. length	181	187	182.5	186.5	172.5	178	176	179.5	181	182	177	192	187	175	188	185	177	177
Length-breadth index	74.03	73.8	73.9	69.1	77.9	71.9	75	76.3	72.3	67.8	74.5	76.04	74.5	74	72.3	73.4	74.8	75.1
Nasal index	44.9	50	52.5	58.06	55	50	57.6	52.04	53.06	54.08	51.5	54	48	47.8	54.7	47.4	60.4	59.3
Grave	514	5	14A	14B	14C	14D	14E	14F	14G	18	23	24	26A	27A	27B	35	36A	36B
Cemetery	74	76	76	76	76	76	76	76	76	76	76	76	76	76	76	76	76	76

Appendix IIa

Cemetery	Grave	Nasal index	Length-breadth index	Max. length	Max. breadth	Front. Breadth	Bas. Height	Auricular height	Bizygomatic breadth	Total facial height	Upper facial height	Cranial base	Facial base
76	44A	45.1	70.7	186.5	132	90	133	111	119	~104	~68	98	96
76	52A	48.3	76.02	171	130	83	124.5	106	114.5	110	63.5	93	93
76	55	45.8	75.4	181	136.5	95	134.5	107	134.5	130	76	106	102
76	58	44.1	72.9	174	127	84.5	131	108		105	65	97.5	90.5
76	72	59.3	76.06	175.5	133.5	94	128	109.5	116	110.5	67	92.5	98
76	74	55.1	74.04	183	135.5	91	128	109	120.5	113	70	94	94.5
76	76	55.5	73.5	176	129.5	89	112.5	104	114.5		59.5	94.5	98
76	77	58.4	72.2	178.5	~129	95.5	128.5	108	124	112.5	65	98	96.5
76	81	53.8	73.7	183	135	97	134	119	114.5	109	64	98	98
76	82	48.08	72.3	188	136	89.5	135.5	117	126	125.5	71.5	98	96
76	83	54.1	73.7	177	130.5	86.5	130.5	111	129.5	116.5	66	95.5	103
76	87	45.1	70.4	183	129	87.5	128	114	119.5	115	70	99	104
76	89	57.7	75.3	170.5	128.5	86	116	101	116.5	100	57.5	95	96.5
76	99	53.3	71.8	174	125	84	130	109	114.5	~103.5	62.5	94	101
76	106	49.4	71.5	184.5	130	96	132	109	120	110	63	105	104.5
76	108	44.8	76.1	~186.5	142	93				127	75		
76	116	61.6	73.6	180	132.5	92	126	106.5	118	100	67	95	98.5
76	124	49		189		96	138	116.5		116.5	67	105	96

Facial base		94.5	99.5	95	95			98	99.5	87.5	104	96			97	110	95
Cranial base		97.5	92.5	98.5	101			97	101	92	107	103			95	109	93
Upper facial height		64	63.5	56	65			62		68.5	72.5	68		69	65	72	62.5
Total facial height			110.5	115.5	116			107.5			121	119		116	112	125.5	106
Bizygomatic breadth			127.5		131			122	130.5		~125			117	138		118
Auricular height		119	114		113	111.5		113	107.5		~121	119.5					
Bas. Height		135	130	134	133.5	131		128.5	130.5	130.5	144.5	142			135	150	130.5
Front. Breadth		97			101.5	93.5		93.5	87		100.5	99.5			88		89.5
Max. breadth	~133	137	136		137.5	131		130	128.5		~138	~133		125	129		130
Max. length	175	185.5	~185.5	176.5	181	170	189	185	176	171	190	~192	185.5	194	202	176	~195	171
Length-breadth index	76	73.8	73.3		75.9	77.06		70.2	73.01		72.6	69.2			61.8	73.3		76.02
Nasal index		45.1	47.2		46.4			44.6	51.02		52.3	53.6			52.1	50	54.8
Grave	125	127	130	133	134	142	143	1	115	18	2	3	7	10A	25	66A	97	130(a)
Cemetery	76	76	76	76	76	76	76	77	77	78	79	79	79	79	79	79	79	79

Appendix IIa

Facial base		92		93	96	93	100		105	101	95	90	95	108.5	94	93	106.5	111
Cranial base	112.5	98.5		100.5	102	100	102.5		103	101	99	95	92	109.5	96	98.5	103.5	112.5
Upper facial height		66		74	71	66.5	69		60		56.5	63.5	68	68	70	68	70	67.5
Total facial height		~113		126	120	108.5	114		104.5		99.5	107.5	106.5	108.5	125	110	116	110.5
Bizygomatic breadth		129		130.5	127.5	~112			128.5	129.5	118.5	128	121	129	122	117.5	132	132
Auricular height																		
Bas. Height	135	141		141	140	136	133.5		131	135	134	131	123	130	125	135	136	138
Front. Breadth	97	100		92.5	100	90.5	92		92	87	96	96.5	87	89.5	89	94	91.5	93
Max. breadth	137.5	140		144	137.5	132.5	139		132	136.5	137	130.5	125	133.5	128.5	128	137	135
Max. length	192.5	180		187	181	177	181		182.5	182	179	173	172	172	174	175.5	186	197
Length-breadth index	71.4	77.7		77.01	75.9	74.8	76.8		72.3	75	76.5	75.3	72.6	77.5	73.8	72.8	73.6	68.5
Nasal index		47.9		48.1	52.9	44.6	45.2		62.2	55.05	52.2	57.1	52.2	50.9		55.5	53	55.2
Grave	135A	135A²	152	157	165(a)	166	166A	168	31A	31B	36	38	43(a)	43B	56	62	34	52
Cemetery	79	79	79	79	79	79	79	79	85	85	85	85	85	85	85	85	86	86

Facial base		108	98	93.5	100.5	100.5	99.5	100	97		99	98.5	98	94			89.5	
Cranial base	98	109	100.5	99	107.5	101.5	99.5	102	103		98	98	104	94			88	
Upper facial height		70	63	57	65	61	69	61	68.5		64	66.5	68	63	67	67	62	
Total facial height		114.5	101	97.5	110	104.5	107.5	104			106	112	119	106	112	113	118	
Bizygomatic breadth	138	145	124	126.5	~134	121	121	123			119	121	121.5		111	117		
Auricular height																		
Bas. Height	136	138.5	124	133	137.5	139	127.5	133.5	145.5	134	135	137.5	131	125.5			128	
Front. Breadth	92	106	89.5	94	~102	92.5	86	97	94.5	92.5	92	94	90.5	100		91	89.5	91
Max. breadth	142	146	128.5	132.5	~139	134.5	127	140.5	140	138	137	128.5	125.5	131.5		121	136	
Max. length	182	195	180.5	184	189.5	177.5	176	181	177.5	182	185	175	184	170		175	172	
Length-breadth index	78.02	74.8	71.1	72.01	73.3	75.7	72.1	77.6	78.8	75.8	74.05	73.4	68.2	77.3		69.1	79.07	
Nasal index	61.6	53.8	54.4	66.2	57.4	57.7	46	59.5	49.03		53.4	49.4	56.1	53.3	55.4	46.8	57.4	
Grave	205	206	208	266A	266B	267	295	305	15	25	28	33	42	69	72	73	77	78
Cemetery	86	86	86	86	86	86	86	86	87	87	87	87	87	87	87	87	87	87

Appendix IIa

Facial base	93		101		97	102	105	92.5	103	95.5	87	109	100.5	95.5	96.5	97	95.5	90.5
Cranial base	98.5		101.5		94	101	108	92.5	107	97.5	92	110.5	103.5	101.5	97.5	98	95.5	91.5
Upper facial height	65		66		62	68.5	72.5	62	67	62	64.5	74	69	68	68.5	68	66.5	56.5
Total facial height	113.5		110		107.5	118.5		111	113	102	100.5		120	111	115	119.5	110	99
Bizygomatic breadth	128.5		129.5			133	135.5		120	124			130	122.5	127	131.5	118.5	111.5
Auricular height																		
Bas. Height	135		138	137.5	128	139	146	130	134	130.5	131.5	139	139	131	137	138	131	122
Front. Breadth	95		96.5		89	92.5	86	81.5	90.5	91	87.5	89.5	89	97.5	94.5	96.5	86.5	85
Max. breadth	141		131	~127	125.5	130	128.5	132.5	130	135	122.5	133	136.5	134	144	139	130.5	126
Max. length	181		176	177	172	179	187	171.5	175.5	173.5	172	187	182	180	185	175.5	178	164
Length-breadth index	77.9		74.4	71.7	72.9	72.6	68.7	77.2	74.7	77.8	71.2	71.1	75	74.4	77.8	79.2	73.3	76.8
Nasal index	47.4		52.04		54	53.4	57.8	55.8	50.5	55.1	55.5	49.5	49.5	52.1	58.7	52.7	51.6	50
Grave	79[2]	83	84	85	89	90	93	94	95	96A	96B	98	100	102	103	104	106	110
Cemetery	87	87	87	87	87	87	87	87	87	87	87	87	87	87	87	87	87	87

Facial base	98.5		97	92		97		96.5	101	100	94.5		90	99.5	104	94	102
Cranial base	103		102	96.5		100		100.5	96	105	99		90	98	104	97	99
Upper facial height	65		71.5	62.5	62	66.5	61.5	56	65.5	72.5	65		64	64	66	66	74
Total facial height	110		126	103	~108	115	105.5	102.5	117	120			108.5	111	112.6	123	
Bizygomatic breadth	127		126	111		126.5	112.5	123.5	116		120	123	118	121	126	124.5	129
Auricular height																	
Bas. Height	136		142	130.5		135.5		134.5	125	131	135.5	125.5	123	127	126.5	133.5	126.5	130.5
Front. Breadth	85.5		97	88	87	86	94	88	83.5	88	92	93.5	96	93	98	95.5	97.5	98.5
Max. breadth	124		133.5	128	129	128	123	128.5	130	138.5	132.5	142	133	132	136.5	138.5	135	137
Max. length	175		178	172	181	171	181.5	182	177.5	182.5	185	177	168	180.5	192	183	181	187
Length-breadth index	70.8		75	74.4	71.2	74.8	67.7	70.6	73.2	75.8	71.6	80.2	79.1	73.1	71.09	75.6	74.5	73.2
Nasal index	48.9		42.5	60.4	56.9	59.1	51.1	48.9	54.7	50.8	44		48.9		54.1	53.06	51
Grave	117	121	125	131	153	157	169	173	1A	75A	173	577	583	601A	601B	614	622	627
Cemetery	87	87	87	87	87	87	87	87	89	89	89	89	89	89	89	89	89	89

Appendix IIA

Facial base	95	99	97	122.5	89	91	92			107	101	100	107	105	96	122	97	101
Cranial base	95	97.5	100	116	90	~96	96.5			112	106	103	109	106.5	100.5	101.5	103	105
Upper facial height	72	65	67	61.5	66	63	70			70	67	73	73	71	71.5	69	72	64
Total facial height	118.5	110.5	114	121.5	113	105	119			119.5	111	119.5	121	123	115.5	113.5	113.5	106
Bizygomatic breadth	130.5		133	139	121.5		130.5			140	125.5	128.5	137.5	136	134	128	131	130
Auricular height																		
Bas. Height	128	130	134	142.5	125	127.5	132.5	132	133.5	145.5	135.5	128.5	146	143	132	126	132	133.5
Front. Breadth	95	93	96.5	98.5	94	90.5	93		98	104.5	98.5	97	101	102	98.5	96.5	99.5	88
Max. breadth	129.5	~128.5	131.5	139	131	122	128.5	143	136.5	147	136.5	145	145	145	134	133	136	134
Max. length	179	177.5	176	199	174	173	177.5	~178.5	184	193.5	190	189	196.5	200	175.5	186.5	197.5	186
Length-breadth index	72.3	72.3	74.4	69.79	75.2	70.5	72.4	80	74.1	75.9	71.8	76.7	73.7	72.5	76.3	71.3	68.1	72
Nasal index	49.06	55	47.06	59.3	40	43.2	40.7			56.6	51.9	46.7	52.9	49	54.3	47.5	58.5	55
Grave	647	673A	673B	677	683A	683B	686	687A	687B	711A	711B	711D	731	733	752	754	772	785
Cemetery	89	89	89	89	89	89	89	89	89	89	89	89	89	89	89	89	89	89

Facial base	105	100	93		96	93	99	92	97.5		103	97		90	99	91	103	96
Cranial base	107	103	97		101	96.5	103.5	96	100		99.5	99		91	95.5	91	101	96
Upper facial height	72.5	65		70	68	66	71	70	71		60.5	69	66.5	61	68	63	65	69.5
Total facial height	120	103.5		~115	110	114.5		117.5			98	119	114	110	109.5	110	110	115.5
Bizygomatic breadth	132	122	119	136	129	120.5	134	128.5	136		120	126	128	129.5	123.5	116	124	124.5
Auricular height																		
Bas. Height	143	132	128.5		131	127	136	125	134	136	129.5	130		124.5	126	125	125.5	126
Front. Breadth	98	90.5	88	109.5	96.5	85.5	92.5	87	88	87	85	86.5	94	91	99	87.5	100.5	86
Max. breadth	138.5	121.5	125	139	139.5	126.5	133.5	138	128	139	124.5	128	127.5	~127	124	132	139.5	131.5
Max. length	199	175	173	190	188.5	173	179.5	179	185.5	181	172	174	187	182	175	169	180	180
Length-breadth index	69.5	69.4	72.2	73.1	73.6	73.1	74.3	77.09	69	76.79	72.3	73.5	68.1	69.7	70.8	78.1	77.5	73.05
Nasal index	51.9	51	51.1	54.2	50	46.8	52.9	46	52.1		66.6	46.8	52.9	57.9	48	56.9	47.1	47.4
Grave	797A	797B	797C	802	807	810	812A	812B	819	825	852	855	858	861	880	917	1152	1154
Cemetery	89	89	89	89	89	89	89	89	89	89	89	89	89	89	89	89	89	89

Appendix IIa

Facial base		94.5	96.5	101
Cranial base		94	102	105
Upper facial height		62.5	63	69
Total facial height		106	112.5	115.5
Bizygomatic breadth			139	129
Auricular height				
Bas. Height		128.5	136.5	134
Front. Breadth		82.5	98	96.5
Max. breadth		141	137	138
Max. length		175	190	174
Length-breadth index		80.05	72.1	79.3
Nasal index		53.2	57.4	52.4
Grave	1161A	1161B	1377A	1377B
Cemetery	89	89	89	89

Appendix IIb

Cranial measurements from anatomical recording cards produced by Douglas Derry and Sir Grafton Elliot Smith (part 2)

Circumference						523	487		510	480	515		505	513
Sigmoid	45		44	45	49	46	50.5		46	43	49	49	50	41	47
Height of symphysis	32		31	30	31.5	30.5	26		32	32	32	30	31	32	31
Bigonial breadth	76		83.5	81	83	80	75		93	78	85	75	80		80
Palate	43.5 x 35.5	44.5 x 36.5	43 x 41	39 x 34	43 x 36	39 x 32	41 x 40		44 x 40	39.5 x 35	44.5 x 37	38.5 x 36.5	40 x 38		44.5 x 38.5
Nose	43.5 x 25	42 x 24	50 x 27	54 x 24	44 x 26	50 x 24	49 x 26		52 x 26.5	51.5 x 24	42.5 x 27	41.5 x 26	46 x 26.5	43 x 24	50 x 24
Left orbit	35 x 30	35 x 33	37 x 35	38 x 37	39 x 33	37.5 x 35	37 x 35		36 x 31	35 x 34.5	38.5 x 31	35 x 31	38.5 x 31.5	36.5 x 25	38.5 x 35
Right orbit	35 x 30	35 x 31	37.5 x 35	38 x 35.5	37.5 x 32	39 x 32.5	36.5 x 32.5		35 x 32	35.5 x 34.5	39.5 x 29	36.5 x 29	39 x 32	35.5 x 25.5	38 x 34
Interorbital breadth	21	20	22	18	19	21	22		21	21	22	20	23	24	24
Grave	106A	106B	106C	106D	106E	774	775	832	835	840	846	848	875	2	3
Cemetery	55	55	55	55	55	55	55	55	55	55	55	55	55	58	58

Appendix IIb

Cemetery	Grave	Interorbital breadth	Right orbit	Left orbit	Nose	Palate	Bigonial breadth	Height of symphysis	Sigmoid	Circumference
58	5						74	33	46	
58	8									
58	9	23	39 x 36	38 x 35	53 x 26	43 x 37	94	33	48	503
58	12									
58	13	19		36.5 x 33.5	52 x 22					
58	14	21	37 x 29	36.5 x 31	47 x 26.5	45 x 38	77	33	45	475
58	17	25	37 x 35	37 x 36	49 x 23	41 x 31.5		27	38	495
58	18	21	38 x 28		54 x 27	39 x 35.5	83	34	42	503
58	19	21	36 x 30	36 x 32	51 x 25	41.5 x 33	73	32	47	520
58	20									
58	100	23	36 x 30	35 x 31	46 x 22	40 x 36	76	30	33.5	480
58	101		37 x 34					31	40	513
58	102	22	39 x 31	38 x 31.5	49 x 28	43 x 35.5	72	33	47	511
58	105	19	37 x 30	37 x 30	45 x 26	42 x 34				485
58	106A	25	37 x 30		45 x 26	48 x 37				512
58	106B							31	39	
58	108									
58	109									519

301

Circumference					516	510	488	485	501	490	507	515		505		520		505
Sigmoid	37.5	42	48.5	48		43	40	43	32	47	44	40		48	42	51		45
Height of symphysis	31	29	35.5			36	32.5	32	25	33	33	31.5		34.5	32.5	37		32
Bigonial breadth						75.5	72	72	73	85	76.5	~79		~88	86	79.5		85
Palate					41 x 39	44 x 37	39 x 35.5	48.5 x 32	42 x 36.5	43 x 31.5	41.5 x 32.5	48.5 x 38.5		40.5 x 35	45.5 x 40	42 x 39		44.5 x 34
Nose					53 x 26.5	48 x 25	45 x 24	47 x 23	43 x 26	45 x 26	54 x 25	56 x 24.5		53 x 26		51 x 26.5		52 x 25
Left orbit		37 x 33.5			37 x 33	40 x 36	38 x 33	37 x 30	35 x 30	37.5 x 31.5	37 x 34	38.5 x 34.5		39 x 34.5		39 x 33		37.5 x 32
Right orbit					38 x 32	40.5 x 36	40 x 33	37 x 30.5	35 x 31	38 x 31.5	37 x 32.5	39 x 33.5		39 x 34		40 x 32.5		38 x 31
Interorbital breadth					22	21	20	23	20	24	21.5	20.5		21	24	22		21
Grave	110	111	112B	113	115	116	117	118	119	120	121	122	123A	123B	124	125	126	127
Cemetery	58	58	58	58	58	58	58	58	58	58	58	58	58	58	58	58	58	58

Appendix IIb

Circumference	509	497.5	494	490	481	508	513	505			516.5			475		491	485	514
Sigmoid	45	40	40	39			46	51			44.5			39			40	45
Height of symphysis	34	31.5	29.5	33			29	31.5			33			28		27.5	~26	
Bigonial breadth	84	71	82	79.5			111	98			96			84			97.5	
Palate	55 x 40	49 x 35	55 x 36.5	45.5 x 39	47 x 36	50 x 36	50 x 33.5	53 x 40.5	48.5 x 40	52.5 x 31.5		46 x 37.5	47 x 40	53 x 35		51 x 37		
Nose	42 x 29	42.5 x 26	44 x 25.5	43 x 27.5	41 x 23	52 x 23.5	43.5 x 23	49.5 x 25.5		50 x 26.5	43.5 x 20	51 x ##	42 x 24	48.5 x 23.5	45 x 24	46.5 x 23		49 x 24.5
Left orbit	37 x 31.5	37 x 31	37 x 30	36.5 x 29	36.5 x 29	40 x 32.5	35.5 x 32	38 x 31		37.5 x 32	38 x 32.5	40 x 36	34 x 31	35.5 x 30	36.5 x 31.5	38 x 31.5		37 x 35.5
Right orbit	37 x 32	38 x 29.5	36.5 x 31	36 x 31	35 x 29	38 x 32	35 x 33	39 x 30.5		36.5 x 32.5	39 x 32		35 x 30	36.5 x 31	36 x 31.5	38.5 x 30.5		38 x 34.5
Interorbital breadth	26	20	22.5	23	20	22	21.5	25		22	20		19	21	23	20		20
Grave	1A	1B	2	3A	3B	4	5	UNKN	2	9	10	12	15	20	24	7	12	14
Cemetery	59	59	59	59	59	59	59	62	68	68	68	68	68	68	68	69	69	69

Circumference	515	490	500	~516	507.5		501	503	483	~504	491	488	489			510		504
Sigmoid	50		47	46	43	40	42	49.5		50	43	40	44.5	50	52		52	50
Height of symphysis	30	31.5	33	33.5	33	27	27.5	26.5			29	25	29.5	25.5	33.5		30	32
Bigonial breadth	~115		96.5	92	92.5		~90	~103			~97	81	92	~85	92		80	92.5
Palate	51 x 42.5	53 x 36	54 x 32	55 x 34	55 x 39	49 x 34	49 x 39	52 x ~37	47.5 x 34.5	51.5 x 39	54 x 39.5	49 x 35	53 x 39.5	51.5 x 32.5	54 x 38.5	53.5 x 37	49 x 38.5	48.5 x 43
Nose	54 x 25.5	52 x 26	49.5 x 25.5	47.5 x 26.5	51 x 26	45.5 x 26	48.5 x 26.5	53 x 25	45.5 x 22.5	55 x 24.5	47 x 26	47 x 23.5	49 x 25	43.5 x 24	48 x 28	54 x 24	53 x 22.5	52 x 27.5
Left orbit	38 x 31	36.5 x 30	37.5 x 34.5	37 x 31	37 x 32.5	37 x 29	38 x 33	36.5 x 31.5	36 x 30	41.5 x 33	38 x 32.5	38.5 x 30	37 x 32	35 x 30	37.5 x 35.5	37 x 34	37 x 33	39 x 38
Right orbit	41 x 33	36 x 30	36.5 x 33	39 x 31.5	36.5 x 33	37 x 29	39.5 x 31.5	38 x 32	36 x 30	41 x 32	39 x 32	38.5 x 28.5	38 x 30	39 x 30	37 x 35	37.5 x 33.5	37.5 x 32.5	39,5 x 38
Interorbital breadth	21	23	25	21	18	23	19	20	20	21	23	19.5	21	25	27	24	21	24
Grave	15	16	17	18	20	21	23	24	25	26	27	28	36	40	41	44	45	48
Cemetery	69	69	69	69	69	69	69	69	69	69	69	69	69	69	69	69	69	69

Appendix IIB

Cemetery	Grave	Interorbital breadth	Right orbit	Left orbit	Nose	Palate	Bigonial breadth	Height of symphysis	Sigmoid	Circumference
69	west of 48	20	38.5 x 32.5	36 x 32.5	51.5 x 21.5	48.5 x 37.5	91	28	46	507
69	49	23	37 x 31.5	37.5 x 33	48 x 25.5	56 x 33.5	78	32	46	
69	52	20					66.5	35	48	
69	57	23	35 x 35	35 x 31	46.5 x 25	56 x 35	81	32	41	
69	58						75	24	41	
69	60	23	38 x 33	36.5 x 33	52 x 23	44 x 36		~23.5	49	
69	61	21	36 x 28	36 x 29	41.5 x 23	45 x 35	74	31	40	493
69	64	21	37 x 32	34.5 x 32.5	47.5 x 22	45.5 x 34.5		30.5	34	488
69	66	24	41 x 32	40 x 35	46 x 27	48 x 32				
69	70	22	35.5 x 27.5	32.5 x 29	43 x 26	47 x 36.5	98	28	42.5	~488
69	71	19	35.5 x 34	35.5 x 34	52 x 24	~43 x 36				497
69	72	24.5	40 x 32	37 x 32.5	47 x 24	50 x 36	89	32	44	518
69	73						79	29	41.5	505
69	74	18	35 x 29.5	34 x 31	49 x 23.5		~84	30	49.5	500
69	81	19	41.5 x 33	40 x 34	54 x 27.5	55 x 36	107	35	46	510
69	85	19	40.5 x 33	40 x 32	54 x 27	54 x 38.5	95	~34	48	498
69	88	21	40 x 33.5	40 x 32	53 x 27			~25	50	605

Circumference	510	496	498		520	492		515	520	500	497.5	503	460	495	537	493	491	493
Sigmoid		41.5		43.5		43.5	48	47	45.5		50	47	45	37	47	39	41	42
Height of symphysis		32		~31		29	32.5	23	32		28.5	~31	28	31	36	31.5	30	24
Bigonial breadth		78				~92.5	97	~90	~114		92	106	82.5	83		95	95	87
Palate	50 x 37.5	47 x 32			57 x 30	50.5 x 33	54 x 36				~47 x 39	55 x 33	54 x 36	~46 x 38	~49.5 x 37.5	51.5 x 35	52.5 x 36.5	~45 x 34
Nose	52 x 23.5	43 x 29	45.5 x 23		50 x 26	50 x 22	52 x 24.5				~50 x 24	45.5 x 26.5	45 x 25	51.5 x 26	~48 x 26.5	52 x 26	52.5 x 25	
Left orbit	38 x 34	37 x 27.5	35.5 x 30		38 x 34	38.5 x 34	39 x 33.5				37.5 x 33	37.5 x 33	36 x 31.5	35 x 34	38.5 x 36	38.5 x 33	44 x 35	35 x 32
Right orbit	41 x 35	36.5 x 27	35.5 x 29		38 x 35	39 x 33.5	39 x 33				37.5 x 33	36 x 31.5	36 x 34		37 x 31		42 x 33.5	36 x 30
Interorbital breadth	22	20	17		24		22	21			19	24	22	17	25	22	25	19
Grave	89	90	91A	92	96	101	200A	200B	200C	200D	UNKN	1	103	16A	16B	17A	17B	18
Cemetery	69	69	69	69	69	69	69	69	69	69	69	71	71	72	72	72	72	72

Appendix IIb

Circumference	497	475	534			505	487		487	535	516	535	488	492.5	488	490		~515
Sigmoid		44	50.5			39	34		42.5	44	48	55.5	37	43	42	41	42.5	41.5
Height of symphysis		34	38			30	28		23	30	36	34	26.5	30.5	33	28	27	~35
Bigonial breadth		85	108			93	86		89	95	100	110.5	86.5	89		86	86	98
Palate		52.5 x 38	51.5 x 39.5	57 x 44.5			48.5 x 40	45 x 35		44.5 x 35	50.5 x 34.5	57 x ~42.5	51 x 44	46.5 x ~35	51 x 35.5	50 x 36	48 x 31	46 x 35.5	52.5 x ~35
Nose		44 x 39.5	43.5 x 27	51 x 26.5			47 x 25	44 x 26.5		44 x 23	51.5 x 25	49 x 27	50 x 22	45.5 x 21.5	43 x 24	44 x 26	45.5 x 25.5	50 x 26	46 x 26
Left orbit		37.5 x 34	37 x 32	40 x 30			37 x 35	38 x 32		35 x 32	42 x 35	39 x 33	40 x 35	36 x 31	39 x 31.5	38 x 32.5	35 x 32	38 x 31.5	38 x 33.5
Right orbit		38 x 33	35 x 31.5	41 x 30			38.5 x 34	36 x 30.5		35 x 31.5	41.5 x 33	40 x 32	40.5 x 35	37 x 30.5	39 x 31	39 x 32	35 x 32	39.5 x 30.5	38 x 33
Interorbital breadth	24	28	20			20	20.5		21	20	21	~21	20	15.5	20.5	25	26	21.5
Grave	19A	19B	19C	19D	19E	20	22	24A	24B	25A	25B	41	44	48	49	54	59	60
Cemetery	72	72	72	72	72	72	72	72	72	72	72	72	72	72	72	72	72	72

Grave	61	64	77	79	88	90	91	93	106	112	114	150	162	166	177	180	226	237
Cemetery	72	72	72	72	72	72	72	72	72	72	72	72	72	72	72	72	72	72
Circumference	489	508.5	484	508.5	488	513	485	~525	508	495	530	507.5		510	469	519	486	495
Sigmoid	36	39	40		44		43	39	30	50.5	49	46		53	38.5		44	50
Height of symphysis	25.5	28.5	32		30		25.5	33.5	32	33	~31	33		34	29	37	34	31
Bigonial breadth	94	96	93		88		90	92	84	99	~118	90		93	91.5		82	~83
Palate	47 x 35.5	52 x 39	49.5 x 35	53 x 33.5	52.5 x ~37	Cleft	57 x ~37	50.5 x 32	51.5 x 35.5	52 x 38	53 x 35		47 x ~37.5	55 x 32.5	54 x 37.5		56 x 35	
Nose	44 x 22.5	46.5 x 27.5	42 x 23	52 x 26	46 x 25		50 x 23	49 x 25.5	45 x 23.5	52 x 23.5	48.5 x 38	54 x 25.5		50.5 x 27.5	44.5 x 23	~50 x 23		49 x 27.5
Left orbit	37 x 30	39 x 33	36 x 28.5	40 x 32	38 x 34	39 x 35	37 x 32	37.5 x 31.5	39 x 31	39 x 35	41 x 33	40 x 35		37 x 28	38 x 35	38 x 35		37.5 x 33
Right orbit	37 x 29	39.5 x 32.5	37.5 x 29.5	39 x 30.5	38.5 x 34		37 x 31.5	39.5 x 32	39 x 30	39 x 35	41 x 32	39 x 35.5		37.5 x 29	38.5 x 35	39 x 34.5		37.5 x 32
Interorbital breadth	18	26	20	23	20	20	21	25	20	19	23	26.5		~22	23	24		25

Appendix IIb

Circumference	495	479		483.5	510	496	492		499		503.5		507		469	528.5	517.5	496
Sigmoid	43	40.5		45.5		42.5		45	46.5		44		48.5				49.5	44
Height of symphysis	26	25		30		35		29	31.5		35		26				30	27
Bigonial breadth	~77.5	84		68		88		~74	84		88		84			89		
Palate	54 x 34.5	45.5 x 35	48 x ~35	52 x 34	57 x 35	52 x 39.5	54 x 33.5	55 x 36.5	55 x 35		52.5 x 34	51 x 33	52 x ~36			57 x 36	51 x 39.5	
Nose	45 x 28.5	43.5 x 26	45.5 x 23.5	45 x 26	47.5 x 25	43.5 x 23	44.5 x 20	50 x 25.5	49 x 28.5		47 x 27	44 x 26	46.5 x 25.5			48 x 27	52 x 25	
Left orbit	37.5 x 32	39.5 x 32	40 x 31	36 x 31	40 x 29.5	38.5 x 30	35 x 32	39.5 x 33.5	39.5 x 31.5	~37.5 x 32	36.5 x 30	38 x 31	37 x 28.5	39 x 33.5			39 x 34	39.5 x 33.5
Right orbit	36 x 31	40 x 31.5	38 x 32	37 x 30	39 x 29	36.5 x 30	36 x 32	39.5 x 33	39.5 x 31		37 x 30	37 x 31	38 x 28				40 x 32.5	40 x 32.5
Interorbital breadth	24	22	20	20.5	22.5	19.5	21	21	20		23	19	21	19.5			22	22
Grave	239	241	243	253	257	262	263	268	269	270	271	273	309	310	322	323	327	334
Cemetery	72	72	72	72	72	72	72	72	72	72	72	72	72	72	72	72	72	72

	337	341	342	343	360	362	368	377	378	380	382	383	384	385	387	392	422	425
Circumference	~530	518.5			490		497							498	493.5	497	509	490
Sigmoid		39	44				45.5				43	39.5	57		45	51.5		45
Height of symphysis		31.5	34				31.5				32	~26.5	32.5		30	~32		~32
Bigonial breadth		110					88				90	86	86		83	76.5		~76
Palate							55.5 x 35		52.5 x 36	50 x 32					51 x 31.5	54.5 x 38		
Nose				49 x 25.5			58 x 26.5	47 x ##	43.5 x 22	50.5 x 25					47 x 25	50 x 27		
Left orbit				37 x 32			39.5 x 33	37.5 x 33.5		38 x 29					39 x 30	39.5 x 33		
Right orbit	~39 x 35.5			37.5 x 30.5			39.5 x 34		39 x 33.5	38.5 x 28.5					39.5 x 30	40.5 x 33.5		37 x 31.5
Interorbital breadth			21				24	29	21	21					20	23.5		21
Grave	337	341	342	343	360	362	368	377	378	380	382	383	384	385	387	392	422	425
Cemetery	72	72	72	72	72	72	72	72	72	72	72	72	72	72	72	72	72	72

Circumference	500	494	486.5		479	508	492	472.5	494				499	508			505	482
Sigmoid		51.5			46	41	36	38	41			49	52		40	42	46.5	46	41.5
Height of symphysis		~30			27.5	34.5	~25	28	32			27.5	27.5		29.5	35.5	29	~34	34.5
Bigonial breadth					100	98.5	89	88	84			85			90	95.5	96	97	89
Palate	51.5 x 39		56 x ~35		49 x 36.5	43 x 36	50 x ~35	47 x 36	50.5 x 37.5			48 x 35.5	51.5 x 37	56 x 37.5			49 x 35	51.5 x 35
Nose	46.5 x 23		45 x 26		44 x 24.5	52 x 24	48 x 27	43 x 23	45.5 x 23.5		51 x 25		50 x 25	47 x 26	48 x 22		49.5 x 24	43.5 x 23
Left orbit	40 x 33		38 x 30.5		37 x 31	37 x 33	36.5 x 32	37.5 x 32	35.5 x 33		39 x 31.5		39.5 x 31	39 x 31.5	39 x 34		39.5 x 30	38.5 x 30
Right orbit	39 x 32.5		38 x 31		38.5 x 30.5	39 x 33	38 x 32	37.5 x 30.5	37 x 30.5		37.5 x 31		39 x 31	39 x 31	39 x 33		38 x 29.5	38 x 28
Interorbital breadth	20		20.5		20	22	20	21	21		~23.5		22	21.5	21.5		21	20
Grave	426	430	433	440	445	464	474	476	5	8	10	25	60	72	88	90	102	107
Cemetery	72	72	72	72	72	72	72	72	73	73	73	73	73	73	73	73	73	73

Circumference	491	505	500	478	507.5	520	488	522	497.5	524	501	515	522.5	492	493	510		
Sigmoid	40	43	35.5	40	41.5	51	46	47			45	43	56	36.5	45	40		41
Height of symphysis	28	28	28	34.5	27	28	35	32.5			33.5	29	35	25	25.5	35		25
Bigonial breadth	82	84	92	85	97	100.5	94	102.5			97	82	91	87	89	78.5		93
Palate	43 x 33	46.5 x 35	49 x 34	51 x 38	47 x ~37.5	52 x 38.5	51.5 x 38.5	55 x 38.5	50 x 31.5	55 x 38	50 x 38	48.5 x ##	53 x 40	48 x 35	50.5 x 36.5	54.5 x 37		46 x 36.5
Nose	48.5 x 22	46 x 24	42.5 x 21	45.5 x 24	44 x 25	52.5 x 23.5	51.5 x 27.5	56 x 28	45.5 x 24	50 x 25.5	50 x 26	47 x 28	52 x 31	45 x 25	42.5 x 21	47 x 31		47 x 21
Left orbit	34.5 x 33.5		37.5 x 33.5	35 x 34	36 x 33	39 x 32.5	39 x 35.5	38 x 30	37 x 32.5	41 x 32	38 x 35	38 x 38	42 x 33.5	37 x 33.5	37 x 31.5	37 x 35		35.5 x 31
Right orbit	36 x 32	37 x 31	38 x 32	35 x 33	39 x 32	39.5 x 33	41 x 33	38 x 30	36 x 31.5	41 x 33.5	37.5 x 34	38 x 35	41 x 32	36.5 x 35	37 x 32	37 x 34.5		36.5 x 31
Interorbital breadth	21	18	21	23	20	20	20	22.5	23	21	24.5	22	21	21	15	26.5		21
Grave	108	3	5	6	12	13	15	19	25	53	58	61	68	70	81	84	169	506
Cemetery	73	74	74	74	74	74	74	74	74	74	74	74	74	74	74	74	74	74

Appendix IIb

Cemetery	74	74	74	76	76	76	76	76	76	76	76	76	76	76	76	76	76	76
Grave	507	511	514	5	14A	14B	14C	14D	14E	14F	14G	18	23	24	26A	27A	27B	35
Interorbital breadth		22	21.5	23	24	23	24	22	22	21	21	20.5	21	25	22	18	19.5	20
Right orbit	40 x 32	36 x 32	37.5 x 31.5	38 x 27	36.5 x 31.5	40 x 32	37 x 36	38 x 32	36 x 29.5	37.5 x 33.5	39 x 33	40 x 30	36.5 x 31	37 x 29.5	40 x 31	37 x 33	38 x 34.5	35.5 x 28.5
Left orbit		37.5 x 30.5	37.5 x 32	36.5 x 26.5	36.5 x 31	40 x 31	35.5 x 37.5	38 x 32	35 x 29	35.5 x 34	37.5 x 34	39 x 30	36 x 33	36 x 31	39 x 32.5	37 x 33	38 x 35	35 x 27.5
Nose	47.5 x ##	47 x 26.5	49 x 22	51 x 25.5	49.5 x 26	46.5 x 27	50 x 27.5	48 x 24	42.5 x 24.5	49 x 25.5	49 x 26	49 x 26.5	48.5 x 25	50 x 27	50 x 24	46 x 22	47.5 x 26.5	48.5 x 23
Palate			50 x 37	52 x 37	50 x 40.5	51 x 35	46.5 x 40	50 x 36		44.5 x ~31	50 x 37.5	56 x 38.5	49 x 36	50 x 37		48 x 36.5	53 x 38	55 x 40
Bigonial breadth		88.5	86	93.5								96	89.5	84.5		94.5	94	105.5
Height of symphysis		26.5	30	28.5								32.5	35	34.5		37	30.5	32
Sigmoid		39.5	50	49								43	41	46		48.5	43	43
Circumference	499		505	522	504	505	488.5	485	486	505	502	494	495	533	515	485	511	493

Circumference	490.5	489	503	476	508.5	482	503.5	514	491.5	495	510	520	489	501.5	478.5	481	510
Sigmoid	45.5		49	47.5	57.5	46	35	40.5		39.5	35.5	50	46.5	35	37.5	45.5	43	47
Height of symphysis			26.5	31	34.5	25	30	30		31	30	~34	35	30	23.5	28.5	28.5	32
Bigonial breadth			76	80	98.5	92.5	86	83.5		89	81.5		96.5	89	85.5		87.5	91.5
Palate	53.5 x 38.5		46 x 35.5	43.5 x 33	52.5 x 39	50 x 37.5	52 x 38.5	52.5 x 35	51.5 x 37	47 x 36	51.5 x 30	50 x 35	55.5 x 31	58.5 x 35	51 x 32.5	56 x 39.5	48 x 35	53 x 36
Nose	43 x 26	43 x 25.5	51 x 23	45.5 x 22	54.5 x 25	51 x 22.5	48 x 28.5	49 x 27	45 x 25	44.5 x 26	45.5 x 24	52 x 25	48 x 26	51 x 23	45 x 26	45 x 24	47.5 x 23.5	53.5 x 22
Left orbit	35 x 31	37.5 x 30.5	37.5 x 33.5	35 x 30	39.5 x 34	35.5 x 34	36 x 30	39 x 38.5	37.5 x 33	38 x 33	36 x 32	36 x 33.5	37 x 33	37 x 33	36.5 x 33.5	34 x 29.5	39 x 31	37 x 36
Right orbit	36 x 29.5	38 x 31	37 x 32.5	34 x 30.5	40 x 33.5	36.5 x 33	38.5 x 30	37.5 x 34.5	38.5 x 32.5	39.5 x 33	36.5 x 30.5	38.5 x 32	38 x 31.5	37 x 32.5	37.5 x 33	35.5 x 29.5	39 x 30.5	39 x 35
Interorbital breadth	20	20	22.5	18	24	~18.5	23	21	20	22	24	21	20	19.5	22	22	22.5	21.5
Grave	36A	36B	44A	52A	55	58	72	74	76	77	81	82	83	87	89	99	106	108
Cemetery	76	76	76	76	76	76	76	76	76	76	76	76	76	76	76	76	76	76

Appendix IIb

Circumference	503.5			521			506	482.5		505	487		504					498
Sigmoid	42	45.5	43.5	44	47.5	45	50.5	47		38	45		51.5	54			54	41
Height of symphysis	27.5	29.5	33	32	32	28	29	26		31	31		36.5	35.5			31	32
Bigonial breadth	82	86	77.5		88		83	~83		85	93.5		93	~103.5			89	
Palate	50 x 33			51 x 37		47 x 35	47 x 35			50 x 32			55 x 38	51 x 33				50 x 36
Nose	43 x 26.5	50 x 24.5		51 x 23	~45.5 x 21.5		49.5 x 23			47 x 21	49 x 25		53.5 x 28	48.5 x 26				47 x 24.5
Left orbit	37.5 x 33	38.5 x 30.5		36 x 34	35.5 x 30	39 x 33				37 x 31	35.5 x 29		39 x 34	36 x 30.5				37 x 32
Right orbit	38 x 33.5	39 x 32		37 x 35	35 x 26	40 x 33				38 x 31	37.5 x 30		42 x 31.5	37.5 x 28.5				35 x 32
Interorbital breadth	21.5			24		21.5	24			22.5	21		21	22				20.5
Grave	116	124	125	127	130	133	134	142	143	1	115	18	2	3	7	10A	25	66A
Cemetery	76	76	76	76	76	76	76	76	76	77	77	78	79	79	79	79	79	79

Circumference	Sigmoid	Height of symphysis	Bigonial breadth	Palate	Nose	Left orbit	Right orbit	Interorbital breadth	Grave	Cemetery
	56.5	38		56 x 37	52 x 26	40 x 32.5	40 x 33	23	97	79
478	43	29	84	49 x 32	46.5 x 25.5	35 x 30	36 x 31	21	130(a)	79
									135A	79
510	46.5	33		48.5 x 34.5	49 x 23.5	35.5 x 32.5	40 x 32	20	135A²	79
									152	79
525	50.5	33	96.5	50.5 x 36	54 x 26	36.5 x 33	36.5 x 33.5	21.5	157	79
515	52.5	31	89	51 x 35.5	51 x 27	36 x 35	36.5 x 34.5	19.5	165(a)	79
495	45	26	88	45.5 x 36.5	51.5 x 23	36 x 36	37.5 x 37	23.5	166	79
507	42.5	30	88.5	54 x 38.5	53 x 24	36 x 33.5	36 x 34.5	23.5	166A	79
									168	79
505	53.5	28	92	56 x 41	45 x 28	39.5 x 32	40 x 30.5	24	31A	85
501.5	52	30.5	85.5	50 x 36	44.5 x 24.5	39 x 30	40 x 29	20	31B	85
505	42	28		55 x 39.5	45 x 25.5	37.5 x 29	38 x 29.5	19	36	85
489.5	43	30	87.5	46 x 34.5	45.5 x 26	37.5 x 32	38.5 x 32	20	38	85
473.5	40	29	90	50 x 36	44 x 23	38 x 31	39.5 x 31	20	43(a)	85
492	42	30	87	50 x 36	52 x 26.5	38 x 33.5	38.5 x 34	18.5	43B	85
486	50.5	34	87.5	47.5 x 29.5		35 x 30	36 x 30	20.5	56	85
490	39.5	27.5	87.5	48.5 x 35.5	49.5 x 27.5	35.5 x 35	37 x 35	24	62	85

Appendix IIb

Circumference	524	526.5	513	547	499	509	525	500	487	515	502	517	514	488	496	491.5	488
Sigmoid	48	46		50	42	47	48.5	46.5	46.5	42.5			43	44.5	43	38.5	40	38.5
Height of symphysis	32.5	36.5		31.5	26	28.5	32	29	30	27			33	32	31.5	28.5	33	31
Bigonial breadth	103.5	91		106.5	95	95	96.5	80.5	82.5	95.5			90	98	~99	84	91.5	79.5
Palate	59 x 36.5	55 x 33		53 x 39	48 x 33	46 x 39.5		54 x 31.5	53.5 x 38.5	52.5 x 34.5	47.5 x 35		52 x 35.5	52 x 32.5	53 x 37	49 x 34	55 x 37.5	55 x 29
Nose	50 x 26.5	48 x 26.5	43 x 26.5	52 x 28	45 x 24.5	40 x 26.5	47 x 27	45 x 26	50 x 23	42 x 25	52 x 25.5		43 x 23	44.5 x 22	49 x 27.5	45 x 24	46 x 25.5	48 x 22.5
Left orbit	37 x 30	39.5 x 31.5	37 x 32	41 x 31.5	35.5 x 31	36 x 28.5	40 x 30	37 x 32.5	36 x 30	36 x 27.5	36 x 32.5		37.5 x 31	36.5 x 34	41.5 x 31	39.5 x 33.5	36 x 33	36.5 x 31.5
Right orbit	37 x 30.5	40.5 x 29	39 x 32.5	41 x 32	36.5 x 31	37 x 28.5	42 x 31	37 x 33	36.5 x 29	36.5 x 27.5			37 x 32	38 x 32	42 x 31	40.5 x 34	37 x 33	38 x 30
Interorbital breadth	24.5	20.5	23	26.5	20	22.5	22	24	19.5	24.5	22		23.5	24.5	22	24	22	21
Grave	34	52	205	206	208	266A	266B	267	295	305	15	25	28	33	42	69	72	73
Cemetery	86	86	86	86	86	86	86	86	86	86	87	87	87	87	87	87	87	87

Circumference	497		516.5		499		482		506	489	491.5	500	483.5	506.5	502.5	506	525	510
Sigmoid	38	48	44	40	54	47	38	54.5		34	42	45.5	40		55	37	45	48
Height of symphysis	27	28	35	32	32.5	34	31	30.5		32.5	33	27	34.5		33	32	35	36
Bigonial breadth	80	89	94	103.5	89	96	78	101.5		88	88.5	85.5			95	89	89	93
Palate	47.5 x 33		50 x 33.5		56 x 38.5		51.5 x 36.5	52 x 35.5	57 x 37.5	50 x 37	53.5 x 35	49 x 31	46.5 x 34	56 x 35	56.5 x 35.5	48.5 x 38	51 x 38.5	51.5 x 34.5
Nose	43.5 x 25		48.5 x 25		49 x 25.5		43.5 x 23.5	50.5 x 27	47.5 x 27.5	43 x ~24	46.5 x 23.5	43.5 x 24	45 x 25	53.5 x 26.5	50.5 x 25	46 x 24	46 x 27	45.5 x 24
Left orbit			35.5 x 34		38 x 33		38 x 30.5	40 x 33	40 x 30		35 x 31	35.5 x 33	35.5 x 35.5	39 x 32.5	38 x 31	37 x 31.5	37 x 32	36.5 x 30
Right orbit	37.5 x 35		36 x 33		39 x 32.5		37.5 x 31	43 x 32.5	39 x 31	34 x 30.5	38 x 32	37 x 33	35.5 x 35	37 x 32.5	39 x 30	37 x 30.5	37 x 31.5	37.5 x 31
Interorbital breadth	22		22		20		20	22	23	20.5	23.5	19	22.5	22	25	23.5	23	23
Grave	77	78	79[2]	83	84	85	89	90	93	94	95	96A	96B	98	100	102	103	104
Cemetery	87	87	87	87	87	87	87	87	87	87	87	87	87	87	87	87	87	87

APPENDIX IIb

Cemetery	87	87	87	87	87	87	87	87	87	87	89	89	89	89	89	89	89
Grave	106	110	117	121	125	131	153	157	169	173	1A	75A	173	577	583	601A	601B	614
Interorbital breadth	21	18	22.5		20.5	24.5	19.5	27	21.5	19	25.5	22	18.5		22.5	22.5	20.5	
Right orbit	38.5 x 31	34 x 28	37 x 32		38.5 x 33	37 x 31.5	38 x 34	38 x 34	38 x 32	37 x 30	36 x 30	43.5 x 35	38 x 32.5		38 x 31	38 x 30	40 x 31.5	
Left orbit	38.5 x 31	34 x 30	37 x 32.5		37.5 x 33.5	37 x 31.5	37 x 33.5	38 x 33	38.5 x 32	37 x 29.5	34.5 x 30	42 x 35	38 x 33		36.5 x 30.5	37 x 30	37.5 x 31.5	
Nose	46.5 x 24	41 x 20.5	48 x 23.5		54 x 23	43 x 26	43 x 24.5	46.5 x 27.5	45 x 23	46 x 22.5	47.5 x 26	59 x 30	50 x 22		47 x 23		48 x 26	
Palate	55 x 33	45 x 31	49.5 x 35.5		51 x 35	47 x 31	51 x 30	53 x 42	46 x 35	49.5 x 36	56 x 34.5	47.5 x 38	47 x 33		50 x 34	53 x 32.5	57.5 x 31.5	
Bigonial breadth	85.5	81	85	86		81		92	86.5	85.5	84.5				89.5	93	88	
Height of symphysis	34.5	27.5	30	32	35.5	29		30	29.5	28	33.5	26.5			33	31.5	31	
Sigmoid	41	37	51	53	47.5	42.5		48.5	48	43	44.5	55			39	44	45.5	
Circumference	487	459	478		494	481	500	483	491.5	500	488	504	510	505.5	481.5	495	526	518

Circumference	511.5	516.5	498		485	543	492.5	470	501.5			547	528	535	547	542	500.5	515
Sigmoid	41	51.5	44	47	52.5	53	44.5	45	47.5			51	57	44.5	55	54	46.5	45
Height of symphysis	30	40	34	28.5	33	33.5	26.5	30	30			33	30.5	32	35	36	35.5	~27
Bigonial breadth	79	87.5	87	85		99	78.5	81.5	90.5			101.5	92.5	96	108	90	97	99
Palate	49 x 35.5	61 x 35	53 x 35.5	54 x 38	52.5 x 37	52 x 41	54 x 34	49.5 x 31	56.5 x 36.5			50 x 42	50 x 40	51 x 43.5	55 x 38.5	56.5 x 36	48.5 x ~39.5	57 x 34.5
Nose	49 x 26	50 x 25.5	53 x 26	50 x 27.5	51 x 24	48 x 28.5	52.5 x 21	48.5 x 21	54 x 22			53 x 30	51 x 26.5	54.5 x 24.5	51 x 27	52 x 25.5	46 x 25	51.5 x 24.5
Left orbit	38.5 x 32	40.5 x 34	36.5 x 33.5	37.5 x 32.5	37 x 34	43 x 33	36 x 35	36 x 33.5	40 x 38			38.5 x 32.5	38 x 35	38 x 34	39 x 33.5	40 x 31	39 x 34	39 x 35.5
Right orbit	40 x 32	41 x 33.5	37.5 x 32	38.5 x 32.5	39 x 34.5	44.5 x 31.5	36 x 35.5	37 x 33.5	40 x 37.5			39.5 x 33	38.5 x 36	39.5 x 35.5	41 x 33	40 x 31	40 x 33.5	39 x 36
Interorbital breadth	21	22	20	19	20.5	26.5	19.5	23.5	20			30	26.5	18.5	23	26	27.5	20
Grave	622	627	647	673A	673B	677	683A	683B	686	687A	687B	711A	711B	711D	731	733	752	754
Cemetery	89	89	89	89	89	89	89	89	89	89	89	89	89	89	89	89	89	89

Appendix IIb

Cemetery	Grave	Interorbital breadth	Right orbit	Left orbit	Nose	Palate	Bigonial breadth	Height of symphysis	Sigmoid	Circumference
89	772	24	39 x 31	39 x 32	47 x 27.5	48 x 39	110	28	45	541
89	785	20.5	40 x 30	39.5 x 32	50 x 27.5	52.5 x 34.5	87.5	27	45	503
89	797A	20	42 x 32.5	41 x 35.5	51 x 26.5	60 x 36	96	38	50	547
89	797B	20	39 x 33.5	39.5 x 33	48 x 24.5	50 x 36	83	28	42	481
89	797C	17	38 x 30.5	37 x 31	45 x 23	48.5 x 35				482
89	802	28.5	41 x 31	41.5 x 31	53.5 x 29		104	33.5	52	539
89	807	23.5	39.5 x 35	38.5 x 33.5	50 x 25	54.5 x 34.5	83			528
89	810	17	38 x 32	35.5 x 32.5	47 x 22	49.5 x 40	92	29	42.5	482.5
89	812A	23.5	41 x 31.5	38.5 x 32	51 x 40	53 x 40		33.5	50	502
89	812B	18.5	37 x 33.5	36.5 x 33.5	50 x 23	49 x 36	96.5	31.5	42	505.5
89	819	22	35.5 x 30.5	37 x 31	48 x 25	53 x 38		32.5	56	506.5
89	825	26.5	35 x 28.5	34 x 28.5	43.5 x 29	52 x 37.5	93	27	39.5	507
89	852	25	36.5 x 30.5	34.5 x 31	48 x 22.5	55.5 x 38	~91.5	33	48	478
89	855	21.5	36 x 28.5	37 x 29	51 x 27	49.5 x 36	95.5	30	44	480
89	858	20	36 x 30	35.5 x 31	44 x 25.5	50 x 37		30	41	502
89	861	19.5	39.5 x 30	39 x 29.5	51 x 24.5	51.5 x 35	88.5			500
89	880	20.5	36 x 28.5	35 x 29.5	43 x 24.5	49 x 35		32	42.5	482
89	917									475

Cemetery	89	89	89	89	89	89
Grave	1152	1154	1161A	1161B	1377A	1377B
Interorbital breadth	20.5	21		18	24.5	19
Right orbit	39 x 35	39 x 30.5		35 x 32.5	39 x 32	39 x 32
Left orbit	39 x 36	38.5 x 31		33.5 x 32.5	39 x 31	39 x 32.5
Nose	52 x 24.5	49.5 x 23.5		47 x 25	47 x 27	51.5 x 27
Palate	51 x 38	55 x 32		52 x 35.5	51 x 39.5	53 x 43
Bigonial breadth	89.5	94	95.5	81	104	94
Height of symphysis	29	~32	35	34.5	33	32
Sigmoid	48	50.5	47	43	50	50
Circumference	508.5	498		501	535	485

Appendix IIIa

Lower appendicular skeletal measurements from anatomical recording cards produced by Douglas Derry and Sir Grafton Elliot Smith

Cemetery	Grave	R Femur (Max)	R Femur (Obl)	R Femoral Head	L Femur (Max)	L Femur (Obl)	L Femoral Head	R Tibia	L Tibia
55	774	441	437.5	47	442	438	46	344	348
55	840	399	393	40.5	398.5	395	40.5	312	313
55	846	418	414	43	417.5	416	43	347	350
55	848	384	381	36	384	384	35	316.5	317.5
55	875	446	442	41.5	450	448	42	363	363
58	2	447						359	
58	3	463	460	42	462	460	42	368	366
58	4				402	402		315	317
58	5								
58	7	487	476.5	46.5				392	395
58	8							336.5	336.5
58	9				~435	435		361	364
58	10	422	420					348	
58	13	378.5	376	39				293	290
58	14	430	428		429	426.5		350	351
58	16	434	432						
58	17	424	420		424	421		345	
58	18	439.5	436.5		442	439		~335	333
58	19	456	456		458	455		359	359
58	100	440	436		441.5	436.5		345	
58	101				453	447		350	
58	102							~359	
58	105	448	444		448	446			367

Cemetery	Grave	R Femur (Max)	R Femur (Obl)	R Femoral Head	L Femur (Max)	L Femur (Obl)	L Femoral Head	R Tibia	L Tibia
58	108								380
58	109	~465	463		~476	474		378	376.5
58	110							359	361.5
58	111	426	424		424	423	35		338
58	112B				484	~480		384	385.5
58	113			39			39	329	
58	115	482	479		~480	~476		380	382
58	117	408	406		413	409		328	327
58	118	400	394.5	38	399	394.5	39	320	321
58	119	420	415		427	423		354	
58	120	464	459		465	459		378	380
58	121	400	396		401	398		315.5	316
58	122	460	458	42.5	464	460	44	385	387
58	123B	444	440		444	440		360	360
58	124	471.5	470		473	471.5		391	390
58	125	464	462	44	463	461	44	391	392
58	127	435	430	42	434	430	42	351	351
59	1A				410.5	405.5			336
59	1B	455	450	42	456	453	42	381	380
59	2	404.5	402	39				325	
59	3A	400	399	38	400	399	37	317	317.5
68	1	469	468	44	463	460	43.5	385	376.5
68	2	471	469	46.5				367.5	366
68	5		423.5	39.5		426		332	331.5
68	6				407	404	38		
68	8							326	326.5
68	9				~394		40		316
68	10	~456	447	42	455.5	448.5	42		360
68	15				463	458	39.5		

Appendix IIIA

Cemetery	Grave	R Femur (Max)	R Femur (Obl)	R Femoral Head	L Femur (Max)	L Femur (Obl)	L Femoral Head	R Tibia	L Tibia
68	20	398	394	36.5			35.5	328	329
68	24			44	414.5	411	43	~322	
69	7								
69	12							339	
69	14	~437	~437	45	~445	~442.5	45	349	349
69	15	478	474	48	479	476.5	47		386
69	16	467	462.5	43.5	469	465	43.5	368	369
69	17	439	~433	41	436	429	41		
69	18	449	442	44.5	447	441	44.5	370	370
69	20	436	426	40	435	426	40	360	361
69	21	415	410		418	412			341
69	23	398		39	403		39	339	
69	24	455	449	45	455.5	449.5	46.5		
69	26	~434	~432.5	44	~433.5	~432	44	374	
69	27	418	414.5	39.5	415.5	413	39	341	338
69	28			39			39	332	334
69	36	426	426	39	430	425.5	39.5	356	356
69	40	431	~430	41			41	352	354
69	41	415.5	412	40			40	331	
69	44	493	488	43			43.5		
69	45							390	390
69	48	~454.5	~454	42.5	462.5	460.5	42.5		372
69	West of 48				479	476	42.5		
69	49	429	425	36.5				354	355
69	52	441	439	44			43	354	357
69	57				446		39		369
69	58	410	406.5	38			38	326	330
69	60			40					

Cemetery	Grave	R Femur (Max)	R Femur (Obl)	R Femoral Head	L Femur (Max)	L Femur (Obl)	L Femoral Head	R Tibia	L Tibia
69	61	406.5	403	36.5	406	403	36.5	326	329
69	64			39	437	431.5	38	360	359.5
69	66	425	422	42	428	425	42		
69	70			43	449	447	44	362	
69	71	415	413		417	413.5	40	313	317
69	72	~455.5	~454	42	~450	~446	42		~370
69	73			40	441	434.5	40		
69	81	468.5	465	46				~390	394
69	85			47.5			47		
69	88								348
69	89								365.5
69	90	393	391	36	393.5	391.5	36	318	317
69	92			44.5	443	443	45	361.5	360
69	95								
69	96						40		
69	101	401	398	37.5	402.5	~401	37	332	332.5
69	200A	~456	~455	44			45	~375	
69	200B				~433	~431	41		
69	200C	472	469.5	42	~473	~469.5	41		
69	UNKN								
71	103			37			37	350	352
72	16A	392	391	49.5	401	399	39	315	315
72	16B	450	448	46	449	446	46.5		
72	17A	422	422	41.5	426.5	426	40.5	344	346
72	17B	399	398	41.5	396	396	41.5	308	308
72	18	393	389	39	393	388	40	329	
72	19A	481	477	43	479	474	42	378	378.5
72	19B	516	512	44	518.5	516	44	429	427
72	19D	376.5	376	38.5	384.5	382	38	302	304.5

Appendix IIIa

Cemetery	Grave	R Femur (Max)	R Femur (Obl)	R Femoral Head	L Femur (Max)	L Femur (Obl)	L Femoral Head	R Tibia	L Tibia
72	20	430	425	42	431	425	41.5	356	356
72	22	431	425.5	39	427	420	38	341	341
72	24B							371	382
72	25A	459	455	43	460	454	44	371	382
72	25B	456	454	48	458.5	453.5	48	353	352
72	27B	448	445.5	40	451	448.5	41	382.5	382.5
72	41	440	436	45	440	437.5	45	357	363
72	44				424	420	41	344.5	348.5
72	48	408	405	42.5	411.5	406	41	335	334
72	49	420	418	38	417	415	37.5	344	342.5
72	54	406	403.5	39	413	410.5	39	336	338
72	60	438.5	436	40.5	438	436	40	343	343
72	61	416	413	36.5	416	413	36.5	334	333
72	77	403.5	399.5	39	403	399.5	39	325	321
72	79	489	483.5	47	483.5	478	46	385	383
72	88	406	404.5	40.5	405.5	403	40.5	337	336
72	90	393	386.5	39	398	387	39	303.5	303
72	91	445	440	37	446	440	37.5	370	373.5
72	93	472.5	462	42	473.5	466	42.5	372.5	376
72	106	404	399	40	404	400	41	340	338.5
72	112	450	445.5	47	454	450	46	361.5	368
72	114	452	450	45	451	450	45.5		376
72	150	436	432	39	435.5	430.5	39	380	377
72	166	490.5	484	44	500	493.5	44	403	404
72	177	449	446	43	449	445.5	43	355	358
72	180	399	391	38	395	392	38	323	323
72	226		392	40	400	400	40.5		318.5
72	237	474.5	469	46	483.5	478.5	47		374
72	239	424	423.5	40.5			40		

Cemetery	Grave	R Femur (Max)	R Femur (Obl)	R Femoral Head	L Femur (Max)	L Femur (Obl)	L Femoral Head	R Tibia	L Tibia
72	241	414	410	37.5			38	333	334
72	253	444.5	444	39	451.5	447.5	39.5	370	369
72	262	473	465	42				386	385.5
72	263	456	454	39			38.5		383
72	268	454	450.5	43	452	449	43	375	378
72	269	455	451	43.5	~470	~462	42	380	
72	270						40.5	380	376.5
72	273	448	445.5	40	451	448.5	41	382.5	382.5
72	275			47			46		
72	278			41.5	453	453	42		381
72	279	443.5	439	41					352
72	288	412	410	37				335	
72	289	397.5	396	39				329.5	
72	306				521	511.5			433.5
72	308	430	425	37	433.5	427	37	361	365
72	309	405	403	37			36		335
72	310	489	486	41	492	488	41		394
72	311	496	491.5	47	506	500	46		403
72	312	485	477.5	41	484	477	40	391.5	396
72	317	428.5	428	42.5	427	426	42	345	344
72	322	420	416.5	37				335	338
72	323			47	494.5	493.5	46	431	431.5
72	324	473	471	46	478	474	46	396	394
72	337	455	450.5	40.5			41	377	377
72	339	452.5	450	40	456	452	41.5	368	366
72	341	420	415	41			41		
72	342	451	447.5	45	456	452	46	360	
72	343								335
72	346			43	482.5	475.5	43	393	

Appendix IIIa

Cemetery	Grave	R Femur (Max)	R Femur (Obl)	R Femoral Head	L Femur (Max)	L Femur (Obl)	L Femoral Head	R Tibia	L Tibia
72	351	442	440	42			41	366	
72	356				450	442			369
72	360	460	457	38			39.5		368
72	361	468	464	46	480	471.5		381	
72	362	440	437	42.5	441.5	437	43	362	361
72	365				430	426	39		345
72	366				455	453	42		365
72	367	435.5	431	39.5	430.5	424.5	39	346.5	350.5
72	368	477.5	475	45	476	474.5	44	386	387.5
72	369				440	436	38	374	
72	375	442	442	42	447	447	42	351	351
72	377	~492	~488	46	~495	~489	45.5	394	394
72	378	466.5	464	42	468.5	462	42	372	
72	380	402	399	35	403	399.5	35		350
72	382	508	501	48			49	408	403.5
72	383	405	403	39.5	409	406	39	325.5	331.5
72	384	482.5	479	44	~481.5	477	43		373.5
72	385	455.5	453	41	460	456	41	359	359
72	387	523	520	47			47.5	428	425
72	388	547	544	49	550	549	48.5	441	441
72	422	462	459	40	461	457.5	42.5		
72	426				497.5	494	45		
72	440								
72	445	434	430	44.5	~430	~427	44	345	341
72	474	415	412.5	38			39	335	335
72	476	379	376.5	36	383.5	382.5	38	304	303
73	8	454	452.5	43	458	455.5	44	376	376
73	10								
73	25								

Cemetery	Grave	R Femur (Max)	R Femur (Obl)	R Femoral Head	L Femur (Max)	L Femur (Obl)	L Femoral Head	R Tibia	L Tibia
73	37	475.5	475	40.5	479	477	42.5	392	392
73	38	447	444	42	446.5	444	42	369	
73	60					~453		372	373
73	88	505	501	49	510	506	49	423	426
73	90	439	438	43			42.5	354	
73	107	427.5	425.5	38.5	427.5	421.5	38.5	338	
74	3							317.5	
74	5	415	414	40	414	412	39	337.5	337.5
74	6	397	394.5	38	398	394.5	38	329.5	329
74	12				425	423.5	44	337	335
74	13	456	453	44	454	453	46		363.5
74	15	457	456	42	456	454.5	43	368	366
74	19			45	462	459.5	45		
74	25			37			36	344.5	346
74	53	437.5	433	43	439.5	437	43	358	359.5
74	58	437.5	434	43.5	438.5	435	44	344	344
74	61	395	393	39.5	397	395	38	321	322
74	68			48.5					
74	70	432	430.5	39	432	429	38.5	350	348.5
74	84	421	418	39.5	425.5	421	39		
74	506	401.5	397	36			36	324.5	
74	507	408	405.5	40.5	412	409	39.5	323	324
74	511			36	422	416	36		345
74	514				439	434	37	348	350.5
76	5	463	461	44	463	462.5	44	380	382
76	18	442	436.5	39.5	442.5	438	39.5	350	
76	23	402	397		405	401		307	307
76	24	473.5	473					386	
76	26A	424.5	423.5	39	426	424	38.5	343.5	346

APPENDIX IIIA

Cemetery	Grave	R Femur (Max)	R Femur (Obl)	R Femoral Head	L Femur (Max)	L Femur (Obl)	L Femoral Head	R Tibia	L Tibia
76	35	408.5	407	42	411	407	40		326
76	55	469	465	46	472	469.5		366	371
76	58			36	381.5	377	36		
76	72							324	
76	76	405		36.5	405	402	35.5		318
76	77						39.5		351
76	81	403	400	39	403.5	399	39	319.5	322
76	82	438	437	42	442	440	42.5	367	362.5
76	83	437.5	436.5	43	437.5	436.5	42		
76	87	432	430	37	428	427	37	349	350.5
76	89				378.5	377	34	312	316
76	93			39.5		425	38.5		
76	98			43.5			44		
76	99	415	411	36.5	420	415.5	37	336	336.5
76	106			39	446.5	443.5	39	352	353
76	108				497	491	45		
76	116								
76	125			38.5			38.5		
76	127	416.5	411	40.5			41.5	325	331.5
76	130				439	437.5	42		
76	134					436	44		
76	139			43	453	450	43		350
76	142	442.5	438.5	40.5			40.5	367	366
76	143			43		474	41.5		
77	1	396	390	36	399.5	393.5	36	325	
77	115	455	452.5	43.5			42	351	354.5
78	18	437.5	436	41			40.5		
79	2	452	449	47.5	~460.5	~457	47.5	372	369
79	3	455.5	451.5	42.5			43.5	364.5	364.5

Cemetery	Grave	R Femur (Max)	R Femur (Obl)	R Femoral Head	L Femur (Max)	L Femur (Obl)	L Femoral Head	R Tibia	L Tibia
79	7				435	~431	42		
79	9			36.5			36.5		
79	10A			45.5			45.5		
79	12	454.5	449.5	45	454.5	451	44	361	360
79	13	469.5	468.5	48.5			48		378
79	15						42		
79	23								
79	25	450.5	450	45			45.5	344	
79	29(a)	444	441	37					
79	29(b)				456.5	453	40		
79	29(c)			45.5					
79	33			49	462	457		351.5	
79	48(a)			42.5			44		
79	48(c)			40			39		
79	65(a)	477	471	45	481	476	45		
79	65(c)			37			38		
79	66A			35			36.5		
79	111				457	456	48		
79	113			39.5		433	39.5		
79	124(a)						41		
79	124(b)						47		
79	130A			41			40		
79	135A	534	530	54.5	~521.5	~517.5	52.5	413	416
79	144			45.5			45.5		
79	147						42		
79	148		464	48			47		
79	152			42			42		
79	157	480	478	46.5			46	401	408.5
79	159(a)		446	44.5	456	452	46		

Appendix IIIa

Cemetery	Grave	R Femur (Max)	R Femur (Obl)	R Femoral Head	L Femur (Max)	L Femur (Obl)	L Femoral Head	R Tibia	L Tibia
79	159(b)	445	444	42.5			44		
79	160			45.5	453	448	45.5	357	356.5
79	161			44.5					
79	164			48			48		
79	165A			47.5			47	357.5	
79	166			46.5		427	45		331
79	168			50		525	50.5		
79	201			47		452	47.5		
85	29				422.5	421	45		341.5
85	31A	460	456	43.5				360	
85	38	409	404	40.5	412.5	410.5	40	328.5	329
85	56	462	460	44	464.5	462	44	363	368.5
85	62	435	430	44				345.5	
86	34	527	521.5	47.5	524	521.5	47.5		
86	205	432	430	51.5	435	432	52	333.5	337
86	206	434	431	46.5	433	431	46	326	327
86	208	406	404		398.5	396		325	326
86	266A	434	430.5	43	433	431	41	366	362
86	267	428	423	43.5	428	424	43	332	334
86	295	416	411		421	416		360	360
86	305	406	404.5		408	405.5		321.5	323
87	12			43.5			43.5		
87	14			38					
87	17			48.7		459	46		
87	19			37					
87	25						48		
87	28								
87	33	392	389	39	396	392.5	38		322
87	35	419	417	38	424	421	38	356.5	356.5

Cemetery	Grave	R Femur (Max)	R Femur (Obl)	R Femoral Head	L Femur (Max)	L Femur (Obl)	L Femoral Head	R Tibia	L Tibia
87	36			36			36		
87	42	444.5	439.5	43	451	442.5	42.5	360	363.5
87	46	464	464	44	468	466	44	376	
87	57			43			43		
87	72					473.5			375
87	73			39			39		
87	74	414	411	38			38		
87	76	447	446	37.5	445	444.5	37.5	355	353
87	77				415	412	37	344	340
87	78			48	465	463	48	396	389
87	79	420	419	42	423	421.5	44.5	339	338
87	81	455	450	37.5	456	453.5	37.5	387	489
87	83	508	506	47.5	500	497	48	393	
87	84	456	454	42	456.5	453	42	378.5	355.5
87	85	420	419	38	424	420	40	352	353
87	89	440.5	438	39	444	439	39	344	345
87	90	494	487.5		493.5	485.5		398.5	400
87	93	515	512.5	49	517	513	48.5	424	425
87	94	409	407	37	413	408	36	330	325
87	95				430	428	41.5		
87	96A	406	403.5	34.5	405	402	35	333	333
87	96B	424	423	37					
87	98	464	461	47	467	465	47.5	385	386
87	99	488	485	45	482	480	44.5	421	414.5
87	100	476	475	45	481	480	46	395	392
87	102	422	419	39.5	423	418.5	40.5	337	336
87	103	438	435.5	40	440	438.5	40	339	341
87	104	443.5	440	43	445	440	44	359	361.5
87	105	430	428	37.5	435.5	432	37		

Appendix IIIa

Cemetery	Grave	R Femur (Max)	R Femur (Obl)	R Femoral Head	L Femur (Max)	L Femur (Obl)	L Femoral Head	R Tibia	L Tibia
87	106	453	451	42	459	455	41	367	364
87	107	415	415	40.5	421	420.5	42	339	339
87	110	412	405	34	415	408	34	340	340
87	116	467	463	45	471	465	45	384	378
87	117	431.5	430	41.5	421.5	419.5	41.5	354	354
87	121	456	456	41	462	460.5		364	356
87	125			47			44		
87	153				457.5	456	41.5		
87	157				436	434	43.5	380	
87	163			39			39		
87	169	420	417.5	35			35	340.5	340
87	173	450	447	48	458	455.5	47	359	359
89	546	424.5	413.5	37.5	419.5	414.5	37.5	339.5	341.5
89	570	430	428	45	431	430	45	333.5	335
89	575				351	349	35	264	263
89	577							345	
89	583				442	437.5		357.5	358.5
89	601B			45.5	452	449	47	370	
89	614	448	446	43.5	455	452	43.5	360	360
89	622	446	439	39	445	443	39	360	359
89	627	472	467	43	481.5	478.5	41	388.5	
89	647	470.5	467	43	466	464	42.5	382.5	381.5
89	673A	489	487.5	44	488	486.5	43.5	382.5	384.5
89	673B	454	452	43.5	457	455	45	357	359
89	683A	424	417	37	421	415	36.5	346	342.5
89	683B	435	426	39.5	434	431	39.5	354	355
89	686	490	482	45	489.5	486	45	401	405
89	687A	478	475	42.5	484	480	42	406	406
89	687B	423	420	43.5			43.5		327

Cemetery	Grave	R Femur (Max)	R Femur (Obl)	R Femoral Head	L Femur (Max)	L Femur (Obl)	L Femoral Head	R Tibia	L Tibia
89	711A	497	493.5	52	508	505	52	399	400
89	711B	477.5	473	48.5	480	475	47.5	376	380
89	731	508	505.5	53	502	499	53	410.5	412
89	733	454	452	49.5	456	453	50	359	355.5
89	764	421.4	416	39.5	421	416	39.5		346
89	772	420	418	44.5	422	420	44	342.5	340
89	785	455	454	48	459	458	45	366	369
89	797A	425	419.5	45	423	419	44		334
89	797B	422.5	417	41.5	423	419.5	40	342	336
89	797C	410	408	42	418	415.5	41	325	325
89	810	423	417.5		420	416		322	321
89	812A	495	490	49	493	492.5	50	388	385
89	812B			42	429	424			330
89	819	441	437	46	432.5	430.5	45	362	359
89	855			46			44.5	378	379.5
89	858			45	435	433	45	347	344
89	861			40.5	405	403	41	323	323.5
89	917	395.5	390	37	393.5	385.5	37.5	307	307
89	1154	411	408	42	406	405.5	41.5	328	327
89	1161A	448	445.5	43	450	447	43	364	367
89	1377B	452.5	452	43.5	454	453.5	44	355	353

Appendix IIIb

Upper appendicular skeletal measurements from anatomical recording cards produced by Douglas Derry and Sir Grafton Elliot Smith

Sacrum	108.5 x 115.5			106 x 108	102 x 107											
L Scapula	146.5 x 100	135 x 86	156 x 98	141 x 86					127 x 96				148 x 94		139 x 88
R Scapula	147 x 103	134 x 87	150 x 95	138 x 88					136 x 99			129 x 96				
L Clavicle	140	131	144	125	144		155		133		133	150	130	125		131
R Clavicle	141	133.5	127 #	126	137		155		134	151	131		126	123		129
L Radius	222	199	231	209	243	250	248	207	204		223	248	241	185	224	227	215
R Radius	224	195	232	210	243	252	248	210	208		223	252	239	188	229		214
L Humerus	311	266.5	291	271	305	315	324		275		286			262	289		284
R Humerus	315	269	290	272	306.5	319	323		283	334	282	310	302	267	292		290
Grave	774	840	846	848	875	2	3	4	5	7	8	9	10	13	14	16	17
Cemetery	55	55	55	55	55	58	58	58	58	58	58	58	58	58	58	58	58

Cemetery	58	58	58	58	58	58	58	58	58	58	58	58	58	58	58	58	58	58	58
Grave	18	19	100	101	102	105	108	109	110	111	112B	113	115	117	118	119	120	121	122
R Humerus	306.5	319	294	298	298	318	318		293			288	327	301.5	284	293.5	328.5	280	307
L Humerus	306	320	291		~294	316.5		315				290	332.5	293	277	290	327	280	314
R Radius	219	233.5	232	226	234	241	246	243			223		~220	205	227.5	249	211	247
L Radius	216	236.5		227	227	245		243.5		~231				217	203	225	248	212	245
R Clavicle	144	155	127.5		146	146		142						140	134	138	159	145	141
L Clavicle	142	154	129	135	144	148		151				128		140	132	141	163	149	149
R Scapula	145 x 108							157 x 104							130 x 99			148 x 97	
L Scapula		154 x 100						161 x 104							132 x 99				155 x 99
Sacrum				87 x 88											99 x 84		104 x 90	113.5 x 122	

Appendix IIIb

Sacrum	110 x 105		104 x 98	102 x 96								109 x 96					92 x 105.5		
L Scapula	142 x 105		162 x 107		103 x 138		92 x 132	155 x 105											
R Scapula			159 x 107		102 x 130			153 x 105							143 x 92				
L Clavicle	144	150	150	152					152	152.5	136			135	146				
R Clavicle	132	145	151.5	146					156.5		138				146	130	120		
L Radius	234	253	253	229		234.5	204.5#							241	213			217.5	
R Radius	238	253	258	227		236	214.5	253	249	217.5			208	242	216		205.5		
L Humerus	301	327	335	301	292	310		270	327	317			269	314	278.5			293.5	
R Humerus	307	320	333	302		312.5	291	280	327	322.5	285			279	318		290		
Grave	123B	124	125	127	1A	1B	2	3A	1	2	5	6	8	9	10	15	20	24	7
Cemetery	58	58	58	58	59	59	59	59	68	68	68	68	68	68	68	68	68	68	69

The Archaeological Survey of Nubia Season 2 (1908-9). Report on the Human Remains

	12	14	15	16	17	18	20	21	23	24	26	27	28	36	40	41	44	45	48
Sacrum			99 x 102	104 x 98	123.5 x 99	124 x 97	104 x 116	97.5 x 111.5			85.5 x 110			99 x 100			100 x 109		101 x 99
L Scapula											155.5 x 111								
R Scapula						154 x 105.5													
L Clavicle		147		148	143	142	144		139		153	140		150		151		174	146
R Clavicle		146	167	146	137	138.5	136				155	139		146.5	133	140		165	140
L Radius	217.5	225	257.5	247.5	223	233	225		220.5		257	224	203	230	235		241		243
R Radius	223	231	259	251	225	236.5	221	225						236	216.5	246			243
L Humerus	308	294.5	330	316	298		~304.5				310.5	302.5		319	310	296	327.5	341	334
R Humerus		304	335.5	320	300	316	~308	291	288.5		312.5	301	288	320			330		329
Grave	12	14	15	16	17	18	20	21	23	24	26	27	28	36	40	41	44	45	48
Cemetery	69	69	69	69	69	69	69	69	69	69	69	69	69	69	69	69	69	69	69

Appendix IIIb

	West of 48	49	52	57	58	60	61	64	66	70	71	72	73	81	85	88	89	90
Sacrum		95 x 101		104 x 111		114 x 106			96 x 93	108 x 95	97.5 x 107			107 x 107				117 x 86.5
L Scapula																		
R Scapula																		
L Clavicle		134	125	131		142.5			146		140	130		143		128		
R Clavicle		139	116	125	123.5						127		135	148		128		
L Radius	241.5	219.5	229	225	210	249.5	230		252		231	223	239	244	236		202	
R Radius		223	228	224	211		214	234	252	206.5	236	228		239			210	
L Humerus		293.5	296	303.5	283	312	276	314				299	315.5	315			272.5	
R Humerus	317	298	296			315	278		315	271.5	308	301	318	304		308		279
Grave	West of 48	49	52	57	58	60	61	64	66	70	71	72	73	81	85	88	89	90
Cemetery	69	69	69	69	69	69	69	69	69	69	69	69	69	69	69	69	69	69

The Archaeological Survey of Nubia Season 2 (1908-9). Report on the Human Remains

Sacrum				89 x 87				93 x 105		104 x 106	91 x 103		106 x 112		124 x 112	95 x 101
L Scapula				144 x 92	172 x 106				128 x 99	155 x 96		134 x 95		130 x 87	123 x 105	136 x 85
R Scapula				142 x 90				131 x 100		154 x 95		130.5 x 93	154 x 96		124 x 102	135 x 90
L Clavicle			143	134		170	140	148	122	151	142	134	134	145	133	124
R Clavicle	159					167	153	140	126	146	145	131	135.5	133	142	133	121.5
L Radius	219	240		209			226	226	207	225	229.5	227.5	233	261	199	231.5	215
R Radius	231			210	263	~221.5	265	228	228.5	211	228	228	210	245	265	201	236	218
L Humerus	308	365		287		289		301	305	282	306	295	279		336.5	266	295	290
R Humerus	312	364		323		340	309	313	287	314	311	299	283	327	339.5	267	299	293.5
Grave	92	95	96	101	200A	200B	200C	UNKN	103	16A	16B	17A	17B	18	19A	19B	19D	20	22
Cemetery	69	69	69	69	69	69	69	69	71	72	72	72	72	72	72	72	72	72	72

Appendix IIIb

Cemetery	Grave	R Humerus	L Humerus	R Radius	L Radius	R Clavicle	L Clavicle	R Scapula	L Scapula	Sacrum
72	24B									
72	25A		307			142	145		144 x 105	130 x 106
72	25B	331	332		246.5	145	150			
72	27B		311							
72	41	310	308	241	241.5	156	152	166.5 x 100	166 x 103	
72	44	295	292	232	225	128.5		135 x 90		93 x 108
72	48			212	211					
72	49	296.5	290	220	216	135	136	138 x 90	146 x 89	101 x 107
72	54	296	293	223		125	125	141 x 94		
72	60	310	305	228	223	142	146			
72	61	301.5	295	229	229		136			
72	77	299	290	211	207.5	128		133 x 98	134 x 97.5	66 x 98
72	79	316			251		145			
72	88	288.5	285	227	219	144	142	135 x 99	140 x 98	102 x 111
72	90	277	271	199	193	120	120	130 x 89	131.5 x 90	
72	91	309	303	235	232			129 x 90	130 x 92	
72	93	308	305		228	145		140 x 97	140 x 97	97 x 116
72	106	372	368	220	217.5	122		138 x 91		98.5 x 110
72	112	327	320	234	234		152	157.5 x 107.5	159 x 108	

Sacrum			129 x 110.5							108 x 102		103 x 119							
L Scapula		164 x 105	159 x 109.5			135.5 x 92													
R Scapula			160 x 109		135.5 x 92														
L Clavicle	150		161																
R Clavicle			155		134	134													
L Radius			254.5	238	214	202	244.5			233			244						
R Radius	246		255	235		246				236								236	
L Humerus			350	304	278	276	328.5			317	336		316		322	311			
R Humerus	338	307	354.5	307		278	328.5	293.5		321		321	309	325					314.5
Grave	114	150	166	177	180	226	237	239	241	253	262	263	268	269	270	273	275	278	279
Cemetery	72	72	72	72	72	72	72	72	72	72	72	72	72	72	72	72	72	72	72

Appendix IIIb

Cemetery	Grave	R Humerus	L Humerus	R Radius	L Radius	R Clavicle	L Clavicle	R Scapula	L Scapula	Sacrum
72	288	284								
72	289	277		209						
72	306	296.5	293							
72	308			214						
72	309	334.5	350	245	281	140	155.5		122 x 98	90 x 106
72	310	310.5				154			135.5 x 94.5	
72	311	344.5	301	230	225.5	126.5				
72	312	333		225	275					
72	317	311	311	275.5	254		163			84 x 99
72	322	317	322.5	242						
72	323	299			237.5	138			157.5 x 101.5	
72	324			240						
72	337									
72	339									
72	341									
72	342									
72	343									
72	346									
72	351									

Sacrum		123 x 104.5					110 x 107							99 x 110	80 x 99				
L Scapula								172 x 103						167.5 x 101	157.5 x 107				
R Scapula								169 x 101						162 x 102					
L Clavicle								159.5						163					
R Clavicle														166	139	154			
L Radius								261	245					211	253				
R Radius	248						227	257.5						214	257	242			
L Humerus							~339.5	299	315.5				283	337		324	321	370	373
R Humerus	319						302.5	312		348			287	337	276.5	316		367.5	
Grave	356	360	361	362	365	366	367	368	369	375	377	378	380	382	383	384	385	387	388
Cemetery	72	72	72	72	72	72	72	72	72	72	72	72	72	72	72	72	72	72	72

Appendix IIIb

Cemetery	Grave	R Humerus	L Humerus	R Radius	L Radius	R Clavicle	L Clavicle	R Scapula	L Scapula	Sacrum
72	422									
72	426									
72	440	371		269	273					
72	445	298.5	300.5	217	212	137	133	129 x 97.5	130 x 99	
72	474	296	288	219.5	214	131	128	133 x 88.5	133.5 x 88	96 x 110
72	476	267	263	197	193	125.5	126.5			90 x 103.5
73	8	321	302	230	228.5		147.5			
73	10			231	217					
73	25	321.5		253	248	165	161			111 x 103
73	37	325.5		250		158.5	156			
73	38	325	346.5	258	236	155	153			
73	60	344	316	236	234	129	124.5			
73	88	312	279	235	215	146.5	143			95 x 107.5
73	90	281	278.5	221		120	122	141 x 83	137.5 x 89	89.5 x 95.5
73	107	287	283.5	215.5	218.5	123	127.5	125 x 92	127 x 91.5	94.5 x 96.5
74	3	274	274	222	216.5	114	129		137.5 x 97	106 x 111
74	5	301	295	222	218.5					
74	6			220						
74	12									

347

Cemetery	74	74	74	74	74	74	74	74	74	74	74	74	74	74	76	76	76	76	76
Grave	13	15	19	25	53	58	61	68	70	84	506	507	511	514	5	18	23	24	26A
R Humerus	329	317	312.5		304.5	307.5	273.5		301	310		283.5	295.5	308	321		274.5	333	296
L Humerus		316.5	310	292	302	310	269		299	298	274.5	286		298			273	333	291.5
R Radius	261	242	255		237	243	217		225	230	224	211	225	226	241		199	248	217.5
L Radius	256		253.5		235	241	213		220			213	223		238		198.5	244.5	
R Clavicle	155	142.5			141.5	150	124.5		131	128		144	129	153	150		129		
L Clavicle		159.5			150	148.5	127		130	129		144.5	137	153.5	147.5				
R Scapula	170.5 x 106	159 x 102			155.5 x 98	142.5 x 105	133 x 91		144.5 x 94.5	142 x 94									
L Scapula	170.5 x 106	167.5 x 102.5			155 x 98	145 x 104	138 x 89		146 x 96	140 x 93									
Sacrum		109 x 112	111 x 98.5	84 x 106	99.5 x 107				105.5 x 108.5		114 x 105		104 x 117.5	118.5 x 122	106 x 102				

Appendix IIIb

Grave	Cemetery	R Humerus	L Humerus	R Radius	L Radius	R Clavicle	L Clavicle	R Scapula	L Scapula	Sacrum
35	76	299	297		223	137	135	165.5 x 97.5	164 x 97	104 x 102
55	76	323.5	326	246	246		~165.5			99 x ~112
58	76			218	213					
72	76		276	209.5			133			
76	76			200.5						
77	76	274	299.5							
81	76	304	271.5	207	204	144				121.5 x 86
82	76	298	310	241.5	237.5			139.5 x 99	143 x 96.5	
83	76	306	302	245.5	242.5			140.5 x 97.5	141 x 98.5	
87	76	264.5	300	236.5	231.5	153	158	155 x 95.5	147.5 x 100.5	97.5 x 95
89	76	300	264.5	191.5	189	130.5	128.5			90.5 x 93
93	76				220.5					
98	76	284.5	280	225	222	133.5	133	143.5 x 91		101.5 x 101.5
99	76	301	299.5	229.5	225.5		158			105.5 x 104.5
106	76			240						
108	76	298	297	221	216.5	130.5	133.5			
116	76		294	222	219					105 x 107
125	76	297	299	225	224					79 x 97
127	76									

Sacrum				114.5 x 102.5		98 x 101	101.5 x 110												
L Scapula	157 x 100					140 x 90			155 x 104										
R Scapula				145.5 x 101		131.5 x 90.5													
L Clavicle		148	138	144.5		125	152.5	136.5	160.5	146		119		143				144	
R Clavicle			136			118.5	149.5	132	152	141				136.5	130				
L Radius	238	228				210	240.5	217.5	235	234					246		240		
R Radius		230	242	233		212.5	243	221	239.5	238	230.5				245		243.5		
L Humerus		304.5	289			282	319.5	302	320	309					324		314		
R Humerus	321.5		288	303		286		324		306.5					327				
Grave	130	134	139	142	143	1	115	18	2	3	7	9	10A	12	13	15	23	25	29(a)
Cemetery	76	76	76	76	76	77	77	78	79	79	79	79	79	79	79	79	79	79	79

Appendix IIIb

Sacrum																		
L Scapula																		
R Scapula																		
L Clavicle			127															
R Clavicle			126.5															
L Radius			237					215										257
R Radius								216					291.5					256
L Humerus								286					348.5					
R Humerus			320.5					292					353.5					329
Grave	29(b)	29(c)	33	48(a)	48(c)	65(a)	65(c)	66A	111	113	124(a)	124(b)	130A	135A	144	147	148	152	157
Cemetery	79	79	79	79	79	79	79	79	79	79	79	79	79	79	79	79	79	79	79

Cemetery	79	79	79	79	79	79	79	79	79	85	85	85	85	85	86	86	86	86	86
Grave	159(a)	159(b)	160	161	164	165A	166	168	201	29	31A	38	56	62	34	205	206	208	266A
R Humerus		~318.5					299			229	291		321.5		371	302	306	283	303
L Humerus			302				292			292.5	284			305	367.5	302	305	289	297.5
R Radius		242	239				222			235	235	218.5	250		270	220	223	211.5	231.5
L Radius			236							233.5		218.5		223	219	229.5	214	228	
R Clavicle							136			165		143	142	152	150	161.5	158	154.5	139
L Clavicle		147.5								164		143	145.5		151	164	154	158.5	139
R Scapula														152 x 109.5	156 x ~114	153.5 x 108	146 x 107	139.5 x 96	
L Scapula																160 x 108	154 x 108	142.5 x 98.5	
Sacrum										108 x 118		103 x 110							

Appendix IIIb

Grave	267	295	305	12	14	17	19	25	28	33	35	36	42	46	57	72	73	74	76
Cemetery	86	86	86	87	87	87	87	87	87	87	87	87	87	87	87	87	87	87	87
R Humerus		297	283						292	272			317.5	323		318.5		316	
L Humerus	290	291.5	280						295.5	270			313			323.5		313	
R Radius	216	228	211										246			250		241	
L Radius	204	224	207						227				244	252		250			
R Clavicle			141						145.5	134.5						155	137		
L Clavicle			137						146.5	136.5				150		156	138		
R Scapula																			
L Scapula																			
Sacrum									105 x 118.5				105.5 x 120						

Sacrum	97 x 104		121 x 111			112 x 111	103 x 101.5	105 x 110.5		100 x 106			78 x 108		100 x 118.5	98.5 x 114.5	103.5 x 103.5		
L Scapula																			
R Scapula																			
L Clavicle	140		131			149		146	149		135		134.5	140		159	137		131
R Clavicle	132		129.5			147		144			132		130.5	142.5	157	160	130		125
L Radius	219.5		234			244		225	281		213.5	228	224.5			265	223		223
R Radius	219	256	232.5		268	248	232	228	289.5		219	229	225		243		266	226	226
L Humerus	287	312	294	325.5		310		301.5	344		279	293		320	341.5	335	293		301
R Humerus	291.5	313	287	322	332	311.5		303	353	365	282.5	293.5	287		317.5		332	294	303
Grave	77	78	79	81	83	84	85	89	90	93	94	95	96A	96B	98	99	100	102	103
Cemetery	87	87	87	87	87	87	87	87	87	87	87	87	87	87	87	87	87	87	87

Appendix IIIb

Sacrum					81 x 97	116.5 x 109	104 x 104	101 x 113			98.5 x 106	98 x 110						
L Scapula																		
R Scapula																		
L Clavicle	148		139.5	145		158	161.5	151		154.5	137							
R Clavicle	147		136.5			150	152	139		145	138							
L Radius	246		237	232.5	218	251.5	241		238	248	231.5	227	240					
R Radius	248		241	229.5	221	251.5	242.5	246	237	258	232	242.5	220	213.5				
L Humerus	320		319	295	282	325	~313	307	317	317.5	297		313.5		296.5			
R Humerus	316.5		320	298.5	283.5	325	299	309		326.5	302	309	316	299	300	252	302	
Grave	104	105	106	107	110	116	117	121	125	153	157	163	169	173	546	570	575	577	583
Cemetery	87	87	87	87	87	87	87	87	87	87	87	87	87	87	89	89	89	89	89

Sacrum					105 x 105	101.5 x 103		97 x 118.5									
L Scapula																	
R Scapula																	
L Clavicle	155	156	135.5		163	136		135			150	161.5	135	162	146		141	152
R Clavicle		153.5	129		137	152	133.5		129.5	149		148.5	164	135.5	159	135		141	147
L Radius		246	235		243	252	233.5	222	226	263	258	221	261	243	261.5	234		228	241
R Radius	238	244.5	236	249	247	254	236	224		259.5		259.5	244.5	265	236	221	228	242
L Humerus	303	308	291	339	317	329.5	310	287.5	293	349	335.5	289.5	357	328	355	323		304	324
R Humerus	311	307	291	332	318.5	329	313.5	296	306	325.5	336.5	296.5	348	337	352	319		299	324
Grave	601B	614	622	627	647	673A	673B	683A	683B	686	687A	687B	711A	711B	731	733	764	772	785
Cemetery	89	89	89	89	89	89	89	89	89	89	89	89	89	89	89	89	89	89	89

Appendix IIIb

Sacrum										79 x 97			
L Scapula													
R Scapula													
L Clavicle	139.5	131	132	144	161	141		141	136	137	126.5	146.5	145	156
R Clavicle	143.5	132	127.5	142			138	143	132	129.5	119	144.5	142	158
L Radius	220	212	211	216	257	222.5	235.5	252	234.5	226.5	212	209.5	227.5	237
R Radius	224	217.5	212.5	215	258		234	253	238	228	212	214	232	238
L Humerus	299	285	288	285.5	346	291	302	324	294	293	264	282	303	331
R Humerus	301	286	293	292	350		300	323	295	293	270.5	285.5	304	329
Grave	797A	797B	797C	810	812A	812B	819	855	858	861	917	1154	1161A	1377B
Cemetery	89	89	89	89	89	89	89	89	89	89	89	89	89	89